The Emergence of Multinational Enterprise:

American Business Abroad
from the Colonial Era to 1914

Mira Wilkins

Cambridge, Massachusetts, and London, England

Contents

Tables

This study is designed to present the early history of American multinational enterprise—the U.S.-headquartered company that does business in two or more foreign countries. It covers the formative years from the colonial era to 1914. A second study—which is forthcoming—will bring the history up to date. This book's originality should lie in the fact that it is the first attempt to pull together the elements that comprise the history of American business abroad before World War I. The text should serve to refute the oft-repeated, too well-established myth that early American direct foreign investment was "confined largely to the extractive industries and utilities" and that American manufacturing companies became concerned with foreign investment later than did the American extractive and utility enterprises. The book will show that well before the First World War, American direct foreign investment was not merely in extractive industries and utilities; indeed, by 1914 a surprising number of "genuine" U.S.-headquartered multinational manufacturing companies had already come into existence. By "genuine" multinational manufacturing companies I refer to corporations that had direct investments in more than just sales abroad, that adapted to and respected foreign local traditions, and acted under foreign rules and regulations in the nations abroad where they operated.

In tracing the history of American business abroad I have undertaken an awesome task. The relevant literature is plentiful and becomes more so daily. Where there has been published material available, I have used it; where it has been absent, I have plunged into company records, the National Archives, and university manuscript and financial record collections. I have interviewed hundreds of businessmen around the world—in the United States, Latin America, Africa, the Middle East, Southern Asia, the Far East, Europe, and Canada. Most of these men are too young to know the pre-1914 histories of their companies, but they have supplied me with corporate histories and records. I have visited installations of American companies in many of the places mentioned in this book: from Tokyo to Chuquicamata, from London to Talara.

This study is confined to foreign investments by U.S. businessmen and business organizations which involved managerial responsibility, the possibility of a voice in management, and direct business purpose. I do not include foreign investments made by corporations or individuals simply to obtain added revenue. This is not a book about foreign loans or about bankers' investments in foreign securities. I am not interested in investments in bonds that carried no voting power. My concern is with the American operating company as it has gone abroad. The distinction is between direct and portfolio investments, and my interest is in the former.

In a 1960 publication the U.S. Department of Commerce defined direct investment as including United States equity in the following types of enterprises:

1. Foreign corporations, the voting securities of which were owned to the extent of 25 per cent or more by persons or groups of affiliated persons, ordinarily resident in the United States, and analogous interests in partnerships and other organizations.

2. Foreign corporations, the voting stock of which was publicly held within the United States to an aggregate extent of 50 per cent or more, but distributed among stockholders so that no one investor, or groups of affiliated investors, owned as much as 25 per cent.

3. Sole proprietorships, partnerships or real property (other than property held for the personal use of the owner) held abroad by residents of the United States.

4. Foreign branches of U.S. corporations.

In this definition, the word "persons" includes individuals, corporations, partnerships, associations, estates or trusts. "Foreign branches" are defined not only as branches of an American-based corporation, but also as foreign operations of a United States corporation "even if the operations in question constitute the sole activity of the corporation."

I have followed this definition as a rule of thumb. The materials, however, have led me to several departures: 1) Rather than deal with United States residents, I consider United States citizens. 2) I have not confined myself to the 25 per cent figures (neither, in fact, did the Department of Commerce, despite its definition); if a foreign investment of a corporation or individuals fell under 25 per cent but was clearly made for direct business reasons I include it. 3) I do *not* include foreign investments by corporations resident in the United States but controlled by foreign capital; I do include foreign investments by corporations *not* resident in the United States but controlled by United States capital. In short, I try to follow the investment chain back to its origin. In the 1960s, the Department of Commerce reduced from 25 to 10 per cent the figure given in item 1 of its definition. On review of my data, I found I had no need to alter my text to incorporate the new numbers. The reason lay in my flexibility in using the 25 per cent figure.

For this book I have not developed any new statistics; I have used statistics compiled by others to give a "sense" of the importance or lack of importance of certain investments at particular times and in particular places. The longer one works with these (sometimes conflicting) data, the surer one becomes that the figures are far from sacrosanct. Those that I have used are to be recognized as *guidelines only*; I have not spent time trying to revise the figures of others. Bookkeeping of different companies is dissimilar; the revaluation of assets occurs at different times in different companies; how companies handled dollar conversions varies. The errors in the statistics may be immense, because they are based on nonanalogous information. Nonetheless, I include "the best available" data.

In selecting companies for inclusion, I have focused on the most important enterprises—important in that they had large-scale operations for their time, were "typical of their time," had significant impact on foreign countries (either in the period covered by this book or later), or had major influence on U.S. policies (again, either in the period covered by this volume or later). I hope this study will give the reader a sense of when, why, how, and where early American businesses went into direct foreign investment; it should suggest the innovative industries as well as the innovative business leaders and corporations. It should give some indication of the problems American companies met as they attempted to do business in foreign lands in the years before World War I. It should, in short, provide the reader with insights into the origins of today's multinational corporations.

July 1969   M. W.

Acknowledgments

Courtney C. Brown, then Dean of the Graduate School of Business, Columbia University, arranged that I be supplied with Ford Foundation funds to make feasible this book; I am most grateful to him and to Ford Foundation. The research was done under the auspices of the Graduate School of Business at Columbia. Allan Nevins, Clarence Walton, Philip Mosely, and Roy Blough helped forward the early stages of this effort. Professor Blough's own work on international business as well as discussions with him stimulated my thinking. Sanford Rose, Yair Aharoni, Emile Benoit, Ronald Schneider, Frank Tannenbaum, and Juan Linz assisted in clarifying difficult points. To Professor Raymond Vernon of the Graduate School of Business Administration at Harvard University, I owe an immense debt; not only did he share a wealth of novel, brilliant ideas, but he gave me a sense of confidence when my spirits ebbed. His suggestions on the first draft of this manuscript were truly superb. His aide, Mrs. Joan P. Curhan generously supplied me with substantial material, which provoked me to fill in gaps in my research. Professor Arthur Johnson of the Graduate School of Business Administration at Harvard University read the first draft of this book with scrupulous care, making invaluable criticisms, which I thoroughly appreciated. Professor Allan Mitchell of Smith College gave fine advice from the standpoint of a "Europeanist." To Mr. Max Hall of Harvard University Press, I want to express wholehearted, genuine appreciation for the attention he has given this work and his constant encouragement. My thanks to my husband, George B. Simmons, are legion; he has been marvelous—offering sage and perceptive comments throughout and most important providing me with a happy world in which to write.

The bibliography indicates the aid of many writers. A few have been especially helpful: Cleona Lewis (her pioneering book on *America's Stake in International Investment*), Herbert Marshall and his colleagues (their excellent study of foreign investment in Canada), Frank A. Southard, Jr. (his splendid volume on U.S. investment in Europe), Edith Penrose (her ideas in *The Theory of the Growth of the Firm*), Alfred D. Chandler and Thomas C. Cochran (their work in business history), and Ralph and Muriel Hidy, George Sweet Gibb and Evelyn H. Knowlton (the four authors of Standard Oil of New Jersey history).

Hundreds of businessmen, whom I interviewed and who gave me time and access to their company's records, contributed significantly to my conception of how business organizations function. Without their assistance, this book would have been impossible. Likewise, patient librarians and archivists—harassed by my incessant demands for books and documents—commanded my admiration. Last, but not least, to my typists, Mrs. Joan Schmidt, Mrs. Athena Prescott, and Mrs. Esther Lanzello, I want to say thank you.

One

The Early Years

The Trader Becomes an Investor

From the period of the earliest known civilization in 2500 B.C., Sumerian merchants found in their foreign commerce that they needed men stationed abroad to receive, to store, and to sell their goods. Later, the Roman trader made contacts at distant points. Much later, the East India Company, chartered in London in 1600, established branches overseas—"outposts of progress." In the mid-seventeenth century, English, French, and Dutch mercantile families sent relatives to America and to the West Indies to represent their firms. So, too, in time, American colonists found in their own foreign trade that it was desirable to have correspondents, agents, and, on occasion, branch houses in important trading centers to warehouse and to sell American exports as well as to select goods for import.[1] The Americans knew of the East India Company's methods and those of other European traders, but the model was not what was relevant. Rather, simply having representatives abroad emerged as a requirement for successful trade. The installation of American mercantile houses overseas, the branching abroad by merchants, and the transformation of traders into investors in other foreign businesses constituted, as we shall see, the initial phase in the history of American business abroad. The colonial merchants of the late seventeenth, and especially of the eighteenth century, pioneered; they planted America's first stakes in foreign lands.

2

Colonial America depended on foreign commerce. Essentials had to be imported. Goods had to be exported to pay for the imports. Exports included North American furs; New England cod fish, whale oil, lumber, and naval stores; New York and New England rum; Virginian wheat, beeswax, and ham; and Maryland and Virginian tobacco. Imports were West Indian sugar and molasses, Portuguese and Spanish salt, lemons, and wine, as well as English manufactured products. In a land with a small population, poor internal communication, and therefore a limited domestic market, foreign trade offered to colonial businessmen the best prospects for wealth.

The typical "businessman" of New Englaɪd and the middle colonies in the seventeenth and eighteenth centuries built his own ships. Frequently, he was himself the captain on voyages abroad. He bought and sold in a number of ports and dealt in many commodities. In his main foreign ports he used agents, who handled his goods on consignment and resold them. The agent might also trade on his own account. In most instances the American would have no direct financial interest in the agent's business. On the contrary, often it was the colonist who was in debt to the British merchant. In a reciprocal manner, the colonial trader not only dealt on his own account, but might serve as agent for American and European sellers.[2]

Sometimes individual Americans would travel to Europe or to the West Indies to do business for their countrymen. They would migrate to the foreign land, retain their American loyalty, and set up enterprises; their operations abroad would have no American home office. An example is American-born Francis Wilks, who served Boston merchant Thomas Hancock in England in the 1730s. Hancock's next agent in London, appointed in 1740, was Massachusetts-born Christopher Kilby. Neither Wilks nor Kilby opened a branch of any particular American company; instead, each traded for many firms. They also represented the Massachusetts Colony in London, combining business and politics. Such "transplanted" Americans formed one category of American business abroad; they were independent agents who started the first American firms overseas.[3]

Some colonial merchants—preferring not to depend on independent agents abroad—dispatched members of their families to England to act for their concerns. This is the first approximation of a foreign branch house, for in most cases the overseas representative was installed at the expense of the American enterprise. The sons of merchant Gerardus

Beekman—William and Gerardus G.—for example, were stationed in Liverpool. Dirck Vander Heyden set up shop in London in 1752 and was the representative for his father in Albany and his brother in New York. Henry Cruger, Jr., of the Cruger family of merchants, became an agent in Bristol. The businessman who established British headquarters —like the independent agent—often acted for a number of American traders, not just his own family firm.[4]

This practice of sending, when possible, a member of the merchant's household to foreign ports seems to have been even more important in the profitable West Indian trade. Sons, cousins, nephews, and brothers of the head of the firm went to the sunny islands of Jamaica, Curaçao, Antigua, St. Eustatius, St. Croix, and others in the Caribbean, to serve the New York houses of Lloyd,* Ludlow, Cruger, Livingston, Van Ranst, Cuyler, Beekman, and Gouverneur.[5] By dispatching a relative abroad, the merchant at home obtained greater control over his business. With such a foreign representative, actions could be taken expeditiously. Distances were spanned, information was more reliable, and thus trading risks were minimized.

In areas where the volume of business was not large enough to warrant an outpost, these same American merchants used independent agents, generally of British nationality. Some British firms had houses in locales where Americans traded and would receive and sell the imports of the colonists, remitting the proceeds in the form desired. Accordingly, the New York merchant John Van Cortlandt, when planning to send some three thousand bushels of wheat from Virginia to Madeira, notified Newton & Gordon, a British concern in Madeira, to sell the wheat and "ship me the proceeds in good Madeira wines."[6]

American merchants engaged in the international movement of peoples as well as commodities. Often, the eighteenth-century trade would be in Negroes from Africa—and still more frequently in indentured servants. The redemptioner trade, in which the shipper financed the passage of the white bonded servant and "sold" the servant on the Virginia rivers, was one means by which America became colonized and also became a source of profit to American businessmen. Yankee merchants had men in Europe to round up "gangs" to bring to the new

* Not Lloyd's of London, but the merchant firm of Henry Lloyd of New York.

world. From the documents on the traffic in African slaves, it seems the New England and middle colony merchants did not have trading outposts in Africa; instead, the captains would stop up and down the West Coast just long enough to collect the slaves. The role of the southern colonies in the commerce was as market, not as shipper.[7]

In sum, by the eighteenth century the typical colonial trader engaged in foreign commerce used either independent agents abroad—generally British but on occasion a transplanted American—or appointed a member of his own family as an agent overseas. In dealing in men the merchant had in some instances representatives in Europe to act as recruiters.

3

Until the time of the Revolution, the American colonies were subject to British mercantile policy. Basic to this policy were these premises: (1) foreign trade was essential; (2) so too was the building of a strong navy and merchant marine; (3) equally crucial was a favorable balance of payments for the mother country; (4) the American colonies were not political entities or communities with needs and interests of their own, but rather "agricultural areas or tenancies, chiefly of importance to England as farming lands, outposts of trade, and sources of wealth"; (5) manufacture in the colonies should be discouraged or prohibited; (6) the colonists were to confine their trade within the empire; and (7) the British government had a role in directing the course of empire commerce.

English laws that attempted to curtail American colonial trade in accord with this philosophy never proved successful; Americans openly flouted the restrictions. Actually, rather than hobble American commerce, the cloak of preferential treatment offered by the British may well have assisted the colonial merchant.[8]

After the Revolution, American businessmen had to adjust to new economic as well as political conditions; no longer were American merchants given empire preference. To compensate for the reduction in dealings with England right after the Revolution—"the embarrassments which have obstructed the progress of our external trade," as Alexander Hamilton put it—Americans tried to develop local manufacture and to expand internal trade. They also sought new and distant markets. Over time new products came into the trade. By 1801 cotton was an important U.S. export, and by 1803, when the value of cotton exports surpassed tobacco, cotton became America's greatest export.[9]

As business expanded, American commission merchants, brokers, shippers, marine insurance companies, and banks developed specialized functions. The specialization that accompanied the growth in trade volume was also reflected in the multiplication of stakes abroad. As American merchants went farther afield, they needed more men overseas to aid them in pursuing their commerce. The "transplanted" American continued as before the Revolution. In the Pacific, Americans established themselves in the Sandwich Islands, 1787, Nootka Sound, 1788, Marquesas, 1791, Fanning, 1797, and Fiji, 1800. American interest in the North Pacific was in whale fisheries, which encouraged the start of an American settlement in Honolulu. The consul to Canton, Major Samuel Shaw, started the firm of Shaw & Randall in that city in 1786, only two years after the Chinese port had been opened to American trade. Shaw & Randall served merchants unfamiliar with the Far East.

The sending of relatives to alien lands continued in the national period, but now the representatives went to more distant locales. In 1803 the Boston merchant, Thomas Perkins, sent his partner and John P. Cushing, his nephew, to start a branch house in Canton. The partner died, and the 16-year-old Cushing continued the enterprise—to make a success of Perkins & Co., Canton.[10]

In the early years of the American republic, trade in the Pacific Northwest was "foreign" business. John Jacob Astor initially handled dealings personally. Then, in 1808, Astor organized the American Fur Company, a limited liability corporation with an initial capital of $1,000,000, which sum he furnished. He installed his own employees at trading posts across the continent; his commerce became an international business extending westward to Canton and eastward to London, Rotterdam, and Liverpool (from whence came drygoods, hardware, gin, and other products needed in the fur trade with the Indians). By the time of the war of 1812, Astor had trading stations on the northwest coast of what would become the United States, and by 1817 he had established a branch in Canton.[11]

Across the Atlantic Ocean new trading commitments were made. Books on the organization of the cotton trade throw little light on the American merchant in Liverpool. Most deal with British firms—importers, commission agents or factors, brokers, and dealers—because, as Norman Sydney Buck put it, "the material necessary to make a fairly complete picture is more abundant for the British agent of trade" and not because the American merchants and factors were less important. An American Chamber of Commerce in Liverpool (the center of the cotton commerce) was formed in 1801, under the presidency of James Maury, American consul. American businessmen in Liverpool seem to have included both merchants collecting goods for sale in the United States and some representatives of American mercantile houses handling cotton.[12]

In general, as their business volume and their profits grew, the largest American-based trading enterprises saw advantages in having their own foreign houses. While the use of independent agents overseas and the sending of members of the family abroad persisted, outsiders (partners, associates, employees) were also dispatched to foreign lands. The late eighteenth- and early nineteenth-century trader seems to have approached his decision on whether to use an independent agent or to establish his own representation abroad with criteria that bear striking resemblances to those used by later and very different types of businesses. In each case there was the question of utilization of scarce resources. For the trader this meant mainly: did he have a man or men available who could be sent overseas to act for his firm? It might also mean, did he have the extra money to station a man abroad? Then, there was the crucial consideration of the adequacy of existing agents. If independent agents in foreign countries were present and were trustworthy and if the trade and profit opportunities were small, the U.S. concern found it preferable to use existing independent agents (either European or American), who would buy and sell, sometimes on order and sometimes on consignment; under such circumstances, aside from the goods involved in each transaction, no investment was made by the U.S. enterprise.

On the other hand, should the volume of business grow, should the profit opportunities seem tempting, the seller often felt the trade would increase even more rapidly if he put it under closer supervision. With a member of the family, a partner, or a salaried representative in the foreign locale, the American enterprise could expect more personal attention to its goods, more satisfactory storage facilities, more information on markets, and more beneficial credit arrangements. Most significant, profits remained within the organization.

Juxtaposed against such advantages were major disadvantages. Branch offices were costly: the profits to the partner or the member of the family, or the salary of the representative abroad, plus the expenses of an office and warehouse, would have to be paid even when there was no trading; thus each business had to be large enough to cover such costs. A second disadvantage was that the independent agent abroad often knew a particular market, which was not true of a man sent from New York or Boston or Philadelphia. Although the latter could learn, the learning process might mean additional cost. Likewise, if the American merchant had depended on the independent foreign agent for financing, this would be eliminated by the new arrangements. In general the home firm had to be prosperous, and the business in a particular foreign country had to be of considerable volume and profitable, or there had to be a basic noneconomic arrangement (such as a relative who wanted to live abroad or a member of the family who was a thorn in the side of the company and who was to be exiled) to justify the investment in a trading post overseas.

By 1836, of the fifty-five foreign firms in Canton, only nine were American. The small number of American houses reflected (1) the size of American trade (2) the position of American commerce relative to British business, and (3) the fact that Americans frequently used British agents. Of the nine American establishments, some, such as the famous Russell & Company (formed in 1824), were autonomous transplanted American firms that acted for any trader who desired their services; some had a direct link with an American company (that is, had a partner in common or were run by a relative of the head of the American firm); and several were branch houses of Boston or New York concerns.[13]

By the 1820s Honolulu had a coterie of "resident traders" who carried on the twofold function of retail merchants and agents of American companies in the sandalwood trade. By that decade there was at least one American house in Manila. As early as 1824 Alsop & Company was in Valparaiso, Chile; Alsop, Wetmore & Co. occupied a building in Lima, Peru, by 1828. That year, or possibly earlier, Boston-born Augustus Hemenway had a trading outpost in Chile. In 1833 S. B. Hale & Co., an American firm, started business in Buenos Aires for trade with the Argentine. Boston-born George Peabody, who made his fortune in trade in Baltimore, in 1837 established himself in London as a mercantile banking house—as "a competitor to Baring Brothers." In the fall of that same year, a director of the Bank of the United States, May Humphreys, and a son of Nicholas Biddle formed a partnership (under the name of Humphreys & Biddle) in Liverpool to serve as agent of the bank and as representative of the Philadelphia firm of Bevans & Humphreys in selling produce shipped to Liverpool. By the 1830s a large number of American merchants resided in England. At the end of that decade or earlier, Americans who acted for U.S. traders were resident in Majunga (Madagascar), Zanzibar, Smyrna, and Bombay. Were a roster available for the 1820s and 1830s of American houses in Cuba, the West Indies, Canada, and Newfoundland, it would include a substantial collection of independent American trading agencies and branches of American commercial concerns. Nonetheless, in spite of the increase in U.S. trading outposts in foreign countries, U.S. merchants in general continued to use independent European—mainly British—houses as their foreign agents. What is important is that the forms were mixed; the same merchant who had direct representation in one port might well use an independent agent in another.[14]

4

At the time when Americans were making some direct foreign investments in trading houses, their country was a net recipient of foreign capital. The interest of individual traders and trading firms in overseas establishments was by no means responsible for the main outflow of funds in the colonial period and in the early years of the Republic. Besides payment for imports, there was dollar outflow covering dividends and interest paid to service European investments in America, capital sent abroad for investments in bonds and stocks of European (mainly English) enterprises (portfolio investments), repatriation of European investments in America, and monies sent home by immigrants (to encourage new immigration). While no figures exist on American direct foreign investment by individual traders and trading firms in these years, evidence indicates that the capital outflow for this purpose was negligible. Yet studies of American mercantile activity seem to demonstrate that these stakes abroad netted for this nation many times the foreign investment.[15]

By several thin threads the business operations of the early traders overseas are linked with today's American international investment. The first such thread is tenuous: the surplus capital accumulated as a result of these trading ventures went for the most part into such American domestic enterprises as real estate, transportation, industry, and mining. Railroads made possible national and then international markets. Manufacturing and extractive ventures—and to a lesser extent railroads—later started their own wave of United States business abroad.

A second link between the early American merchants and subsequent multinational businesses lies in the continuity of a few branches of trading firms. While none of the colonial connections lasted, a small number of the post-revolutionary pioneer American businesses abroad continued for years as permanent trading posts. Harvey & Outerbridge (founded in 1787) and Bowring & Company (founded in 1811) are exceptional in that their houses in Newfoundland survived into the twentieth century. Russell & Company, Canton, 1824–1891, had a relatively long life span, as did Olyphant & Company, also of Canton, which existed over forty years (until 1878). Augustus Hemenway's trading business and his outpost in Chile continued after the founder's death, and there was a direct tie between his enterprise and that of Wessel, Duval & Co., which started in 1906 and exists today. Arkell & Douglas, begun in New York in 1833, established branches abroad, and by 1912 had houses in Europe, South America, Oceania, and Africa. Such firms, and others that could be cited, are rarities; most early foreign outposts of trading houses had short histories.[16]

By the mid-nineteenth century, the continuity of such trading companies became more common. Firms such as W. R. Grace & Co. and American Trading Company still exist in the 1960s. Some concerns— for instance, W. R. Grace, started in Peru in 1854, and Melchior, Armstrong, and Dessau, established in Copenhagen in 1795—began as foreign-based companies and became Americanized in the course of their commerce with the United States.[17]

When large American industrial companies began to sell abroad, most started by using established American trading firms as *their* agents. Then when foreign business in American-manufactured products expanded, industrial corporations began to handle the overseas marketing themselves. This is a significant link between today's multinational enterprise and the export houses.

A third thread that connects the trader and the latter-day giant investor lies in the metamorphosis and merger of particular mercantile businesses into more diversified and sometimes entirely different enterprises. Sometimes this change took place abroad and sometimes at home. Of most interest was the change that occurred overseas. The foreign trader became an investor abroad in other ventures besides commerce. For example, in the 1750s, David Beekman, son of the New York merchant Gerardus Beekman, went to St. Croix to represent his family's firm. Beekman dealt in sugar; with his profits, he purchased sugar estates on the island. His is an early case (the first we have found) of an American trader turning investor and making a direct foreign investment in an agricultural enterprise.[18]

The pattern became typical. It is easy to cite case after case, but a few instances will suffice. Ladd & Company, an American commercial house in Honolulu, was established in 1833; two years later it integrated its business by obtaining a 50-year lease on almost one thousand acres of sugar lands. This firm planted sugar, built a mill, and exported its output to the United States. By the late 1830s, American traders, transformed into plantation owners, were taking the lead not only in developing the sugar industry in Hawaii, but in "virtually every aspect of the economic development of the islands."

Drake Brothers and Company in Cuba in the late 1840s is another example of a trader turned investor in sugar plantations. Augustus Hemenway spent funds he earned in trade to start both a smelting establishment at Caldera, Chile, and small copper mines at Carrizalillo, Chile. Frequently a trading concern would acquire properties in return for bad debts. Thus a Bolivian citizen, Pedro Lopez Gama, came to owe the American firm, Alsop & Company, of Valparaiso, Chile, more than a million dollars. To pay his debt, Lopez Gama assigned to Alsop & Company some claims and rights he had obtained from the Bolivian government. In 1876 the government acknowledged its indebtedness to Alsop & Company; to meet its obligation, it agreed to grant the firm a lien on certain Bolivian customs duties, a guarantee of 40 per cent of the net profits of all mining sets of silver belonging to the Bolivian government (with one exception where the firm would get 50 per cent), and the right to select within three years several silver mines and to work them on the basis of a 25-year concession. In this manner Alsop & Company developed a sizable investment. A predecessor of United Fruit in the Caribbean that started in trading and shipping invested out of earnings in banana plantations, exemplifying the trader turned investor. The activities of W. R. Grace & Co.—contemporaneously with the predecessor of United Fruit—in developing a stake in sugar in Peru provide another illustration of this pattern.[19]

The nineteenth-century trader who established himself abroad in agriculture, mining, and to some extent in railroads and in industry, did so either by accident (that is, through extending credit and acquiring property as a result of the debtor's default) or purposely (by intentional integration of the business). In neither case was much, if any, capital exported from the United States. The foreign investment was made either through the credit line or through the reinvestment of profits accrued abroad.

If some traders invested in agriculture, mining, transportation, or industry abroad, others took a different course. The earliest American private banks to go overseas also had their genesis in trading enterprises. The House of Morgan, with its London connection, evolved from the mercantile business of George Peabody. Samuel B. Hale's Argentine trading firm moved into banking and, in connection with Baring Brothers, J. P. Morgan, and Morton Rose & Company, floated loans for the Argentine national government and several of the provincial governments. From the late 1840s on, the American firms, Lazard Frères, Seligman, and Morton, Bliss & Co., set up branch banks in Europe; their financial dealings also emerged out of mercantile endeavor. These houses found trading in money to be more lucrative than dealing in goods.[20]

5

In summary, in the colonial period American direct foreign investment was made either by independent merchants or by members of a trader's family. The stakes thus established appear to have been confined to England and to islands in the West Indies. All were short-lived. After independence, trading firms set up more outposts in alien lands, spanning an increasingly wider geographical area. The branch house form of direct investment abroad took on importance in the post-Revolutionary years, as merchants sought control over their distribution network. The capital exported to start and to maintain the units outside the United States was minimal. As the nineteenth century progressed, there came to be threads connecting certain of these U.S.-owned overseas businesses and present-day enterprises. While many such foreign concerns existed only for a short time, some came to develop their own histories. Some broadened their functions, integrating into mining, agriculture, industry, transportation, and banking. Measured by the number of ventures (relative to other contemporary American direct investments abroad), the foreign trader-foreign investor—a perennial in American history—was most significant in colonial times and in the first seventy-five years of the republic.

New Stakes Abroad
(1800–1860)

In Mexico they [Americans] are building railroads and cutting through mountains. In Lima they are projecting turnpikes. . .In Brazil people from the States are growing cotton and showing how it can be manufactured without taking it all the way to Liverpool or Manchester. In the States of the Plata, Edward A. Hopkins is building an 'American wharf.'—"American Enterprise Abroad," *Merchant's Magazine,* 36:263 (February 1857).

The first three decades of the nineteenth century saw slow economic growth in the United States as the nation created the preconditions for rapid advance. The country was shaping a stable and viable political structure, accruing revenues from rising exports of cotton, establishing an important textile industry, and starting to build canals as a link between the coast and the interior.

In the thirty years prior to the Civil War, America experienced great economic progress, scarred only by the Panics of 1837 and 1857. Americans introduced revolutionary new inventions: the telegraph, the reaper, and the sewing machine. Manufacturing enterprises—still of small scale —dotted urban centers in the Northeast and Midwest. Miners found gold in California, and entrepreneurs began to extract basic industrial minerals (coal in Pennsylvania, copper and iron ore in Michigan, and oil in Pennsylvania). The nation's population more than doubled, rising from 13 million to 35 million. The boundary of Oregon was set in 1846. California and the Southwest joined the United States in 1848. Internal transportation expanded rapidly. Unquestionably Americans devoted their main investments to domestic development. Capital was scarce and was primarily used at home; opportunities for profit abounded in the new nation. Yet, at the same time—and while America attracted sizable amounts of European funds—some U.S. citizens (besides the merchants) made direct *foreign* investments. As we shall see, there were three distinct groups of Americans who invested abroad.[1]

In the years 1800–1860 the United States government began to define very tentatively its role in relation to American business abroad. Its new diplomatic offices in foreign lands were places for businessmen to call.

It installed consuls overseas concerned with commercial activity and protection of United States citizens living or conducting business in the consular district. A number of the consuls engaged in foreign business on their own. On occasion the State Department and even the President of the United States—before the Civil War—dealt with problems involving American business investment abroad.

Some American treaties concluded in the pre-Civil War period directly affected, or would come to affect, American business abroad. America's entrance into commercial treaties with friendly nations became important in creating congenial conditions for future investors. The first such treaty, the Treaty of Amity and Commerce, was signed with France in 1778. Of a different character was the Treaty of Wanghia (1844), whereby Americans gained full trading privileges in treaty ports in China and most-favored-nation guarantees. Under this treaty Americans, for the first time, gained explicit extraterritorial rights in China: an American accused of crimes in China would be tried by an American consular official. Initially this was primarily of interest to traders, but later became important to investors. Other pre-Civil War treaties directly relevant to business abroad included the Treaty with New Granada, signed in 1846 and approved by the Senate in 1848, and the Clayton-Bulwer Treaty, signed and approved in 1850. Their impact will be evident in the text to follow.

The mood in Washington during the 1850s of "Manifest Destiny," and the official mission of Commodore Matthew Calbraith Perry to Japan in 1853 to open that country to trade, would at a later date have impact on American investment. (In the 1850s there was no American investment in Japan.)

Before the Civil War, the United States government neither sponsored, guaranteed, nor wholeheartedly supported American business abroad,* but neither did it do anything to thwart it. It did defend businessmen before claims commissions when their properties were lost abroad (sometimes with success and at other times unsuccessfully). Like-

---

* When the British Superintendent of Trade in Canton visited merchant Robert Forbes in 1839, urging him to cooperate with a British blockade and close his firm, the American manager stoutly replied, "I should remain at my post as long as I could sell a yard of goods or buy a pound of tea . . . we Yankees have no Queen to guarantee our losses" (Forbes, *Personal Reminiscences*, p. 149).

wise, by the 1850s there were certain instances of gunboat diplomacy. There were also instances when business would have welcomed more aid from the United States government and did not receive it.[2]

2

The first category of direct investors abroad (excluding the traders) in the years 1800–1860 comprised individual entrepreneurs. These men went overseas to do business in a variety of industries, agriculture, and mining, as well as banking, transportation, and public utilities. Table II.1 gives examples of such enterprises.[3]

Table II.1. Early American entrepreneurs abroad

Place	Date	Activity by American citizens
CANADA:		
St. Andrews, Quebec	1804	Two built a paper mill
Montreal, Quebec	1820	Started a small bank
Ontario	Late 1830s & 1840s	Opened tanneries, foundries, and carriage works
Ontario	Before 1840	Participated in the lumber industry
Sherbrooke, Quebec	1840s	Helped start a cotton mill
Ontario	1840s	Took part in copper mining
Windsor, Ontario	1850s	Massachusetts-born Hiram Walker erected a distillery
Ontario	1850s	Started to manufacture agricultural implements and sewing machines
ENGLAND:		
Manchester	1810	Joseph C. Dyer with other Americans brought from U.S. about 12 machines, which Dyer subsequently undertook to manufacture in England
MEXICO:	By the 1820s	Were mining precious metals, planting coffee, and operating sawmills
Vera Cruz-Mexico City	1830	Three New Englanders established Mexico's first stagecoach line
Tabasco	1831	Aaron Leggett got an exclusive grant to run steamboats in state waters for 10 years

Table II.1. (continued)

Place	Date	Activity by American citizens
CUBA:	By 1834	Owned sugar plantations and mills as well as iron mines
ARGENTINA:	1813	One obtained rights from the Argentine government to make bricks, another to provide boat service
	About 1821	Stephen Hallett arrived in Buenos Aires, opened shop as publisher of books, magazines, and newspapers (in English and Spanish). He was said to have written his own copy, erected his own press, cast his own type, "and actually fabricated his own paper and ink when the occasion demanded it"
PARAGUAY:	1853	Edward A. Hopkins built a sawmill and cigar factory
HAWAII:	By late 1840s	Value of American property estimated at $1,000,000, including homes, shops, a newspaper printing house, and land
	1850s	Controlled roughly ¾ of Hawaiian business
RUSSIA: St. Petersburg	1857	Several from Baltimore, Maryland, were building locomotives, cars, castings of cannon, and making a variety of machinery for the Russian government

Source: See note 3.

It would be possible to document hundreds of other individual Americans who went to foreign countries and established businesses. The evidence is clear: not only in Canada, England, Mexico, Cuba, Argentina, Paraguay, Hawaii, and Russia, but in many other spots around the globe, individual Americans migrated and initiated new ventures. The sum total of such Americans in the years 1800–1860 probably numbered under six hundred. They do represent, however, an early planting of stakes abroad.

These heterogenous enterprises each involved only a small amount of American capital. Often American entrepreneurs went abroad and used British capital. For instance, Americans built—while the British financed —the first Cuban Railroad (1837). Massachusetts-born William Wheelwright (1798–1873), considered by Latin American historians to be the most prominent early American entrepreneur in Latin America, moved to Valparaiso, Chile, in 1830, where he constructed lighthouses, port facilities, and gas and water works. In 1838 he obtained a concession to operate a steamship line on the west coast of South America. When he could attract no United States capital, he obtained British funds and founded the Pacific Steam Navigation Company. Wheelwright developed a Chilean coal supply; between 1849 and 1852 he built the first railroad in Chile from the port of Caldera to the coal mines at Copiapó—also financed by British money. In 1850, because of Wheelwright, Chile was the first South American country to have a telegraph line. In 1863 he began to build, on the Argentine side, a railroad to link Argentina and Chile. His is the fascinating story of American talent and ingenuity, with little American capital. Only to the extent that he invested *very small sums* of his own can his activities be called direct investment.[4]

This was likewise the case with Henry Meiggs, who arrived in Chile in 1855 and by 1858 was a contractor on bridge buildings for the Southern Railway in Chile. The railroad was financed by British interests.[5] There are many instances which indicate that when large amounts of capital were needed in these years, Americans—operating abroad— turned to European sources. It appears to have been American individuals rather than American capital, in the quotation at the head of this chapter, who were in 1857 building the railroad in Mexico, the turnpike in Peru, and the wharf in Argentina.

What motivated such Americans to go abroad? If they invested their own money, why did they do so? Their motives were diverse, and often highly personal. Some individuals visited a foreign locale to see a relative or friend, to tour, or to represent the United States government, and while there saw business possibilities. Others, in the United States, heard of specific opportunities in a foreign land and went to seek them. Some were employed overseas by a foreign firm and reinvested money *earned abroad* in an overseas enterprise of their own (in case of trouble, the United States government considered this stake to be an "American" foreign investment). Others were fugitives from American justice.[6]

The Americans who emigrated to start foreign enterprises as private businessmen or to work for firms financed by foreign capital (and then to make direct investment on their own) generally operated in a single country.* They transmitted more skills and talent than capital. Many of their businesses were short-lived, lasting only their lifetime or that of their sons. Some, especially those in underdeveloped countries, found themselves hounded by host nation governments and their concessions canceled. Others—in Canada, for example—had no difficulty operating in a foreign environment. If these businessmen had problems with the host country they would call on the U.S. government, which acted on claims commissions to try to gain compensation for lost American investments.[7]

3

The second set of direct investors in pre-Civil War America, unlike the first group, did not "transplant" their businesses. This category of direct investors had foreign investments that aided *American* development. Their foreign investments were, like those in the first category, highly diversified. For example, the American banking enterprise of Peabody-Morgan in London (started in 1837) had as its main aim to attract British capital to the United States rather than to finance American expansion abroad.[8]

Similarly, when Chicago was being settled, Daniel H. Hale went to Europe, formed two companies (one Scottish and the other English), and lured immigrants as well as funds to the midwestern wilderness. William F. Harnden, in the 1840s, established an international express service, with agencies in leading cities of England, France, Scotland,

* An exception was American-born machine builder Joseph C. Dyer, who established a factory in Manchester, England, and then in the late 1820s or early 1830s, since machinery export was prohibited by British law, installed his sons under the name Dyer Frères, as machine makers and cotton spinners in France. (Testimony Matthew Curtis to Select Committee, *Parliamentary Papers*, 1841, VII, 114–115).

Ireland, and Germany. His was also a popular immigration company, arranging for the passage of Europeans to the New World.

Erastus Corning, John Murray Forbes, and John W. Brooks in 1849–1850 invested in the Great Western Railway in Canada. The line would serve, they hoped, as a connecting link between the New York Central and the Michigan Central Railroads. New York railroads and stockholders of the Michigan Central invested about $800,000 in the Great Western with this intention. Their plan was defeated. In 1851 the Great Western adopted a 5′6″ gauge, over the vigorous protests of the American stockholders; thus the railroad did not connect with the American roads, which had a 4′8½″ gauge.

In 1854 the American Cyrus W. Field raised $1,500,000 from New York "merchants and capitalists" for the New York, Newfoundland & London Electric Telegraph Company. The company obtained a charter and subsidy from the Newfoundland legislature and two and one-half years later completed a telegraph line across Newfoundland and a cable to Nova Scotia. Since telegraph connections from Halifax, Nova Scotia, to New York already existed, the new lines shortened by about forty-eight hours the time for news carried by European steamers to reach New York. Field next sought funds to lay a cable between Newfoundland and Ireland. American investors were uninterested; apparently Field himself bought about 88 shares in his new company, the Atlantic Telegraph Company, Ltd. (The 88 shares were worth about £88,000, or $444,000.) The rest of the stock for his new British-incorporated company (capital £350,000) was sold in England. Ten years later (1866) the Atlantic Telegraph Company, Ltd. completed the first transatlantic cable.

The American publishing firm of Wiley and Putnam in 1841 opened a branch in London, planning to sell American books in Great Britain. This sales branch became derivative; its manager found the most remunerative business was the purchase of English books for sale in the United States.[9]

The investments by George Peabody, Hale and Harnden, the U.S. railroadmen, Cyrus Field, and Wiley and Putnam, seemingly isolated examples of pre-Civil War American foreign investments, had one common feature: they sought to supply the United States with funds, immigrants, railroad connections, news, and books. The Americans who invested in Europe found in the early 1840s, when Pennsylvania and Maryland were defaulting on interest payments on foreign-held bonds, that, as one wrote home, they were subject to "mortification, obloquy, and disgrace" because the state governments had reneged on their obligations. The Americans abroad were given a "tongue lashing." [10] There is no evidence that the United States government played any role whatsoever on behalf of these early American investors—either in encouraging or discouraging them.

4

In this second category of American direct foreign investments—those aiding *American* development—were two giant enterprises, giant by the standards of the 1840s and 1850s. These were investments in transportation. Here, in contrast to the earlier mentioned ventures, the government of the United States did take on an important role. In December 1846 the American minister in Bogotá (capital of New Granada*) thought it dangerous "to let the golden moment pass" and signed a treaty to guarantee United States transit rights across the Isthmus of Panama. The American Senate approved the treaty on June 3, 1848. That year Congress authorized mail contracts for two steamship lines, one on the Atlantic and one on the Pacific side of the Isthmus. Although the Isthmus would temporarily be crossed by mule and small boat, President James K. Polk envisaged a railroad or canal. In 1848 the United States Mail Steamship Company accepted the Atlantic contract, and the Pacific Mail Steamship Company took the West Coast contract. William H. Aspinwall of the Pacific company agreed to build a railroad spanning the Isthmus.

Accordingly, in 1848 Aspinwall, joined by two other Americans, Henry Chauncey and John L. Stephens, made a contract with the New Granada government. The 49-year contract gave the Americans the exclusive right to construct a railroad, free use of all public lands lying on its path, and 250,000 additional acres of public land. It stipulated the railroad company would have the right to set tolls. New Granada was to

* In 1830 the name "New Granada" was given to the area now comprising Colombia and Panama. The region was renamed in 1858 the Granadine Confederation, in 1861 the United States of Colombia, and in 1866 the Republic of Colombia.

receive 3 per cent of the profits of the new business. Aspinwall agreed to complete the work within eight years. He echoed President Polk in declaring the railroad would spur trade to California and Oregon, as well as to China, Australia, and the East Indies.[11]

The demand for fast, safe passage to the American West was stimulated by the discovery of gold in California in January 1848. The alternatives to crossing the Isthmus were the westward trip by covered wagon or the treacherous 9,000-mile voyage by boat around Cape Horn. When the Panama Railroad Company was chartered by the New York legislature (April 7, 1849), Aspinwall found it easy to raise the authorized capital of $1,500,000 (shortly hiked to $5,000,000). This was clearly an attractive investment, with prospects of profit immediate because of the fervent desire of Americans to go west. Research indicates that the stake in the Panama Railroad was the first truly large American direct foreign investment. This enterprise had the then unique characteristic of combining the export of American skills, techniques, *and money* on what was for the time a mammoth scale.

Dense jungle, malaria-infected mosquitoes, and sand flies impeded progress on the line. The sultry tropical sun made for cruel working conditions, as did the six months of rain. The company had difficulty getting labor—must less efficient labor; the resources of Panama could not feed the imported work force, and food had to be imported. By August 1850, however, in spite of such obstacles, the construction of the Panama Railroad was under way.[12]

Meanwhile, other Americans sought to provide transport between the two oceans. Many people in the United States wanted free transit rights over the Isthmus of Tehuantepec in southern Mexico included in the Peace Treaty signed at the end of the Mexican War (1848). Mexico refused, insisting the privilege had been granted to a Mexican contractor, who in turn had ceded it to a British company. Not to be outdone, the American-owned Tehuantepec Railroad Company, in 1849, acquired the concession from the British firm. General John G. Barnard, on behalf of the American company, made a survey, and the company prepared construction plans; but before the work began the Mexican government, in 1850—consistent with its earlier refusal—declared the company's concession void.[13]

Another scheme was developed by E. G. Squier, then a United States consul in Central America. Squier planned in 1850 to construct a railway across Honduras. He formed a company in 1853, but because of opposition from the owners of the Panama Railroad Company, his railroad was never built. The estimated financial loss to his backers was about one-half million dollars.[14]

A fourth American endeavor to link the Atlantic and Pacific oceans became the first success.[15] In August 1849 the Nicaraguan government gave Commodore Cornelius Vanderbilt's newly formed American Atlantic and Pacific Ship Canal Company a contract for a canal. The document specified that if the company found it impossible to build a canal, it would "construct a railroad, or rail and carriage road." The company set out almost immediately to pave a macadam road and to establish a carriage-steamboat route. "New York merchants and capitalists" invested more than $2 million. On July 3, 1851, the route was opened. No plans were made for a canal. On August 14, 1851, the Nicaraguan government chartered the Accessory Transit Company, formed by stockholders in the canal company and controlled by Vanderbilt. The transit company acquired certain rights granted the American Atlantic and Pacific Ship Canal Company: first, the exclusive rights of crossing the Nicaraguan isthmus by means *other than* a canal; and second, an agreement to pay the Nicaraguan government 10 per cent of its profits. From July 1851 into 1852 the Nicaraguan route operated by the transit company was the best approach to the American West.

Vanderbilt put aside his plans for a canal. The British, with interests in the West Indies and British Honduras, eyed American intentions with alarm, believing the British should control any canal that went through Nicaragua—or elsewhere in Central America. In the Clayton-Bulwer Treaty (April 19, 1850) the United States and British governments bound themselves to cooperate in the construction of an isthmus canal, but no cooperation was forthcoming. Thus, in the 1850s it was left to private enterprise to cope with interoceanic traffic.

Because American investments in the Accessory Transit Company and the Panama Railroad were so large (in terms of the 1850s), it is worth viewing the experiences of these two companies in detail. As already noted, the Accessory Transit Company was the first of the two to begin operations; it was also the first to conclude operations. The company did business at a profit but did not pay to the Nicaraguan government 10 per cent, as specified by the contract. During 1852 the transit company and the Greytown, Nicaragua government also started to dispute the occupancy of a particular tract of land over which each claimed sovereignty. When, early in 1853, the Greytown city government insisted the company remove its establishment from that land, an agent of the transit company "craved" protection from George N. Hollins, captain of the United States sloop-of-war *Cyane*. Hollins, who could not "permit any depredations on the property of the Accessory Transit Company," sent ashore twenty-four marines. The dispute was settled temporarily by compromise, but in Nicaragua hostility to the company remained over the unpaid sum due the government.

Then, on May 16, 1854, the captain of a company-owned steamboat shot a native boatman after their ships collided. When Greytown authorities tried to arrest the captain for murder, the American minister, Solon Borland, intervened. Later that evening, Nicaraguan officials attempted to take Borland into custody, and in the confusion, the minister was hit with a fragment of a broken bottle. United States Secretary of State W. L. Marcy felt Nicaragua should apologize to Borland; the U.S. Secretary of the Navy dispatched Hollins and the *Cyane* to protect company property and redress the insult. After consultation with transit company officials, the American commercial agent at Greytown demanded $24,000 for damages to transit company property and insisted on the apology. When the demands were not met, Hollins on July 13th bombarded Greytown, destroying the entire town. The United States Department of State did not rebuke Hollins, and President Franklin Pierce justified the captain's action in his message to Congress in December 1854. Such incidents of gunboat diplomacy muddied the waters of American-Latin American relations for many years. But what followed was worse.

In the summer of 1853 Vanderbilt had lost control of the Accessory Transit Company to two Americans, Charles Morgan, a Connecticut Yankee who had been in shipping and in railroads in the American Southwest, and Cornelius K. Garrison, who owned a profitable mercantile and banking house in Panama. After growing increasingly discontent with political conditions in Nicaragua, Morgan and Garrison saw their answer in William Walker, a California adventurer who hoped to extend American sovereignty to Central America. Walker had no State Department support. On May 4, 1855, he arrived in Nicaragua. With the financial assistance of Morgan and Garrison and with aid from them in the movement of troops and supplies, Walker in October 1855 overthrew the antagonistic Nicaraguan regime.

Meanwhile, unknown to Morgan and Garrison, Vanderbilt began repurchasing shares in the transit company and by February 1856 had regained control. Not to be outwitted, Morgan and Garrison demanded that Walker annul the transit company's charter, seize its property on the grounds of Nicaragua's unsatisfied financial claim,* and grant them a new charter! The Walker government complied. Vanderbilt countered: declaring the Accessory Transit Company's route through Nicaragua closed, warning people not to take the passage because of political turmoil in Nicaragua, extracting payments of $40,000 per month from the Pacific Mail Line and the United States Mail Line in return for promises not to compete on the Panama route and not to permit Morgan and Garrison to succeed in Nicaragua, and asking the United States government to intervene to "wrest from the aggressors their plunder and to restore to us to the enjoyment of our outraged rights." He stated the property confiscated was worth between $700,000 and $1,000,000. His pleas notwithstanding, the United States government took no action. Later, in 1856, Vanderbilt personally sponsored a successful rebellion against Walker, fulfilling his promise to the steamship lines and blocking forever the plans of Morgan and Garrison. Then as a final touch Vanderbilt submitted a claim against Costa Rica—which had aided him in the overthrow of Walker—for destruction of the property of the bankrupt Accessory Transit Company. He also submitted a claim against Nicaragua. In neither case was there compensation. The Nicaragua route was closed. "The stockholders' money has been wasted," complained in vain the receiver for the Accessory Transit Company.

In the years from 1851 to 1855, when the Accessory Transit Company operated, it carried some 20,000 people annually across the isthmus and

---

* Other, more spurious grounds were also included.

made modest profits.* After 1856 the jungle closed in over the road. This early foreign investment, and Vanderbilt's ancillary activities in connection with it, yielded him a personal fortune. On the other hand, the New York residents who invested in the company had not received their money back and much ill-will persisted in Nicaragua. In 1862 a new company—not affiliated with Vanderbilt interests—was formed with a capital of $3,000,000. It sought to reopen the Nicaragua route, but because of conflicts with the Nicaraguan government the effort proved a failure. The idea of a canal traversing Nicaragua was contemplated frequently—until in 1903 the United States government selected the alternate Panama Canal route.[16]

Meanwhile, the Panama Railroad had become passable in October 1851, and as conflicts in Nicaragua gained publicity in the United States, American travelers chose to take this slightly longer route. The railroad paid its levies to the New Granada government, and there was no strife. In 1855, the first year of full operation, the railroad brought in gross receipts of $1.1 million; in subsequent years its revenues mounted. The line had cost $8 million to construct. After 1856, with no other route across the Central American isthmus, the Panama Railroad provided the undisputed best means of getting to the American West. Both Presidents Pierce and Buchanan felt it the duty of the United States to provide for safe transit in Panama, and the U.S. government intervened militarily at least twice before 1861 to keep the right of passage clear.

Until the completion of a United States transcontinental railroad in 1869, the Panama Railroad continued to be the best route from the American East to the American West. By the end of 1867 it had carried more than 400,000 passengers. In 1868 alone its gross receipts, including freight and mail as well as passengers, totaled $4.3 million. Its profits that year, after all fixed charges, totaled $2,307,483, equal to nearly 33 per cent earned on the $7,000,000 stock. (The capital had been increased from $5,000,000 to $7,000,000 in 1865 by an issue of a 40 per cent stock dividend.)

---

* The Nicaraguan government claimed as due it $40,000, which if a valid claim, by extrapolation would mean the company made $400,000 in profits during the years 1851–1855, or an average of roughly 4% per annum on the $2 million invested.

When in 1869 the first transcontinental railroad across the United States was completed, it obtained the traffic. Even so, the Panama Railroad Company could have continued to be profitable, for it had a sizable trade in goods passing between the West Coast of South America and Europe, but a quarrel over rates with the British-owned Pacific Steam Navigation Company reduced this business. The Panama Railroad was on the brink of disaster. The subsequent history of this company—how in the 1870s it joined in a freight pool with American railroads and once more became a profitable concern; how in 1881 a French Canal Company acquired the line; how the French tried and failed to build a canal; how in 1904 the American government purchased the properties of the French company—are all part of a later story. The Panama Railroad stands out, however, as an exceptional, early, large, and profitable investment of American capital in foreign lands. From 1852 to 1905 inclusive, a total of $36,377,068 in cash and $2,146,772 in stock was returned to the company's stockholders, a respectable performance for 48 miles of railroad.[17]

American funds spent on the Panama Railroad and on the Nicaraguan carriage-steamboat line were by far the most important pre-Civil War direct foreign investments of United States citizens. The money had been spent in underdeveloped countries. Although the activity of the American minister in Bogotá in 1846 had cleared the way for the transit rights across the Isthmus of Panama, and on a number of occasions American forces intervened to keep the right of transit clear, the building and operation of the railroad had been in private hands and privately financed. In Nicaragua in the pre-Civil War years the American government with its gunboat diplomacy, played a dubious role. To be sure, Washington disclaimed William Walker's efforts in Nicaragua, but ultimately the opposition of Cornelius Vanderbilt's transit company defeated the adventurer. Walker had been encouraged by the transit company under Morgan and Garrison, and overthrown by the same company under Vanderbilt.

In Panama the railroad had for many years important consequences in bringing trade and revenue into the country. United States citizens established mercantile and banking houses in the free ports. The American Carl B. Franc started planting bananas near the railroad in the late 1860s. American enterprise made important contributions. In Nicaragua the situation was the opposite; American business showed itself at an early point in shabby garb.[18]

5

Companies in the third category of U.S. foreign investors were the forerunners of the multinational corporate stakes of later years. Before the Civil War, America was basically an exporter of primary products. Some American manufacturing companies, however, aspired to export. By the 1850s American technology was so developed that in certain metallurgical industries linked with mass production (machine tools, guns, reapers, and sewing machines) this country already had world leadership.

When in 1851 Americans demonstrated their wares at the Crystal Palace exhibit in London, many Europeans saw for the first time the technical accomplishments of the New World. Among the exhibitors were Day & Newell (locks), Wetherill Brothers (chemicals), C. H. McCormick (reapers), John R. St. John (compasses), Samuel Colt (repeating firearms), Lippincott, Grambo & Co. (books), Colgate and Co. (starch). Not one of these firms in 1851 had foreign branches, subsidiaries, or affiliates; in time many of these, or their successors, would have large international businesses.[19]

Some of the exhibitors had exported and had discovered their products were not competitive in Europe. Cyrus McCormick found this true of the American reaper. Accordingly, in 1851 he made a licensing arrangement with the British firm, Burgess & Key, to manufacture and sell his reaper. Burgess & Key contracted to make the reaper, "to take charge of the machine at Lincoln for exhibition and to exhibit it in operation in Ireland and in the north of England and also in Scotland." The firm paid McCormick a royalty on sales.[20]

On the other hand, Samuel Colt, "to protect himself from the destructive effects which would follow the introduction of . . . spurious arms into use in England, where he had no patent," decided to set up a foreign branch plant. Colt had established the Colt Patent Fire Arms Manufacturing Company in Hartford, Connecticut, in 1848. Four years later he built his London factory, introducing American methods and machinery. According to his biographers, Colt "would have preferred to buy his machinery in England to create a favorable impression among prospective customers, but no machinery made in England was exact enough for the work necessary to turn out the revolvers." The guns Colt manufactured in Britain were replicas of those produced at his Hartford plant. His London manufacturing enterprise appears to have been the first foreign *branch plant* of any American company. It is significant that the investment was in the leading industrial country of the world.

The factory was a financial failure. As early as December 1853 Colt considered it a "constant drain on [his] resources and energies." Four years later he sold the British facility to a few Englishmen, who took the name of London Pistol Company and who continued to manufacture Colt guns. Soon their business went bankrupt. Meanwhile, on the continent of Europe, Colt licensed arms to be made by other manufacturers. Although these revolvers never reached the high standards of the American-made unit, Colt had little incentive to start a manufactory on the continent after his discouraging experience in England.[21]

Three years after Colt had started his London factory, five Americans, partners in the firm of J. Ford and Company, of New Brunswick, New Jersey, acquired a mill and began to produce vulcanized rubber in Edinburgh. Their 1856 Scottish plant was American-financed, designed, equipped, and managed. They invested in Britain because they envisaged higher profits than they could earn by expanding in the United States; one commentator explains that "the specific choice of location was strongly influenced by the fact that, at that time, English patents were not protected in Scotland, and could thus be exploited there without the payment of royalties." Like Colt's enterprise, this U.S. venture was shortlived; by the second half of the 1860s, the five Americans had sold out to British interests.[22] The manufactories of Colt and of J. Ford and Company in Britain were to our knowledge exceptional as American direct investments in foreign "branch" factories before the Civil War. There appear to have been no others.

6

To summarize, by the time of the American Civil War, this country's businessmen had made various types of direct foreign investments. The direct investments had been in industry, agriculture, mining, banking, and public utilities (as well as trade), with the largest sums involved in transportation. If we exclude the investments of the traders (discussed in Chapter I), the others were

1. investments by individual American entrepreneurs, who emigrated and started their own small businesses abroad;

2. investments by American men or companies in foreign countries to aid American domestic development; and

3. investments by American manufacturing firms or their stockholders in overseas "branch" factories—to supply a foreign market (only two and both failures).

These categories, while not completely exclusive, provide the range of nonportfolio foreign investments made by Americans before 1860. The order offers a key to the *numerical* prevalence of each type.

By 1860 American businesses had obtained concessions from foreign governments in Nicaragua, Panama, Argentina, and Mexico. Americans had invested in both underdeveloped and developed nations, from Paraguay to England. American businessmen had learned from experiences in Nicaragua and elsewhere that the political climate for foreign investment might be different from what it was at home. They had found themselves in competition with the British in such third-country areas as Mexico and Central America. American entrepreneurs in underdeveloped regions had discovered the United States government would act in some instances, but not in others, to protect their properties from damages—for example, in Panama and only in part in Nicaragua.

Regrettably, the data are not good enough to establish a schedule of the *value* of U.S. direct foreign investment in the years before 1860. The statement in *Historical Statistics of the United States* that the U.S. direct foreign investment in the pre-Civil War years was "negligible" is not disputed here.[23] It seems true both in the absolute amount of money involved and on any realistic comparative basis.* The only sizable for-

* That is, compared with the United States domestic investment, compared with U.S. GNP, compared with British foreign investment.

eign investments (over several million dollars) were in Panama and Nicaragua; these investments related entirely to the growth of the American economy. It is clear, however, that by the 1860s Americans had demonstrated they were ready to start establishments beyond the frontiers of their own nation.

The Appearance of Modern International Business (1865–1892)

Although American traders, individual citizens, and some corporations had made foreign direct investments before the Civil War, two prerequisites for international business * were absent: the first was speedy transportation and communication to distant places; the second was the transformation of the American corporation into a national enterprise.

In the mid-nineteenth century, sailing-packets made the trip from the United States to Europe in about 21 days, and the fastest clipper ship took 14 days. Steamships in the 1850s crossed the ocean in 9 to 10 days. By the 1880s, passenger-carrying steamships made the trip in 5 to 6 days. As noted earlier, the first transatlantic cable was completed in 1866. We will see in this chapter that other cables followed—making possible speedy communication.[1]

As railroads crisscrossed the United States in the years 1865–1892, U.S. companies began to market their products nationally. Not until businessmen thought of national sales (as distinct from local, state, or regional sales) did they consider international expansion. Sometimes their international aspirations coincided with their national plans; sometimes their international endeavors started immediately after their domestic distribution network had been established; sometimes foreign projects were long delayed. It was, however, the American companies with national sales plans and unique products that discovered the attractions of business abroad and were the first to be successful in undertaking such activities.[2]

---

* Henceforth, when I use the term "international business," I no longer refer to the international trader, but instead to the American-based corporation with *investments* in foreign branches, subsidiaries, and/or affiliates.

This chapter examines the foundation from which developed today's multinational enterprises—the initial foreign investments made by U.S. companies to enlarge their sales abroad. We shall not be concerned here with American businesses' investments abroad to obtain sources of supply. The reason is that while Americans were quick to make investments worldwide in order to sell, they were slower to do so in order to obtain raw materials. America had a large domestic market, yet this in no way deterred businessmen from seeking still more opportunities abroad. The United States also had rich natural resources; and Americans looked first at home for oil, copper, iron, lead, silver, and timber; that they did so deterred foreign investment. Why was there the difference?

Marketing abroad involved only a negligible foreign investment, and sometimes none at all. It could be started with virtually no outflow of monies from the United States. On the other hand, the capital required to exploit resources was larger. Scarce capital in the United States found satisfactory employment at home. Companies hesitated to make sizable investments abroad when domestic raw materials were available.

Because of the small capital requirements, companies that marketed abroad often sold world-wide, although they did pay special heed to the regions where the per capita income was the highest and the ability to consume was the greatest. On the other hand, before the 1890s, when some businesses ventured abroad to invest in railroads, or copper, iron, lead, silver, or timber, they generally went to nearby areas—Mexico, Canada, or the Caribbean—as will be evident later.

For most American companies, the investments abroad between 1865 and 1892 were made with an eye to filling foreign demands. Most extensions were in marketing. Some companies began to manufacture and to refine outside the United States to fill foreign requirements. There were also, as we will see, some investments in selling services—in utilities and insurance—again to cater to the needs of foreign consumers.

Balance-of-payments statistics do not reflect the early extensions of American business abroad. With the exception of 1877–1879 and 1881, in the years 1865–1892 America was a net recipient of foreign funds. The net capital outflow from 1877 to 1879 and in 1881 cannot be attributed to large direct investments, but rather to repatriation of European funds invested in this nation. Even if our balance-of-payments statistics were better, they would not explain the business abroad undertaken by the nascent American international enterprises. United States business developed abroad gradually; the capital outflow was initially minute. Only if we look at the characteristics of the foreign expansion in some detail can we understand the emergence of American business commitments in foreign lands. No general estimates have been made of the book value of our direct investment abroad before 1897.[3]

Little will be said in this chapter about the U.S. government's influence on the development of these businesses' stakes in foreign lands; my reading of the evidence indicates that its role was peripheral. The government did aid Commercial Cable Company and other cable companies in arranging to land cables abroad, but such aid was exceptional. The typical American company went abroad "on its own."

2

Singer * was the first American international business, anticipating the Standard Oil companies, General Electric, National Cash Register, and International Harvester. It started its international business on the heels of its domestic plans. Its machine came to be sold in villages, towns, and cities. Throughout the world it came to have substantial foreign investments. The early presidents of Singer, I. M. Singer (1851–1863), Inslee Hopper (1863–1876), Edward Clark (1876–1882), George R. McKenzie (1882–1889), and F. G. Bourne (1889–1905) paid personal attention to foreign business. We will look carefully at the Singer case—an exemplar.[4]

Late in August 1850 I. M. Singer saw some primitive sewing machines in Boston and decided "if I could make the sewing machine practical, I should make some money." His friend George B. Zieber offered him forty dollars to build a model machine; another friend provided workshop space. Singer himself later recalled "I worked at it day and night, sleeping but three or four hours out of twenty-four . . . The machine

* From 1851–1863, this unincorporated unit was called I. M. Singer & Company; in 1863 Singer Manufacturing Company was organized as a New York company; it became a New Jersey company in 1873. In 1904 Singer Sewing Machine Company became the *sales* company for Singer Manufacturing Company.

was completed in eleven days. About nine o'clock in the evening we got the parts together and tried it; it did not sew . . . Sick at heart, about midnight we started for our hotel. On the way, we sat down on a pile of boards, and Zieber mentioned that the loose loops of thread were on the upper side of the cloth. It flashed upon me that we had forgotten to adjust the tension on the *needle* thread. We went back, adjusted the tension, tried the machine, sewed five stitches perfectly, and the thread snapped. But that was enough." [5]

Singer had invented his sewing machine. By 1851 he had applied for both domestic and foreign patents. That year Edward Clark entered the newly established firm of I. M. Singer & Company, contributed no money, providing only his financial and legal abilities. Singer recollected: "In March 1852 Mr. Clark and myself bought Zieber out and continued to manufacture machines." In subsequent patent litigation, Clark's background in law proved indispensable.[6]

Aside from taking out foreign patents, Singer apparently did nothing in international business until 1855. Then I. M. Singer & Company sold its French patent for the single-thread machine to a French merchant, Charles Callebaut; the terms were 10,000 francs cash and 20,000 francs to be paid as soon as Callebaut had received orders for 30 machines. Callebaut was to pay 15 per cent royalty on the sale of 4,700 machines. The Singer company wanted a fee of 1000 francs per machine; Callebaut refused, stating that it would "prevent him from lowering his price to meet competition." [7]

"We are happy to know that you have become the purchaser of our French patent, although the price presently paid is very inadequate compared with the real value of the invention," a company official wrote the merchant. The letter continued, "It shall now be our study to manage affairs here, on this side of the Atlantic, as to promote the success of your enterprise." The Singer enterprise agreed to furnish Callebaut with an assistant for his "manufacturing department," so that he could "produce perfect machines." It also sent Callebaut tools and machinery and instructed its own representative that "no reasonable effort shall be wanting on our part to get you fitted out with an establishment which shall be a model one, and a credit to American skill in the mechanical arts. At the same time we must say that we wish M.

Callebaut to forward funds as fast as possible. Our very large expenses last year and small business comparatively makes it necessary to use all our resources. If M. Callebaut finds himself cramped for means it will be well for him to associate [with] some capitalist of good business habits. The business will no doubt be a large one." [8]

By the end of 1855 Callebaut's manufactory was operating. But for the Singer organization in the United States, this first attempt at foreign business caused only frustration. Callebaut was reluctant to pay what was due the Americans, handled competitive sewing machines, became involved in litigation with Singer and others, and refused obdurately to tell the New York company how many sewing machines he had made or sold.[9] This proved the first and last time that I. M. Singer & Company or its successor, Singer Manufacturing Company, ever sold a foreign patent to an independent businessman.

Meanwhile, in the United States the company had sold "territorial rights" to independents. By September 1855 it discontinued this practice, because, in its words, "We have had cause to regret it." In 1856 Singer began "demonstrating and servicing" its products in its own domestic sales rooms; the company also started to sell on installment. Three years later, Singer had 14 branch sales offices in the United States; in addition, it used franchised agents. By 1863 it had become fully committed to marketing through its own domestic sales offices and to the installment system of payment.[10]

How did these changes in domestic policies affect Singer's foreign operations? First, the company never sold territorial rights abroad as it had in the United States; it had learned from its poor American experience. With the exception of the Callebaut relationship, in its foreign business Singer started by using independent franchised agents who sold and advertised the American-made product in a given region. By 1858 the firm had independent businessmen as foreign agents in Rio de Janeiro and other cities overseas. From September 1860 to May 1861 the company exported 127 machines, mainly to independent intermediaries in Mexico, Canada, Cuba, Curaçao, Germany, Venezuela, Uruguay, Peru, and Puerto Rico.

By this time Singer had also sent a salaried representative to Glasgow, and at least as early as the fall of 1861 had a man in London. In short, the company began to follow in international operations its domestic policy of having its own sales offices. It also began to finance sales in Great Britain. Alonzo Kimball was the "agent" * in Glasgow, Singer's headquarters for Great Britain and Ireland. W. E. Broderick took charge in London in 1861 and from there arranged for sales in Belgium and Spain—"pioneers for the places mentioned."

Soon London replaced Glasgow as Singer's British sales center, and Broderick wrote to his home office: "There can be no doubt, if we were properly represented, orders to very large amounts from the continent would come to us and in a short time, we should sell more in that locality than in England, where all sorts of machines are made, even [imitations of] our own." [11]

In 1862 Broderick was already meeting competition from imitators of the Singer machine, a problem that would continually plague Singer representatives around the world. During the years of the American Civil War, foreign sales of Singer machines mounted steadily. The company could sell in England at prices lower than in the United States because the premium on foreign exchange would cover the difference. Its main competition in England was William Thomas, who had years before purchased Elias Howe's English patents. The American firm, Wheeler & Wilson, was another formidable rival.[12]

From London Broderick remitted funds to New York on the sale of the sewing machines; if trade were poor one week, he would apologize that no money had been sent home. Slowly, the British manager began to establish additional branch offices in England, to each of which he initially sold on commission. Here he was following the U.S. pattern.

With Broderick and Kimball flourishing in the United Kingdom, the company sent Frederick Neidlinger to Hamburg in 1863: "I shall try and gett [sic] your machine started wherever there is a prospect of making money," this representative advised New York. In Germany, he wrote, "Competition is very high and Machines are sold cheap, but when your Machines are operated other dealers fall back and confess that the Singer Machines are the Best." [13]

In 1864 George B. Woodruff, formerly in charge of the company's Boston office, was dispatched to London to replace Broderick, who re-

* He was called an "agent" even though on a salary.

turned to head Singer's San Francisco office. Woodruff rationalized the British business, aiming at "system" and "order" and opening new offices for retail sales.[14]

Meanwhile, Neidlinger actively established branch offices in Germany and Sweden. Requests came into New York from firms in Latin America to represent the company on that continent. The only block to progress by 1864–1865 seemed to be the company's involvement in litigation in the United States, France, and England over its patents.[15]

During 1866, despite the financial panic in England, although manufacturing businesses that purchased sewing machines were in distress, Woodruff could not obtain enough machines from New York for his "family" trade. Competition from Wheeler & Wilson grew stronger, "*But but*" wrote Woodruff from London, "here comes the nub. We are out of stock . . . I declare we are now in a worse position than any time heretofore. *I am completely done for.* The last four or five months trouble in this way has completely shattered [?] *every nerve out of my delicate little body.*" Why New York could not or did not supply the machines is not clear, but it may have been because of brisk domestic sales. All year long the London manager complained: "We are harassed to death with agents and customers, countermanding orders, giving up agencies, in fact our business for this year has been utterly ruined. I am powerless to help it . . . About A Machines [family models] I can only say send me any number *less than twenty thousand.*" The trade connections he had made, he claimed, were falling apart: "it kills me to see it going to the dogs." "*We have beat the bush and others are picking up the game.*" Still, New York did not send adequate supplies.[16]

In January 1867 he wrote that Wheeler & Wilson were "certainly whipping us bad in Glasgow." Then in the spring of 1867 Woodruff visited the United States, where he learned that the directors of the Singer company proposed to "manufacture" in the United Kingdom. Vice President George Ross McKenzie traveled to Britain to investigate "the whole subject of labor, shipping, etc." [17]

Why Singer decided to build a factory abroad does not appear in the company's correspondence. A subsequent Singer president, F. G. Bourne, almost thirty years later, explained that since United States currency after the Civil War was being restored to its normal specie value, premiums on foreign exchange were cut. At the same time wages in America were increasing. "Thus the cost of the domestic manufacture became too high to enable competition in the world markets . . . Therefore some of the American manufacturers established factories in foreign countries." [18]

Contemporary records show that when Singer decided to build its first foreign plant, it did expect major economies. Woodruff wrote to New York in December 1867: "I earnestly hope the progress of your new Factory will be such as to warrant us *very soon* in giving up one warehouse at a saving of £100 per annum." In another letter he noted the new factory would reduce "our enormous freight bills, storage, and various incidental expenses." The branches in the United Kingdom were operating at a $33,000 loss in 1867, which made this step imperative.[19]

Singer's first factory in Glasgow was "a very small experimental affair, so as to make it safe to discontinue if it did not succeed." The balance sheet of 1868 shows its total assets as $262,539.89. It was an assembly operation, "receiving parts from America in a partly finished state." Initially, its orders were for 100 machines every other week, then 200 every week, but soon its output mounted. By 1869 the company required a larger factory, and Singer Vice President George McKenzie recommended the American company "send Tools to Glasgow to manufacture all the Parts there for a production of 600 Machines per week."

Inslee Hopper (President of Singer, 1863–1876) visited Britain in 1871, and the next year a supplemental Singer factory rose in Glasgow. Six years later the company acquired additional space. All this expansion was the result of a continued growth in demand for Singer sewing machines.[20]

Woodruff in London had undertaken extensive marketing programs in England, Spain, Portugal, Italy, Belgium, and in the 1870s, in France (when Callebaut's patent expired, the Singer company went into competition with him). In Hamburg, F. Neidlinger's brother, George Neidlinger, had taken charge of the business, extending it throughout Germany, Scandinavia, Russia, and Austria-Hungary.[21]

Around the world, Singer was gradually forming what would become its famous international business network. The rationalization of this marketing structure occurred after the American company had adopted its domestic sales organization, following the same pattern. It began after the company awoke to the realization that foreign business made a crucial contribution to its profits.

By 1874, with poor economic conditions in the United States, Singer was selling more than half its sewing machines abroad (126,694 out of 241,679). Woodruff became convinced "that we can never make our business solid except by Branches at all great centres—and wherever we must work by local agents we must bind and tie up the affair within our own controll [sic] and constant direction." The advantages of the salaried-plus-commission agent over the locally financed independent agent were multifold. The independent agent did not pay sufficient attention to the product; he did not bother to instruct the buyer how to use the machine; he did not know how to service it; he failed to demonstrate it effectively; and he did not seek new 'customers aggressively. Independents were not prepared to risk their capital to sell goods on installment nor would they risk carrying large stocks. Woodruff was convinced that the company must keep "the controll [sic] of the business in our hands." [22]

In 1878 Singer's main competitor, Wheeler & Wilson, also took its business from independent agents and opened central offices in key European cities. But whereas the Singer company had moved into this method "little by little," Wheeler & Wilson made an abrupt transition. "I am certain," wrote Woodruff to Edward Clark, now President of the Singer company, "the W & W will lose by these operations this year more than £50,000. This business cannot be made in this slap bang style." [23]

Woodruff's prognostications proved right, and by the end of the 1870s Singer's sales at home and abroad far surpassed those of the former leader, Wheeler & Wilson. The latter company never recovered its lead.* Singer had become pre-eminent in the American and worldwide industry. By 1879 Singer's London headquarters had 26 central offices in the United Kingdom, and one each in Paris, Madrid, Brussels, Milan, Basel, Capetown, Bombay, and Auckland. Each central office in turn had suboffices under its control. The offices sold at wholesale and retail, providing several types of cash discounts and provisions for

* Years later the Singer Company acquired Wheeler & Wilson.

installment sales. Each suboffice had canvassers to peddle the machine, "shopwomen" to sell from the showroom, "instructresses" to teach the customers, and "collectors" to obtain the installment payments.[24] George Ross McKenzie, who became president of Singer Manufacturing Company in 1882, had in 1879 reorganized the foreign operations, putting a "second man" in all the central offices, "so that neither sickness, death, nor any other circumstances may interfere with the smooth workings of the business to any great extent." McKenzie laid down rules for the auditors, who visited all offices, checked stock, studied the books, and observed the performance of employees to judge whether their salaries were "too high or too low." The auditors were admonished "not [to] take favors" and to "be careful to distinguish in the report what is known to be positively true & what is rumor." [25]

By the 1880s a formidable Singer foreign sales organization existed: The London headquarters took charge of Singer sales in Australia, Asia, Africa, the southern part of South America, Great Britain, and a large part of the European continent. Hamburg was the center for northern and middle Europe,* while the New York office directed export sales to the Caribbean, Mexico, northern South America, and Canada. In the 1880s the London office set up sales centers in Australia, China, the Philippines, and Brazil, in each case employing salaried officials in these locales. The new offices not only reflected the mounting business but in turn spurred company sales.[26]

By 1881 the company's three separate Glasgow factories were congested and inadequate. They had grown "like Topsy." The Singer directors in the United States decided to erect at Kilbowie, near Glasgow, a modern plant equipped with the latest American machine tools and with a capacity equal to that of the company's largest American factory.[27] This full commitment to foreign manufacturing was entirely different from the steps taken in 1855 to have the independent Callebaut manufacture or the tentative steps taken by Singer in 1867 to establish a foreign assembly unit. The company had learned from experience that it could produce for European and many other markets more cheaply in Scotland than in the United States. On May 18, 1882,

---

* The Hamburg office did a sizable business: Neidlinger's remittances in 1880 totaled almost one million dollars.

the ground was broken for the company's own large Kilbowie manufacturing plant.[28]

According to Tom Mahoney, author of *The Great Merchants,* Singer
began assembly in Montreal in 1873 (we have found no other evidence
of such a facility). Company records do indicate that in 1883 Singer
started a small manufacturing plant in that Canadian city to supply
the Dominion market. This plant was required because Canadian customs duties raised the price of Singer machines to a noncompetitive
level. In 1883 the company also began to manufacture stands in Austria because of the "enormous duty." The operations in Canada and
Austria were minute compared with the giant manufactory at Kilbowie.[29] In short, by the 1880s, Singer had a worldwide organization—
with a vast sales network and foreign manufacturing plants.

3

The Singer company was exceptional because by the mid-1880s it
already had three decades of involvement in the foreign field and because of the size of its multinational business. Yet by the 1880s Singer's
commitment to expand abroad was *not* unique. In the 1870s and 1880s
many American companies sought export markets to dispose of surplus
output and obtain economies of scale. This was true of companies producing screws, harvesters, cash registers, elevators, steam pumps, locomotives, locks, and guns. All of these metal products were superior to
those sold by European firms. As American prices declined in the 1870s
and 1880s these goods became more competitive abroad. There does
not appear to have been "dumping" of U.S. exports, but instead comparable prices (plus transportation). The reason for the exporting was
to broaden the companies' market. After the establishment of national
sales organizations, many metal products companies created international
sales networks. They began in the main by selling in Canada and across
the Atlantic, for Canada and Europe provided the most customers.

There seems to have been an evolutionary pattern in the growth of
the foreign business of most of these metal-working companies, although
companies might skip a step or several steps in the process. In stage
one, the U.S. concern sold abroad through independent agents (an
export man in New York, export or commission houses in the same

city) or, on occasion, filled orders directly from abroad. Companies
frequently started to export, using the facilities of the international
trading firms—and their successors—described in Chapter I. Next, in
stage two, the company appointed a salaried export manager and/or
acquired an existing export agency and its contacts. This stage might
also involve the appointment of independent agencies in foreign countries to represent the company. The foreign agent would sell on his
own account or handle shipments on consignment. In the third stage,
the company either installed one or more salaried representatives, or
a sales branch, or a distribution subsidiary abroad, or it purchased a
formerly independent agent located in a foreign country. At this point,
for the first time, the company made a foreign investment. In the
fourth stage, a finishing, assembly, or manufacturing plant might be
built abroad to fill the needs of a foreign market.

By the mid-1880s all these stages had emerged. Baldwin Locomotives
was in stage one: an exporter with no foreign investments; the National
Cash Register Company was in stage two, having appointed an independent agent in London; in stage three were predecessors of International
Harvester, with some salaried representatives abroad. Remington had
sales branches in Europe. Otis Bros. & Co. (later Otis Elevator Company)
had purchased control of a formerly independent agent in England.[30]
In stage four were Hoe printing presses (1867) and Babcock and Wilcox
boilers (1881), with manufacturing facilities in England, while American
Screw Co. (1876) had a plant in Canada. In Canada between 1876 and
1887, 47 verified American branch, subsidiary, or controlled affiliated
manufacturers were established, many of which were in the metal-working
fields.[31]

These U.S. companies sent Americans abroad with experience in
marketing and service; the companies exported American ingenuity
and technical know-how. Their capital exports were minimal. Too
often, studies of U.S. foreign investment ignore the evolution of business abroad and neglect the growth of the sales establishments. For an
understanding of the multinational corporation, the marketing activity
cannot be forgotten, since it was from such initial forays that there
grew the large contemporary international investments. Profits earned

abroad could be and were reinvested to develop over time giant foreign investments. Just as the Singer company started acting on its own with a marketing network, so did many other metal-working companies. Plants were built later to fill market requirements.

4

American corporations in the electrical industry * were also pioneers in establishing stakes abroad. Their foreign investments sometimes made them operators of and sometimes suppliers of utilities, and sometimes both. We will see electrical companies introduced producer and consumer products abroad and invested to sell both. As noted earlier, speedy communication was a prerequisite for international business. American companies participated in providing better communication links. The telegraph was an American invention; U.S. capital had been involved in introducing the telegraph to Newfoundland and installing a cable connection to Nova Scotia (see Chapter II). In 1856 Western Union Telegraph Company was formed in the United States; in the following two decades, it became "the largest and most powerful corporation" in this country. Before it completed its transcontinental telegraph line (1862), Western Union envisaged connecting the American system with a cable to Russia. These plans collapsed in 1866 when Cyrus Field's British-financed Atlantic Telegraph Company laid the first cable across the Atlantic, joining Western Union's land lines with Europe. Western Union had no investments in European telegraph systems; in fact, in many European nations the telegraph was a state monopoly. By the 1860s Western Union had large interests in only one foreign nation, Canada, its leading associate being the Montreal Telegraph Company.

In 1866 the International Ocean Telegraph Company, promoted by the New Yorker James A. Scrymser—apparently with American financing—installed the first cable to Latin America (Florida-Havana). Jay Gould in 1878 seized control of the company, and Scrymser turned to other ventures, organizing the Mexican Cable (later Telegraph) Com-

---

* We define the industry to include both utilities and producers of electrical supplies, equipment, and final products.

pany (incorporated May 6, 1878) and the Central and South American Cable (later Telegraph) Company on May 29, 1879.* [32]

In 1879, Jay Gould, after obtaining control of the International Ocean Telegraph Company, went into his second international venture, forming the American Union Telegraph Company. The latter leased for 99 years the Dominion Telegraph Company (established in 1868 by Canadians to develop a telegraph system in the provinces of Ontario and Quebec). Soon the Dominion Telegraph Company merged into the Great Northwestern Telegraph Company, which consolidated the major Canadian telegraph lines and was in the main financed by Canadian capital; American Union Telegraph Company retained a small stake in the new enterprise.

Then in 1881 Jay Gould gained control of Western Union. He arranged for Western Union (1) to obtain a 99-year lease on his first acquisition, International Ocean Telegraph Company, and (2) to acquire the American Union Telegraph Company and through it the Canadian holdings. In short, by 1881 the Western Union system was linked physically with the transatlantic cable and physically and financially with the Canadian system as well as with cables uniting the United States and Latin America.

At this point John William Mackay entered the picture. He had made a fortune on the Comstock lode bonanza, and with James Gordon Bennett set out to break Gould's telegraph and cable monopoly. On December 12, 1883, they founded the Commercial Cable Company, which in 1884 laid two submarine cables to Europe.† Meanwhile, remaining independent of Western Union and Mackay interests were the U.S. investments in the Mexican Cable Company and Central and South American Telegraph Company.[33]

5

Next came the introduction abroad of the American invention, the telephone. Alexander Graham Bell went to England in 1877 to seek

---

* Central and South American Telegraph Company became All America Cables in 1920 (*Moody's 1920*).

† In 1886 Mackay founded the Postal Telegraph and Cable Company and started to fight the Gould-Western Union monopoly on land.

a patent. He appointed Colonel William H. Reynolds of Providence, Rhode Island, to act as his representative in England; he deputized him to attract English capital to a new British company to "work the invention."

Competing with Bell was Thomas Edison, who had an American, Colonel George R. Gourard, as his agent in England. Gourard formed the Edison Telephone Company in London in 1879. It held Edison patents on the telephone and like the Bell venture, was financed by British capital. Edison gained an interest in this company in exchange for his knowledge, technical aid, and patents. In 1879 the Edison Company began to install in London the first European telephone exchange.

The two English telephone companies—both headed by Americans, operating under patents taken out by Americans—proved bitter rivals, until in May 1880 they merged into the United Telephone Company, Ltd. Meanwhile, under the Telegraph Acts, the British government in 1879 had declared telephonic communications a state monopoly. Thus, under British government license the United Telephone Company, Ltd. imported American-made apparatus and completed the installation of the telephone system in London. Through sublicensees, telephone exchanges began elsewhere in Britain. The extent of American financial interest in these ventures is not clear. Edison had sold his initial holdings to Gourard, who may in turn have resold them. What Bell did with his stock is unknown.[34]

In France, in competition were Bell, Edison, and other companies that used the equipment of the American Frederick Gower. In 1880 all these interests combined in the Société Generale des Téléphones, with a five-year concession (later extended another five) from the French government to start and to operate a telephone system.

American Bell and Edison interests made energetic efforts to introduce the telephone elsewhere in Europe, Latin America, Asia, and Africa. With this purpose the International Bell Telephone Company, Ltd. (1880), the Continental Telephone Company (1880), the Tropical American Company (1881), and the Oriental Telephone Company (1880) were formed. W. H. Forbes, President of American Bell Telephone Company, was involved in the International Bell Telephone Company, and the Continental Company. The International Bell Telephone Company, Ltd. obtained franchises in seven cities in Belgium, six in Russia, four in Holland, three in Italy, two each in Norway and Sweden, and one each in Denmark and Switzerland. In these enterprises, I.B.T.C. generally held a minority interest. In the early 1880s the Tropical American Company purchased from the Continental Company the latter's telephonic rights in South America; by the mid-1880s Tropical American was selling American-made telephones, transmitters, telephonic instruments and supplies to some eight Latin American telephone companies, in five of which it had a minority stock holding. The Oriental Telephone Company participated in operating companies in Cairo, Alexandria, Hong Kong, Shanghai, and five Indian cities.

The fate of the Oriental Telephone Company is unknown. The Continental and Tropical American companies went out of business in the 1890s, the latter after selling its holdings in the operating companies in Latin America to English businessmen. International Bell Telephone Company found its revenues dwindling as European governments chose to own and operate their national telephone systems. By the end of the 1890s, I.B.T.C. was disposing of its stakes in its remaining European subcompanies; the shell of International Bell remained until July 23, 1920,* when the corporation was formally dissolved.[35] These early involvements in telephone exchanges overseas brought few financial rewards to their American sponsors.

In Canada in 1880 the American Bell Telephone Company itself started, and initially controlled, the Bell Telephone Company of Canada. The American company's policy toward the Canadian business was expressed in a letter dated July 13, 1880, from W. H. Forbes, President of American Bell, to C. F. Sise, the American managing director of the Canadian enterprise:

> While we believe that the telephone business can be made of great value in Canada . . . it is our policy there, as in the states, to bring in local capital, influence, and management, since the whole field is far too large for us to undertake to cover.

---

* This date was about three weeks after the International Telephone and Telegraph Corporation was incorporated. The coincidence in dates is remarkable, but I.T.T. has *no* corporate records on the International Bell Telephone Company in its Secretary's Office; nor is there any overlap in personnel between I.T.T. and the officers who signed the dissolution certificate of I.B.T.C.

The plan was to sell part of the stock as soon as possible. The Bell Telephone Company of Canada made steady progress. By the end of 1885 there were 9614 subscribers, and the parent American Bell Telephone Company reported to its shareholders that it was "much encouraged with the future of the [Canadian] Company." [36]

6

There are two basic parts to the telephone business: the first is to operate the telephone system, and the second to manufacture apparatus for the system. In 1882, when the International Bell Telephone Company was still hopeful about its prospects for European business, it decided to build a factory in Antwerp, Belgium. Western Electric Company made telephones for the American Bell Telephone Company, and it offered to join with International Bell Telephone Company to construct and operate the Antwerp facility. The main reason for the plant seems to have been to locate near the customers. A Belgian manufacturing unit could supply European telephone exchanges far more rapidly than an American source. Antwerp was selected, since it was the European headquarters of I.B.T.C.

Thus in 1882 a new Belgian *manufacturing* company was organized, owned 55 per cent by Western Electric and 45 per cent by I.B.T.C. and "its friends." Western Electric provided the management. This was Western Electric's first factory outside the United States. The next year, Western Electric opened a sales branch in London that was supplied by both the Antwerp facility and Western Electric's Chicago plant. In 1890 Western Electric obtained 100 per cent control of the Antwerp factory and made plans to manufacture in Paris, Berlin, and London. "This multiplication of factories is an evil imposed by the necessity of working for governments, which refuse to buy outside their own countries," Western Electric's foreign representative, F. R. Welles, wrote his company's president, E. M. Barton, in January 1890. With plants in the key European cities, Western Electric would be able to sell to European governments even after they had nationalized their telephone systems. Meanwhile, in Canada in 1882 the American-controlled Bell Telephone Company of Canada began to manufacture telephone equipment in Montreal. Canadian patent laws required local manufacture.[37]

7

In the planning of business stakes abroad, the flow of information is important. An investor must know of an opportunity and he must place someone overseas to develop that opportunity. Edison had Colonel Gourard in London. Not only did Gourard form the Edison Telephone Company, but he presented other unique Edison products. "The public interest . . . continues unabated in connection with his [Edison's] other known inventions—phonograph, megaphone," wrote Colonel Gourard from London in 1879. The Edison phonograph had been sold in Europe in 1878 (through exports from the United States); then the microphone had been introduced, next the telephone, and finally, in 1879, Edison made plans to present his incandescent lamp. Edison's research on the incandescent lamp in the United States had been financed by a syndicate headed by J. P. Morgan interests, which took part in introducing the lamp overseas. Likewise, men who had acted on behalf of the telephone for Edison in Europe were enlisted to promote the lamp. From country to country and region to region, different methods of entering the markets were used. In England, for example, a newly constituted Edison company began to import lamps from the United States; Edison wrote his bankers, Drexel, Morgan & Company in October 1881,

> I think that ultimately we shall have to establish a factory in England but for the first thru our own stations the machinery can be supplied from here at lower cost and much better made than were we to start a factory in England to do the work right away.
> We will supply the lamps for the Isolated business . . . at fifty-cents each, when a station is started I will supply them at forty-cents each for the purpose of lighting up a district. I am certain it would not pay for a long time to come to start a lamp factory in England as freights being low and there being no duties it would be impossible to compete with our lamp factory here as we have established such a perfect system of manufacture and trained men who are now very skilled and experienced.

The Edison Electric Light Company, Ltd. in England (formed in 1882) served at first exclusively for sales, installation, and licensing of subcompanies. Its authorized capital was divided into A shares, equal to £100,000, which were paid in full by British capital, and B shares equal to the same amount which were allotted to Thomas Edison and his American partners.

Edison paid personal attention to the business in England, giving instructions on how to manage the unit: "Do all business by personal solicitation, wherever possible. Whatever orders you do get execute quickly and well. Don't be in a hurry to make money. Don't interfere with the head of your Isolated department in details of business—don't hamper him with red tape of a Board of Directors."

The English corporation started to license subcompanies, and as it did so, met difficulties: low-priced gas was highly competitive with electricity; municipal institutions hesitated in granting permission to an electrical company "for taking up the streets"; competition from other light companies proved intense. The British directors wanted to manufacture the lamp in England, but Edison objected.

In Britain competition came from the Swan interests; but as early as 1881 Joseph Wilson Swan, who had his own lamp patents, was talking to Edison representatives on "whether we are going to be open enemies, or secret friends or what." G. P. Lowrey, a lawyer on behalf of Drexel, Morgan interests, favored a coalition of the Edison and Swan companies. On the other hand, Edison's representative felt, Swan "can be anniahilated [sic] easier than he can be bought." By 1883 the indecision was resolved in a merger of the Edison and Swan groups and the formation of the Edison and Swan United Electric Company, Ltd. Edison interests had a large minority holding in the new corporation.[38]

Meanwhile, Edison arranged to grant local capital "the exclusive right to make, use and vend and to license others to make, use and vend in Switzerland (but no other country) all his inventions relating to . . . his system for furnishing light and power from electricity for the term of fifteen years." Edison was to get 50 per cent of the net profits, and not be liable for any losses. He made separate arrangements for Sweden and Norway, and others for Portugal.

For the rest of Europe, a parent New York company, Edison Electric Light Company of Europe, Ltd.* formed three French affiliates: 1. La Compagnie Continental Edison (capital 1,000,000 francs), with offices in

---

* Edison was president and the largest shareholder in Edison Electric Light Co. of Europe (capital: $2 million).

Paris, which was "charged to make available the processes . . . in countries for which we are authorized to treat." Eighty per cent of the profits of this company were to go to Edison interests, after cash subscribers were reimbursed for their contribution. 2. La Société Industrielle et Manufacturie Edison, capital 1,500,000 francs, "profits to be divided half to us and half to capital," after deduction of annual provisions for retiring capital. This company would manufacture in the vicinity of Paris, and would be under the direction of Charles Batchelor, an American coworker of Edison's. It would be controlled from America. 3. La Société Electrique Edison, with a capital of 1,000,000 francs, and with 60 per cent of the profits pledged to the Edison group after capital was reimbursed. It would set up isolated plants for the purpose of lighting large stores, railroad depots, printing establishments, and so forth. The working capital for all three companies was provided by a strong banking group that included Seligman Frères & Co., Drexel Harjes & Cie, Bank l'Escompte de Paris, Banque Central (France), and Speyer Brothers. Thus, in Europe, Edison enterprises began under the aegis of the international bankers.[39]

In 1881, at the Paris Exposition, Emil Rathenau saw the Edison lamp. He wanted to introduce it in Germany and soon brought German banking interests into his plans. In the fall of 1882 Edison's French representative—Charles Batchelor—wrote home: "I think there is no doubt now that our friend Siemens will sue us in Germany for [patent] infringement." Negotiations with Siemens & Halske were deemed imperative—and in 1883 Edison interests reached an "understanding" with the competitor. That year Emil Rathenau formed Deutsche Edison Gesellschaft to exploit Edison electric light patents in Germany; he was the new managing director. This company was licensed by the Compagnie Continental Edison and Société Electrique Edison in Paris. The Compagnie Continental Edison received founders shares entitling it to 20 per cent of the German profit.

From the start the Germans wanted a lamp factory in their nation (the Italians, with a similar licensing arrangement, did also). Batchelor in France wrote to Samuel Insull, Edison's secretary, on April 25, 1882:

> I want to ask Edison if he wants me to *press for factories* in every European country, or do what I can for the factory in America.

My opinion in this is that the only way to bring the Edison lamp down to proper price is to establish factories in each country so as to get at the cheapest method of manufacture, and save the enormous *customs* and *freight rates*.

No response to this letter is to be found in the Edison archives, but there is evidence that Edison preferred to export from America to Germany and elsewhere at reduced prices and to hold the market for exports. A year and a half later, however, another Edison representative in Europe (J. F. Bailey) was writing the inventor to report on the German company's new lamp factory. This correspondent noted that he would have tried

to induce the Germans to take their lamps from the States, if economy had been the only consideration. But there are two others. . . . (1) National feeling; (2) the Patent laws. You may think that national feeling does not weigh against economy, but that is a complete error. Any German interloper would have all the national sympathies and would hold the German market against a foreign lamp that should be both cheaper and better.

In the next place the patent laws require that manufacture shall be started and adequate to the supply of the market within three years from the date of the granting of the patents.

From the German company came plea after plea to Edison to send a man from the States to set up their new factory. The Germans wrote directly to Edison for drawings and blueprints. Although the French Edison companies were its parents, the management of the German enterprise bypassed France and noted in its letters, "We prefer as far as possible to deal directly with you in [America on] these [technical] matters."

Edison was consulted for skills and knowhow, but he was not supreme over the financial structure of the European business. By the end of 1883, Edison's representative in France was expressing fears that they had been taken advantage of by the European bankers. He noted that the percentage on profits guaranteed to Edison interests was "worth very little." "There are so many ways of making no large profits, and these jews are so keen that it is doubtfull [sic] in my mind if we get anything from that in 10 years." [40]

As 1884 progressed it was clear Edison interests were being betrayed.

The American parent company, Edison Electric Light Company of Europe, Ltd., which had carried all the costs of taking out the patents, found that in its four years of existence it had received no profits from its European affiliates and as a result was in serious financial straits.

With the business crisis in the United States in 1884, the company's bondholders clamored for payment—at least of the coupons due—but the American company was unable to pay even the interest on the bonds, much less the principal.

At this point, the Europeans made new demands on the parent company. In what appears to this author as shrewd (and immoral) financial manipulations, the Europeans declared that the Compagnie Continental Edison had lost half its capital—and the bankers urged the consolidation of the three French enterprises to "hide" this disaster from the public and certain stockholders. At the same time, the Europeans proposed to deprive the Americans of their veto powers over the foreign business—the only major advantage the Edison Electric Light Company of Europe, Ltd. still retained. The Americans naturally objected, but the European bankers countered, threatening to liquidate Compagnie Continental, which they casually remarked would result in such a scandal as to "destroy all possibility of anything ever coming to the shareholders or bondholders of the Light Company."

Faced with blackmail—and it was nothing else—the bondholders of the Electric Light Company of Europe meekly acquiesced to the consolidation of the three French units and to relinquishing their company's control. With an eye to obtaining some cash return, the bondholders agreed that Compagnie Continental would transfer patents to Deutsche Edison Gesellschaft and grant the German firm such other major concessions as more territory in which to conduct its operations. In exchange, the German company would pay 50,000 marks to Compagnie Continental, one half of which would go to the Electric Light Company of Europe (the funds to be used to meet its obligations to the bondholders). Edison himself, the largest shareholder in the Electric Light Company of Europe, derived no benefit from this action and lost control over the European enterprises. Nonetheless, the company's board of directors approved the recommendations of the bondholders.[41]

Meanwhile, the South American business was undertaken by the agents,

Fabbri and Chauncey. Arrangements for India, New Zealand, and Australia were made directly through Drexel, Morgan and Co.; Frazar and Co. was made the agent in Japan; American Trading Company was active in Korea on behalf of Edison; in 1883 an Edison Electric Light Company was established in Canada.

By the early 1880s Edison interests were exporting to Brazil, Chile, and Argentina, and setting up lighting systems in Latin America. As in Europe, so in Latin America, Edison established the foundation for a big business but gained no financial satisfaction. In 1884 Edison was writing on the top of a letter from Brazil, "Refd to C. W. Johnson by the Busted-Disgusted South American Dept. Edison." With 1885 came the failure of Kendall & Company, Edison's agents in Valparaiso, Chile, that exposed "the worst swindle ever known in Valparaiso." [42]

In the mid-1880s Edison retired from the business activities of all the Edison Electric Light enterprises; from this point his interest in the foreign business was taken up by others. What is important is that it was due in large part to the inventor's own initiative that his electric light, as well as his telephone, microphone, and phonograph, were given worldwide introduction. He reaped little profit from such international business, and much disappointment. It seems likely that it was his experiences with international bankers that later influenced his admirer Henry Ford to be so hostile to this group. (Ford in *his* international business dealings never had anything to do with international bankers and did his best to malign them at every opportunity.)

The actual consolidation of the French Edison companies did not take place until December 1886 because the Europeans still sought to squeeze more concessions out of the very dry lemon—the Edison Electric Light Company of Europe, Ltd. The Deutsche Edison Gesellschaft in 1885 had obtained its demands, including ownership of the patents for Germany, making it no longer a licensee of the Compagnie Continental. In 1887 the German company changed its name to Allgemeine Elektrizitäts Gesellschaft (A.E.G.), translated as the German General Electric Company. It became one of the two major companies in the German electrical industry.

Paradoxically, when the Edison General Electric Company was incorporated in the United States in 1889, A.E.G. was a parent in its formation as one member of the German syndicate involved. The tail was wagging the dog. Edison General Electric Company by that time had no foreign holdings. All the equity holdings that Edison had had abroad were purchased either by foreign interests or by Americans, for whom they became portfolio investments.[43]

Meanwhile, Thomson-Houston Electric Company and Brush Electric Company, two other U.S. concerns with unique products, also presented their wares abroad. Brush had designed improved dynamos with constant current and high-voltage characteristics, and then had led in introducing the arc lamp. In 1880 Brush Electric Company concluded a licensing agreement with Anglo-American Brush Electric Light Corporation in England. Thomson-Houston Electric Company, formed in 1883, held important patents in arc lighting. It exported, made foreign licensing agreements, and in 1884 started an international subsidiary company; it also made commitments in Canada. In 1887 it acquired Brush Electric Company. By 1891 Thomson-Houston had annual sales of $10.3 million, compared with Edison General Electric Company's volume of $10.9 million.

General Electric Company was incorporated in 1892, merging the Edison General Electric Company, the Thomson-Houston Electric Company, and the latter's subsidiary, Thomson-Houston International Electric Company. Despite all Edison's preliminary efforts abroad, it was from the Thomson-Houston acquisition rather than from the Edison Company that G.E. obtained its initial foreign holdings. General Electric acquired all the stock of the Thomson-Houston International Company for $1,212,000, most of which can be regarded as foreign investment. In addition, at the time of the organization of G.E., the Canadian General Electric Company, Ltd., a manufacturing and selling company, was formed. For $1,000,000, G.E. obtained majority control of the Canadian General Electric Company, which acquired the Edison and Thomson-Houston patents in the Dominion; Edison's and Thomson-Houston's former Canadian interests were consolidated into Canadian General Electric Company.* Thus, from its origin, General Electric was involved in international business. Its president, C. A. Coffin, formerly

---

* At the time of formation, the minority Canadian stockholders got an option to purchase G.E. holdings in this enterprise.

chief executive of Thomson-Houston, had none of the unhappy experiences abroad of the Edison group and was encouraged to expand worldwide. It is to Coffin that credit for General Electric's early foreign business must go.[44]

8

George Westinghouse was another enthusiastic American entrepreneur involved in international business in the 1880s. Three years after he introduced his air brakes in the United States, he sold them in Europe. In 1872 Westinghouse organized an export company to handle his foreign trade in air brakes. This firm installed a technical and sales staff with shop facilities in England. The American-made brake was adapted for use abroad. Then in 1879 Westinghouse started a shop in Paris to manufacture brakes, sending over to France an American from Pittsburgh to act as chief foreman. Customs duties, freight rates, and, of key importance, the stipulation in French railway contracts that supplies must be locally made were the reasons for his foreign manufactory. In 1881 Westinghouse incorporated a wholly owned subsidiary, The Westinghouse Brake Company, Ltd., in England to manufacture brakes for sale in Britain. In the next two decades he formed companies in Germany and Russia to manufacture for each host country's consumption.

Meanwhile, in 1886 Westinghouse had incorporated in the United States the Westinghouse Electric Company. It soon became involved in foreign business, starting in 1889 The (London) Westinghouse Electric Company, which obtained from its American parent patent rights for the whole world outside of the Western Hemisphere. This fully owned subsidiary began as a trading, constructing, and installing company and did not at first manufacture. Its successor would do so at the turn of the century. In the Westinghouse case—as in all other cases in the electrical industry—it was American companies with unique products that went into foreign business.[45]

9

United States chemical companies likewise became involved in enterprise abroad. Here we are using the term "chemical companies" broadly, to include medicinal preparations, film, and explosives. All these types of businesses invested abroad, seeking foreign markets. For example, Pond's Extract Company, which marketed a "pain-destroying and healing" remedy, started a London subsidiary in 1872 to direct sales and distribution of the extract in England and on the continent.

Wyeth & Bros.,* founded in 1860, sent to England in 1877 the American-born Silas M. Burroughs. Burroughs established an independent London agency to market Wyeth products. Henry S. Wellcome, another young American, became Burroughs' partner. Wellcome had been granted the exclusive agency for all the world (except the United States) for McKesson & Robbins' new line of gelatin-coated pills. These two men formed Burroughs, Wellcome & Company, incorporated in England on September 1, 1880. They introduced compressed medicines and other American drugs in Britain. English firms still sold pills in big bottles, and British prescriptions called for huge doses of bitter-tasting medicines. By contrast, the Burroughs, Wellcome containers of pleasantly flavored tiny pills met high favor. The two Americans adopted aggressive sales techniques, making personal calls on doctors and handing out samples (they were the first to do this in the United Kingdom). They advertised extensively in medical and trade journals—with 10- to 20-page inserts, instead of the typical one-page advertisement. In time, Burroughs, Wellcome made more of its own preparations in England rather than importing from America, and soon was appointing its own agents in foreign countries to market *its* output. It was independent of Wyeth & Co.; but Wyeth & Co. did go into business in Canada directly. According to the Canadian *Monetary Times,* Wyeth opened a Montreal plant in 1879.

Other American drug companies established Canadian factories in these early years. Frederick Stearns & Company † began to do business in Canada in 1884 (probably manufacturing); Parke, Davis began manufacturing in 1887 in Walkerville, Canada (near Windsor). Why the manufacturing began so early is not known; possibly the Canadian Patent Act of 1872 (which required working of patents) had an influence (see Chapter VII).[46]

* Purchased by American Home Products in 1931.
† Purchased by Sterling Drug in 1944.

American-born George Eastman obtained his first patent in England for an apparatus for coating photographic plates on July 22, 1879. By the winter of 1879–1880 he was arranging U.S. and foreign distribution of the U.S.-made photographic plates. By the mid-1880s he had direct representation in London in the person of one of the largest shareholders in his American company, William H. Walker, who started a distributing branch in London. By the fall of 1885 Eastman opened up the French trade. By decade's end (November 28, 1889) he had incorporated in London the Eastman Photographic Materials Company, Ltd., which would manufacture film, continuing, however, to import Kodak cameras from the United States. This new company took over the business and goodwill of Eastman's New York company in London, Paris, Milan, St. Petersburg, Melbourne, Sydney, Shanghai, Canton, Constantinople, and Japan, and all other countries outside the Western Hemisphere—so extensive had Eastman's business grown in ten years. Eastman's Rochester, New York, company held the majority of the stock in the English subsidiary, while the preferred shares and a portion of the common stock were sold to the English public. The funds raised through the sale of stock in England were used for building a new factory at Harrow, Middlesex.

The expansion of foreign business, George Eastman declared, would "distribute our eggs and pad the basket at the same time." Eastman's biographer is not explicit on the specific reasons for the Harrow factory, but it seems likely that (1) the company had a clear demand for its output as well as patent protection; (2) the Rochester plant could not supply enough film to fill the demand; (3) film spoiled, and it was preferable to have it produced as near the consumer as possible; (4) materials were available in England at a lower cost than in the United States; and (5) the factory could be financed out of capital raised and borrowed in England. Thus, in 1890 construction began on the Harrow factory—which was run by American management and equipped with American-produced machinery. When completed, it handled most of the foreign trade in Kodak film.

Another facet of U.S. business abroad in the "chemical industry" was the expansion of the American explosives companies into Canada. In

1876 the Windsor and Hamilton Powder Mills became part of the American powder trust group of companies.* [47]

10

The best known of all international companies by the late 1880s was Standard Oil. In the decades after Drake's drilling of oil in 1859 in Titusville, Pennsylvania, Standard Oil companies took leadership in the world's oil industry. John D. Rockefeller had started refining in Cleveland, moved in the 1870s into the acquisition of additional refineries in the United States, into pipelines and transportation, and also into direct marketing.

In the years from 1862 to 1865, between 28 and 59 per cent of all American-refined oil was exported; it was sold through commission agents, export houses in New York, and jobbers abroad. No American refiner had foreign investments. In 1866, 69 per cent of all American-refined oil was sent abroad, and in the years to 1885 this percentage never dropped below 64 per cent; in one year, 1871, it soared as high as 77 per cent of American output. Clearly, such trade was vital. In 1866 William Rockefeller, brother of John D., formed Rockefeller & Co. in New York to handle foreign business. This was four years before the organization of the first Standard Oil Company—Standard Oil of Ohio. Yet despite this measure, and a few other tentative steps, most oil exports continued to be sold in domestic transactions to independent export merchants or representatives of foreign importers.

In 1879 Standard Oil of Ohio made its first foreign investment—in a refinery in Galicia; the investment by 1881 equaled $32,300. That year, the company also had $123,000 in foreign facilities for restoring second-hand barrels, and it had an interest in Meissner, Ackermann & Company of New York and Hamburg, a partnership of export merchants, with a "long" history in the oil business. This was the sum total of the foreign interests. The investment in Galicia proved short-lived, owing to the antagonism against the Americans from local producers, and by 1886 the first Standard Oil refinery abroad was out of business.[48]

---

* In 1872 the Gunpowder Trade Association (later known as the American Powder Trust) came into being, coordinating sales practices of independent powder companies in which du Pont had investments; it came to unite all the important black powder companies in the United States east of the Rockies.

Meanwhile, in 1882 the Standard Oil Trust was formed—a holding unit for some 40 companies. By this time many of the component companies were separately becoming involved in foreign business. Thompson & Bedford Company, Ltd., sold pressed paraffin lubricants and wax abroad, and in the 1880s opened sales branches overseas. Chesebrough had offices to market vaseline in Montreal, London, Paris, Barcelona, Hamburg, Rio, and Buenos Aires. Vacuum Oil, which manufactured lubricants, had by 1885 established offices in Montreal and Liverpool.

New York Standard (organized in 1882) took over Ohio Standard's earlier investment in Meissner, Ackermann & Co., and through this company consigned Standard Oil-refined products to Henry Funck & Co. in the United Kingdom. In addition, it developed the Oriental trade in kerosene. Jersey Standard (formed in 1882) had a number of directors who showed special interest in the export business. The Standard Oil affiliate, Waters-Pierce, built up in the mid-1880s an extensive marketing network in Mexico; because of the duties on refined oil, it began to refine imported Pennsylvania crude oil in Mexico City and Vera Cruz. Archbold and Conill for the same reasons established two refineries in Cuba. Standard of Ohio, Standard of Minnesota, and Standard of New York marketed kerosene in Canada. Nonetheless, most kerosene exported continued to be sold through outsiders: commission houses, jobbers, foreign merchants.

Then in the mid-1880s came the so-called "oil war" between American and Russian oil. In January 1880 the Russian government awarded a concession for a railway from the rich Baku oil fields to Tiflis, from which a railway already ran to the port of Poti on the Black Sea. When the Baku-Tiflis line was completed in 1883, Russian oil became competitive in Europe. It was cheap, produced by inexpensive labor, and geographically nearer to European markets than American oil. Russian oil was owned by foreigners and extracted by modern methods. The Swedish Nobel brothers (Robert, Ludwig, and Alfred), the French Rothschilds, and the American Herbert W. C. Tweddle were among those who brought Russian oil into competition with Standard Oil exports.

Standard Oil had several alternatives in meeting the challenge of Russian oil. It could buy controlling interests in the companies producing in the Russian fields; it could arrange for agreements on prices and trading territories with the producers and refiners of Russian oil; it could strengthen its marketing organization in the places where the rivalry was strongest and meet the competition directly.

Apparently it did not consider the first tactic, for even in the United States it was only beginning to invest in production. It was still primarily a refining, transporting, and marketing concern. Thus, when in 1884 the American Herbert W. C. Tweddle offered his stock holdings in an integrated oil company in Russia to Standard Oil, Standard Oil turned it down. (French financial interests took it happily).

Standard Oil could have arranged agreements on prices and trade with the Russian oil concerns, but in the 1880s it was not yet prepared to take this step. Instead, Standard Oil's main strategy was to meet the competition with a renewed vigor. First it cut prices, and when this proved inadequate, it established foreign subsidiaries to watch carefully over the trade. Thus, on April 24, 1888, the Anglo-American Oil Company, Ltd. came into being. It marketed the American-refined oil and put the British business under Standard Oil's direction and control. The same policy was adopted in Germany, where Standard Oil formed an affiliate in 1890. Here Standard entered into a joint venture with German oil merchants, who knew the Deutschland trade and who brought into Standard Oil's possession tankers, warehouses, tank cars, and trained employees. The new British Standard Oil affiliate found it could supervise the East of Suez trade better than the American companies. In 1890 it started to consign in its name Standard Oil products to traders in the key ports East of Suez. So, as the 1890s began, Standard Oil, after gaining dominance in foreign markets, had been pushed by competitive pressures to extend its marketing investments as well as its exports beyond the national borders. Its few refineries (in Mexico and Cuba) were all built with marketing considerations in mind. It had no investments in foreign oil production.[49]

11

By the 1880s, Equitable, New York Life, and Mutual—the Big Three in American insurance—were similarly active in foreign business. New York Life Insurance Co. led the way first into Canada,* and then in

---

* New York Life started selling in Canada in 1858, discontinued in 1860, and started again in 1868.

1870 it began to sell insurance in England. By the close of the 1870s the company also did business in France, Germany, Scotland, West Indies, Mexico, British Guiana, Belgium, Venezuela, Russia, Ireland, Switzerland, Italy, and Austria. In the next decade it added forty more countries to its list of foreign nations in which it sold insurance—countries ranging from China to Peru, from South Africa to Australia. By 1885 almost one third of its total business was done outside the United States and Canada.

The insurance companies spent large sums in marketing insurance and in real estate that must be considered as direct investments. Equitable Life Assurance Society purchased a Paris building to demonstrate it was a stable, reliable concern. New York Life Insurance followed, its Board of Trustees in 1882 recommending the purchase of a Paris edifice to give confidence to intending insurers. With the same motive, New York Life in 1884 bought lots in Berlin and Vienna to build in those cities. The reason behind this extension was that foreign business brought in good receipts; from 1876 to 1882 the income to New York Life from business on the European continent was $6,626,568.96.

During the 1880s governments abroad began to insist that American insurance companies make investments locally in order to do business. New York Life Insurance's first concession in Russia in 1885, for example, required a deposit of securities to cover the policies issued, so that even the securities purchased abroad were more a part of a marketing than an investment program. By the mid-1880s, American insurance companies were negotiating directly with foreign governments on doing business; their willingness to take foreign securities was considered a token of good faith. Sometimes their relations with foreign governments went even further: for example, in 1884 Equitable made Mexican President Porfirio Díaz head of its company's Mexican advisory board.[50]

12

The conclusion is obvious, yet no single historian has previously documented it: by the start of the 1890s, leading American inventors, manufacturers, and marketers were concerned with international business. American marketers of sewing machines, harvesters, typewriters, elevators, printing presses, boilers, electrical apparatus, drugs, explosives, film, petroleum, and insurance already had investments outside the

United States. Such men as Isaac Singer, Alexander Graham Bell, Thomas Edison, George Westinghouse, George Eastman, John D. Rockefeller, J. P. Morgan, and others less well known had vision to see beyond the national horizon. The U.S. triumph abroad was one of ingenuity: new products, new methods of manufacturing, and new sales and advertising techniques. Americans who made overseas commitments had something distinctive to offer foreign customers. They sought not only to cater to, but to create, foreign demand. From sewing machines to drugs to oil to insurance, aggressive and imaginative marketing gave Americans an advantage. Americans went abroad when they discovered their advantage.

In making their foreign enterprises a success, the early American businessmen exported skill, knowhow, patents, machinery, and, most important, confidence in new products and sales methods. If added capital to support these exports were needed (as in the case of the electrical industry and in the film industry), such funds might well be raised abroad. Only the American insurance companies made substantial foreign investments.

These early international businesses established their foreign stakes—as we have seen—first and foremost in the areas around the world where there were customers—in Europe and Canada primarily. They made their principal investments where there was demand for their offerings —in the wealthiest nations in the world. The businesses described in this chapter went abroad to sell and to make profits through sales in the countries in which they made investments; if they went into manufacturing, refining, or real estate, it was with marketing considerations paramount. They did not go abroad for supplies or to produce abroad for sale in the United States. They were not all successful; Edison was certainly not financially successful in his worldwide ventures. Nonetheless, all of them introduced American goods and talents worldwide.

An analysis of the cases presented in this chapter makes it clear that the post-Civil War foreign investments in sales operations were made to broaden markets, obtain better control over distribution, and meet competition, all strategies similar to those followed by the same companies in the United States, except that entry abroad in some instances sought to avoid strictly national business cycles. More specifically, the reasons

why each enterprise decided to invest in a finishing, assembling, manufacturing, or refining facility (*beyond the sales investment*) were individual. Abstracting from the above cases and analyzing the results leads
us to conclude that here, too, some considerations were identical with
contemporary *domestic* investment decision making. For example, just
as at home, investments abroad were made to save on transportation
costs and warehousing expenses, to obtain superior customer service and
to avoid damage in shipping a perishable product. Likewise, businessmen invested in foreign manufacturing when the costs of production
were cheaper abroad than in the United States. A domestic counterpart
of this decision might be the building of a plant, based on regional cost
differentiations. Some of the foreign investments involved acquiring or
merging with a foreign competitor, who had manufacturing facilities;
acquisition of or merger with competitors at home provide a domestic
parallel. On the other hand, in this period, there were some business
decisions in the foreign field distinctive to international businesses. No
basic decision on whether or not to invest involved any action taken by
the U.S. government.* Many decisions, however, were made in response
to foreign government actions. Thus, foreign customs duties, which
made imports not competitive with locally produced articles or made
their price prohibitively high, prompted investments to make products
behind the tariff walls. Differential customs duties, which encouraged
foreign processing, prompted U.S. investments in foreign petroleum refining. Government patent requirements in Canada and Germany,
which required "working the inventions," meant new investments in
those nations to comply with the requirements. Foreign governments
insistence on local purchases of equipment stimulated U.S. investment
in the European electrical industry. Nongovernmental reasons for U.S.
manufacturing abroad involved insistence by foreign stockholders that
the company manufacture within a foreign country because of "national
feeling," special product needs abroad, and availability of foreign capital to finance the manufacturing outside the United States. Clearly
there were varied reasons for these early forays into direct foreign investment, and, as we have seen, the reasons were not mutually exclusive.

* Unless U.S. government's monetary policy in the immediate post-Civil War years
be considered a cause for deflation and for the Singer investment; see p. 41.

After decisions were made to invest, circumstances often changed. The initial decisions provided the basis for a long chain of subsequent decisions that would be shaped by U.S. company strategies, strategies of the managers of foreign branches, subsidiaries, and affiliates, occasionally by U.S. government policies, and continually by foreign conditions (actions of foreign governments, consumers, competitors, and partners). Market conditions abroad influenced the course of the U.S. enterprises in each foreign nation in which they did business. Companies adjusted to circumstances abroad. One early adjustment is clearly evident. In the 1880s, if an American company made a commitment to establish itself or to manufacture in Britain, often much of its foreign trade came to be handled from there—for the British were far more sophisticated in this business than the Americans; it proved far easier to handle worldwide trade from a London headquarters than from New York—or any other American city.

Investments made abroad grew abroad. The case of Singer was not atypical. The records of the Singer company indicate that its foreign operations developed gradually and that this firm does not seem to have exported any large sums of money until it built the Kilbowie plant in 1882. Yet by that time it already had a sizable investment accumulated outside the United States. New offices were opened, when the business "could afford to carry the expense." This was the case with American reapers, typewriters, cash registers, pumps, telephone apparatus, film, and so on. Standard Oil's investments pre-1890 were almost entirely in marketing and refining, and the sums remained relatively small; here, too, reinvested earnings provided a basis of growth. In certain facets of the electrical industry, where large amounts of capital were needed, the aid of international bankers was sought; the result was that the foreign companies became quite separated from the parent concerns.

As already noted, no figures exist for American overseas direct investment in the 1880s. Paradoxically, in this decade, when foreign capital flowed into the United States to finance our railways and to develop our mines, we can truly speak for the first time of American international business—business involving more than trading, more than one country, and direct stakes in foreign nations. While British investment in the United States was primarily portfolio investment, American business was already involved in direct investment abroad. The Singer sewing machine, the McCormick reaper, the Kodak camera, as well as the name of Standard Oil, became symbols of America abroad long before the Ford, or Coca Cola, much less IBM, the Boeing 707, or Helena Rubinstein.

Factors Influencing the Growth of American Business Abroad
(1893–1914)

The extension of business abroad before 1893 was dwarfed by what
followed. The 1890s saw a steady growth of U.S. enterprise in foreign
lands, involving not only the companies considered in Chapter III but
many others as well. At the turn of the century there was a veritable
"wave" of new U.S. corporations introducing operations beyond the
American boundaries; United States direct investment flowed into Canada as never before. Between 1897 and 1902, Europeans pointed to "the
American invasion of Europe"—an invasion of American-manufactured
goods. The phrase "American invasion" was first used by the Austrian
minister of foreign affairs; it came to be frequently repeated. Thus, an
Englishman, writing in 1901, explained that men sometimes spoke of
"the dramatic coup of a Morgan when he acquired control of our greatest shipping lines" as the "American invasion." This, to the Englishman,
was "mere sensation." "The invasion," he recorded, "goes on unceas-
ingly and without noise or show in five hundred industries at once.
From shaving soap to electric motors, and from shirt waists to telephones,
the American is clearing the field."

The sensation to which the writer referred was the purchase in 1901
by J. P. Morgan & Company of part ownership in the Leyland shipping
line—an old English enterprise. The London press declared America
was using its "boundless resources of capital" to snatch away Great
Britain's supremacy of the seas. In the face of popular clamor in England, the Chairman of the Leyland Company reported to his shareholders that Morgan's offer "was so extravagant that no management

had the right to refuse it." * In London, in 1901–1902, three publications appeared, entitled respectively *The American Invasion, The American Invaders,* and *The Americanization of the World.*[1]

Expansionist fervor existed in the United States. Whether it was the chairman of the American Steel and Wire Company, who declared that merger had taken place in his industry because the organizers "wished to be the wire manufacturers of the world," or the General Electric Company *Annual Report* (Jan. 31, 1898), which more modestly stated, "Our increased business in foreign countries has disclosed the fact that in design, cost and efficiency our machinery compares most favorably with that of European manufacturers," or the slogan "Sherwin-Williams Paints Cover the Earth," or Chauncey Depew's exhortation, "Let production go on . . . let the factories do their best, let labor be employed at the highest wages, because the world is ours," American businessmen at the turn of the century clearly thought in international terms.[2]

This was the era when an 1899 letterhead of New York Life Insurance Company proclaimed it "The Oldest International Life Insurance Company in the World. Supervised by 82 Governments." It was the time when Herbert Hoover began his career as a mining engineer, with trips to some fifteen different countries, including Australia, China, India, and Egypt; † and when the Guggenheim Exploration Company (organized in June 1899) sought to "prospect, explore, improve, and develop mining properties in any part of the world."[3]

2

In the 1890s, expansion of the railroads, the growth of new urban centers, and the rising population opened up new domestic markets for American businesses. Corporations broadened their scope at home, and

* In October 1902 the International Mercantile Marine Company was incorporated in New Jersey. It acquired a number of foreign shipping lines, including the Morgan interest in the Leyland Company. Morgan tried without success to bring the Cunard Line into the I.M.M.—but the Cunard Company "pledged themselves to remain in every respect British."

† Hoover was hired in 1897 by the British mining firm of Bewick, Moreing and Company, which wanted an American mining engineer, since "American machinery and American technical practice in gold mining were far ahead of those of the British." In 1908 Hoover organized his own international mining-engineering consulting service—with offices in New York, San Francisco, London, Petrograd, and Paris (Herbert Hoover, *Memoirs,* I, 28ff).

many of those that did so made investments abroad. On the other hand, between 1893 and 1897, the depression in the United States served to limit domestic demand. This had two pronounced influences on the foreign endeavors of U.S. enterprise. The first was a direct effect: companies with surpluses saw external markets as a way to get rid of goods that could not be sold at home. Exports rose. Then to maintain exports, companies started sales branches abroad, and soon the firms were making further foreign investments to hold and increase their foreign markets. A second consequence of the 1893–1897 depression was that many American companies failed, but those that survived grew mighty (taking advantage of low depression prices) and expanded into giant corporations. Such enterprises were in a position to do more abroad. The development in the United States of large banking houses and the rise of stock market prices at the end of the 1890s aided the turn-of-the-century mergers. In this merger movement, huge American corporations came into being; many of these looked for sales, and in some cases raw materials, in foreign lands. New companies, organized in the years between 1902 and 1914, fitted into the tempo of the times; frequently they looked for sales and then made investments abroad as well as at home.[4]

In America the merger movement at the turn of the century occurred at the same time as this country became (for a short interval) a net exporter of capital. The heaviest capital exports were in the years 1898–1901; the United States continued as a net capital exporter through 1905, although the U.S. remained a debtor nation on international accounts. The coincidence between the turn-of-the-century merger wave and the new posture of the United States as a net exporter of capital was no accident. The availability of a large-scale capital market in this country made possible the mergers and also provided for the expansion of direct investment abroad.* The same personalities involved in the crea-

---

* I am not claiming that all the export of capital went to direct investment, but I would put more emphasis on direct investment than Friedman and Schwartz in their *Monetary History of the United States*. There were of course other reasons for the net export of capital: repatriation of European holdings in U.S. securities at good stock prices; the outbreak of the Boer War in October 1899, which led to the recall of British investments; American portfolio investments abroad; but my reading of the evidence indicates that the increase in U.S. direct investment was important (Milton Friedman and Anna Jacobson Schwartz, *A Monetary History of the United States*, pp. 142–149).

tion of big business at home carried U.S. business to foreign lands; Standard Oil representatives, J. P. Morgan, the Guggenheims, James B. Duke, and George Perkins are examples. Later, when Ford Motor Company and General Motors were formed, they too sought to develop stakes abroad.[5]

Most of the activity of American business in foreign lands was either forward integration into sales or horizontal integration. This was mainly in the industrial or industrializing countries. Some U.S. enterprises integrated backward, investing in foreign raw materials; or, if they were mining companies integrated horizontally, entering into mining outside the U.S., generally in the Western Hemisphere. We will see that U.S. railroad leaders also extended their operations outside the national boundaries, primarily in this hemisphere.

Just as the growth of big business at home affected the rise of international business, so too political changes in the United States had their impact. For example, the Sherman Antitrust Act of 1890 forbade agreements in restraint of trade. This act has been called "the mother of trusts": since agreements among independent companies were illegal, the companies turned instead to mergers; nothing forbade mergers, which as we have seen accelerated at the turn of the century. As also noted, the giant merged enterprises became most active in international business. This extension to foreign lands was perhaps an indirect consequence of the Sherman Antitrust Act. But the act had more direct impact on the contours of U.S. business abroad. In the early twentieth century, antitrust suits against American companies—dealing mainly with their domestic activities—had repercussions on their foreign business. In the next chapter we will see clear evidence of this in the oil, aluminum, and tobacco industries.

American foreign policy (including commercial policies) also influenced this nation's investors abroad. In these years the federal government expressed a desire to aid U.S. business in foreign lands. Consular services offered assistance to businessmen who sought markets outside this country. Exuberant politicians, who edged America into war and victory over Spain, who forced from the British the cancellation of the distasteful Clayton-Bulwer Treaty, and who made plans for the Panama Canal, hailed U.S. companies' expansion abroad. Politicians who advocated the acquisition of Hawaii saw it as opening great business opportunities. The conquest of the Philippines was viewed by them, and by many businessmen, as a stepping stone to trade in the Orient. They imagined that if each Chinese should buy one biscuit a day, U.S. plants would run twenty-four hours a day to fill Chinese needs. Secretary of State John Hay's Open Door Notes of 1899—his insistence on equal commercial opportunities and his dictum that China was not to be divided by Europeans and Japanese into spheres of influence or partitioned—were part of the vibrant, expansive mood. In 1909 President Taft declared his administration was "lending all proper support to legitimate and beneficial American enterprises in foreign countries" and that the Department of State was being reorganized to "make it a thoroughly efficient instrument in the furtherance of foreign trade and of American interest abroad." The United States government—at least until the Wilson administration—clearly sought to assist American business operating outside the country. Moreover, it came increasingly to be in a position to do so as the United States emerged as a world power.[6]

Yet historians often look at U.S. government intentions and not at the other side of the coin. One has to ask how much aid the burgeoning U.S. international businesses actually got from the U.S. government and how decisive such help was in shaping their plans. More research on this is needed, but in reviewing the experience of U.S. companies in various activities, industries, and countries in the years from 1893 to 1914, it seems that for manufacturing enterprises the aid rarely proved to be decisive. International manufacturing corporations received mainly information along with some assistance on trademarks, patents, and import restrictions—all useful, but usually not key factors in the businessmen's decisions on whether or not to invest, or to expand existing investments. When the oil companies were distributing abroad, they appear to have acted in general on their own. In their search for oil concessions in foreign lands, on the other hand, the State Department frequently became involved (sometimes as an observer, sometimes on a particular request, sometimes in either arranging or participating in the negotiations). Yet the historians of Standard Oil of New Jersey indicate that when that important unit embarked on a major search for foreign oil properties, "at no time in the 1912–1917 period was effective diplomatic action taken to back Jersey Standard in its efforts to acquire oil reserves." The insurance firms, which dealt with European governments, handled most of their own discussions; in fact, explicit comments appear in their records that the State Department was not helpful. Businesses that invested in less developed areas, where disorder prevailed, were the ones that sometimes (but not *always*) obtained significant U.S. government advice and aid. Bankers who planned to float loans and who received important guidance and support from the U.S. government are out of the scope of our study because they were not direct investors. Those bankers who established branches and houses abroad for the most part did not in these years require U.S. government aid,* although a U.S. bank in Nicaragua did join in asking the State Department to defend its enterprise.[7]

On the other hand, certain U.S. foreign policies clearly altered the course of American business abroad. For example, the final abandonment of unequal treaties with Japan (1899) gave that nation the opportunity to introduce tariff protection, which created a situation wherein certain American businessmen had either to invest in manufacturing or lose their markets. We will see other U.S. trade and tariff policies that had substantial (sometimes inadvertent) impact on U.S. enterprise abroad. Here we must stress that the relationship between the American government and American business in foreign lands was complex. While U.S. corporations that invested abroad in the decades before World War I were unquestionably affected by U.S. foreign policies, for most of them in most countries the role of the U.S. government seems to have been only one of many influences, and generally not decisive. Those instances in which it was important will be noted in the chapters that follow.

3

The environment abroad far more than circumstances in the United States influenced the strategies of American businessmen who were making or who already had foreign direct investments. Americans continued to place their largest foreign investments in market-oriented facilities in industrial or industrializing countries—where there was a large existing

* In the case of the national banks, they could not expand abroad until the Federal Reserve Act (December 1913) gave them authority to do so. Whether they would have done so, however, is questionable.

or potential demand for their goods. On the other hand, they made their largest foreign investments in raw materials in nearby regions and in areas where the raw materials were available.

As Americans planted stakes abroad, they found foreign competitive practices were often unfamiliar. This was not so much the case in Canada, where American businessmen encountered relatively well-known conditions (though a smaller market than that at home). Frequently, U.S. corporations' chief competitors in the Dominion were American enterprises that invested across the border. On the other hand, in Europe Americans discovered the acceptance of what has been called a "negotiated environment." * European firms often preferred cooperation to competition at home and also in overseas markets. Usually—though there were exceptions—American corporations when they went abroad sought to act independently. Europeans would suggest alliances. On rare occasions, as will be evident in Chapter V, Americans initiated such proposals. In the United States the law was clear: the Sherman Antitrust Act of 1890 forbade agreements in restraint of trade. The act contained three passages dealing with "restraint of trade . . . with foreign nations"; the courts were slow, however, to interpret this phrase. No international law forbade worldwide accords to control commerce.

Thus, many American businesses (as they exported, entered into foreign licensing arrangements, and made foreign investments) joined with others, especially Europeans, in restrictive international agreements. These agreements varied. An American company, or its subsidiary located abroad, might make a pact (1) with an otherwise independent firm; (2) with a licensee; or (3) with a foreign company in which it had obtained some equity, from minority to controlling interest. Such accords might include exchanges of patents, technical knowhow, general information and skills; protection of the home market and sales territories of each participant; export quotas; consultation on bids and price controls; standardization of product; output quotas; and joint purchase of materials.

Before World War I, most of the restrictive international agreements linking American industrial corporations (or their wholly owned sub-

* The term "negotiated environment" is used by H. van der Haas to mean an environment protected from the free play of competitive forces (van der Haas, *The Enterprise in Transition*, 18–19, 30–31).

sidiaries) with *independent* foreign firms proved short-lived, limited in scope, and difficult for the participants to enforce. In the next chapter we will see such agreements in the copper, oil, aluminum, and explosives industries. American companies that made agreements *with foreign licensees* found these more durable than the ones with completely independent concerns. These agreements usually covered a specific number of years or the life of the patent(s); some, however, had a long history. When the U.S. firm licensed a foreign company, it might or might not obtain an equity interest in the licensee; licensing always involved some kind of "relationship" agreement that was in most cases restrictive. In the next chapter, we will see such agreements in the electrical, office equipment, and roller bearings industries. The third type of international agreement—that between an American company and its *affiliates* —defined the tie between the parent and its offspring. Such pacts were apt to be of the longest duration. Often, they had no time limitation, for they might well be integral to the formation of the overseas unit. The receipt from the parent of patents, skills, technological knowhow, and allocation of a market territory gave value to the foreign affiliate. These features were advertised as a means of attracting foreign capital to invest in the new business. Frequently, American corporations that expanded abroad (in Canada as well as in Europe) and wanted to attract host country capital made this sort of arrangement. We will see examples of this in the tobacco, electrical, and automobile industries.

On the other hand, some U.S. companies which did not seek joint ventures with foreign capital and which had products clearly superior to those made abroad in the particular market avoided entangling alliances. There is considerable evidence that American companies that formed their own 100 per cent-owned subsidiaries or branches in foreign countries did not make restrictive agreements with such units. Nonetheless, in the case of 100 per cent ownership, restrictions at any particular time may have been made explicit in correspondence between the home office and the subsidiary.* Companies with 100 per cent-owned subsidiaries or branches were in the oil, aluminum, tobacco, electrical, office equipment, automobile, fertilizer, and farm equipment industries.

---

* This is important. When subsidiaries were tightly controlled by the parent, they could be used according to the parent's needs. Detailed relationships did not have to be spelled out in contracts.

None of the above four types of relationships (with independents, licensees, affiliates, and wholly owned subsidiaries) was a "pure type." Typically, a U.S. company entered into one kind of relationship in one foreign market and another in a second foreign market. Likewise, it is important to see process in business abroad: independent foreign firms might become affiliates; independent foreign licensees might become affiliates; affiliates might become independent or, alternatively, 100 per cent-owned; 100 per cent-owned subsidiaries might become affiliates. These processes were already in evidence before 1914.[8]

If foreign competitive practices were important in shaping American business practices abroad, so too were the nationalistic policies of foreign governments. In the chapters that follow we will see that in Canada "national policies" spurred U.S. businesses to invest in manufacturing, while European and Japanese national tariffs and demands of governments for local production of goods purchased prompted American companies to make foreign investments.[9] Foreign government legislation often meant that for a U.S. company to gain or maintain a market abroad, it had to make investments in the host country in assembly, manufacturing, or refining; in the case of insurance companies, it was necessary to make security deposits abroad. It was insufficient for a company merely to have a stake in a sales establishment outside the United States.

American companies made few investments in countries colonized by the European powers. When they did, they frequently found that Dutch or British government officials acted to curb their activities. In independent, less developed nations, host government policies also influenced American business. In our discussion of U.S. investments south of the Rio Grande, we will see that the policies of dictators—whether favorable or unfavorable to U.S. business—had profound impact on investment decisions and conditions of operations of the companies in those lands.[10]

4

It is apparent that American and foreign economic and political conditions shaped the investment activities of Americans outside this country. The next chapters will consider some of the leading foreign investors, indicating specifically how the domestic and host-country environments influenced U.S. business abroad. Note how often the U.S. firm did not operate "essentially [as] a national corporation operating extra-nationally, insisting on the primacy of the methods . . . [used] at home, and even the laws of the home country." Instead, the American company often—but not always—made adaptations that showed it to be a "genuine multinational enterprise . . . sensitive to local traditions and respecting local jurisdictions and policies."[11]

V

Expanding Abroad
(1893–1914)

The evolution of enterprises in key industries calls for specific attention in order to make the generalizations of the previous chapter meaningful. One key industry was copper. By the mid-1880s European mine owners had become alarmed at the large exports of American copper. "Our French friends have been very anxious to have us united with them and try and control the product[ion] of the world—they to take care of Europe and we of America, but I would have nothing to do with the scheme," wrote Channing Clapp of Calumet & Hecla, the largest Michigan copper company, in March 1886. A year and a half later M. Secretan of Paris determined to corner the world's output of copper, and this time the major American copper companies entered into agreements with him to curtail production. The Secretan syndicate proved a notorious failure. By 1891, because of low prices Calumet & Hecla took the initiative in entering into arrangements with independent European producers to limit output and to restrain American exports, with the goal of price stabilization. Such agreements had only partial success.

Then, in 1895–1896, the British Rothschilds gained control over Anaconda Copper Company, by that time America's largest copper company. Through this and other properties, they controlled roughly 40 per cent of the world's copper. They were able to exert some influence on price, but no evidence exists that they negotiated pacts with other American independents.[1]

In the turn-of-the-century merger movement Amalgamated Copper Company was formed (in 1899); it acquired Anaconda, and in the process, Anaconda's ownership returned to American hands. Amalgamated declared *its* aim was to dominate the world's copper industry. To do so, it would need an effective marketing structure. Before it considered investing in foreign copper mines, it turned attention to selling its output at home and abroad. It looked to the Lewisohn Brothers, dealers in copper for many years. At least as early as 1899, Lewisohn Brothers had a London house. On January 29, 1900, the United Metals Selling Company, incorporated in New Jersey, was organized to take over and to continue the metal business of the Lewisohn Brothers, retaining that firm's management. Initially this sales unit was not directly owned by Amalgamated group.* At its formation, United Metals was the largest dealer in copper in the world. It continued to do business through its branch house in London. In 1906, Amalgamated became interested in a small extent in Mexican mining. Despite the size of Amalgamated and United Metals, neither could control world-wide copper prices.

Meanwhile, the Guggenheim brothers had come into the copper trade, acquiring copper mining properties in the United States, Mexico, and Chile, and establishing a London branch to handle their copper distribution. By 1914 United Metals Selling Company had lost first place in the world copper industry to the Guggenheims. The latter found that they too were unable to stabilize world prices.[2]

All the American copper exporters discovered that European buyers, unfettered by antitrust laws, combined to force down prices. The Americans, who exported some 45 to 55 per cent of United States copper production, could not under the Sherman Act join together to counter the European cartel. Thus, John D. Ryan of Amalgamated became an articulate advocate of legislation to let American *exporters* combine to *meet* foreign cartelization.†[3] By the time of World War I, American

---

* In 1911–1912 Amalgamated Copper Co. completed its purchase of the selling unit.

† Ryan insisted on *legislation* and not simply that the Federal Trade Commission be given the power to authorize combinations and exempt exporters from the provisions of the Sherman Act. The latter would be undesirable, he believed, because the Federal Trade Commission would only allow association when there was no political advantage in refusing it. Ryan thought the Federal Trade Commission would prohibit combinations among the large producers—and only let the small ones combine. This was not what he desired, or for that matter, what he felt the country needed. (Ryan to J. H. Perkins, Vice President of the National City Bank, Sept. 29, 1914, Vanderlip Papers, Special Collections, Columbia University). Ryan hoped to get the exemption in the Clayton Act; he was not successful in this, but when in 1918 the Webb-Pomerene Act was passed, he obtained his victory.

copper exporters had prepared the ground for cooperation in foreign trade. The Guggenheims had made extensive investments in foreign copper properties, while Amalgamated had a small Mexican mining investment. Other mining companies, such as Phelps, Dodge, also had stakes in Mexican mining. The short-lived agreements of the late 1880s and early 1890s had been only preliminary trials for this industry in its associations with foreign enterprises. In the process of making contacts with European businessmen the American companies were also extending their own business abroad.

2

Oil continued to be a giant U.S. export business. From 1892 to 1914, U.S. oil exports equaled more than half this nation's production. Standard Oil companies handled the bulk of this trade. We have noted that in the 1880s, when Standard Oil was faced with intense competition in Europe from Russian oil, it chose to expand its foreign sales organization—through investment in distribution facilities. Thus it met competition with more competition.

By 1892, however, John D. Archbold—second only to John D. Rockefeller in the Standard Oil organization—wrote to Rockefeller that he had entered into extensive and confidential interviews with the Rothschilds, who had major interests in Russian oil. They told Archbold that they would take steps toward control of the oil business in Russia and were quite confident of success. Archbold wrote Rockefeller: "We reached a tentative understanding with them on the basis of [here the letter runs into cipher] . . . for the first year, and thereafter in the increase of the world's business the Americans are to have [cipher again]." He admonished Rockefeller to keep the matter "exceedingly confidential. It was thought best that we should not see the Nobel people [who had large production facilities in Russia], but that the approach be made to them on the subject by the Rothschilds."

Despite this evidence, historians of Standard Oil are convinced no "general agreement" was ever reached between Standard Oil and the Russian producers, although in certain markets Standard Oil affiliates did conclude understandings with sellers of Russian oil.[4] What characterized Standard Oil's foreign operations was versatility. Standard

Oil companies continued to invest in their own distribution network abroad—starting or buying marketing firms in which they would own 100 percent of the stock or only part of the stock. In a few instances, when foreign tariffs on refined oil were high, Standard Oil built or purchased foreign refineries. Standard Oil also bought foreign oil in certain producing countries where the price was lower than that of American output. In addition, by the turn of the century Standard Oil was beginning for the first time to consider purchasing foreign *oil-producing properties* as well as merely buying foreign oil. This was after the unit had been an international investor for over two decades.

By 1900 Standard Oil was a giant multinational concern. As for international agreements with independent foreign oil companies, Standard Oil in the first decade of the twentieth century continued its policies of the 1890s. It did not scorn local agreements. Thus, although from 1903 through 1905 Standard Oil affiliates participated in cutthroat price wars with the Deutsche Bank-Shell group in Europe, in 1907 press reports noted agreements covering European markets between Standard Oil affiliates, the Deutsche Bank-Shell group, and Nobel-Rothschild interests. Similarly, in the Far East, Standard Oil of New York (which marketed kerosene in the Orient) engaged in sporadic price wars with the Royal Dutch-Shell group * until 1905. Then there were understandings, but after five years of agreement stiff competition resumed in 1910 and 1911. In short, the accords were on an "on again–off again" basis.† [5]

The pacts that Standard Oil companies made in foreign countries did not stop Standard Oil from extending its investments abroad. By the end of 1907, Standard Oil had established or acquired control of fifty-five foreign enterprises with a capitalization (not excluding duplication arising from the fact that some companies held shares in others) of roughly $37,000,000. In most of these units Standard Oil, directly or

---

* The Shell Transportation and Trading Company, an English concern, was organized in 1897. It had emerged from M. Samuel & Company, merchants and carriers in the eastern trade. Royal Dutch Company was a producer of oil in the Netherlands East Indies. By 1903 the Shell Company and the Royal Dutch Company were working closely together in far eastern markets. The two firms merged in 1907.

† To analyze or even mention each agreement and each termination is beyond the scope of this study. Rationales for agreements and their breakdown differed in each instance.

indirectly, held over 50 per cent of the stock. Most were for marketing; some had transportation facilities; some had refineries; and two (the wholly owned Româno-Americana Company—capitalized at $2,412,500 in Rumania—and the majority-controlled Imperial Oil Company, Ltd.— capitalized at $4,000,000 in Canada) were fully integrated foreign producers.* Standard Oil by this time had also tried to get into Far Eastern production. In 1898 it attempted to buy shares in the Royal Dutch Company to obtain a stake in oil production in the Netherlands East Indies, but the directors of Royal Dutch barred this move.† In 1899 Standard Oil sought—and continued to seek—concessions in the Dutch East Indies, only to be blocked by the Dutch government's support of its own business. Its attempt to explore in Burma (1902) was thwarted by British opposition. Lord Curzon declared, "It is not desired by the Government of India to introduce any of the American oil companies or their subsidiary companies, into Burma." Standard Oil's efforts to produce through a subsidiary in Japan proved prohibitively expensive and were abandoned after seven years.[6]

By 1911, before the U.S. Supreme Court decision to split up the giant concern, Standard Oil had 67 affiliates engaged in foreign trade.[7] Most of its foreign business was done through its own companies abroad. The result was effective control and management of its own distribution, but not of world commerce, where occasional competition from foreign oil companies proved severe.

When in 1911 the United States Supreme Court decided Standard Oil was a monopoly and ordered its dissolution, the effect on the organization of the company's foreign business was dramatic. Of the 34 companies into which Standard Oil was split, nine retained foreign facilities:

1. Jersey Standard obtained the largest foreign assets, comprising oil wells in Rumania and Canada; refineries in those two countries and in Germany and Cuba; a marketing network in Canada, every important Western European country (except Britain), and in all Latin America (except Mexico).

* Imperial's production was very small.
† The directors of Royal Dutch issued 1500 "preference" shares, which gave sole voting rights to existing members of the Board; the shares could not be transferred without consent of stockholders of this class of stock, which effectively barred Standard Oil participation.

2. Anglo-American Oil Company, Ltd.,* marketed in Britain.

3. New York Standard † controlled Far Eastern oil distribution.

4. Chesebrough Manufacturing Company,‡ makers of lubricants and specialty products, kept the European marketing network it had developed since the 1870s. By 1911 it had sales subsidiaries in England, Spain, France, and Germany, sales branches in Latin America, and a manufacturing subsidiary in Montreal, Canada.

5. Vacuum Oil operated in Portugal, France, Austria-Hungary, Germany, Sweden, England, Italy, Russia, and Canada (many of its subsidiaries in these countries had blending plants and refineries for lubricating oil). It also was in the lubricating oil trade in Asia (India), Africa, Australia, and New Zealand. By 1911 its product range in these regions (except India) also included kerosene, naphtha, and to a lesser extent gasoline and fuel oil. It used the trademark "Mobiloil."

6. Borne, Scrymser Company sold lubricants and specialty products in various foreign markets.

7. Colonial Oil Company marketed through direct investment outposts in certain South American nations.

8. Galena Signal Oil Company exported railroad oils.

9. Waters-Pierce Oil Company had major stakes in Mexican marketing and refining; it also had petroleum lands in Mexico.[8]

Practically all these companies continued to expand abroad after 1911. This was especially true of Jersey Standard and New York Standard. The former enlarged its foreign marketing, refining, and producing facilities because it feared antitrust action were it to expand at home. Its foreign deliveries exceeded its domestic deliveries of refined products. Most of its foreign sales were made through exports of American-refined products and sold through wholly owned or affiliated sales companies or branches, but deliveries from its refineries abroad also rose rapidly between 1912 and 1914. In 1911 Jersey Standard's foreign crude oil production was small; in subsequent years it turned more attention to developing foreign sources of supply. Through its Dutch marketing affiliate, Jersey Standard in 1912 was able to make its first investment in

---

* Reacquired by Jersey Standard in 1930.

† New York Standard and Vacuum Oil merged in 1931 to form Socony-Vacuum.

‡ Chesebrough Manufacturing Company in 1955 merged with Pond's to become Chesebrough-Pond's, Inc.

oil concessions in the Dutch East Indies. The next year—again through a foreign affiliate—it made its entry into oil production in Peru. It also made "overtures" to acquire Lord Cowdray's lucrative Mexican oil properties, but "legal and political difficulties" thwarted the Mexican plans.[9]

New York Standard added to its sales network throughout the Orient and sought to acquire producing properties in Palestine, Syria, and Asia Minor. On February 10, 1914—with the aid of the State Department *— it entered into an agreement with the Chinese government by which it obtained the first opportunity to explore oil deposits in North China, in the Provinces of Chihli and Shensi; later development, it was envisaged, would take place under a joint Standard Oil-New York–Chinese government venture.[10]

At the time of the dissolution of Standard Oil in 1911, the separate companies were not competitive with one another; each under the old structure had its specific region, function, or products, which it retained. Some would become highly competitive. Standard of California, which would become one of the major international oil companies, had no foreign business in 1911.

With the court decision, certain existing independent American oil companies saw increased possibilities abroad as well as at home. This was not the case with Pure Oil. Pure Oil had had foreign sales establishments earlier, and had at one period offered competition to Standard Oil in Germany and the Low Countries. In England, Shell had acquired Pure Oil's stakes in 1905 and in 1911 Jersey Standard bought the rest of Pure Oil's foreign marketing organization (in Switzerland, Germany, the Low Countries, and Scandinavia). Pure Oil gave up foreign marketing. On the other hand, the Texas Company—later Texaco—formed in 1902, had started in 1905 to establish overseas sales offices; by 1913 Texaco products were sold through its own outlets in Europe, Latin America, Australia, Africa, and Asia. Between 1911 and 1914, many American oil companies—including the Texas Company and Gulf— began to invest in the prolific oil fields in Mexico (these investments bore no relation to the break-up of Standard Oil and were predicated on new oil finds in Mexico).[11]

* State Department officials followed the events closely and were involved in the negotiations.

In short, in the years 1892–1914, American oil interests abroad had expanded. The most influential U.S. government action, affecting the foreign business, had been the Supreme Court dissolution decision. In Burma and China, the U.S. government had sought to assist the oil companies in their negotiations with the foreign governments; these instances seem to have been exceptional. When the American oil companies went abroad, they had been confronted by the possibility of combination overseas. Standard Oil had entered into certain cartel relationships; it had generally acted in these agreements from a position of strength. Before and after the dissolution, Standard Oil companies and some independents had enlarged their foreign stakes in distribution and, to a lesser extent, in refining and production. Primarily because of foreign tariffs, American companies had built or purchased refineries in certain consumer countries in Europe, Canada, and Latin America. To supplement U.S. supplies of oil, companies had begun to seek foreign reserves. With the exception of Burma, and for a while the Dutch East Indies, the Americans' hunt for foreign oil had not been seriously curtailed by European governments; in Burma, a European government—nationalist in intent—had successfully blocked the American investment.

3

In aluminum, as in copper and oil, American enterprise—seeking foreign business—had to adjust to European methods. The predecessor to Aluminum Company of America (Alcoa),* Pittsburgh Reduction Company, was formed in 1888, and faced this problem early in its history. In 1891–1892 the company built a plant in France to try to compete in Europe, but it was not successful. Then, for one year (1895–1896) Pittsburgh Reduction Company made an agreement with the giant Swiss aluminum company. The American firm pledged not to sell in Switzerland, Germany, and Austria-Hungary, while the Swiss unit agreed not to sell in the United States. This pact proved of short duration and was followed by aggressive marketing activity by Pittsburgh Reduction Company in Europe. At the same time, the company boldly moved into Canadian business (1899), starting a plant at Shawinigan Falls, Quebec.

By 1901, the American aluminum company's young president, A. V.

* Alcoa was—until World War II—the only major company in the U.S. aluminum industry.

Davis, was traveling to Europe regularly to supervise the expanding overseas trade. Davis discovered that "if one attempts to sell in Europe without participating in European cartels, he is at once faced with the competition of the European producers operating as a unit." Davis therefore decided to enter into accords with European industrialists. He recognized that an arrangement might be vulnerable under the Sherman Antitrust Act, so Pittsburgh Reduction Company formed a new, wholly owned subsidiary in Canada (Northern Aluminum Company) to act on behalf of the American parent. The Dominion subsidiary, in addition to operating its own plant, would handle all the American company's export business. In 1901 it concluded an agreement with the Swiss, two French, and one British company, wherein each national group reserved its home market exclusively for the domestic producers. The United States was a "closed market," while the rest of the world was an "open market" (that is, each party to the agreement was assigned a fixed quota in the "open market"). This accord was renewed and strengthened in 1906; the Pittsburgh Reduction Company was expressly required to stop its *customers* in the United States from reselling aluminum abroad. The new strictures proved unworkable, and the pact was canceled in 1908. In its place that year a new agreement was made between the Canadian subsidiary of Alcoa (the name was changed from Pittsburgh Reduction Company to Aluminum Company of America on January 1, 1907) and the Swiss aluminum company, which indicated that each would act as sales agent for the other in certain markets. Each pledged once more not to invade the other's "territories." The Swiss, it was understood, would stay out of the U.S. market.

Alcoa, at home, now found itself facing prosecution on antitrust violations, and on June 7, 1912, signed a consent decree which, among other things, prohibited it from making any agreement restricting exports from or imports into the United States. This served to void the 1908 agreement of Alcoa's Canadian subsidiary; whereupon, with the full knowledge of the U.S. Justice Department, the Canadian subsidiary of Alcoa made a new pact with the foreign producers, regulating the aluminum trade *outside* the United States. Alcoa officials noted that this was to permit the Canadian subsidiary "to do business in Europe, the European way." Explicit in the agreement was the stipulation that it would not in any way affect U.S. export and imports.

Thus, while the American copper producers in the pre-World War I period sought to change U.S. law to permit Americans to combine to *meet* European cartels, while Standard Oil in particular foreign countries on occasion joined in European cartels and in other areas was aggressively independent, Alcoa took a third approach: acting at first directly, and then through its Canadian subsidiary, it made agreements with independent European companies in 1895, 1901, 1906, 1908, and 1912 to regulate foreign business. Called upon to justify its action, an Alcoa spokesman declared: "The difficulties inherent in the development of any foreign market are great enough without insisting upon doing it in a way that the Europeans consider abnormal, and in the face of a unified competition from the foreign companies banded together in a cartel." Alcoa's relationships with the European companies involved marketing and not procurement of raw materials. On November 29, 1912, Alcoa organized Bauxite du Midi—a French bauxite company; by 1913 Alcoa was looking to South American sources of supply (see Chapter IX). The investment in foreign bauxite came after the company had been involved in international business for more than two decades.[12]

4

Sometime before 1890 (the exact date is unknown), the Gunpowder Trade Association (made up of America's leading makers of explosives) agreed with English and German manufacturers of the same product that the American companies would not sell in the Eastern Hemisphere if the Europeans would keep out of the United States, Mexico, and Central America.

In 1896 an American company, Aetna Powder Company, shipped dynamite to South Africa. Britain's major explosive manufacturer, the Nobel-Dynamite Company, claimed South Africa was "its territory." To counter the American company's intrusion and to provide competition, the British and German producers of black powder, detonators, and high explosives announced in 1897 that *they* would build factories in New Jersey.

Faced with this threat, du Pont, Aetna, and other associated American companies sought out the Europeans and reached a new accord with them on October 16, 1897. The American factories (du Pont, Laflin and Rand, American Powder Mills, Aetna Powder Company, and others) pledged to the British and German companies "to avoid anything being done which would affect injuriously the common interest." The Europeans agreed not to build factories in the United States, and the Americans in turn promised they would not erect factories in Europe. Both agreed to discuss prices. For high explosives, a more explicit pact was made, elaborating territories. There was to be an *exclusive territory of the American factories,* including the United States, Mexico, most of Central America, Colombia, and Venezuela. A *common territory* was defined to comprise the rest of South America, British Honduras, and the Caribbean islands (excluding Spanish possessions); in this territory there was to be no competition, for trade was to be carried on in a joint account, and neither Americans nor Europeans were to build factories without consultation. Canada and the Spanish possessions in the Caribbean were labeled a *free market,* exempt from the agreement.* The remainder of the world was the *exclusive territory of the European factories.*

This 1897 accord continued in effect for ten years; when it expired in 1907, the same parties made a new pact (with only minor alterations). Du Pont and the British Nobel Company in 1910 jointly formed the Canadian Explosives, Ltd., which acquired the four or five Canadian explosives firms in which the parent companies already had interests. In 1914 the European and American companies again affirmed their agreement, making trivial modifications; because of the outbreak of war, the new contract did not go into effect.†

* By 1897, the American powder group already had plants in Canada; the initial investments were made in 1876 (Marshall et al. *Canadian-American Industry,* 83). Although I have not been able to confirm this, it is possible the group also had operations in Cuba at this time.

† In the meantime, on June 13, 1912, du Pont and a number of other American powder companies (three of which were involved in the agreements with the Europeans) were found by a U.S. district court to be in a "combination in restraint of interstate commerce" in powder and explosives; they were "enjoined from continuing said combination and monopoly." The decree stipulated that two new competitive corporations were to be created (these were later formed and called Hercules Powder Company and Atlas Powder Company). The decree said nothing whatsoever about the restrictive

As in the copper, oil, and aluminum industries, the pre-World War I agreements made by the American explosive producers dealt exclusively with market plans and had nothing to do with the procurement of raw materials. Just as the Guggenheims did not ask permission when they went to look for foreign copper, just as the oil companies did not consult with their temporary allies when they went to look for overseas oil, and the aluminum company did not talk to its European associates when it considered bauxite investments, so too du Pont apparently did not have to ask for approval when in 1912 it made small investments in Chilean nitrates.

Whereas the international agreements made by the copper and oil companies did not limit their international investments, while the aluminum company's international agreements may have, in part, curtailed its investments, it seems unquestionable that the pacts entered into by the American explosives makers severely restricted their foreign investments.[13]

5

James B. Duke's American Tobacco Company (formed in 1890) came to be among the most impressive American firms abroad. Like every company we have so far considered, it began as an exporter. In response to foreign tariffs and existing or potential competition, it organized subsidiary companies in Australia, Canada, Japan, and Germany. It did not disdain joint ventures and frequently purchased majority interests in large foreign manufacturing companies. By 1901 its four Australian factories were turning out 200 million cigarettes annually, its Canadian factories 100 million, its Japanese plants 8 million, and its German unit 3 million. In addition, it was exporting over one billion cigarettes made in America—nearly one third of its entire output. Duke testified in 1901, "We are always selling direct from factories here [in the United States], unless there is some discriminating duty against us that forces us to manufacture [in a foreign country]."

Because of the discriminatory duty on manufactured tobacco, Amer-

---

agreements with the Europeans, nor did it deal with the joint-venture company, Canadian Explosives, Ltd. (William L. Stevens, ed. *Industrial Combinations and Trusts*, 463–471, and du Pont, *Annual Report 1912*).

ican Tobacco decided it required a factory in England, and in 1901 purchased Ogden's Ltd., a leading English producer, paying for the concern over $5 million. This action aroused the wrath of British competitors, thirteen of which combined into Imperial Tobacco Company. For roughly a year, vigorous rivalry existed between American and Imperial; then in the fall of 1902, an accord was reached. American Tobacco and its affiliated enterprises ceded their entire business in Great Britain and Ireland to Imperial. Imperial agreed not to sell in the United States, its dependencies, or Cuba—all of which were to be the "territory" of American Tobacco. American Tobacco and Imperial Tobacco organized a third company, British-American Tobacco Company, to handle the tobacco business in the rest of the world. American Tobacco Company and its affiliates received two thirds of the stock of British-American Tobacco, while Imperial Tobacco Company got the remaining one third. American and Imperial transferred their foreign factories, foreign subsidiaries, and foreign trade to British-American Tobacco.

The new British-American Tobacco Company proved to be a successful international business. Imperial Tobacco, in which American Tobacco acquired a minority interest, operated in its restricted territory, while American Tobacco confined itself to its designated territory. In 1902 American Tobacco invested for the first time in tobacco growing in Cuba and Puerto Rico.

In 1911 in *U.S. v. American Tobacco,* the Supreme Court ordered the dissolution of American Tobacco Company. The Court insisted that all American Tobacco's foreign restrictive covenants must be abrogated. The ruling stated that by January 1, 1915, American Tobacco must "sell or otherwise dispose of, or distribute by way of dividends to its common stock holders" all its holdings in British-American Tobacco Company and Imperial Tobacco Company. Thus, as in the Standard Oil case, the Court broke up a multinational enterprise. Out of this dissolution came American Tobacco (a new company), Liggett & Myers Tobacco Co., P. Lorillard, and R. J. Reynolds Tobacco Company. At this time, none of these four companies showed special interest in foreign business. Duke himself, who had created the giant tobacco combine, became chairman of the board of British-American Tobacco

Company. Under his leadership, the company (still controlled by American capital) expanded business *without* selling in the United States, although it did manufacture within this country for export. So, despite the antitrust action, the markets remained delineated. Since British-American had headquarters in London, the U.S. Court set the stage for the later drift of the company's ownership into British hands. This occurred in the early 1920s, but until then British-American must be considered a multinational *American* company.[14]

7

Agreements involving foreign patents made by the predecessor companies of General Electric had restricted the regions in which licensees could operate. All Edison's early relations with affiliated foreign companies had involved accords, limiting sales territories. After the German General Electric Company (A.E.G.) obtained full independence from control by Edison companies, it began to market on an international basis. Edison in 1888 had received protests from his agents and companies abroad, insisting that the inventor "stop" the entry of A.E.G. into their "territories." Edison wrote to do this, but the Germans, separated from the Edison group, refused; they felt no obligation to comply.

When in 1892 the Canadian General Electric Company, Ltd. was organized (controlled by the new General Electric Company), the minority Canadian stockholders held an option to purchase General Electric's holdings. In time the option was exercised, and the purchase by the Canadians included an agreement which conveyed to the Canadian General Electric Company, Ltd. "in perpetuity the exclusive right to manufacture and sell in Canada" products developed by General Electric. By 1900 the General Electric Company's *Annual Report* no longer recorded any stock holdings in the Canadian unit, and the Canadian General Electric Company, Ltd.'s *Annual Report for 1905* reported that the capital was "entirely Canadian." The independent company had exclusive rights in Canada.*

* When, in 1906 and 1907, the Canadian General Electric Company, Ltd. needed additional financing, it sold shares in *London* to obtain funds! G.E. may have maintained a *small* minority holding in the Canadian firm, although I have no evidence of this.

In 1892 the Thomson-Houston Company—a subsidiary of G.E.—started an affiliate which would manufacture in France. The Thomson-Houston Company obtained an interest in that affiliate in exchange for patents, know-how, and the exclusive right to sell Thomson-Houston products in French territory. General Electric saw to it that none of its other foreign subsidiaries or affiliates competed in the French Thomson-Houston company's territory. A similar procedure was followed when the British Thomson-Houston Company, Ltd. was formed in 1894.

While General Electric sold its holdings in the Canadian enterprise and maintained only a minority interest in the French Thomson-Houston company, it gradually increased its participation in the British affiliate. In 1905 G.E. signed an agreement with British Thomson-Houston providing for an "exchange of patents, information, and selling rights in specific territories." By 1906 G.E. owned 97 per cent of the stock in the British manufacturing company.

Meanwhile, in 1903, General Electric and Allgemeine Elektrizitäts Gesellschaft made an agreement whereby A.E.G. would sell exclusively in much of Europe, Turkey, and in Asiatic Russia, while G.E. would have exclusive sales in the United States and Canada.* Both companies could sell in such "neutral areas" as Mexico, Central America, South America, and Japan. Many countries (including France and England) were not mentioned in this agreement, presumably because General Electric and A.E.G. had separate commitments. The next year, A.E.G. purchased G.E.'s interest in Union Elektrizitäts Gesellschaft (one of the companies established earlier by Thomson-Houston); in return, G.E. obtained a small stake in A.E.G.

That year, 1904, G.E. made patent agreements with an existing Japanese concern that manufactured electric lights—Tokyo Electric Company, Ltd. The agreements were followed by G.E.'s acquiring in 1905 a controlling interest in Tokyo Electric. Then, in order to expand its operations in Japan, G.E. in 1909 made a patent agreement with another existing Japanese business, Shibaura Engineering Works, Ltd., manufacturers of heavy electrical power equipment—a firm backed by the House of Mitsui. The next year G.E. acquired a minority interest in Shibaura Engineering.[15]

* But note G.E. had ceded Canadian rights to the Canadian General Electric Company.

In short, as a General Electric executive later described it, the concept of organization was one in which General Electric would be the center, and then there would be foreign satellite companies, with exclusive rights, patents, and agencies. General Electric would restrict British Thomson-Houston to sales in England and not allow it to sell elsewhere, unless it had permission and then only through an associated company. All G.E.'s patents for England would go to the British affiliate, and in turn B.T.H. would give back to G.E. all rights to manufacture, use, and sell its products outside of its exclusive territory. This procedure was followed many times over, and General Electric became the residual legatee of everybody's exclusive rights. General Electric thus could effectively say, "You can't sell in a particular territory because we hold the patents—your patents too—and have granted them to others."

There were many sound business reasons for such a structure. Each foreign company could serve its local markets far better than General Electric. If each company developed a separate market, this would maximize the coverage and increase the total sales. The General Electric Company was not large enough—did not have sufficient depth of management—to cover the world; on the other hand, if friendly companies abroad cooperated with General Electric, all the companies would benefit.

By the outbreak of World War I, General Electric had "associated" manufacturing operations in Canada, England, France, Germany, and Japan—with a range of investments from 97 per cent to small minority holdings.* In many other parts of the world, from Mexico (1897) to South Africa (1898) to Australia (1898) G.E. had wholly owned sales subsidiaries and branches.[16]

Westinghouse Electric Company likewise established new foreign manufacturing enterprises. As noted in Chapter III, George Westinghouse had in 1889 organized a British subsidiary to trade and install machinery on contract. When in 1899 George Westinghouse decided to move into manufacturing electrical equipment in England, he formed a new corporation—the British Westinghouse Electric and Manufacturing Company, Ltd. The American parent obtained all the common shares in return for granting the enterprise the existing Westinghouse electrical business in England and also "the exclusive right to operate under its

* It is not clear that it had any interest at all in the Canadian business.

[the U.S. parent's] patents in England and its dependencies (except those in North America)." Most of the preference shares were offered to the British public. In the main, then, British capital financed the expansion, while the American company retained control through holding all the common and some of the preference shares. By 1914 Westinghouse had manufacturing plants not only in England but also in Germany, France, Russia, and Canada. Everywhere Westinghouse built huge plants. Whereas General Electric's foreign business developed less precipitately, took on a local guise, and proved profitable, Westinghouse soon found its large foreign assets were an incubus.[17]

7

International Business Machines' predecessor companies also started their foreign enterprises before World War I. In 1911 the Computing-Tabulating-Recording Company (C.T.R.) was formed in the United States (the company was renamed International Business Machines in 1924). C.T.R. was a merger of International Time Recording Company, Tabulating Machine Company, and Computing Scale Company. At the time of the merger, International Time Recording Company had sales representatives in foreign countries; Tabulating Machine Company had licensing arrangements with companies in England and Germany; Computing Scale Company had a factory in Toronto (started in 1902) and was apparently exporting to Europe. The licensing agreement that Tabulating Machine Company made in 1908 with the independent British Tabulating Machine Company had profound effects on the later foreign business of I.B.M.: the agreement gave the British unit an exclusive license to make and sell the products of the American Tabulating Machine Company, and later of I.B.M., in all the British Empire except Canada. Because of this accord, I.B.M. could not for years market certain of its products in the United Kingdom, Australia, New Zealand, India, or Australia.[18]

8

The early twentieth century witnessed the creation of an American automobile industry; it also saw the industry establish sales abroad. The automobile manufacturers—like other U.S. businesses before them—

sought first to export. Faced with tariffs, the enterprises sought to get behind the tariff barriers and assemble or manufacture in major markets. The first factories built by U.S. automobile companies or their affiliates outside national boundaries were in Canada. In 1904 Gordon M. Mc-Gregor, a Canadian maker of carriages, visited Henry Ford and suggested to him that Ford cars be manufactured in the Dominion. Ford agreed. McGregor raised the capital in Canada and in the United States to finance this venture. Henry Ford and the Detroit stockholders in the Ford Motor Company got controlling interest (51 per cent) in the new Canadian Ford unit in exchange for patents, drawings, and Henry Ford's services. The Dominion enterprise was to handle Ford business in the entire British Empire, excluding England and Ireland; it started at once to manufacture Ford cars in Canada—behind the Dominion tariff wall.

Other car manufacturers followed Ford across the border. By 1906 advertisements were appearing in *Canadian Motor* for "Canadian-made Oldsmobiles." In 1907 the Canadians Robert McLaughlin and his sons organized the McLaughlin Motor Car Company to make Buicks in the Dominion. By the time General Motors was formed in 1908 (and acquired Olds Motor Works and Buick), it already had affiliated foreign plants. In 1909 Everett-Metzger-Flanders (later merged with Studebaker) started to assemble cars in the Dominion. All these new entries were to be behind the Dominion tariff barrier.

Olds had by 1904 developed a quantity export business through regular dealers and direct sales representatives in England, France, Germany, and Russia. Buick started overseas sales in the early 1900s—and apparently had introduced some direct representation. Thus, when General Motors was formed, it took over this foreign business of Olds and Buick, and in 1911 established the General Motors Export Company to develop a more extensive overseas distribution network.

Ford had begun in England with agents, then developed a sales branch, and in 1911–1912 built a British assembly plant, with a small amount of manufacturing. By 1914 the Model T had become the "best seller" in England. By then Ford also had a small assembly unit in France, and in that same year became the first American automobile company to establish a direct sales outlet in Latin America—a sales branch in Argentina.[19]

9

Thus far in our discussion of American international businesses we have emphasized those companies that first went abroad to sell; some of these, as we have seen, were also beginning to seek foreign raw materials. Other companies from the start gave their chief attention to obtaining overseas raw materials that were not available in the United States, or were available at lower cost abroad. A number of such companies will be discussed in detail in Chapters VI–IX. Here we will look at one industry only—one that had major problems with European cartels; the fertilizer industry.

In the years 1893–1914 potash was almost exclusively "found and mined in Germany." At the turn of the century the output was controlled by a German syndicate. In an attempt to break this control, the Virginia Carolina Chemical Company, a large American buyer of potash, obtained in 1902 a majority interest in a new German mine in the province of Hanover. In 1909 another American company, International Agricultural Corporation, to secure a supply of potash salts independent of the Potash Syndicate, acquired the entire stock of the Sollstedt potash mines in Germany—one of the largest potash properties. It made contracts to deliver potash at below-syndicate prices to other American buyers. Its investment in 1909 was carried on its balance sheets at $4 million.[20]

The German government would not tolerate this substantial intrusion, and in 1910 the Reichstag enacted a law regulating prices and production of potash and imposing a compulsory cartel. Up to this time, International Agricultural Corporation had found its German investment "extremely profitable." Now the American contracts became "burdensome"; the Agricultural Corporation sold one half its holdings to a German concern with an option to that company to purchase the remainder. The option was not taken up before the outbreak of war in 1914. Clearly, however, the requirements of operating under host government restraints were not satisfactory to this American company.[21]

On the other hand, Virginia Carolina Chemical Company apparently found it could conform to the German regulations, and moved in the other direction. Its president, S. T. Morgan, informed the stockholders in July 1911 that "the German potash properties are in good condition . . . and will probably make more money than they have heretofore." The next year the company purchased additional German potash holdings. Morgan wrote in June 1914 that "by owning a large interest in potash mines in Germany, it [the company] is always able to get its potash on the most favorable terms." * Its subsidiary had become a member of the syndicate.[22]

By 1914, Virginia Carolina Chemical Company's interest in foreign business was not only in the potash mines but in sulphur mines in Mexico; its principal subsidiary, Southern Cotton Oil Company (makers of 'Wesson' oil) had "stock interests in [cotton] oil refining and manufacturing plants in Europe." [23] Virginia Carolina, unlike International Agricultural Corporation, had come to terms with European operating conditions.

10

Because European "competition" (or lack of it) had such pronounced effects on the course of U.S. businesses that moved abroad, it is worth tabulating a few more American enterprises that made restrictive agreements with foreign independent companies, with licensees, and with affiliates abroad. Some of these are listed in Table V.1. The table includes only those companies that had direct foreign investments and one for which the agreement later evolved into a direct investment (Timken Roller Bearing). Clearly, a number of U.S. companies found it essential to cooperate with Europeans rather than do business independently. Indeed, in the process of growth abroad, American business had to come to terms with European practices either with strong new competitive tactics or with cooperation—or retreat.

In the foreign investment decisions of executives in the copper, aluminum, and explosives companies, foreign government action and nationalist feeling seem to have had little impact, although when com-

* Nothing indicates the actual dollar investment. After World War I, Virginia Carolina Chemical Company presented a claim for $508,320.79 to the Mixed Claims Commission (U.S. and Germany) based on the compulsory wartime sale and liquidation of the Chemische Werke Schoenebeck, G.m.b.H., in which it owned 90 per cent of the stock. An award was made of $337,957.00. Mixed Claims Commission (U.S. and Germany), *First Report of Marshall Morgan*, 32–33; Mixed Claims Commission (U.S. and Germany), *First Report of Bonynge*, 42.

Table V.1. Miscellaneous agreements between United States and foreign companies made before 1914

U.S. company	Parties to the agreement	Nature of agreement	Fate of agreement
American Radiator	German subsidiary and independent foreign producers	Stabilized German market *only*	Lasted until World War I
Union Sulphur	German subsidiary and Sicilian producers	Apportioned world markets	Canceled January 1913. U.S. management feared it might violate N.J. antitrust laws
International Nickel	Company and Rothschild operations in New Caledonia	Price and market sharing agreement	Lasted through World War I
Diamond Match	Company, independent Swedish Match Co., and Bryant & May Ltd., England (partly owned by Diamond Match)	Divided world markets	Canceled in 1914, presumably as a result of American Tobacco case and the election of Woodrow Wilson, advocate of a strong antitrust policy
United States Steel	Company and English and German independent producers of rails	Regulated selling districts; U. S. Steel agreed not to interfere with German trade	Appears to have been terminated with U.S. entry into World War I
Timken Roller Bearing	Company and its independent British agent	Licensing agreement	1909 agreement continued into 1920s

Sources: On American Radiator: Nationale Radiator Gesellschaft m.b.H., Minutes of the Board of Directors, 1904–1912, in files International Division, American Radiator and Standard Sanitary Corporation, New York. On Union Sulphur: Ervin Hexner, *International Cartels*, Chapel Hill 1945, 272 and Temporary National Economic Committee, *Hearings*, Washington, D.C., 2217ff. On International Nickel: Hexner, 234; O. W. Main, *The Canadian Nickel Industry*, Toronto 1955, 19, 35–39, 46, 64, 73–74, 100; and *Mineral Industry 1903*, 492. John F. Thompson and Norman Beasley, *For the Years to Come*, New York 1960, 93 notes the personal friendship of Robert Thompson of International Nickel and Baron Adolphe de Rothschild. On Diamond Match: Report of Commissioners, Combines Investigation Act, Dept. of Justice, *Matches*, Ottawa 1949, 7. On U.S. Steel: Federal Trade Commission, *Report on Cooperation in American Export Trade*, Washington, D.C. 1916, pt. II, 75. On Timken Roller Bearing: *U.S. v. Timken Roller Bearing Co.*, 83 F. Supp. 284.

panies in the aluminum and explosives industries built plants in Canada, they may have been in part motivated to do so by the Dominion tariff.

On the other hand, in the foreign expansion of the companies in the oil, tobacco, electrical, automobile, and fertilizer industries, host government tariffs, preferences for national businesses, support of local cartels, and so on, influenced U.S. corporate strategies abroad. American firms in these industries were profoundly affected both by European business *and* political conditions.

Nationalism as an influence on the course of business abroad is too important to leave buried amidst these case studies. Before 1914 numerous American companies felt the impact of foreign nationalism and nationalistic government measures as they established plants in foreign countries. Thus, the *1897 Annual Report* of Diamond Match reads: "Your directors . . . thought it wise to sell the Liverpool property and business to the Diamond Match Company, Ltd. of England. One of the main reasons for doing so was to overcome English prejudice against Yankee products by making it an English company." The new corporation had English shareholders, but was controlled by the American Diamond Match Company.[24]

In Germany hostility to foreigners grew so intense, tariffs rose so high, and patent laws were so framed, that American businesses in search of sales often found it wise to manufacture there.[*][25] France was not as antagonistic to aliens as Germany in these years, but its tariffs were high enough that some American businesses considered local manufacture a wise step. American companies frequently started their first European sales branch in London, had their largest foreign market there, but built their first European *factory* in Germany or France. Then, if they found it was economical to manufacture in Germany or France, they would subsequently start a factory in England, based purely on cost considerations. Generally, each factory served the particular foreign country in which it was located.[26]

---

* On Feb. 23, 1909, a convention between the United States and Germany was concluded under which the nonworking provisions of the German patent laws were made inapplicable to American patents. Up to this time, Americans either had to work their patents or have them voided. The Taft administration undertook negotiations in 1909 for similar conventions with other European governments "whose laws require the local working of foreign patents." (*Foreign Relations of the United States 1909*, xii). This was a clear case of U.S. government assistance to American business abroad.

In Russia intense nationalism meant that businesses operated under close government supervision. A director of Westinghouse Air Brake Company in Russia told F. A. Vanderlip in 1901 that his company had been unsuccessful, having lost from $200,000 to $300,000 in the previous year: "Every act of the company is dependent on the approval of the Finance Minister . . . The government is almost our only customer," complained the director.[27]

When in 1909 International Harvester—faced with high tariffs— contemplated a factory in Russia, President Cyrus H. McCormick, Jr. visited St. Petersburg. He explained to the Russian Ministers of Finance, Commerce, and Agriculture that his company and its predecessors had been selling in Russia for twenty-eight years, through agents and branch houses, and that the company had at that time eight branch houses in the Empire. He told them International Harvester planned a Russian plant, but that his associates in Chicago hesitated to invest in the Empire, because "they feel that foreign capital might not receive the protection and encouragement which is accorded in other countries where they welcome foreign capital." McCormick told each minister: "We . . . need the approval and the cooperation of the Russian Government and officials in every reasonable way."

The Minister of Agriculture, Krivochein, replied to McCormick that he thought "the plan is an excellent one which will benefit Russia." The Minister of Commerce, Timiriazeff, was equally sympathetic, indicating that he was an advocate of high tariffs and would put one on harvesting machines * if International Harvester established a factory there. The Minister of Finance, Kokoctsoff, who described himself as a "rabid protectionist," also looked with favor on the proposal; he pointed out, however, that "those of us, like myself and the Minister of Commerce . . . who feel that Russia should have a tariff to encourage home industries are really in the strange position of fostering *foreign industry* in agricultural machines."

McCormick declared that International Harvester planned to form a company under Russian laws, employ Russian labor, use Russian lumber, iron, and other resources as far as possible, "and in every way pos-

---

* The tariff on certain harvesting machines had temporarily been suspended. There was still a high level on mowers and other implements.

sible to conduct the enterprise as a Russian Company." To this Kokoct-soff replied that what was important to him was that the capital and all the affairs of the company remain in American hands—that is, not pass to western Europeans. Clearly, western European capital was a threat to Russian sovereignty; American capital, small as the entry was, constituted no such threat. With the ministers' full encouragement, the International Harvester Company purchased property in December 1909 to build a Russian plant.

By 1911 International Harvester had five foreign plants—in Canada, Sweden, France, Germany, and Russia. Each had been built because of tariffs and the possibility of competition developing behind the tariff walls. In that year, foreign business constituted 40 per cent of International Harvester's entire business, and contributed more proportionally to the net earnings.[28]

Between 1898 and 1912 American Radiator Company, which had sold in Europe since 1892 and had had a branch in London since 1895, incorporated subsidiaries and started factories in many European countries. With the exception of its plant in England, all of its factories were built because of the need to vault high tariffs. The company's subsidiaries in Europe took on names such as Compagnie Nationale des Radiateurs, Nationale Radiator Gesellschaft m.b.H., and National Radiator Company, Ltd. to avoid the word "American" in their titles and to appease nationalist feeling.[29]

Japanese nationalism prompted some American companies to invest in manufacturing plants there. In 1899, with the end of unequal treaties, Japan exercised its newly won right to set its own tariffs. American businesses—such as Western Electric, American Tobacco, and others—sought to get within the barrier, just as they were doing in European countries.[30]

11

United States insurance companies operating abroad were far less concerned with foreign competition than with coming to terms with foreign governments' nationalistic policies. As noted earlier, certain countries required that as a condition of doing business, foreign life insurance companies keep a legal reserve within the host nation, that companies buy specified host country securities, and that such securities and cash be placed in depositories designated by the host government.

The Swiss, Austro-Hungarian, German, and Russian governments, especially, policed the business of the U.S. insurance companies. Faced with threats of hostile legislation, Equitable Life Assurance Society in 1891 withdrew from selling in Switzerland. When New York Life Insurance Company lost its license to do business in Switzerland, its president, John A. McCall, visited with Swiss authorities in October 1892 to convince them to relicense his firm. The Swiss government agreed, but only after insisting on larger deposits within the Republic.[31]

By 1896 New York Life Insurance Company's vice-president, Darwin P. Kingsley, was writing from Paris that "the question is nothing less than full reserves on the continent, or extinction of continental business . . . It seems tough to quit the place where the best business we have is being gotten—the best in quality. We have $125,000,000 of as firm business here as stands on the books of any Company in the world."[32]

When Austrian legislation required full deposits, Equitable, in 1897, stopped doing new business in Austria. New York Life Insurance Company's vice president, George Perkins, went to Vienna to negotiate. Mutual Life Insurance Company also wanted to stay. As a result of Perkins' efforts, both New York Life and Mutual were able to continue in business.

In Germany, as in Switzerland and Austria, Equitable withdrew because of nationalist pressures. The company stopped doing business with Prussia in July 1894 rather than invest half of its Prussian premium returns in local bonds as a deposit. New York Life and Mutual also refused to abide by the regulations, and in 1895 the Prussian government "threw them out." The talents of Perkins were called upon again. He employed Guidon von Nimptsch, who was a school friend of the German Minister of Foreign Affairs, Count Bernhard von Bulow.* In the summer of 1899, Perkins wrote the president of New York Life: ". . . in Austria and Switzerland our respective Embassies did not do one solitary thing for us. In both cases we were handed our concessions on the side and not through the Embassy and this is the programme I am

* Count Von Bulow became German chancellor (1900–1909).

working for in Berlin." The skilled diplomacy of Perkins was clear. When the Germans demanded that the American company not hold stock in industrial concerns, the *American* by-laws of the New York Life Insurance Company were altered to meet German requirements.[33]

Meanwhile, in Russia Perkins, "greatly impressed with the future of the country," undertook direct discussions with government officials. In October 1899 he met with Minister of Finance Serge Witte in St. Petersburg. Perkins explained "it was just possible" that New York Life Insurance Company might market some Russian bonds; Witte discussed the matter directly with the Czar, and Perkins obtained his reward. On October 27, 1899, Witte addressed the New York Life Insurance Company:

> I have this day ratified the contracts concluded between your establishment and St. Petersburg International Bank of Commerce on the one part, and the South-Eastern and the Vladicaucase (sic) railroad on the other part, which contracts bear on the purchase of $10,000,000 . . . worth of 4% bonds guaranteed by the State.

It was agreed that New York Life would participate directly or indirectly to the extent of 20 per cent in any Russian-American business concluded in the next two years. The letter from Witte added, "As regards the wish expressed by you to be protected against rival companies . . . I must inform you that I shall be opposed to any issuance of further permission relating to the establishment in Russia of American insurance companies."

Thus, in return for the large portfolio investments in Russian bonds and for aid in marketing them in the States, Perkins gained the right to do business in Russia as well as protection from competition. In Berlin, too, he was able to get New York Life readmitted to Germany while Mutual was still barred. In October 1899 Perkins, on a train from St. Petersburg to Berlin, was writing New York Life Insurance Company President John A. McCall:

> We are now on the same pleasant and friendly relations with the Russian [Insurance] Department that we have heretofore established with Austria, Switzerland, and Prussia, and I wouldn't give a man five kopecs to guarantee us against trouble in any one of these four Governments . . . They are our friends—they believe in

us and even want to help us. The entire complexion of things, as existing four or five years ago, is changed and our future could not be brighter.

At the turn of the century, New York Life Insurance Company was firmly committed to doing business abroad, while Equitable was withdrawing from foreign sales and Mutual was fighting an uphill battle. In their attempt to maintain their position abroad, both New York and Mutual were making large foreign investments.[34]

In 1905 came the famous Armstrong investigation of American insurance companies with its damaging disclosures of their abuses. The investigators recommended that the companies should be limited to $150,000,000 of new business each year. The limit was imposed on January 1, 1907. Thus, Equitable, Mutual, and New York Life curtailed domestic and foreign sales. Each decided to eliminate unprofitable overseas business, or activity in areas where there were "unsettled conditions, arbitrary exactions, excessive expenses, or unsatisfactory mortality." Mutual decided not to make any more deposits abroad. Equitable by 1912 resolved "to cease entering" foreign countries.[35]

Only New York Life retained a firm commitment to international business. In June 1908 its new President, Darwin P. Kingsley, speaking in Paris, declared that while under the regulations the company had trimmed its sales in both Europe and the United States, it had retired from only two "juristics:"—"from Portugal, because of conditions with which we could not comply, and . . . from Texas . . . where laws were passed worse than anything ever written on any Statute Book of Europe or covered in any Ministerial Decree." A law passed in Italy on April 4, 1912, made life insurance a state monopoly; as a consequence, Equitable and New York Life withdrew, transferring their business to the Italian government.[36]

While the policy of Equitable and Mutual was one of retreat, New York Life Insurance continued to enlarge its foreign business. By 1913 the total amount of American insurance in force abroad (outside of Canada) had declined from its peak of $1,142,000,000 in 1905 to $1,049,178,223 in 1913. On the other hand, the amount of New York Life insurance in force in foreign countries rose from $494,383,349 in 1905 to its high point of $525,081,511 in 1913. Thus in 1913 New York

Life Insurance Company carried over half of all American insurance in force abroad, outside of Canada. It alone of the three big American insurance firms still proudly proclaimed its international character.[37]

12

Neither European competition nor European governments shaped the course of American direct investment in banking in these years. The earliest investments in American banking abroad had been in houses in London and on the continent to market American bonds. By 1912 such key private banking houses as J. P. Morgan, Lazard Frères (an American firm), Lee, Higginson & Co., and Speyer & Co. had had London and/or Paris houses for many years. With few exceptions, the new branch banking in the years 1893–1914 was mainly to provide services for American individuals and companies abroad. Only a few commercial banks were international—that is, did business in two or more foreign countries. American Express—which got into the business of travelers' checks in 1891—moved into banking in Europe when a representative opened a Paris branch in 1895. By 1900 American Express had offices all over England and the continent—14 such offices by 1912. The International Banking Corporation, which began operations in 1902 in China, initiated American banking in the Orient, hoping to aid America's China trade. Its board of directors included steel magnate Henry C. Frick, railroadmen E. H. Harriman and Edwin Gould, and mining and smelting entrepreneur Isaac Guggenheim. I.B.C. spawned branches throughout the Far East; it also opened branches in Panama and Mexico. A 1912 publication indicated it had 17 branches. One estimate notes that 26 foreign branches of American banks existed in 1913; * obviously the majority were branches of I.B.C.

Until the end of 1913, U.S. national banks were prohibited by law entry into foreign banking. This changed after the enactment of Section 25 of the Federal Reserve Act (December 23, 1913). Thereafter, national banks with capital and surplus of $1 million or more were allowed to start branches in foreign countries and U.S. possessions. National City Bank was the first to do so, organizing a branch in Buenos Aires in 1914

* It apparently excluded the American Express offices.

(see Chapter IX). Its branch was to provide a service for American business abroad.[38]

13

The foregoing account should make it evident that in the years 1893–1914 many American enterprises were involved in foreign operations. Many developed investments abroad in marketing, manufacturing, and raw materials; space limitations have precluded consideration of numerous other industries—from drugs, to machine tools, to food. "Even in pickles and sauces one Pittsburgh firm Messrs. Heinz has recently covered the English market," wrote an Englishman in 1901. He continued, "Its preparations are today to be seen in half our restaurants and in practically every grocery's in the country." Also omitted are many companies that failed in their attempts to move abroad. Not only did International Agricultural Corporation and Equitable Life Insurance retreat from foreign business but S. M. Horton Ice Cream Company tried to introduce its product to the British public. A reporter explained its failure: "The British public is not educated up to the ice-cream habit." [39]

The United States companies that went to foreign lands introduced American money, technology, products, and management, but they also used in their foreign operations European and Canadian money, European technology and products (less often), and European and Canadian management (quite frequently). They were flexible in the process of expanding abroad; in the rare case, they were even prepared to enter into joint ventures with foreign governments (as, for example, Standard Oil of New York in China).

For the most part the investments grew in spite of agreements made with competitors abroad, although in some instances (the explosives industry, for example) foreign investments were severely curtailed because of such accords. We have noted that a number of companies in the copper, oil, explosives, and nickel industries came into contact with Rothschild and Nobel interests and had to come to terms with these European giants.

As we have seen, firms had to shape their strategies because of foreign governments' nationalistic actions. This was apparent when the British government acted on behalf of British companies in Burma, blocking the entry of U.S. business. In Germany the government's support of cartels was onerous to one U.S. firm; in another case, adjustments were made. Most American companies came to terms with nationalism by incorporating in the host country, changing from sales operations to manufacturing and refining abroad (thus bypassing tariffs), hiring local personnel, purchasing locally, adopting "national" titles, and making security deposits (in the case of the insurance companies). Most of these adjustments were made in Europe and Canada—the large markets. Sometimes adjustment was impossible, and the U.S. firm withdrew. American banks began to offer services abroad for traders and international investors.

Chapter X will contain a summary of the point that the expansion of international business had reached by 1914. Here, it need only be said that there was indeed a penetration by U.S. companies into foreign business. Table V.2 gives Cleona Lewis's estimate of the book value of U.S. direct investments abroad in the years 1897, 1908, and 1914. Such bare figures do not reflect the dynamics of the growth of the international companies—as their leaders shaped a course, responding to economic and political change at home and, to a far greater extent, to the unique economic and political environments abroad.

Table V.2. Estimates of U.S. direct foreign investments for the years 1897, 1908, and 1914 (book value in millions of U.S. dollars)

Country or Region	(1) Total [a]			(2) Railroads			(3) Utilities			(4) Petroleum [b]			(5) Mining [c]			(6) Agriculture			(7) Manufacturing			(8) Sales Organizations [d]		
	1897	1908	1914	1897	1908	1914	1897	1908	1914	1897	1908	1914	1897	1908	1914	1897	1908	1914	1897	1908	1914	1897	1908	1914
Mexico	200	416	587	111	57	110	6	22	33	1	50	85	68	234	302	12	40	37	—	10	10	2	2	4
Canada and Newfoundland	160	405	618	13	51	69	2	5	8	6	15	25	55	136	159	18	25	101	55	155	221	10	15	27
Cuba and other W. Indies	49	196	281	2	43	24	—	24	58	2	5	6	3	6	15	34	92	144	3	18	20	4	5	9
Central America	21	38	90	16	9	38	—	1	3	—	—	—	2	10	11	4	18	37	—	2	1	—	1	1
South America	38	104	323	2	1	4	4	5	4	5	15	42	6	53	221	9	11	25	—	2	7	10	16	20
Europe	131	369	573	—	—	—	10	13	11	55	99	138	—	3	5	—	—	—	35	100	200	25	30	85
Asia	23	75	120	—	—	10	—	15	16	14	36	40	—	1	3	—	—	12	—	5	10	6	12	15
Africa	1	5	13	—	—	—	—	—	—	1	2	5	—	2	3	—	—	—	—	—	—	—	1	4
Oceania	2	10	17	—	—	—	—	—	—	1	2	2	—	—	4	—	—	—	1	6	10	—	2	5
Banking	10	20	30	—	—	—	—	—	—	—	—	—	—	—	—	—	—	—	—	—	—	—	—	—
TOTAL	635	1638	2652	144	161	255	22	85	133	85	224	343	134	445	720	77	186	356	94	296	478.	57	84	170

Source: Cleona Lewis, America's Stake in International Investment, Washington, D.C.: Brookings Institution, 1938, 578ff. Many of these figures are questionable, but they do present the general pattern. The Mexican figures, for example, may be too low for 1908 and too high for 1914. The railroad investment in Central America (1897) is too high since Miss Lewis erroneously included the Panama Railroad. The European 1908 and 1914 totals are substantially larger than the sum of columns 2 through 8. On the other hand, Miss Lewis does not itemize the direct investments of the U.S. insurance companies, which may make up a large part of the difference. The investment in Canadian utilities is probably low. The oil investment in Asia in 1914 excludes Jersey Standard's investment in the Dutch East Indies.

[a] Total includes sum of columns 2 through 8 plus miscellaneous investments.

[b] Petroleum includes exploration, production, refining, and distribution; the bulk of this is in distribution.

[c] Mining and smelting.

[d] Excludes petroleum distribution; includes trading companies and sales branches and subsidiaries of large corporations.

[110]

Three

The Western Hemisphere

The "Spillover" to Mexico
(1876–1914)

The basis for much of today's international business was established by the enterprises considered in the preceding chapters. There is a direct line of evolution from many of those companies to the multinational corporations of the present day. The story of business abroad is, however, not so simple. Certain nearby areas—because they *were* nearby—attracted the special attention of American investors: Mexico, Canada, and—of less importance in dollar sums—the Caribbean.* These regions drew some investors with interests limited to the neighboring lands and others whose interests were multinational.

Mexico, Canada, and the Caribbean are singled out for separate consideration in the next three chapters, not only because they are nearby, but for other reasons as well. Mexico is significant because from the 1870s to roughly 1912 it attracted more U.S. direct investment than any other single country.† Canada ranked second only to Mexico in the level of U.S. direct investment during those years, and rose to first place by 1914. As for the Caribbean, while the region stood relatively low in terms of the size of U.S. direct investment, of all areas, U.S. stakes there attracted the most public attention in America.[1]

In these three regions in the early 1870s, only several dozen U.S. companies had interests. The last two decades of the nineteenth century saw the entries grow rapidly: by the turn of the century—as the U.S. frontier appeared to be closed—a dramatic upturn occurred in U.S. direct investment in the nearby areas. The surge coincided with the general

* Henceforth the term "Caribbean" includes the islands, Central America, northern Venezuela, and northern Colombia.
† See Table V.2.

heightening of U.S. business interest in worldwide investment—a phenomenon noted at the beginning of Chapter IV. Here we turn specifically to the rise of U.S. stakes in Mexico and consider which American businesses went there, why they invested, why Mexico particularly attracted so much U.S. capital, and what conditions influenced American individuals and corporations as they moved their operations across the Rio Grande.

2

The forty-six-year-old Porfirio Díaz in November 1876 marched his troops into Mexico City, forced an election, and in May 1877 assumed leadership of that country. Mexico lay in abject poverty; mining and agriculture had fallen into neglect.[2] Díaz was born poor and had risen in the army through his own accomplishments. He determined to bring Mexico out of *its* penury. One method was to use foreign capital, and in 1877 he made his first offer of subsidies to railroad builders.[3] Foreign investors were not interested until Díaz provided order, stability, and protection for their property. He did, forming the *rurales*—a strong rural police to keep the peace and crush opposition. To the dictator (as Díaz became), the rurales served as a gestapo, a cheka, and a palace guard all in one.

Beginning in 1879, a stream of American capital flowed into Mexico. Then a group of Boston capitalists incorporated the Sonora Railway Company. The Bostonians planned to extend the Atchison, Topeka, and Santa Fé to the Pacific Coast in order to break the monopoly of Collis P. Huntington and provide an alternate route to the American West. Like the earlier large U.S. foreign investments in transportation in Panama and Nicaragua,* these entries were part of the entrepreneurs' domestic plans rather than specifically *foreign* ventures.[4]

From the end of 1880 to 1884 Díaz was not in office, but his successor followed his policies; when in 1884 Díaz resumed national leadership (which he retained until 1911), there had been no discontinuity.[5] In 1880 as Díaz closed out his first term, American railroad construction began in Mexico—in Sonora and elsewhere. Fred Wilbur Powell, in *The Railroads of Mexico*,[6] documents each railway. This is unnecessary

---

* See Chapter II.

here. What is important is that the same business leaders who built the American railways crossed the border to create the Mexican system. In 1881 Collis P. Huntington and Southern Pacific interests obtained a concession.[7] In time, Jay Gould, Russell Sage, and E. H. Harriman made investments in Mexican railways. British, French, Dutch, and German capital came too, but American money predominated.* [8]

The progress was phenomenal: whereas in 1877 Mexico had only 417 miles of railway, ten years later there were 4,106 miles; in 1897, 7,311 miles, and by September 1901, 9,600 miles. The government subsidies granted to foreign railway interests in cash, certificates, and bonds up to December 31, 1899, equaled $101,656,378.15.[9]

The large number of concessions to foreigners, as well as the liberal terms of the grants, caused murmurs of discontent within Mexico, but the Díaz government insisted "it was necessary to make an extreme effort, even to making sacrifices, rather than lose the opportunity of gaining by the investment of foreign capital in Mexico, the impetus that would bring prosperity." [10] The boom of railway construction and of the Mexican economy at the turn of the century emphasized his point.

Railways served many of the same functions in Mexico as they had in the United States. They opened new lands and provided possibilities of new mining enterprises. There followed a proliferation of investments in mining and later in land. Engineers, promoters, and working miners traveled the railways to remote districts. The railroad meant lower freight charges on transporting of ores from the mines and they made feasible the introduction to the mining regions of bulky and heavy modern machinery.[11]

Foreigners found the Mexican mining laws of 1884 and 1892 were satisfactory. The 1892 law gave the miner his property "in an irrevocable, perpetual and secure form through the payment of a yearly tax, with full liberty as to method of work and amount of work done." [12]

With peace and order maintained by the *rurales,* with the railroads, with the satisfactory legislation, and the rich untapped deposits of silver, gold, lead, zinc, and copper, literally hundreds of U.S. mining companies invested in Mexico. Then, after the passage in the United States of the high McKinley tariff (1890) and the imposition of new duties on

---

* Some of the American enterprises were joint ventures with European capital.

the entry of lead ores *into* the United States, Americans found it profitable to build smelters across the Rio Grande.[13]

To read the *Engineering and Mining Journal* or *Mineral Industry* of that period is to learn about the opening of mines and smelters in Chihuahua, Sinaloa, Durango, San Luis Potosí, Aguascalientes, Michoacan, Zacatecas, Puebla, Guerrero, and elsewhere. Typically, a few Americans would form a syndicate and would raise money from a number of investors. To develop the mines, the founders frequently sought funds from Boston or New York financial houses. Americans often purchased old abandoned mines from Mexican owners. These could not be operated without considerable capital, which required the entry of Eastern money and American big business.[14]

The Guggenheim brothers became prominent in Mexico in the 1890s. In October 1890 they obtained a Mexican government concession to build smelters; they completed their first one (for lead only) at Monterrey in 1892 and a second one (for copper and lead) started operations at Aguascalientes in 1893. These smelters stimulated mining in the region, and the Guggenheims invested in a copper mine in 1893 and then in many other Mexican mining properties—in copper, lead, silver, an zinc.[15]

In 1904 Mexico became second only to the United States as the most important copper-producing country in the world.[16] The richest copper mines were those of Greene Cananea (discovered in 1896 by the American adventurer and cattleman, "Bill" Greene, and after 1906 managed by interests associated with the Amalgamated Copper Company);[17] the Moctezuma mine at Nacozari in Sonora (opened by the Guggenheims but purchased in 1895 by Phelps, Dodge[18]); and the Boleo mine in Lower California—the only non-American one of this group (controlled by the French Rothschilds).[19] By 1906 the Greene Cananea Company alone had an authorized capital of $60,000,000.[20]

In lead and silver American funds came to be equally evident. In 1902 Mexico passed the United States to rank first in the world's silver output. The Consolidated Batopilas Silver Mining Company of New York, organized in 1880, was an early venture; in 1887 it merged with five other American silver companies to form a new Batopilas Mining Company (capital, $9,000,000).[21] Robert S. Towne of the Consolidated Kan-

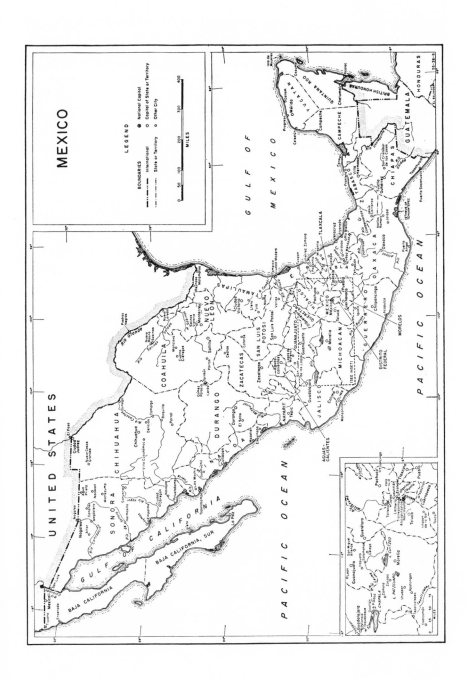

sas City Smelting and Refining Company purchased lead and silver mines in the 1880s in Sierra Mojada and then in Chihuahua; in the 1890s he built a smelter in Mexico. The giant American Smelting and Refining Company, known as ASARCO, with a capital of $65,000,-000, became the key company in Mexican mining and smelting. This company was organized in 1899 by men and capital associated with Standard Oil; initially, practically all its properties were in the United States, but among its first acquisitions was Towne's Kansas City company with its Mexican mines and smelter (Towne became a director of ASARCO).

In April 1901 ASARCO acquired the Mexican smelters of the Guggenheims. The Guggenheim brothers, independent of ASARCO, retained their own Mexican lead and silver mines, but that year they gained control of ASARCO. The properties under the Guggenheims' authority made them the largest U.S. investors in Mexico. Towne left ASARCO and on his own mined and smelted lead and silver in Mexico; his stakes were small compared with those of the ASARCO organization.[22] A map included with the ASARCO *Annual Report* for 1904 shows that the company and associated Guggenheim-controlled concerns owned or operated some 64 properties in Mexico, mainly in the states of Chihuahua, Durango, and Nuevo Leon, but also dispersed in other states.[23] At many of these locales the Americans established company towns.

Railroads opened new possibilities in Mexican coal, and in June 1899 the Mexican Coal & Coke Company was founded. This New York-directed firm had its property in the state of Coahuila, Mexico, and boasted a self-contained government. The company typically put in a machine shop, hospital, drugstore, schoolhouses for the children of American and Mexican personnel, a jail, post office, and telegraph office.[24]

The processing of Mexican ores usually went only so far as smelting; then the product would be exported. The investment in Mexico's first steel plant by the New Yorker Eugene Kelly was exceptional. Kelly, in a rare joint venture with key Mexicans, in May 1900 organized the Compañía Fundidora de Fierro y Acero de Monterrey (capital $10,000,-000 U.S.).[25]

Far more typical were the mounting U.S. interests in mining and smelting. That the American Institute of Mining Engineers held its

1901 annual meeting in Mexico signifies the keen attention paid by Americans to Mexican mining.[26] Euphoria intoxicated U.S. investors; nowhere, declared a representative newspaper article in April 1903, were life and property as secure as in Mexico. The country was attractive because of its wondrous undeveloped mineral wealth and its great economic progress. There was, declared a contemporary, "absolute freedom from strikes and labor trouble" and the "immense advantage of cheap labor." In 1903 when labor unrest plagued managers of several of the principal mining camps in the United States, Díaz's *rurales* prevented similar disturbances in the same companies' Mexican operations. From a wage standpoint, the yearbook *Mineral Industry* (1902) estimated that a ton of ore could be mined in Mexico for 40 per cent of the cost of mining similar ore in the United States, assuming the American miner did twice as much manual work as the one in Mexico. *Mineral Industry* in 1903 reported that mine prospecting and development in Mexico required less capital than in the United States.[27]

There were, to be sure, Mexican import duties, export levies on silver and gold, imposts on certain business transactions, and property taxes, yet many of these could be reduced or waived through negotiated concessions.[28] Actually, labor conditions were not always harmonious; but in the main the *rurales* kept order better than American police. By 1908, however, wages were rising; miners were no longer content to work for 50 to 75 centavos (Mexican) per day. At Cananea, Mexicans objected to 3 pesos a day! * On the other hand, no labor unions organized Mexican mine workers.[29]

As U.S. investments in railroads and mining rose, Díaz and his finance minister, José Yves Limantour, acted to forestall criticism of foreign domination of Mexico. The government began in 1903 to buy railroad securities to give it the controlling voice in the management of Mexican railroads. Between 1903 and 1909, Limantour gained control for Mexico of the most important national railroad lines; a new company, National Railways of Mexico, in which the government held majority interest, started operations in 1909. There continued to be sizable U.S. investments in Mexican railroad stocks and bonds, but the

---

* Three pesos equalled $1.50. Cananea's wage was exceptionally high.

major railroads had for all practical purposes been "nationalized." The price was satisfactory; there were no complaints at this point from American investors in the railroads. An official government publication assured the mining industry, "Since the government has acquired the controlling interest in the trunk lines, it is safe to assume that 'feeder' tracks will be built in all directions." [30]

At the same time, the Mexican government had become sensitive to the dominant role of American Smelting and Refining Company in northern Mexico and an "authorized" government report in 1908 declared,

> The grievous situation created by the predominant power of the Trust will probably be modified when the concessions granted by the government expire. In the meanwhile, independently of the trust a number of smelters have been built for the purpose of treating customs ores, and the entrance of the United States Smelting and Refining Company into Mexico will probably cause such competition as to give fair play at last to the mining fraternity.

This same report estimated that in 1908 there were 840 American companies mining in Mexico, out of the total of some 1000 foreign mining companies.[31]

In 1897 the largest amount of American direct investment in Mexico had been in railroads, the second largest in mining. By 1908 because of the rising stakes in mining and because of the "nationalization" of the key railroad lines, the book value of the direct investment in mining far exceeded that in railroads.* American investors also entered into land speculation, cattle raising, and planting in Mexico.

George Hearst—father of William Randolph Hearst—purchased a thousand square miles of land in Vera Cruz, Campeche, and Yucatan, as well as the million-acre Babicora ranch in Chihuahua. The largest part of the chicle producing land in Mexico—approximately 3 million acres —was operated by the international American Chicle Company,† which relied on the raw material to make its chewing gum. Examples of other large land holdings in Mexico are listed on Table VI.1. Smaller haciendas abounded, some owned by U.S. companies and others by individual

---

* See Table V.2 for all figures on direct investments.
† See p. 212 for American Chicle's other foreign holdings.

Table VI.1. Some large U. S. landholdings in Mexico—1911

Company	Location in Mexico	Activity	Size
Flores, Hale (of San Francisco)	Lower California	Growing orchilla	"Thousands of square miles"
Palomas Land and Cattle	Chihuahua	Cattle raising	2 million acres
Sonora Land and Cattle (of Chicago)	Sonora	Cattle raising	1.3 million acres
Morris & Co.	Chihuahua	Cattle raising	1.26 million acres
Piedras Blanca Ranches	Coahuila	Cattle raising	1.24 million acres
Rascon Manufacturing and Development of Louisiana	San Luis Potosí Tamaulipas	Sugar	1 million acres
Corralitos	Chihuahua	Cattle raising	800,000 acres

Source: See note 32.

Americans. Land was cheap in Mexico, and as acreage became more expensive in the United States, Americans moved southward. The land was used for growing bananas, coconuts, pineapples, and limes, plus fibers, coffee, and rubber, as well as for raising cattle and planting chicle, flowers, and sugar. Investments ran into many millions of dollars.[32]

The United States stake in rubber deserves special attention. In 1899, with the British creating plantations in the Far East, President William McKinley proposed that Americans participate in growing rubber to fill their country's domestic needs. The suggestion provoked a spree of speculation. Hundreds of companies were organized. While some went as far afield as Brazil, most sought rubber in Mexico. Bernard Baruch tells of the genesis of one significant investment. The inventor William A. Lawrence had developed a process for extracting rubber from guayule, a shrub found in northern Mexico. Baruch wrote later: "The more I explored the matter the greater my interest. Here at our very door, and in a healthful climate, it seemed, lay a possible source of rubber." Accordingly, in 1904, Baruch, Senator Nelson W. Aldrich, Dan Guggenheim (who, as we have seen, was already taking part in mining and smelting ventures in Mexico), and Thomas Fortune Ryan went into the Mexican rubber business; * John D. Rockefeller, H. P. Whitney, Levi P. Norton, and C. K. G. Billings participated. Through various companies they purchased 2 or 3 million acres of land in Mexico and erected a factory at Torreon to obtain rubber from the guayule plant. The companies involved were acquired by Intercontinental Rubber Company in 1909. Others also considered the guayule shrub. On May 26, 1906, the Mexican Crude Rubber Company was formed. It acquired land in Mexico and started factories at Viesca, Coahuila, and Cedril, San Luis Potosí. Many Americans planted the traditional rubber tree in southern Mexico.[33]

As for U.S. investment in Mexican utilities—compared with U.S. stakes in railroads, mining, or land, it was not substantial. We mentioned in an earlier chapter that the Mexican Telegraph Company was American-managed and financed; so too was the newer Mexican Telephone and Telegraph Company (1905). The American engineer, F. S. Pearson (not to be confused with the British oilman, Sir Weetman Pearson), was active in Mexican Light and Power Company, serving Mexico City; † the bulk of the capital for Pearson's operations was Canadian, not American. There were other miscellaneous U.S. interests in Mexican utilities—many linked with operations in the mining industry. For example, the Greene Cananea Company owned waterworks, the public lighting system, and the telephone connections in its company town. The giant American stakes in Mexican utilities were for the future; in 1914, English and Canadian money predominated in this activity.[34]

There was one other sector in which U.S. interests in Mexico became significant. As early as 1876 a Boston ship captain had purchased tar at Tuxpam for use on his vessel. He organized a company, went back to Tuxpam, acquired leases on land, and drilled two or three wells. When he found a small quantity of oil, he built a refinery; its kerosene output he sold in Mexico. Since his funds proved limited, he sought more capi-

---

* This was almost the same group that several years later invested in the Belgian Congo.

† He also had interests in Chihuahua railroad and lumber companies; by 1914 his holdings in Mexico were said to equal $25,000,000.

tal on State Street. No Bostonians, however, shared his optimistic predictions of bonanzas in oil, and his requests were rejected. The downcast captain returned to Tuxpam to commit suicide—the first of many frustrated investors in Mexican oil.[35] Meanwhile, Standard Oil had been exporting kerosene to Mexico. We noted earlier that because of the duties on refined oil, its affiliate, Waters-Pierce Oil Company, had by 1885 built refineries at Vera Cruz and Mexico City. These units processed imported Pennsylvania crude. Before 1900 Waters-Pierce was the most important oil company in Mexico. Henry Clay Pierce, its chief executive, also had interests in the then American-controlled Mexican Central Railway, which carried his products.[36]

A new stage in the history of the Mexican oil industry began in 1900 when Edward L. Doheny, an independent oil man from California, visited Mexico on the invitation of A. A. Robinson, American president of the Mexican Central Railway. Robinson recognized that if oil were abundant near his line, its transit would add to his profits. Doheny and his staff investigated. "We felt that we knew, and we did know, that we were in an oil region which would produce in unlimited quantities . . . fuel oil," Doheny later recalled. Accordingly, in 1900, Doheny incorporated in California the Mexican Petroleum Company; it started to drill for oil the next year.

No doubt stimulated by Doheny's efforts, Waters-Pierce Oil Company acquired some oil lands in 1902. Yet it was Doheny, not Pierce, who took the lead in exploring for and finding oil. Pierce at this point remained most interested in refining and marketing in Mexico. Doheny's Mexican Petroleum Company drilled a well in 1904 that flowed for nine years, yielding about 3½ million barrels of heavy fuel oil. This success was in the so-called "Golden Lane"—a strip of land about one mile long and 25 miles wide on the Gulf of Mexico—which became the principal source of Mexican oil. Doheny's true bonanza came in September 1910. Then a subsidiary of his Mexican Petroleum Company, Huasteca Petroleum Company, "brought in" the well Juan Casiano No. 7; by the end of November 1919 it had yielded 80 million barrels! Later in 1910, the Britisher Sir Weetman Pearson (who on July 16th had become Lord Cowdray) struck oil, and his Mexican Eagle Oil Company (or Aguila Company, as it was called) became the largest Mexican producer. The triumphs of Doheny and Lord Cowdray directed world attention toward Mexico; American and British capital invested in Mexican oil. By 1911 the Mexican oil production that was marketed totaled 34,000 barrels per day, more than half of which was American-owned. That year, Mexico rose to third place in the world's oil industry—following the United States and Russia.[37]

The American railroad, mining, cattle, planting, utilities, and oil companies hired thousands of Americans to work in Mexico, and these individuals looked to U.S. business to supply them. We see vividly in Mexico what often occurs with U.S. direct foreign investment: we will call it the "cluster complex." When Americans move abroad, they remain consumers of American shoes, clothing, and other goods; thus in Mexico, U.S. manufacturers began to sell to the Americans there, and *then* to Mexicans as well.[38] Towns developed American communities. In Cananea, Sonora, for example, a department of the mining company manufactured doors, windows, and moulding for sale to the public. An American, Joseph Krause, made boots and shoes to order, "fit guaranteed." A Boston retail shop opened and advertised "The only Exclusive Gent's Furnishing House in Cananea. Hart, Shaffner & Marks CLOTHING. J. B. Stetson HATS. . . . We are clothiers to the American colony of Cananea." William C. Greene had a cattle business (along with his mining enterprise), which not only served as wholesale and retail butcher, but included a sausage factory as well.[39]

The mining projects attracted chemists, ore-testers, and engineers; such subsidiary interests by 1902 already owned almost $7 million worth of property in Mexico. The machinery builders in the United States opened offices to supply the new enterprises. The multinational U.S. insurance companies did business in Mexico. American banks opened in Coahuila, Nuevo Leon, and Mexico City.[40]

Trade increased. In 1870 our commerce with Mexico had amounted to roughly $8.6 million. By 1910 it had reached $117 million. Writing early in 1911, William Downs concluded

> The linking of Mexico to the United States by lines of railroads, . . . the extension of American banking facilities [there] . . . have made it possible for the American merchant or manufacturer to do business . . . practically on the same terms as in the more remote

parts of the United States. Much of the business is now done directly by the manufacturers, the most successful of whom have established their own branches or selling agencies in . . . Mexico.[41]

American trade and investment in Mexico was a "spillover" from the United States. The American stake was larger than that of the British. The border became meaningless. Profits were to be made, and businessmen sought them. Perhaps the fact that it was so easy to establish enterprises in Mexico made the shock of what came after 1911 the harder to take. There was in this expansion of American business no sense of violation of another's national territory, or of Mexican rights for national self-determination, or of politics in fact. Americans entered Mexico in good faith. Their investment—direct and portfolio—by 1911 totaled, according to various estimates, between $646 million and $1.5 billion (see Table VI.2–VI.4) * [42] My own estimate would choose the middle ground of just under $1 billion, of which roughly $600 million appears to have been direct investment. This latter sum was in large part American money exported from the United States rather than an investment accrued through profits earned abroad, reinvested depreciation allowances, or foreign borrowings. Nowhere in the world outside of the United States did Americans have such large direct investments.

3

Throughout the tenure of Porfirio Díaz, Mexicans in many walks of life muffled their hostility to the dictator. In 1910 the antagonism became overt. The next year, the aging dictator was ousted; he resigned May 25, 1911. Díaz was accused of catering to foreign—particularly American—interests. Mexican newspapers declared American business had exploited Mexico. Mining camps in the United States in the first decade of the twentieth century were rough; so were those in Mexico. South of the border, however, an extra element of conflict existed. Mexicans saw foreigners with wealth; by contrast their own people, living in poverty, were working for the strangers. Company towns— where Americans maintained the roads, post office, schools, and stores,

* The Fall Committee (in 1919) in another estimate put U.S. investment in Mexico at $1.5 billion in 1911 (U.S. Senate, Subcommittee of the Committee on Foreign Relations, *Investigations of Mexican Affairs, Report,* 66th Cong., 2nd sess., Washington, D.C. 1920, 3322).

Table VI.2. U. S. direct and portfolio investments in Mexico—1911
Estimate of William H. Seamon [a]

Investment		Millions of U.S. dollars
Government bonds		52.0
Railways		
Rail stocks	235.5	
Rail bonds	408.9	644.4
Tramway, power & electric light plants		.8
Mining		
Mines	223.0	
Smelters	26.5	249.5
Land		
Timberland	8.1	
Ranches	3.1	
Farms	1.0	12.2
Livestock		9.0
Rubber industry		15.0
Manufacturing		
Soap factories, etc.	1.2	
Breweries	.6	
Other factories	9.6	11.4
Banks		
Stocks	7.9	
Deposits	22.7	30.6
Stores		
Wholesale	2.7	
Retail	1.7	4.4
Oil business		15.0
Insurance		4.0
Theaters and hotels		.3
Professional outfits		3.6
Houses and personal property		4.5
Institutions, public and semi-private		1.2
		1,057.8

Source: U.S. Dept. of Comm., Bureau of Manufacturers, *Daily Consular and Trade Reports,* July 18, 1912, 316.

[a] William H. Seamon, an American mining engineer, made this report on U.S. investments in Mexico in 1911. It is often referred to as the "Letcher Report" because Consul Marion Letcher submitted the figures to Washington.

Table VI.3. U.S. direct and portfolio investments in Mexico — 1908, 1914
Estimate of Cleona Lewis (in millions of U.S. dollars)[a]

Year	Direct	Port-folio	Total	Direct investments by sector							
				RRs	Mining	Oil	Agr.	Util.	Sales	Mfg.	Other
1908	416.4	255.6	672.0	56.8	234.0	50	40	21.6	2	10	2
1914	587.1	266.4	853.5	100.4	302.0	85	37	33.2	4	10	5.5

Source: Cleona Lewis, *America's Stake in International Investment* (Washington, D.C., Brookings Institution, 1938), pp. 578ff.

[a] Miss Lewis has no 1911 estimate. All qualitative evidence indicates total U.S. investment in Mexico was higher in 1911 than in 1914. There are, as is evident, substantial differences between Miss Lewis's estimates and those of Seamon: on the size of the portfolio investments in railroads, on the investment in utilities, and on the direct investment in the oil business. Miss Lewis used Seamon's data when developing her own figures. Note that by Miss Lewis's calculations direct investment constituted between 62 and 69% of U.S. investment in Mexico; by Seamon's data (if we count a portion of the railroad stocks as direct investment), direct investment totaled about half U.S. investment. Miss Lewis's figures on investment in utilities seem large but note that Seamon nowhere accounts for U.S. direct investment in telephone and telegraph systems in Mexico.

Table VI.4. U. S. direct and portfolio investments in Mexico—1911
Estimate of Luis Nicolau D'Olwer [a]

Investment	Millions of U. S. dollars
Government bonds	29.6
Railroads	267.3
Utilities	6.7
Mining	249.5
Land (incl. planting, cattle raising, and timber)	40.7
Industry	10.6
Banks	17.1
Commerce	4.5
Oil	20.0
TOTAL	646.0

Source: *Historia Moderna de Mexico, El Porfiriato, La Vida Económica* (Mexico, 1965) II, 1154.

[a] This 1965 Mexican approximation is far lower than the earlier U.S. estimates. In this estimate the bulk of the U.S. investment is clearly direct investment.

and even paid the wages of the police—were deeply resented. That "millionaire" foreigners should own millions of acres of land created animosity. That oil should be under alien control seemed intolerable. There was, according to one estimate, more American than Mexican money invested in Mexico. Resentment ran rampant because of this lording of one nationality over another. The bitterness was buttressed by memories of the American war with Mexico in 1847–1848. Mexicans repeated their suspicions that the United States sought to acquire all or at least more of Mexico and that the entry of capital heralded the flag. The clash of nationality mixed with politics led to passionate opposition within Mexico to Díaz, because of his concessions to the Americans. Mexican protesters completely overlooked the contributions of American capital: the miles of new railroads (much of which had subsequently been acquired by the government), the development of national resources, the new schools and hospitals in mining and agricultural communities, the new employment opportunities, and the higher wages.[43]

On the other hand, certain U.S. businessmen in Mexico were no longer pleased with the Mexican dictator. Díaz had close relations with Lord Cowdray's British-financed Mexican Eagle Oil Company, and the dictator's preferential treatment of the Britisher annoyed the American oilmen. Moreover, Díaz's finance minister, José Yves Limantour, called himself an "enemy of American monopolies" and "consistently opposed . . . permitting American capital . . . [to get] the upper hand." Limantour, it was said, encouraged British petroleum interests to compete with the leading American oil men (the refiner and marketer, Henry Clay Pierce of Waters-Pierce Oil Company * and the oil producer, E. L. Doheny of Mexican Petroleum Company). Hawley Copeland, a private secretary employed by Waters-Pierce, later wrote to President Wilson that when the Mexican government, under Limantour's prompting, had gained control of the Mexican Central Railway and incorporated it into the National Railways, Pierce saw his friends in the management of the

* Waters-Pierce Oil Company, as earlier noted, was a Standard Oil affiliate until the Supreme Court dissolved the Standard Oil combination in its decision of May 15, 1911. According to the historians of Standard Oil, however, the New York headquarters never controlled its affiliate's chief executive, H. C. Pierce. It is perfectly possible that Pierce took actions without the authorizations or even the knowledge of Standard Oil officials in New York.

railroad replaced. The new management introduced freight charges which discriminated against Waters-Pierce Oil Company in favor of the British. This action—aiding the Díaz-supported British oil interests—enraged Pierce.[44]

In 1911 rumors circulated in England, Mexico, South America, and the United States that "Standard Oil interests" financed the overthrow of Díaz. It was reported (1) that the Standard Oil affiliate, Waters-Pierce Oil Company, hoped a new government would be more sympathetic to American business (and less helpful to the British); (2) that "Standard Oil representatives," or Waters-Pierce, were supporting the revolutionists in order to obtain control of the National Railways, and (3) that Standard Oil felt the revolutionists would give it oil concessions that were not obtainable from the unfriendly Díaz government.[*][45]

One U.S. journalist suggested that the American mining and rubber interests in northern Mexico had much to gain "with Limantour out, and Díaz deposed." This writer indicated that these investors could not dominate the existing government and saw the possibility of dominating

---

* Reports implicating Standard Oil reached the State Department in 1911; at first they were not taken seriously. Then in April 1911 a special agent of the Justice Department in El Paso related the activities of a "Standard Oil representative" named C. R. Troxel. So detailed were the agent's dispatches that Secretary of State Philander Knox discussed the matter with President Taft. Knox maintained, "If the allegations are true we should break up the nefarious business." The Secretary of State penned a stern letter to John D. Archbold, chief executive of Standard Oil in New York. On May 15, 1911—the very day the Supreme Court decreed the dissolution of Standard Oil—Archbold replied to Knox with an "emphatic disavowal" of all statements "connecting the Standard Oil Company with financial negotiations with the leaders of the Mexican Insurrectos." W. H. Libby (in charge of Standard Oil's foreign business) hurried to Washington to confer with the Secretary of State. No memorandum remains in the State Department files to record Libby's discussions, but later department records indicate he denied Troxel represented Standard Oil. If the denial was true, this would effectively refute the evidence of the El Paso agent. (Record Group 59, 812.00/1503, 1542, 1593, 1652, 1790, 1942, 2040, National Archives). In 1912 a subcommittee of the Senate Foreign Relations Committee, headed by William Alden Smith of Michigan, held hearings in El Paso, Los Angeles, Washington, D.C., and New Orleans on whether there had been U.S. participation in the disorders in Mexico. Hearsay evidence was presented implicating Standard Oil; no Standard Oil or Waters-Pierce representative testified. Shelburne G. Hopkins, legal adviser to Madero, stated categorically that neither Standard Oil nor Waters-Pierce money was involved in the revolution (see *Revolutions in Mexico Hearings*, pp. 753–754). Albert B. Fall of New Mexico, who was on the Senate subcommittee (and who was not an impartial observer), concluded rumors of Standard Oil participation "were without foundation" (*Investigations of Mexican Affairs, Hearings*, 2640, Fall's 1913 report).

an alternative one. He does not, however, assert that the overthrow of Díaz was financed by these businesses; in fact, he indicates they had little sympathy for Madero.[46]

When there was a possibility of the U.S. government's intervening *on behalf of* Díaz during the 1911 revolution, E. L. Doheny cabled President Taft opposing such action: "Only gainers thereby would be British and other foreign interests." The United States did not intervene.[47]

After a short provisional government, Francisco I. Madero took power in 1911. Some U.S. businessmen in Mexico found him preferable to the old dictator. Although committed to social reform, the Madero family had wealth, property, and position. Many Americans felt Madero would want stable government and order. One reaction was expressed by a representative of the Cananea company—the large U.S. copper mining company in Sonora: "When the Maderistos came . . . we preserved a strict neutrality. We took the position of supporting the constituted government, whatever that might be, and we supported the Díaz government as long as it was in power." American Smelting and Refining Company, still the largest single American concern in Mexico, made profits in 1912 while Madero was in office. So did other mining companies. Waters-Pierce was prepared to work with Madero. Senator Albert Fall found that when Madero took power, the American oil companies "possibly conferred favors upon members of the Madero family." The legal adviser of the Madero group (Shelburne G. Hopkins), after the success of the revolution, became a lawyer for Waters-Pierce. Thus, important large American corporations came to terms with the revolution.[48]

At the same time, the Madero revolution, and especially the disorderly aftermath, made most Americans cautious about new investments in Mexico. The *Engineering and Mining Journal* in an editorial took a detached view: "Americans residing in Mexico are naturally exasperated by the [revolutionary] situation but there is nothing for them to do but to be patient, continue to restrain themselves, and if possible take themselves out of harm's way." This journal, in February 1912, opposed any propaganda for American intervention, which "would be like pouring gasoline on the flames." On the other hand, it noted that the mining industry found conditions early in 1912 "particularly vexatious."

During 1912 many U.S. investors curtailed, and if possible repatriated, their investments in railroads, mining, land, and utilities. Damage was done to the cattle and mining properties of Americans in northern Mexico, as well as to the Mexico City properties of Mexican Light & Power Company. Equitable Life Assurance Society, which had close ties with the Díaz administration, stopped doing business in Mexico. On the advice of the U.S. Department of State, numerous small businessmen deserted their Mexican facilities. The United States sent warships to transport American citizens who wanted to leave Mexico. The U.S. government embargoed arms to Madero's opponents, while permitting Americans in Mexico to import arms in self-defense. One American from the El Tigre Mining Company in Sonora told a Senate subcommittee in September 1912, "I went to Washington and saw President Taft [about 7 months ago], and he told us he would give us all the arms and ammunition we needed, and we bought the arms here in El Paso." Increasingly, during the course of 1912, U.S. businessmen in Mexico became doubtful about Madero's ability to maintain order. A representative of the Cananea Company, who had long opposed U.S. intervention in Mexico, by September 1912 felt "it has got to come." When the mining engineer from El Tigre Co. saw President Taft he asked only that the President send a man to Sonora to investigate. "We realize that in a foreign country we cannot expect to get the protection of the United States government for our financial interests, but we have felt that if there was going to be any sudden movement we would like to know it in time to get our women out from there." But by September 1912 he too believed U.S. "intervention must come some day." [49]

When the Madero government imposed new taxes on the foreign oil companies, there was immediate protest that the taxes were confiscatory and would impede investment. Yet, unlike most other Americans, the oilmen did not cut back. In 1911–1912, during the Madero era, the Texas Company made its first investments in Mexican oil; so too, Gulf Oil in 1912 invested in Mexico—its first foreign investment of any kind. And what of the Standard Oil companies? In 1912, Magnolia Oil Company (a new company controlled by the presidents of Standard Oil of New York and Standard Oil of New Jersey) purchased 400 acres of land in the Tampico region.* Standard Oil of New Jersey also made purchase

---

* For the two Standard Oil companies this was a short-lived investment in Mexico; in 1913, the Texas court ordered that the Magnolia stock held by the two men be put in trust and that Magnolia Oil Company operate independently of Standard Oil control.

contracts with the two leading producers in Mexico; E. L. Doheny (1911) and Lord Cowdray (1912). In addition, Standard Oil of New Jersey tried unsuccessfully in 1913 to purchase Lord Cowdray's oil properties. The rich oil resources of Mexico lured the oil men.[50]

On February 19, 1913, Mexicans arrested Madero and shot him late in the evening of the 22nd. Victoriano Huerta, who may have authorized the murder, became Mexico's new chief executive. Rumors associated English oil money (which had consistently opposed Madero) with the Huerta *coup*. As for Americans in Mexico, many who had come to lack confidence in Madero's abilities looked kindly on his overthrow. The U.S. Ambassador, Henry Lane Wilson, unquestionably approved the change. On the other hand, Woodrow Wilson, only recently elected President of the United States, was shocked at Huerta's manner of assuming power. In April 1913 Wilson's cabinet concluded that the "chief cause of this whole situation in Mexico is a contest between the English and American Oil Companies to see which would control." [51]

President Wilson dispatched former Governor John Lind of Minnesota to investigate. On October 7, 1913, Lind met with the new English minister to Mexico (Sir Lionel Carden), who favored support of Huerta's administration. Lind found that the British "seemed content with any solution that temporarily enabled them to resume the production and shipment of oil and other products and to sell goods." He told the minister, "We as neighbors, while equally interested in the restoration of business, were compelled to consider the future" and that President Wilson clearly indicated he "would sanction no attempted solution that rewarded treachery and assassination with office and power."

As for American businessmen in Mexico, more than all else they desired stability and order so they could do business. They wanted an end to the continuing civil war. Officials of Phelps, Dodge, Greene Cananea Copper, and Mexican Petroleum recommended to President Wilson that he recognize Huerta if the latter agreed to an early election.* But their suggestions brought forth no results. Meanwhile, H. C. Pierce,

---

* The executives of the two copper companies and the oil company proposed not only that Huerta hold an election in the states he controlled, but that the anti-Huerta forces (the Constitutionalists) be asked to suspend hostilities and also hold elections in the states under their control (Arthur Link, *Wilson*, II, 351).

of Waters-Pierce, ended his feud with Lord Cowdray; the two agreed in 1913 "to an equal division of the [Mexican] trade in all refined oil products." They succeeded in stabilizing the business conflicts.*

The Mexican revolution continued. Transportation in the north was irregular as rebel forces blew up railroad bridges and pilfered goods; fuel and basic supplies grew scarce. Labor shortages plagued American companies, for Mexicans joined rival groups of rebels. Rebel leaders extorted "forced loans" from American businesses, and in September 1913 the Huerta government threatened to do the same. Rebels "commandeered" American-owned facilities for the manufacture of ammunition and for barracks. There was, according to *Mineral Industry 1913*, "a demoralization of the mining industry." The American Smelting and Refining Company's *Annual Report for 1913* commented on the "very unfortunate condition of affairs in Mexico by reason of which so large a part of the Company's property is at present unproductive." ASARCO had its mines and five smelters located in centers of "exceptional revolutionary activity"; the disruption of railroad transportation had devastating effects on that company, with its dispersed operations depending on rail connections. By January 1914, *Engineering and Mining Journal* was reporting sizable American property losses in northern Mexico and estimated that "80 per cent of the Americans in Mexico three years ago have left the country." [52]

Most of the large American plantation properties in the south kept in operation, but under adversity. A number of the U.S.-owned utilities operated at a loss. The oil interests feared depredation; 245 Americans in Tampico on July 14, 1913, appealed, in vain, to President Wilson for protection. The State Department learned on October 1, 1913, that "a movement is on foot to raise a loan from the great petroleum interests under threat of national expropriation." In November a telegraph from Tampico to Washington indicated "Oil Companies will have to pay tax to revolutionists as they cannot afford to shut down." Yet neither disorder nor forced loans nor taxes hobbled the oil firms. Challenged

---

* A year earlier, Lord Cowdray had made agreements with Jersey Standard (as noted) but these did not affect his relations with Waters-Pierce, by this time a completely independent company. Woodrow Wilson seems to have been unaware of the "peace" between the rival U.S. and British oil companies.

by wells that were then the "most prolific producers in the world's history," their output and exports mounted. They continued operations irrespective of civil strife.[53]

Because of its origins in assassination, Woodrow Wilson never recognized the government of Huerta. In April 1914, following an insult to the American flag and as German merchantmen tried to ship arms to Huerta, President Wilson ordered the landing of American marines in Vera Cruz. American businessmen in Mexico were practically unanimous: they were aghast. The action seemed to open the Pandora's box to further disarray. The U.S. oil companies had learned to cooperate with the Mexican government *and* to pay taxes to the revolutionaries. They opposed Wilson's move. The occupation of Vera Cruz by the marines virtually forced Huerta from power.

By this time Huerta's enemies were mobilized under Emiliano Zapata in southern Mexico, in the northeast under Venustiano Carranza, in Chihuahua by Pancho Villa, and in Sonora by Alvaro Obregón. In each area, American businesses were governed by the different authorities; American Smelting and Refining Company was under several jurisdictions at once. Early in July 1914 the armies of Carranza and Obregón converged on Mexico City. Huerta resigned on July 14. That phase of the Mexican Revolution had ended, but civil disruption had not.[54]

In the summer of 1914, for most U.S. investors, the Mexican scene offered little but gloom. Whereas, in 1911, Mexico had ranked as the largest recipient of American direct foreign investment, in 1914—by the start of World War I in Europe—Canada held this position. Only U.S. oil men sent new funds into Mexico—mesmerized by rich oil resources. Most Americans had learned that investment across the Rio Grande was risky. Never again would Mexico rank as the nation with the largest amount of U.S. direct foreign investment. In the minds of executives of American companies, Mexico—which for investment purposes had almost been considered part of the United States—was henceforth a "foreign country."

The "Spillover" to Canada
(1870–1914)

Canada became politically unified in the Dominion of Canada on July 1, 1867. Before this, Americans had invested in various Canadian provinces (see Chapter II); afterward, U.S. stakes increased. Stable and orderly government, together with generally friendly relations, encouraged the flow of U.S. capital, technology, and management across the border.[1]

2

The new Dominion government sought to create national unity through railroad construction. Like the United States and Mexican governments, the government of Canada offered subsidies to railroad builders. Americans were attracted. And, just as in Mexico, so in Canada, they looked first toward stakes in lines that could be linked with an American system. In 1871 a group of Americans, headed by Jay Cooke (president of the Northern Pacific Railroad), sought to obtain a Canadian charter to extend the Northern Pacific northward into the Canadian prairies. The group also wanted to construct a railway in eastern Canada to connect with the Vermont Central, which would give it a route to Boston via Montreal. Cooke, with the Canadian businessman Sir Hugh Allan, soon became even more ambitious and bid for a concession to build the Dominion's first transcontinental railroad. Canadian opposition stiffened against U.S. participation in this "great national work." Sir Hugh believed he would not receive the charter unless he excluded the Americans, and proceeded to do so. The Americans, once spurned, released information on bribery that resulted in the resignation of the conservative government (November 1873). Defeated by this murky incident, Americans nonetheless retained interest in Canadian railroads. Other obstacles were not as awesome. In time, Cornelius Vanderbilt, J. P. Morgan, and James J. Hill (a Canadian by birth) were among the American railroad leaders to acquire stakes in the Dominion railroads. They did not, however, play a major role in building the Canadian system. Whereas Mexican railroads were in large part U.S.-financed, the British supplied the bulk of the vast sums expended in Canadian railroad construction.[2]

3

American capital was also attracted by Canada's mineral and timber resources. The reader would be bored by any attempt to document and unravel the complex histories of the many U.S. entrepreneurs who crossed the border to acquire interests in mining copper, nickel, iron ore, asbestos, lead, zinc, coal, gypsum, manganese, antimony, and phosphate, or for that matter in such precious metals as gold and silver, or in timberlands. The border for these men proved meaningless. The vast majority of such stakes were by individuals who established or acquired small companies—some incorporated in the United States, some in Canada. Only the most important U.S. investors (1870–1914) need concern us.*

In 1877 in the township of Orford, Quebec province, several Americans bought a mining property and in March 1878 they organized the Orford Nickel and Copper Company—capital $300,000. This small company developed the first Canadian nickel deposits to be used commercially. Soon it built a smelter and refinery at Constable Hook (near Bayonne), New Jersey, to process the Orford ore. Meanwhile, in 1881 an Ohioan, Samuel J. Ritchie, seeking hickory for his carriage-building trade, went to Ontario. Near Coe Hill in Hastings, Ritchie found timber and also iron ore and copper. In time, he bought land in the Sudbury district of Ontario. To work his Canadian properties, in Jan-

* I have judged importance by asking: (1) Did the company do something new? (2) Did it have a long history in Canada? (3) Was it an especially large investor? (4) Did the Canadian investment reflect an early multinational interest? and/or (5) Did U.S. capital clearly dominate an important Canadian industry?

uary 1886 Ritchie incorporated in Ohio the Canadian Copper Company (capital $2,000,000) and the Anglo-American Iron Company (capital $5,000,000).* The Canadian Copper Company soon recognized that its mines possessed nickel as well as copper.

Since the Orford company had smelting and refining facilities, the Canadian Copper Company in 1886 arranged for its ore to be treated at the Orford unit's New Jersey facilities. By 1890 the Orford company's mines were exhausted; that company had become solely a processor of others' ores, and in 1890 it agreed to buy exclusively from Canadian Copper Company. By the turn of the century, the latter's mines were furnishing most of the world's nickel. In the merger movement occurring in the United States at this time, the Canadian Copper Company, the Orford Company, and some other units were joined together in the $24,000,000 International Nickel Company, incorporated in New Jersey in 1902. At origin it was the world's largest nickel producer; †[3] it would one day become a key multinational corporation.

Bethlehem Iron Ore Company, which looked to foreign regions to supplement its iron resources, made small investments in Ontario in the 1880s. More substantial were the stakes by a number of U.S. companies in asbestos mining in Quebec, which likewise dated back to the 1880s. About 1910 the Johns-Manville Company of New York acquired control of a leading Dominion asbestos company and American capital came to dominate this Canadian industry. Among the other U.S. participants in Canadian mining were the Guggenheims, who added to their multinational stakes. Their interests in Canada were in precious metals. All these investments and many more, notwithstanding, U.S. direct investments in Canadian mining ($159 million) in 1914 equaled only about half the U.S. stake in mining in Mexico ($302 million); the development of U. S. mining and mining in general in the Dominion was still in its infancy.[4]

Ritchie was not alone in seeking Canadian timber. The International

* Canadian Copper would acquire the properties of Anglo-American Iron in 1898.
† While the major properties of International Nickel Company were in the United States (refining and smelting) and in Canada (mining and also a smelter built by Canadian Copper Company in 1900), the International Nickel Company, in addition, controlled the Nickel Corporation, Ltd. (a British company) and the Société Minière Caldeonienne (a French company), both of which had acreage in New Caledonia.

Paper Company (capital $45,000,000) announced in 1899 that it owned about 1.6 million acres of timberland in Canada, principally in Quebec Province. Americans made investments in timber in Ontario and in the Prairie Provinces. Estimates made in 1909 indicated that about 90 per cent of the available timber in British Columbia was controlled by U.S. citizens or companies. With timberland becoming more limited in the United States as the frontier closed, Americans swarmed across the border. Whereas in Mexico, the U.S. "agricultural" investment comprised everything from rubber to cattle lands to fruit properties, in the Dominion the U.S. "agricultural" stake seems to have included mainly timber and timberlands. Cleona Lewis estimated U.S. direct investments in Canada of $101 million in this sector in 1914.[5]

Americans undertook to process some Canadian resources in the Dominion. There were small, and often ephemeral, U.S. direct investments in smelters to handle Canadian mineral products; most ores were, however, exported to the United States for smelting and refining. The Bostonian H. M. Whitney was active in the formation in 1898–1899 of the Dominion Iron and Steel Company, which contracted to purchase its coal from a Canadian coal company that Whitney controlled.[*] While there was—as far as we can gather—no U.S. direct investment in Canadian wheat-growing, as wheat was "making the Canadian west" after the turn of the century, a handful of Americans crossed over the border to engage in flour milling. Most substantial were the U.S. stakes in lumber and paper and pulp mills.

Americans built lumber and paper and pulp mills for several reasons. First, Canada's abundant water resources meant cheap power. Lumber, and especially paper and pulp mills, could produce cheaply because of the low cost of power and the accessible raw material. Second, Americans wanted the output of these mills. Third, investments were stimulated by the actions by the U.S. government and by the Canadian governments (Dominion and provincial). The Canadians—desiring industry—wanted their raw materials processed locally. In 1886, for example, the Dominion government raised the export duty on timber to encourage domestic sawmill construction. In 1897 the Ontario government insisted

---

[*] In 1901 Whitney sold his interests in the Dominion Iron and Steel Company to Canadian investors.

that all timber logged on Crown lands in that province be manufactured in Canada; this prompted the building of U.S. mills in Ontario. More significant, in sequence the Province of Ontario prohibited the export of pulpwoods from Crown land (1900); the Dominion Parliament forbade pulpwood export from Dominion Crown lands in the Prairie provinces (1907); Quebec took the same measures relating to its Crown lands (1910) as did New Brunswick (1911) and British Columbia (1913). As a result, Canadian *and* American paper and pulp mills sprang up within the Dominion.[6]

Such Canadian rulings by themselves would probably have been insufficient to spur large U.S. investments. However, under strong pressure from American newspaper publishers, the United States in 1911 admitted Canadian newsprint duty-free. This proved the *coup de grace*. Now with the U.S. market wide open, investments in the Dominion looked promising to American businessmen. In 1912 a subsidiary of the *Chicago Tribune* (Ontario Paper Company) constructed a Canadian mill to supply newsprint for the newspaper. Other U.S. firms followed. By 1914, of the $221 million invested by U.S. business in Canadian manufacturing, an estimated $74 million was in paper and pulp. Only a start had been made; the future would see far greater interests in this sector.[7]

Other investments in processing were made by Americans in Canada, based on the availability of cheap and abundant power. Companies in the U.S. aluminum industry and in other electrochemical activities moved across the border to take advantage of the power resources. The plants of Alcoa at Shawinigan Falls (1899), Norton at Chippawa. Ontario (1910), and American Cyanamid on the Canadian side of Niagara Falls (1913) appear to have been motivated by such considerations.[8]

4

Americans developed some interests in public utilities in the Dominion. Western Union retained a limited minority stake in Canadian telegraph lines (see Chapter III). By 1910 American Telephone & Telegraph Company held 38.56 per cent of the shares in the Bell Telephone Company of Canada—an amount sufficient to worry Canadian nationalists. A Dominion Select Committee in 1905 investigated whether their national telephone company's association with U.S. capital was to the country's advantage; the committee considered nationalizing the telephone system, but it made no such recommendation, nor did it make any suggestions which jeopardized the position of A. T. & T. Other investments included those of Bostonians, who put capital in and contributed management to the Shawinigan Water & Power Co.; Philadelphia money developed power facilities around Sault Ste. Marie, Ontario. Additional, smaller U.S. stakes existed in certain light and power plants. In 1914 the total U.S. direct investment in Canadian utilities, according to Cleona Lewis, reached merely $8 million (this seems to the writer too low an estimate).[9]

5

The Dominion's expanding population and prosperity attracted American international business, as noted in earlier chapters. Prominent was Standard Oil. Unlike Mexico, which by 1914 had begun to receive large U.S. investments in oil wells, Canada with no similar bonanzas attracted no comparable "flock" of American oilmen. Before 1914 the main U.S. stakes in Canada's oil industry were in distribution and refining and were part of the over-all expansion of U.S. international business. A number of Standard Oil companies had sold in the Dominion in the 1880s. Other Standard Oil units entered in the next decade, making direct investments in marketing and constructing refineries. These companies met competition from Imperial Oil Company, Ltd. (formed in 1880), which by the 1890s had the largest Canadian refinery, a national marketing network, and a vigorous Canadian management. To cope with the competition, Standard Oil in 1898 bought controlling interest (75 per cent of the stock) in the Imperial Oil Company, Ltd. Imperial in turn acquired most of the companies and plants affiliated with Standard Oil in the Dominion as well as the facilities of several small competing refiners. These steps assured Standard Oil's preeminent position in Canada. When the Standard Oil empire was dissolved by the Supreme Court in 1911, Imperial Oil Company, Ltd. remained an affiliate of Standard Oil Company of New Jersey. Imperial Oil was by this time a fully integrated oil company, but its oil production was small. There were other, minor stakes by Americans in marketing oil in Canada and perhaps some in oil exploration; only the U.S. investment in Imperial Oil was substantial.[10]

Practically every American manufacturing company that exported sought to sell in Canada. As in Mexico before 1910, because the Dominion was a neighbor, American companies often administered their Canadian marketing within the framework of their domestic organization rather than as "foreign" business. Many more U.S. companies wanted to sell in Canada than in Mexico, because of the higher standard of living in the Dominion, which carried an ability to purchase.[11]

United States manufacturing companies seeking sales in Canada usually found it wise to build or acquire factories there. Marshall, Southard, and Taylor's superb study of American-controlled industry in Canada found that the first "branch" manufactory located across the border was started as late as 1870.* [12] In 1909 an American consul in New Brunswick declared:

> It is no longer safe, when recognizing a familiar brand or name, to assume that it is American [i.e. made in America] for numerous manufacturers and others have established permanent branches in Canada, and they put their products under the American brands familiar to the trade, but with the added information "Made in Canada" in small print. Practically every article made in the United States is sold here.

A consul in Toronto that year commented on the marked tendency of large American concerns to establish "branch factories"—with no fewer than fifty in Toronto alone. Windsor by 1909 had four plants making motor cars and one making motor accessories—plus a large number of other new factories fabricating American goods.[13] By 1912 some 200 American "branch" manufactories were present in Canada and the number was rising. In the electrical industry, Westinghouse was well established;† in automobiles, Ford and General Motors had plants in Canada; in rubber, Goodyear and U.S. Rubber manufactured; in explosives, du Pont had manufacturing plants; in harvesting equipment,

* Note this was almost two decades after the first verified American "branch" plant in England—the Colt factory (see Chapter II).

† On General Electric see p. 93 above.

International Harvester had a large factory—and so it went. By 1914 Canada clearly had more U.S.-controlled manufacturing plants than any other foreign nation.[14]

In earlier chapters it was noted that U.S. manufacturing companies frequently invested in foreign plants to meet competition and/or to preclude it, and to appease foreign governments' nationalistic sensibilities. We noted this was true in Canada. More specifically, various Canadian government measures proved significant in spurring U.S. businessmen to change from exporting to manufacturing across the border. Corporate records indicate U.S. companies wanted to sell in the Dominion; they chose to manufacture only when it proved to be the most effective means of entering or maintaining their markets.

Under the Canadian Patent Act of 1872, patents were declared null and void if not worked within two years of issuance. Continued imports also nullified the patents. This influenced U.S. firms in the electrical industry to set up factories in the Dominion.* The Canadian Patent Act of 1903 reaffirmed these principles. A writer on Canadian protectionism in 1908 declared that the patent legislation was "as instrumental as the high duties on manufactured articles imported from the United States in compelling American manufacturers to establish branch factories in Canada—even more directly in many instances than the tariff." [15]

Yet our analysis indicates that the protective tariff was most crucial. American manufacturers of sewing machines, automobiles, automobile accessories, rubber goods, harvesters, radiators, and enamel ware started factories to sell within the Dominion in order to avoid full customs duties (the word "full" is used, because many of these early enterprises depended on supplementary imports from the States). By jumping the tariff barriers, such companies were able to meet existing—or more often to preclude potential—competition.[16]

In addition, in its tariff revision of 1897, Canada introduced a broad British preferential system—the first within the Empire. It gave unilateral concessions to British goods. One authority notes the coincidence of this legislation and the'accelerated movement of American firms across the border and suggests a connection. At least one firm—the

---

* As noted in Chapter III we have not been able to determine whether this was a factor in the drug industry's migration to Canada, but it seems plausible.

Ford Motor Company—acted on the assumption that there would be reciprocity within the Empire; Ford planned its Canadian expansion with that in mind.[17]

The "National Policy" of Canada—first formulated in 1879 and existing throughout the period before World War I—endorsed industrialization. Industry would provide employment and lead to economic growth. This applied to the processing of Canadian resources, as we have seen. It meant tariffs on imports to encourage industry. Likewise, in accord with this policy, Ontario municipalities offered free sites, money bonuses, loans, and tax exemptions to attract new businesses; by 1900, 95 Ontario municipalities had granted aid to Canadian *and* American corporations that came within their boundaries. Quebec municipalities also gave generous rewards to woo industry.

Two typical news stories from 1907 issues of the Toronto *Globe* read:

> Chatham, June 5—The city will make a loan of $20,000 to Cornelius Bros., Grand Rapids, Mich.
> The company will manufacture brass goods and expects to employ 25 hands at the start, increasing in a year to 100.

> Sarnia, July 8—Sarnia voted today upon two bonus by-laws, one to grant $12,000 to the Standard Chain Company of Pittsburg and the other to loan $12,000 to the Jenks Dresser Bridge Company, both American concerns . . . The former company guarantees to employ not less than sixty men and the latter fifty men.

Steel industry bounties were provided in 1897 and 1899 in Dominion legislation, and on at least two occasions American companies took advantage of them to set up plants to manufacture steel rails.* An American promoter who had interests in iron ore and timber resources in Western Ontario and who planned to make steel rails successfully lobbied for a clause in the Dominion Railway Act of 1900 which stipulated that every railroad receiving national subsidies must use rails "made in Canada," if they could be obtained "upon terms as favorable as other rails can be obtained." American-controlled companies in Canada would make the rails! [18]

It is important that all such legislation—involving patents, tariffs, in-

---

* Of the $8,814,835 total bounties paid to June 30, 1905, two American companies (Sydney Company and Algoma Company) received $4,454,962.

dustry incentives, and "made-in-Canada" rulings—would not have been enough to "force" investments by American manufacturing firms in Canada. Just as the Canadian legislation did not force Americans to invest in the processing of paper and pulp (they only invested when the paper and pulp could be exported and used in the United States), so too unless American companies desired to sell in Canada and unless the market was there (or could be created), Americans would not have invested. The presence in the Dominion of a demand for American products was a prerequisite for these expansion moves. Unlike Mexico, where the main American investments were in railroads, mining, and land, in Canada by 1908 the largest single sector of U.S. direct investment was in manufacturing *—and the bulk of the manufacturing was not by processors of raw materials, but by U.S. businesses that "spilled" across the border to sell their wares (see Table VII.1).[19]

Table VII.1. American manufacturing in Canada—1897, 1908, 1914 (in millions of U.S. dollars)

	1897	1908	1914
Paper and pulp	20	55	74
Other manufacturing	35	100	147
TOTAL	55	155	221

Source: Cleona Lewis, America's Stake in International Investment, Washington, D.C.: Brookings Institution, 1938, 595.

In 1911 the U.S. government, preferring freer trade, was prepared to accept a reciprocal trade treaty with Canada. Businessmen in Boston, Buffalo, Detroit, Minneapolis, and Duluth became ardent advocates of such a treaty. James J. Hill even published a book recommending the union of the United States and Canada, and President William Howard Taft, an advocate of reciprocity, cautioned Hill to restrain his campaign lest it jeopardize their mutual cause. The warning of moderation came too late, for although the United States ratified the reciprocity

* See Table V.2.

treaty in 1911, the Canadians rejected it, apprehensive over further U.S. domination of their economy.[20]

Canadians feared their nation would lose commercial independence, and that perhaps the American flag might even follow trade. But what in effect the rejection of the treaty meant was that American manufacturing interests increasingly by-passed the tariff barrier and invested in Canada. Paradoxically, the Canadians' action, designed to secure independence, stimulated U.S. investment and thereby led to an even more extensive integration of the two nations' economies, for at the same time as the Canadians rejected the treaty, they did not express hostility to the U.S. investor in manufacturing and put up no bars to investment.[21]

6

The rise of such U.S. investments in Canada prompted additional American interest. The influx, as a later report has noted, served to shape social and economic similarities between the two countries. American insurance companies went across the border, acting within the context of their U.S. expansion programs. All the major American insurance firms not only marketed in Canada, but invested funds there—not as portfolio investments—but to cover governmental deposit requirements. *The Monetary Times* of Toronto estimated that in 1913, U.S. life and fire insurance companies had stakes amounting to $67,850,000 in Canada.[22]

In these years American banks proved an exception to the general move across the border; they had little concern with Canadian direct investment. American businesses in Canada used U.S., London * or Canadian banking facilities.[23]

7

Whereas the vast majority of U.S. companies in the Dominion before World War I planned that their business would be either for Canada exclusively or for export to the United States, a few enterprises that entered Canada had, or developed, broader plans. Some started in the Dominion with an eye to serving British Empire markets—to take advantage of projected preferential duties (Ford is a case in point). Sher-

* For instance, General Electric in Canada; see p. 93n above.

win-Williams found that its Canadian affiliate would have more value if it owned the stock in the company's English subsidiary (the English subsidiary in turn had branches in London, Liverpool, Paris, Calcutta and Bombay, Durban and Johannesburg, and Shanghai!). Some firms found their Canadian enterprises, while initially designed to handle only Canadian trade, could sell in France to great advantage after the Canadian-French commercial treaty of 1907 (International Harvester is an example).

Certain companies alert to American antitrust legislation discovered their Dominion affiliate was useful for discussions with European competitors to control production and prices—discussions from which the American company was barred (Alcoa fits this case). Jersey Standard employed Canadian affiliates to carry out activities in Peru in 1913–1914. That company's historians give as the reasons: (1) British owners preferred to sell their Peruvian properties to a Canadian rather than an American company; (2) the British government favored this course; (3) British and Dominion companies had more status in Peru than American businesses; (4) "Britain, in contrast to the United States was known for the support and protection it extended to interests under Empire flags" (there were immediate problems to be settled by diplomacy); * and (5) New Jersey's "Seven Sister Laws" of 1913 set restrictions on corporations' holding stock in other corporations. So it seemed best to use a Canadian affiliate to hold the stock in the Peruvian venture. Western Electric in December 1913 put its extensive foreign stock holdings under a Canadian affiliate. Its action might have been taken for tax reasons (in 1913 Canada did not yet have a corporate income tax). Thus, Canadian enterprises of pre-World War I years, as later, often served more than their ostensible purpose. Such "extra use" of the Canadian subsidiary or affiliate rarely seems to have been the fundamental motive for the expansion of U.S. business into Canada; it was instead an afterthought. It reflected flexibility in management of international enterprises.[24]

---

* In 1911 the Peruvian government had issued a decree challenging an earlier decree of 1888, which had determined the tax basis for the property. This was being submitted to diplomatic discussions.

8

As American business "spilled over" the border into Canada, there was no certainty that the newly established enterprises would be wholly owned by American capital or even managed by American citizens. Whereas in Mexico practically every U.S. venture was 100 per cent owned by U.S. capital and managed by Americans, such was frequently not the case in Canada. Whether or not Canadian capital and top management would contribute seems to have depended on the answers to three questions: (1) Did Canadian entrepreneurs participate in the formation of the enterprise? (Note that the one joint venture cited in Mexico—the case of the Mexican-American steel company—had Mexican businessmen involved.) (2) Was an existing Canadian business to be purchased? (In Mexico, Americans often started from scratch or purchased abandoned mines; there were generally no able Mexican entrepreneurs associated with purchased businesses.) (3) Was the project of a type that needed considerable capital for expansion? (In Mexico there was not adequate local capital available for investment; * in Canada there was capital prepared to enter into joint ventures.) If the answer in the case of Canada to any of the above three questions was "yes," more likely than not Canadians would contribute both capital and top managerial talent. In a number of cases, the answer was "yes." On occasion, American corporations would organize enterprises in Canada and sell stock to Canadians, not for public relations purposes, but simply to raise added funds. Often they hired Canadian executives, again not for public relations purposes, but because talent was available.† [25] Frequently, Americans would combine Canadian and American management in running their Dominion enterprise.

Before World War I it was "common knowledge" among Canadians that the type of investment being made in their economy by Americans

---

* In Mexico, sometimes large projects mixed U.S., English, and Canadian capital.

† A recent report on foreign ownership of Canadian industry notes deficiencies in Canadian entrepreneurial ability. Report of Task Force on the Structure of Canadian Industry, *Foreign Ownership and the Structure of Canadian Industry*, 96–97. Actually, the Americans that ventured into Canada before World War I found a number of Canadian entrepreneurs (McGregor and McLaughlin in automobile industry are good examples), who participated in an important fashion in running Dominion units.

differed from the far larger British stake. Writing in 1912, S. Morley Wickett noted that "the great bulk of these [British] investments go into public securities and railway and industrial bonds, comparatively little into industrial stocks, which carry the technical management. The number of cases where Canadian factories are in the charge of British managers and British foremen is remarkably small." Americans, on the other hand, were found to have invested only a comparatively small amount in public securities, while the greatest amount of U.S. capital was in "branch factories" and in other outright industrial investments. Wickett concluded, "Whatever fault may be found with citizens of the American republic they can never be accused of unbelief in the peculiar virtues of American ideas, methods, men and industrial products." [26] It was these America offered along with the capital. By 1914 American business was already playing a substantial role in the Canadian economy, and foundations were being laid for a still greater contribution.[27]

The "Spillover" to the Caribbean
(1870–1914)

The third region into which U.S. capital and management "spilled over" included the countries washed by the Caribbean Sea: the islands, Central America, and northern South America. In Mexico and Canada at the turn of the century there was a surge in direct investment, so too in the Caribbean region. In fact, U.S. direct investments in the Caribbean area seem to have been divided between those made before and those after 1898–1903. The division here relates not only to the surge in investment after 1898 and the turn-of-the-century merger movement in the United States, but also to the Spanish-American War, the U.S. decision to build the Panama Canal, and Joaquin Crespo's actions in Venezuela. These events altered the conditions for U.S. direct foreign investment in the Caribbean.

2

Before 1898 Americans invested rather sparsely in railroads and other transportation facilities in the Caribbean.* United States capital participated in financing Cuban railroads, but the principal ones were owned and controlled by English and Spanish interests. In the Dominican Republic, the San Domingo Improvement Company of New York constructed railroad lines.[1] Minor C. Keith (nephew of the American entrepreneur Henry Meiggs, who engineered awesome railroads in the Chilean and Peruvian Andes in the 1860s) built rail lines in Costa Rica.

The Costa Rican government, when it wanted railroads, had turned to Meiggs and awarded him a concession for the first Costa Rican rail-

---

* See Chapter II for early investments; here we are only concerned with post-1870s stakes.

road (July 1871). At that time no railroads existed in Central America except for the Panama Railroad and a short line in Honduras. Meiggs, before he died in 1877, delegated the work to his nephews, Henry M. Keith and the younger Minor C. Keith. Minor assumed the leadership, and soon Henry withdrew.* In 1892 Minor Keith, who used British money, quarreled with the British directors of the Costa Rica Railway Company. He then obtained another contract from the Costa Rican government for a new line; gradually he gained added concessions, each of which gave him land and rights of way. Through his efforts Costa Rica developed a railroad network.[2]

Other Americans invested in the Central Railroad of Guatemala in the 1880s and 1890s. In Nicaragua in 1887 Americans obtained a concession to construct a canal, incorporated in the U.S. the Maritime Canal Company, but did not build the waterway. Francisco J. Cisnero, a Cuban-born U.S. citizen, and American-born S. B. McConnico secured rights to build railroads in Colombia. These two men planned to use American capital, which was exceptional; in the main, railroads in Colombia were financed either by British or German funds. The Panama railroad, as noted in Chapter II, became the property of French investors in 1881. By 1898 Venezuela had a small railroad in the northern part of the country—American-constructed and financed.[3] In sum, however, the total U.S. direct investments in railroads were not large.†

Similarly, mining attracted only a minimum of U.S. capital to the Caribbean in the years before 1898. In the mid-1880s and early 1890s Americans invested in three iron ore properties in Santiago province, Cuba; ‡ among the investors were Pennsylvania Steel Company and Bethlehem Iron Ore Company. On the island of Trinidad, a U.S.-owned company extracted asphalt, while another, the New York & Bermudez Company, carried on similar activities in Venezuela. Likewise, in Venezuela, The Orinoco Company, Ltd., in which some American capital participated, acquired a concession covering 10,000 square miles of ter-

---

* The first Costa Rican relationships were with Meiggs; then on Aug. 18, 1871, the government made a contract with Henry M. Keith; later relationships were all with Minor Keith.

† See Table V.2 for estimates in 1897 (see also note at end of table).

‡ Juragua Iron Company (1884), Spanish-American (1885) and Sigua Iron Company (1892).

ritory; it planned to develop natural resources along the Orinoco River —possibly iron ore. Individual American citizens (including Minor Keith) put money in Central American and Colombian mining—in much the same manner as small U.S. investors had gone into Mexican and Canadian mining. In the 1880s a "mining boom" occurred in Honduras—with companies seeking gold and silver. At least one of these American concerns, New York and Honduras Rosario Mining Company, which later became associated with American Smelting and Refining Company interests, had a long history.[4]

Of all sectors, agriculture attracted the most American capital in the Caribbean before 1898. The phenomenon of the trader turned investor became increasingly evident. Captain Lorenzo Dow Baker, for example, started in the banana trade in 1870. In 1877 he settled in Jamaica, where he purchased bananas and arranged for their shipment to Boston. Andrew Preston of a small Boston produce firm marketed the fruit in the United States. In 1885 Preston and Baker merged their enterprises, forming the Boston Fruit Company, and soon decided that in order to secure a reliable source of fruit, they should grow as well as purchase bananas. In 1887 Baker bought four banana plantations in Jamaica (1,300 acres); in subsequent years he enlarged this holding. To hedge against hurricane damage, Baker also acquired 40,000 acres in Santo Domingo.[5]

Other American traders integrated backward into sugar. Cuba had had ten years of war (1868–1878) during which the country's sugar estates fell into disuse. American merchants, seeking to maintain their source of supply, lent funds to local—usually Spanish—sugar dealers and directly, or through them, to the sugar estate owners. Defaults on these loans led to U.S. stakes in Cuban sugar plantations. The Atkins family, for example, had participated in the Cuban sugar trade since 1838; not until 1882 did E. Atkins & Company obtain land holdings. It did so because a sugar estate owner defaulted on his debts. Atkins then expanded his firm's investments and by 1898 E. Atkins & Co. was probably the largest American sugar proprietor on the island.

Only the rare agricultural stakes in the Caribbean region were by U.S. industrial companies, integrating backward. H. O. Havemeyer, the most prominent individual in the American sugar refining industry, did, however, make his first small investment in Cuban sugar in 1892.[6]

Minor C. Keith made his initial entry into agriculture in tropical America for a different reason. In the late 1870s, in order to raise revenues for the Costa Rican railway, Keith planted bananas along its route. From that point the entrepreneur acquired added land to start banana farms; in the 1880s and 1890s he obtained 10,000 acres of jungle land near Bluefield, Nicaragua, 10,000 acres on the Caribbean side of Panama, and 15,000 acres near Santa Marta, Colombia. He also seems to have obtained small holdings in Honduras. These ventures were, in the main, financed by funds he obtained in England. When, in 1892, Keith started on the new railroad in Costa Rica, the government required him to introduce banana cultivation along the route. Keith, more than any other individual, was responsible for the spread of banana farms throughout Central America.* Before the turn of the century, Keith participated in cattle raising as well as banana farming, mining, and railroads in Central America.[7] Other individual Americans became involved in sugar, coffee, cocoa, tobacco, cattle raising, and timberlands in the Caribbean region. Some individuals obtained government concessions; others bought land from private parties.

The pace of investments in agriculture was affected by U.S. legislation and by circumstances in the host countries. When, for example, the McKinley tariff (1890) put Cuban sugar on the free list, new U.S. capital went into Cuban sugar investments. In 1894 Cuban sugar was taken off the free list, and between 1895 and 1897 U.S. investment in Cuban sugar languished. This was due in part to the new high duties, and in part to political unrest in Cuba, where demands for autonomy from Spain and attacks on U.S. properties made the investor wary. United States investors in Cuba saw no advantage in Cuban autonomy. They wanted strong government to keep order. Elsewhere in the Caribbean, political disturbances curbed U.S. interests in agriculture. Nonetheless, agriculture received more U.S. capital in the Caribbean than in any other region in the world (see Table V.2). The reason lay in the proximity and potentialities of the region.[8]

Americans made only small investments in utilities in the Caribbean before 1898. A subsidiary of the American-owned Havana Gas Company

---

* He was not, however, the first to introduce banana farming into Central America; the American Carl B. Franc had planted bananas in Panama in the 1860s.

provided light for that city. Americans built the Havana water works about 1893. As noted earlier, International Ocean Telegraph ran a cable from Florida to Havana, and the Central and South American Cable Company had certain interests. Americans owned and managed a small electric light concern in northern Venezuela. Other similar scattered stakes existed—some associated with railroads, mining, and agricultural projects.[9]

American exporters and importers maintained outlets in the Caribbean —as they had throughout the century. The U.S. corporations that were making worldwide investments played only a limited role in the Caribbean. The largest international companies—Standard Oil, Singer, and New York Life, for example—sent out their representatives. As noted earlier, one corporation in the Standard Oil group had refineries in Cuba and Puerto Rico. It has been impossible, however, to verify a single investment by an American company in a manufacturing plant in the entire Caribbean before 1898. The markets were not large enough to warrant such stakes.[10]

In short, by the time of the Spanish-American War, the amount of U.S. capital in this region was small. In 1897 American direct investment in the Caribbean was less than in Mexico or Canada or, for that matter, Europe. Cleona Lewis estimates the total U.S. direct investment in the Caribbean, including Central America (but excluding northern Colombia and Venezuela), as only $70.2 million.* [11]

Despite the low sum, the U.S. government had become involved in protecting American investors. In Nicaragua in the years from 1894 to 1897, U.S. government policy sought to assure that the Maritime Canal Company's concession was not forfeited,† and on several occasions the United States sent marines to keep order in Nicaragua. In March 1895 marines landed to protect American merchants and banana planters in Panama. In May of that year J. N. S. Williams, an American sugar estate manager, was complaining of the political unrest in Cuba. "I should

---

* This figure should be reduced by $9.7 million, which Miss Lewis includes as a direct investment in railroads in Panama. The Panama railroad by 1897 was French-owned; any U.S. investment in it would have been a portfolio rather than direct investment.

† Note that the company—which had obtained its concession in 1887—had not started construction.

think," he wrote, "that there are sufficient American interests centered in and near Cienfuegos to warrant the petitioning of the American government for a man of war to be stationed in Cienfuegos Harbor." No gunboat was sent. Instead, the American estate owner asked protection from the sovereign Spanish government, and the U.S. State Department endorsed his request.[12]

3

When, in 1897, war was threatening between the United States and Spain, the initial reaction of American traders, shippers, exporters, and most American property owners in Cuba was opposition; they wanted peace and order to conduct their businesses. There was enough turmoil in the Caribbean. Then on February 15, 1898, the *U.S.S. Maine* was blown up in Havana Harbor. "Remember the *Maine*" became the chant of yellow journalism. By April 1898 America was at war with Spain. Only when the war became imminent did U.S. businessmen finally support it, and then with reluctance.* [13]

Despite their initial lack of enthusiasm, when the "splendid little war" ended in July 1898, businessmen turned new, close attention to Cuban investment and, in fact, to the entire Caribbean region. Although Congress, in declaring war, had stated, "The United States hereby disclaims any disposition or intention to exercise sovereignty, jurisdiction, or control over said island except for the pacification thereof," this was enough. All investors wanted was "pacification"; they recognized that the American government might take far stronger steps than the Spanish government had to enforce peace and order.

Indeed, the war marked the opening of a new epoch in U.S. direct investment in Cuba. United States citizens saw opportunities for profits

---

* Some U.S. international businesses—Equitable Insurance Company, New York Life, Singer Manufacturing Company, and Armstrong Cork, for example—had investments in Spain and found these in jeopardy when America entered the war. The Valencia newspaper *El Pueblo* ran a series attacking U.S. investments in Spain, quoting at length such tirades as the letter from "A Valencian," June 4, 1898: "While the Yankees in uniform fight our soldiers on sea and land in a manner most savage and beyond all civilized laws, the Singer Yankees exploit our interior, robbing the poor by means of infamous contracts, in order to send money to the United States, and with the greatest shamelessness, with complete tranquillity, keep open their dens in the principal cities of Spain to plunder the unfortunate."!! These Americans would clearly have preferred no U.S.-Spanish confrontation.

in Cuban railroads and mines, but their major new stakes continued (as in the past) to be in agriculture and now increasingly in the processing of agricultural products. In 1898 a group of businessmen associated with the sugar broker, B. H. Howell, Son & Company, thought this the "opportune time" to buy sugar plantations in Cuba. That year, the Boston Fruit Company obtained an interest in the Banes Fruit Company in Cuba. In 1899 the United Fruit Company was formed (acquiring the Boston Fruit Company and its holdings). United Fruit found sugar more profitable than bananas in Cuba; by the summer of 1900 it was spending over a $1 million to equip one of the most efficient sugar mills on the island; in subsequent years, it increased its interests in Cuban sugar estates. When, in 1903, Cuban sugar was granted U.S. tariff preference, U.S. funds poured into Cuba. By 1909 a consular report declared American sugar mills produced about 40 per cent of Cuba's sugar, leaving Cuban and European mills the remainder. United States business involvement continued to rise. The Cuban-American Sugar Company (formed in 1906) had by 1913 an authorized capital of $20 million; through its subsidiaries it became the largest owner of plantations and sugar mills in Cuba. H. O. Havemeyer expanded his Cuban holdings; his stake came to comprise minority positions in four Cuban firms, including Cuban-American. How much control he could exercise through such minority interests is questionable. We have found, however, that American business leaders learned that small stakes in foreign properties frequently gave them important advantages: "friendly" treatment, vital information (including cost data), and the ability to intervene, if necessary, at a time of crisis. Generally, neither management nor routine control went with such holdings, although direct business considerations were clearly involved. Thus, through Havemeyer, the largest American sugar refining company—American Sugar Refining Company—had a *tranche* in the Cuban sugar industry.[14]

Tobacco, after sugar, was Cuba's second industry. Robert P. Porter— dispatched by President McKinley to report on the island's economic conditions—wrote in late 1898:

> Although profits of from ten to thirty-five per cent have been realised on tobacco-raising in Cuba, very few foreigners, excepting an occasional German, have undertaken it. English and German com-

panies own the majority of the manufacturing establishments in Havana and elsewhere, but they have found that it is more profitable to buy the raw material than to raise it, although an English company, manufacturing in Havana, is reported to have paid $1,000,000 for 18,000 acres in the Vuelta Abajo district.

Porter stated that "no American companies" were manufacturing in Cuba, but before his book went into print in 1899, he had to add a footnote. "Since this chapter was written an American syndicate known as the Havana Commercial Company has been formed. This company has absorbed some fourteen factories in Cuba."

In tobacco, therefore, as in sugar, Americans rushed into investment in Cuba at the conclusion of the Spanish-American War. It is important to see another relevant factor. Consolidation in the *American* tobacco industry preceded the expansion of the American Tobacco Company into Cuba and Puerto Rico. In 1899 the giant American tobacco concern had started manufacturing cigarettes and cigars in Puerto Rico. Then American Tobacco's affiliate, the American Cigar Company, organized the Havana Tobacco Company (1902). The latter acquired the stock of Henry Clay and Bock Company, Ltd. (an important British firm), the previously mentioned large but independent Havana Commercial Company, and another independent Cuban concern. In this fashion, American Tobacco, through Havana Tobacco Company, "controlled a large portion of the manufacture of cigars in Cuba." In addition, in 1902 American Cigar Company formed the Cuban Land and Leaf Tobacco Company and the Porto Rican Leaf Tobacco Company to grow tobacco on the two islands.[15]

After the war Americans looked anew at prospects in Cuban utilities. The American Indies Company (did the name have any special significance?), financed by Peter A. B. Widener, Stephen B. Elkins, William C. Whitney, and Thomas Fortune Ryan, bid for electric traction concessions on the island. In 1907 Americans acquired from Canadian investors control of the Havana Electric Railway. And so it went.[16]

As Cuba became more "Americanized," U.S. manufacturers went to sell goods. Trade grew; trading firms proliferated. American manufacturers started direct sales outlets. Some went farther: Pabst Beer opened a bottling plant on the island, while Coca Cola had a branch plant in Havana by January 1906. The rise in total U.S. direct investment in nearby Cuba between 1898 and 1914 was substantial; direct investment more than quadrupled.[17]

Action by the U.S. government created an environment for the sharp surge in investment. Under the Platt Amendment to the Army Appropriation Bill of 1901, in the Cuban Constitution drafted in late 1901, and then in a 1903 treaty between Cuba and the United States, the government of Cuba agreed that the United States could intervene to preserve Cuban independence and to maintain a government adequate for the protection of life, property, and individual liberty. This reassured American investors. So, too, the U.S. tariff preference for Cuban sugar, granted in 1903, was important in stimulating investment.

4

United States stakes on other Caribbean islands and in Central America also rose in the years before 1914, although not as rapidly as in Cuba. A number of U.S. citizens, syndicates, and small companies invested in railroads, mining, agriculture (fruits, sugar, coffee, timber, and cattle raising), utilities, trade, and banking. The decision of the U.S. government to build the Panama Canal (1902–1903) resulted in the influx of Americans into Panama—to meet the needs of construction work and of the workers.

Some American firms got huge monopolistic concessions in the Caribbean. One was granted to the United States and Nicaragua Company, incorporated in Maine on April 20, 1903. Its concession covered more than 10 million acres in northern Nicaragua, and included exclusive mining privileges and the right to build and to operate railroads, telephones, and the telegraph.[18] This concession was atypical in its grandeur.

While a handful of the large companies that emerged during the turn-of-the-century merger movement made investments in the islands and Central America (exempting Cuba, which attracted more than a handful), most were little interested in these small countries. United Fruit Company, which went to the Caribbean to procure its bananas, was the key exception.

Of all the companies in the Caribbean region, the United Fruit Company was from its origin preeminent. Of all the entrepreneurs, Andrew

Preston, President of United Fruit, and Minor C. Keith, First Vice President of the company, were of crucial significance. The story of this company and these men covers vital developments in U.S. direct investment in the Caribbean, not only in agriculture but also in transportation and communications. In 1899 the United Fruit Company (capital $20 million) was formed; it owned or leased at origin, some 322,000 acres of land in Jamaica, Santo Domingo, Cuba, Costa Rica, Colombia, Nicaragua, and Honduras—properties that had been acquired before 1899 by the Boston Fruit Company and by Minor Keith. Compared with the immense U.S. land holdings in Mexico and Nicaragua, this acreage was not substantial; it would rise. For the most part, United Fruit Company had land on which it grew, or intended to grow, bananas. In addition, the company had orange groves, cattle land, coconut trees, rubber trees, cacao, and sugar production. The regional dispersion of its properties throughout the Caribbean gave it an opportunity to spread its risks—risks of hurricanes, floods, droughts, banana diseases, as well as of revolution, riot, and political unrest.

In its early years, United Fruit Company purchased the bulk of its fruit from independent farmers. In some cases it acquired stock holdings in the businesses of independent growers. In 1911 the directors of United Fruit decided that instead of raising 35 per cent of the bananas on its own lands and buying the other 65 per cent on the open market or through contracts, it would purchase additional tropical lands and plantations, aiming to supply 80 per cent of its own fruit. The policy was based on "tropical conditions and lack of respect for tropical contracts." By 1913 the company owned or leased 852,560 acres, of which 221,837 were under cultivation.[19]

Between 1900 and 1913, United Fruit Company or its subsidiaries made contracts with governments in the Caribbean region. For example, in the 1900 agreement between a United Fruit subsidiary and the Costa Rican government, the former promised to increase cultivation of bananas in Costa Rica. In exchange, it received land from the government and a ten-year exemption from export taxes. In 1909, Costa Rica imposed an export tax of one cent per bunch on all bananas shipped out of the country; the State agreed not to levy any other tax on the exportation of bananas or the banana industry. United Fruit made similar contracts with other host-country governments, which specified that in exchange for a one cent per bunch export tax, the company was granted the right to grow bananas, usually additional acreage, exemption from other taxes, and often freedom from conscription for its work force.[20]

United Fruit shipped its fruit in company-owned vessels. In 1899 it claimed to "control over ninety per cent of the [banana] imports into the United States." In the States it had the established distribution network that Preston had earlier organized. By 1902 United Fruit was looking for overseas markets. The company's president announced in August 1902, "We now have the business of handling all West Indian and South American fruits for the British, the French and other European markets." The next year United Fruit bought 50 per cent of the stock of the British concern, Elders & Fyffes Shipping Company (increased to 100 per cent in 1910). United Fruit, in a prospectus for a bond offering, claimed in 1907 that the company was "doing almost all the banana business both in America and in Europe." [21]

Wherever the company planted or purchased bananas, it arranged transportation, not only by steamship but also through ownership of railroads or through contracts with existing railroads. This was essential, for bananas were perishable. United Fruit had acquired the "Keith railroads" in Costa Rica in 1899; two years later the company formed the Northern Railway Company * to consolidate these railroads. On June 15, 1905, the Northern Railway, the Costa Rica Railway (still British-owned), and United Fruit agreed the Northern Railway would operate both railroad systems.† This gave United Fruit excellent transportation for its bananas in Costa Rica. Meanwhile, in 1904 Minor Keith turned to building the Guatemala Railway. To finance this activity, he sold a substantial portion of his stock in United Fruit Company; ‡ he also obtained German and British capital. This railroad, merged with others, became in 1912 the famous International Railways of Central

* Incorporated in New Jersey with headquarters in Boston.

† The stock of the Northern Railway Company was transferred to trustees (one of which was nominated by United Fruit and the other by the Costa Rica Railway Company).

‡ According to data uncovered in a 1959 stockholder suit against the International Railways of Central America, Minor Keith until 1904 owned 60 per cent of the stock of United Fruit Company, when he sold all but 10 per cent to invest in Guatemalan railroads (Ebb, *Regulation and Protection of International Business*, 44).

America (I.R.C.A.). In 1904 the Guatemala Railway had ceded farms along its route to United Fruit; in 1907 the fruit company started its initial plantings in Guatemala. Similarly, in Panama and Honduras, railroad construction, land grants, and banana plantings were closely allied. Keith dreamed of connecting Guatemala, El Salvador, Honduras, Nicaragua, Costa Rica, and Panama with railway lines. His building railroads aided the United Fruit Company. Whereas at origin United Fruit owned only 71 miles of railroad, by 1914 the company had a total of 669 miles of railroad in Costa Rica, Guatemala, Honduras, Panama, Colombia, Cuba, and Jamaica. If we add to this the 163 miles of track of the Costa Rica Railway Company, operated by Northern Railway, the United Fruit Company controlled 833 miles of railroads in tropical America.

Because the company was planting in remote areas, it needed radio communications between its offices and farms, and in 1913 incorporated the fully-owned subsidiary, Tropical Radio Telegraph Company, to develop such communications.[22]

As United Fruit Company fashioned this "Banana Empire," it had to tame the jungle. It installed sewage, drainage, and water systems; it filled in low and swampy country; it cut down forests and created plantations. It established company towns, where no one had ever lived before. Everywhere it operated, it invested in hospitals. Preston estimated in 1913 that United Fruit had spent in cash $190,000,000 in the development of tropical America. In these years before World War I, the company had become a giant, doing business in small underdeveloped countries. Already it played a dominant role in the economies of certain Central American republics.[23]

At this time when American industry was establishing itself in the Caribbean, the U.S. government was also looking more closely at its strategic interests in the area. Victory in the Spanish-American War meant new American government responsibility. In 1901 the Clayton-Bulwer Treaty (under which the United States and Britain would have shared the construction of an isthmus canal) was canceled, and the United States obtained the right to build, own, operate, and fortify its own canal. As America made plans to construct the canal, it became an essential part of State Department policy to support U.S. investments in the region and to try, when possible, to encourage United States rather than German, English, or French business in the Caribbean. The American government felt that it was in the interest of the American nation to keep peace and order in regions near the Canal. The strategic interest of the United States in the area had become well defined.

Because of the policies of Presidents McKinley, Roosevelt, and Taft, American investors in the islands and Central America realized that if they called upon the U.S. government to defend their property rights and their persons whenever there was disorder, they would get support. It was accepted in the State Department that American investments in the Caribbean served U.S. *political* interests and that "by urging on the investors to lend themselves as instrumentalities of foreign policy, the government clothed those investors with rights to protection of especial dignity."

The so-called "Roosevelt Corollary" to the Monroe Doctrine (December 1904) stated,

> Chronic wrongdoing . . . may in America, as elsewhere, ultimately require the intervention by some civilized nation, and in the Western Hemisphere the adherence of the United States to the Monroe Doctrine may force the United States, however reluctantly, in flagrant cases of such wrong doing or impotence, to the exercise of an international police power.

The Monroe Doctrine (1823) had been designed to prevent the intervention of European powers in the "new world." The Corollary justified intervention by the United States. While "gunboat diplomacy" by the United States had occurred before the exposition of the Corollary, it now became more common: in Cuba in 1906 American marines landed at Cienfuegos and were stationed to guard U.S. sugar plantations threatened with burnings and revolution. When Honduras and Nicaragua were at war in 1907, the Navy sent the *U.S.S. Marietta* to protect American properties along the coast of Honduras. In 1909—at the request of the Bluefields Steamship Company—the United States sent a warship to protect U.S. property; 1910 saw the arrival of U.S. forces at Bluefield, Nicaragua, to aid "preponderating American and other foreign interests." [24]

In a law of October 4, 1911, the Nicaraguan National Assembly ordered the cancelation of certain contracts and concessions which it deemed illegal or unconstitutional. At this point, a revolution was threatening in Nicaragua. In 1912, when the National Bank of Nicaragua (an American corporation) asked for protection, when 125 planters, two dozen American trading firms, several banking houses, and the railroad and steamship company petitioned the United States for assistance, Secretary of State Philander C. Knox authorized the landing of 2,700 marines, who occupied the country. From 1912 to 1933 (except for a brief trial interlude in 1925) a small force of marines remained in Nicaragua to keep stability. Woodrow Wilson looked with disdain on "dollar diplomacy," yet he did not remove the marines from Nicaragua, and in 1914 when wild disorder broke out in Haiti, he too sent in marines.[25] The interventions of the U.S. government reassured Americans who sought to do business under perilous political conditions in the islands and in Central America.

5

As American entrepreneurs encountered unrest on the islands and in Central America and persevered, they also did so in Colombia. Because of the secession of Panama and the building of the canal, American investment was unwelcome in Colombia. Nonetheless, Americans made small investments in railroads and mining. The important agricultural holdings of the United Fruit Company (inherited from Minor Keith's earlier entry) were retained. At Santa Marta, on the northern coast of Colombia, American capital built and operated an ice plant as well as a telephone and electric lighting system, which were completed in 1909. United States business also became interested in Colombian oil. In 1913 General Asphalt sought a concession, which it apparently did not get. According to State Department records, in 1914 Standard Oil of New York * entered into an agreement with the Colombian owners of the

* Was this Standard Oil of New Jersey, located in New York? It may well have been. The companies were often confused in 1914. The Secretary's Office of Mobil Oil Corporation (the successor to Standard Oil of New York) has no record of any Standard Oil of New York investments in Colombia at this time and indicates "Our Company first got into direct operations in Colombia in the early 1930s." (J. H. Strohsahl, Assistant Secretary, Mobil Oil, to author, Dec. 5, 1969). While the historians of Standard Oil of New Jersey do not mention the investment, it fits logically into their story. (See Gibb and Knowlton, *The Resurgent Years*, pp. 369–371). Jersey Standard has destroyed many

Cartagena Oil Refining Company to take over the control of their refining interests and to make extensive explorations on their land holdings.[26]

The U.S. State Department, after the secession of Panama, had sought to allay the hatred Colombia had toward the United States. Negotiations were at a diplomatic level. No gunboats were sent to Colombia. At the end of the Taft administration, Secretary of State Philander C. Knox felt the "Government of Colombia has closed the door to any further overtures on the part of the United States." Woodrow Wilson tried to reopen the door. He retained the policy of his predecessor in seeking to keep European investors out of the Canal area, and at the same time sought to abandon dollar diplomacy. Lord Cowdray tried to obtain a large oil concession from the Colombian government in 1913; he attributed to U.S. government pressure Colombia's failure to ratify his concession. President Wilson's Secretary of State, William J. Bryan, in November 1913 wrote the American legation in Bogotá that "on account of friendship," the Department of State "views with disfavor any concessions or grantings of a hampering monopolistic nature which may be sought in Latin America by foreign capitalists whether European *or American*" (italics mine).* The Wilson administration endorsed a U.S. treaty with Colombia to pacify differences; the treaty was signed on April 6, 1914.†[27]

6

In Venezuela, even more than in Colombia, in the late nineteenth and early twentieth century, existing and new U.S. direct investment encountered an unfriendly environment. In 1898 the Venezuelan dictator Joaquin Crespo declared the title of the New York & Bermudez Asphalt Company to be faulty and terminated its large asphalt concession. This started a sorry chain of events. General Cipriano Castro—Crespo's suc-

---

of its early records. Company executives can not find any indication of such an investment (M. F. Kane, Manager, Shareholder Relations Division, Office of the Secretary, Standard Oil of New Jersey, to author, Dec. 19, 1969).

* It has been pointed out that Wilson did not bar "Standard Oil's" agreement with the Cartagena Oil Refining Co.; it can, however, be argued that this was not "of a hampering monopolistic nature."

† The treaty was not ratified by the U.S. Senate until Apr. 20, 1921.

cessor—in 1900 reversed his predecessor's decree, recognizing the validity of the asphalt company's claims, but the stay was only temporary. Later, in 1900, another American company, Warner-Quinlan, sought Venezuelan asphalt land. Intrigue followed between the two American competitors, in which Cipriano Castro participated. National Asphalt (by this time the parent company to New York & Bermudez Asphalt Company *) declared the Venezuelan courts inept and called on President McKinley in 1901 to send a warship. When he did so, Cipriano Castro was outraged. The issue rested in the Venezuelan courts; when the final resolution came, it was to the disadvantage of both Warner-Quinlan and New York & Bermudez. The former retired from Venezuela in 1904; the latter, which refused "to pay" for the quasi-favorable decision in its behalf, was placed in the hands of a receiver. The receiver continued, however, to make small shipments of asphalt. General Castro also voided in 1900 the earlier concession of the Orinoco Company, Ltd.[28]

Undaunted by the experiences of New York & Bermudez and the Orinoco Company, another American concern, the United States & Venezuelan Company, made a contract with the Venezuelan dictator Castro on April 20, 1901. It blithely purchased a large asphalt property some 70 miles west of Maracaibo, built a railroad, erected a sizable asphalt refinery and machine shop, and then started a village for more than 1000 workers. The village was a typical company town, complete with church and school. In all, the company claimed to have invested $600,000. On its completion General Castro declared the company's contract null, on the grounds that the Venezuelan Congress had not approved it. The property was shut down. The U.S. government asked the dictator to submit the case to arbitration, a suggestion he rejected.

Other American investors in Venezuela suffered under similar—and what seemed to them—capricious treatment: the concession of the International Rubber and Trading Company, an American unit, was canceled by the General. Likewise, the American corporation that ran the electric light system at Maracaibo operated under duress. American

---

* The U.S. asphalt company that operated on the island of Trinidad and the New York & Bermudez Company were first merged into the Asphalt Company of America (formed in 1899), then into National Asphalt (1900), and finally into General Asphalt (1903).

businessmen became convinced that Venezuela was not the place to invest: "An American cannot live and do business in Venezuela at the present time, this is certain," declared one businessman in 1907.

Secretary of State Elihu Root's pleas on behalf of the American companies proved futile, and so the secretary in June 1908 notified the American chargé d'affaires in Venezuela "that in view of the persistent refusal of the present Government of Venezuela to give redress for the governmental action by which substantially all American interests in that country have been destroyed or confiscated, or to submit the claims of American citizens for such redress to arbitration . . . the Government of the United States . . . has determined to close its legation" in Caracas.

When, in December 1908, General Juan Vicente Gomez became the new dictator in Venezuela, he indicated immediately that Venezuela would "settle satisfactorily all international questions"; the United States resumed diplomatic relations. "Heartiest congratulations; great work," cabled the new Secretary of State, Robert Bacon, when the Venezuelans took favorable action in February 1909. That summer the claims of the United States & Venezuelan Company and the Orinoco Company were finally settled; the New York & Bermudez got its concession back.[29]

General Gomez created a favorable environment for foreign investment in his country. Soon subsidiaries of General Asphalt (New York & Bermudez Company and the newer Caribbean Petroleum Company) were obtaining two of Venezuela's earliest petroleum concessions (1910, 1912).* General Asphalt lacked the funds to develop these lands and sought money in the United States. Americans, doubtless cautious about investing in the once politically unstable Venezuela, would not provide the capital. Accordingly, in 1913 General Asphalt sold a 75 per cent interest in its Caribbean Petroleum Company to Royal Dutch-Shell. In February 1914 Shell became the first commercial oil producer in Venezuela.† A new era had begun. Whereas the U.S. government had acted to keep the British out of petroleum investments in Colombia, the British had stepped into Venezuela—unimpeded.[30]

---

* The concessions went to an attorney for General Asphalt, who transferred them to the subsidiaries.

† General Asphalt retained a minority interest (25 per cent) in this venture until 1923, and it received its share of the profits; Shell managed the business.

7

In short, despite political unrest, U.S. business investments throughout the Caribbean had risen in the years from 1870 to 1914, especially after 1898. In the Caribbean, more than anywhere else in the world, U.S. government action did play an important role in seeking to provide a favorable climate for U.S. business. The government's support of American enterprises reached its high point under President Taft. Because Taft believed it was a useful function of the U.S. government to advance as well as protect legitimate trade and investment of American citizens abroad, he acted to send gunboats and marines when American property seemed threatened; it was in the Caribbean that this power was exercised. Woodrow Wilson opposed exerting U.S. influence *to advance* business abroad. Nonetheless, as we have seen, the President did not withdraw marines from Nicaragua; moreover, the policy of the Wilson administration in trying to pacify relations between the United States and Colombia—although not so motivated—served to aid existing and future U.S. investors in Colombia.[31]

The landing of marines to create order and to aid American companies in the Caribbean has provoked a flood of books, articles, and symposia. The literature and commentaries have come from students of American diplomacy, economic history, Latin American history, international law, and economics. The Smedley Butler quotation has frequently been repeated: "I helped to make Haiti and Cuba a decent place for the National City Bank boys to collect revenues in . . . I helped purify Nicaragua for the international banking house of Brown Brothers . . . I helped to make Honduras 'right' for American fruit companies." [32] Considerably more attention has been paid to investments in this nearby region than the dollar totals warrant.[33] Far greater in 1914 were the contemporary investments in Mexico, Canada, and Europe; but in these areas American strategic interests were not so much in evidence.* Because of America's "strategic" interests, U.S. stakes in

---

* I have found that the amount of U.S. investment bears no relation to the amount of U.S. government interest in any particular area at any time. The phrase, which was often used to justify American government intervention, "There are U.S. interests involved," is highly ambiguous and can mean anything from strategic interests, to $200,000, to millions of dollars. In understanding the use of the phrase and United States actions, important questions are: 1. What are America's strategic interests? 2. What relation does the American foreign investment in the area have to the host

Table VIII.1. Percentage of total U. S. direct foreign investment in "nearby" areas—Canada, Mexico, and the Caribbean

Investments in	1897	1914
Part A	%	%
Railroads	99	95
Agriculture	95	94
Mining	97	69
Part B		
Selling organizations (excluding petroleum)	27[a]	24[a]
Manufacturing (excluding paper and pulp)	52	44
Oil (producing, refining and distributing)	14	59

Source: Calculations based on figures in Lewis, *America's Stake in International Investments,* pp. 602, 590–591, 583–584, 578, 595, 579, 588.

[a] These percentages are probably low, since many of the selling organizations in the nearby areas were extensions of U.S. domestic sales networks, and it is impossible to find figures separating the domestic from the foreign operations.

the Caribbean rather than in Mexico, Canada, or Europe have attracted sustained public attention in the United States.

Is the concept of "spillover" of U.S. direct investment used in the titles of this and the two previous chapters viable? United States direct investment in nearby Mexico, Canada, and the Caribbean appears to have been distinctive in certain respects, and in other ways to have been part of the general movement of U.S. business abroad. One distinctive feature, as we noted, lay in the quantity of U.S. capital (in Mexico and Canada) and the attention paid to the U.S. stake (in the Caribbean). A second distinctive feature rested in the amount of involvement in railroads. Practically all U.S. direct investment abroad in railroads was in these neighboring areas. Similarly, the vast bulk of U.S. foreign direct investment in agriculture was in these nearby regions. This was also the case with mining in 1897, but was less true in 1914, when the South American mines opened (see the next chapter). Table VIII.1, *Part A,*

government? (The greater the tie between the American company abroad and the host governments—through concessions, or contracts, or loan relationships—the more often the U.S. government tends to become involved in one way or another.) 3. How much disorder is there—and how much "cause" for intervention? 4. What is the role of competitive European interests?

demonstrates these generalizations. An additional distinctive feature was that in every one of the nearby areas, the entry of U.S. capital encountered fear that annexation might follow. Mexicans, warned by the Mexican war experience, worried lest the United States take more territory. The writings of James J. Hill favoring the annexation of Canada were hardly to the liking of Canadians. Similarly, it was unclear whether Cuban independence would be observed; the United States did, after all, annex Puerto Rico; often, too, U.S. actions in the Caribbean impinged on an exercise of national sovereignty. In short, the U.S. direct investment that "spilled across" the border was in a certain fashion unique.

On the other hand, a general feature of the move of U.S. direct investment to the nearby areas was that it represented part of the vigorous worldwide expansion of U.S. business enterprises. The neighboring regions got their share of the total international stakes of traders, manufacturers, and oil companies. Table VIII.1, *Part B,* shows the percentages. The timing of the surge in direct investments—at the turn of the century—to each of the nearby areas also coincides with the general move of U.S. business worldwide.

In all three neighboring regions we have seen what was evident elsewhere overseas—that the economic and political environment in the United States and in the host countries shaped investment strategies. Thus, the rise of big business in the United States influenced the "spillovers." Giant firms, such as American Smelting and Refining Company, International Paper, International Nickel, United Fruit, and General Asphalt (all organized in the United States in the turn-of-the-century merger movement) acquired the foreign business of their predecessor companies and became important in Mexico, Canada, or the Caribbean. The U.S. government's role in altering investment patterns was evident in various ways. President McKinley's urging of American interest in rubber plantations spurred new activity in Mexico. United States commercial policies (in part inadvertently) encouraged U.S. stakes in the nearby areas. As we have seen, in response to the 1890 McKinley tariff, Americans built smelters across the Rio Grande. The end of U.S. duties on Canadian newsprint in 1911 made it worthwhile for certain Americans to invest in the Dominion. The failure of the U.S.–Canadian reciprocity treaty in that same year prompted other U.S. stakes in Canadian manufacturing. U.S. tariff changes influenced the pace of American investments in Cuban sugar. Likewise, action (and often lack of action) by the U.S. government had impact on investment decisions made by many American businessmen in Mexico. Most important, the U.S. government intervened directly in the Caribbean to try to impose order and thus protect and advance U.S. business.

United States companies were attracted to these regions by natural resources and markets; but in each nearby area, the investment pattern differed. In Mexico—an underdeveloped country—Americans moved over the border to seek a source of supply. The largest single sector for investment came to be mining. The mines of Mexico supplemented the output of the U.S. mines. In Canada—a developing nation—Americans sought both markets and sources of supply. The largest single sector for investment was manufacturing, most of which was designed to serve the Dominion buyer. The Canadian market was seen by American business as an extension of the U.S. market. In the less developed Caribbean regions, Americans went mainly in search of tropical produce—agricultural products. The output was exported primarily to the United States, but international marketing had begun. These neighboring areas were included, as we saw in Chapter V, in the regions distributed under restrictive agreements made by American companies with Europeans. With few exceptions, however, they were allocated to the American company, or, in the case of Canada, sometimes shared between American and British companies. Competition in these nearby regions was often among several U.S. firms or among U.S. and European firms rather than with local businesses.

In Mexico, Canada, and the Caribbean, host governments on occasion had encouraged investment. Díaz, as we have seen, paid subsidies to American companies that built railroads, gave police protection to those that mined or had plantations, offered tax incentives to new foreign enterprises, and canceled import duties on materials for mills and smelters. He did this to encourage economic growth in Mexico. Canadians likewise gave subsidies, loans, and bounties to U.S. investors. A British historian described the gains accruing to the Dominion as American goods manufactured in Canada replaced U.S. and British imports: "The

Canadian consumer would be the last to complain [he got cheaper prices], and to the Canadian farmer, the introduction of concerns employing hundreds of hands meant a wider market for his produce; while Canadian manufacturers learned the ways of large scale industry. But it was a defeat for the British manufacturer." Throughout the Caribbean, governments gave concessions to new U.S. businesses, including low taxes, land, and freedom of workers from conscription, hoping their economies would benefit by the influx of American capital.[34]

In other instances, however, host governments acted to discourage investment: for example, the Mexican government nationalized the railroads and examined the preponderant position of the American Smelting and Refining Company. Later it placed "forced loans" and new taxes on U.S. investors and failed to maintain order. The Canadian government refused to let Jay Cooke participate in the transcontinental railroad and scrutinized the U.S. stake in the Canadian Bell telephone company. Governments in the Caribbean canceled concessions and often proved unable to prevent unrest. Thus, in the nearby areas—as in the general case—political conditions abroad affected the entry and growth of U.S. foreign investments.

What of the U.S. firms themselves? Were those companies that operated in these nearby areas simply operating "extra-nationally," or were they "genuine multinational enterprises," as defined at the end of Chapter IV? Some simply operated "extra-nationally—insisting on the primacy of the methods . . . [used] at home and even the laws of the home country." These firms, doing business in Canada, Mexico, and the Caribbean, functioned through U.S.-incorporated companies, used American men and methods, and acted as though their "foreign" operations were simply an appendage of their domestic activities; they made few modifications in their ways of doing business. At times, in the Caribbean and even in Mexico they went so far as to look to the U.S. government for intervention to create order. American businessmen generally had no desire for U.S. political sovereignty in the lands where they operated. Few desired territory for territory's sake. They wanted order, stability, protection of property, and sanctity of contract. If they requested U.S. government aid or intervention, it was to these ends. While there were some requests from U.S. businessmen in Mexico for aid, only in the Caribbean in these years did business leaders ask for substantial U.S. government assistance.*

In the nearby areas, some U.S. businesses altered their conduct to act as "genuine multinational enterprises . . . sensitive to local traditions and respecting local jurisdictions and policies." This was the case of many of the manufacturing firms that invested in Canada. In Mexico, in order to continue to operate, American enterprises paid taxes and conformed to "local jurisdictions and policies," but often they did so only under duress. Among American companies in the Caribbean there was perhaps the least sensitivity to local traditions and the least "respect" for the usually weak indigenous political leaders, although contracts were made with host governments and there is evidence that some companies and individuals in certain countries were respectful in their relationships. In short, as noted at the end of Chapter IV, as in nearby areas, some companies operated simply "extra-nationally," while others were "genuine multinational enterprises." It can be concluded, however, that there were relatively more extra-national companies doing business in the neighboring areas than elsewhere around the world.

Up to the year 1914, adversities in these three regions had not been serious enough to deter U.S. investments, over a long period. Again, as in the general case of U.S. enterprises investing worldwide, the incentives to investments tended to outweigh the obstacles. Key U.S. businessmen—among them John D. Rockefeller, James J. Hill, Collis P. Huntington, E. H. Harriman, H. O. Havemeyer, Henry Ford, the Guggenheims, James Buchanan Duke, and Thomas Fortune Ryan— through their companies or individually, all made foreign investments in at least one of the nearby regions. Theirs were direct investments,

---

* One did, however, get from businessmen extreme comments, such as the following written in 1907 by a man with interests in Venezuela, "The United States encourages immigration into Latin America, and the making of investments there, yet views with indifference the murder, robbery, imprisonment, or expulsion of its own citizens." This businessman resented the fact that the United States government would not "undertake to compel foreign governments to live up to contracts which they make with our citizens. . . The United States must take possession of the worst of those countries [in Latin America]—for their sake, for our sake, and for the sake of the world" (Crichfield, *American Supremacy*, II, 3–4).

related to their specific business requirements. Admittedly, the stake abroad of each man was small compared with his domestic interests; yet the foreign investment symbolized the same alertness to potentials beyond the national boundaries as we have seen among many leading U.S. businessmen.

The South American Experience

M. Guggenheim's Sons in 1898 made a contract with the Compañía Huanchaca de Bolivia, in which the American firm agreed to operate a lead-silver smelter at Antofagasta, Chile, on behalf of the Huanchaca company. This was the first entry of the Guggenheim family into South American business and initiated participation on a grand scale. It familiarized the Guggenheims with Chile and gave rise to a host of new investments in South America; it signaled the entrance of U.S. big business.[1]

2

A flashback to the earlier years indicates that after the 1860s U.S. stakes in South America had expanded slowly. From the 1830s onward such American entrepreneurs as William Wheelwright, Henry Meiggs, William Thorndyke, Edward Dubois, and Colonel George Earl Church, had pioneered in building and promoting railroads in South America, using mainly British capital. They left a heritage. When, for example, Henry Meiggs constructed the Chilean railroads, he hired at least sixty American engineers, some of whom remained in Chile and started their own ventures. Members of the Wheelwright family made South American investments. A few U.S. citizens who worked on the Southern Railroad in Peru later became prominent in business in that country. In the last decades of the nineteenth century, Americans continued to participate in South American railroad building—but the amount of U.S. capital involved remained minimal. Grace Brothers—which began in other businesses—undertook to operate, build, and finance railroads in Peru and Bolivia in the mid-1880s, but here once again the money the firm used was British.[2]

United States interests in South American mining and smelting before the turn of the century were likewise small. Some stakes evolved from the activities of traders who became investors. One such trading unit, Alsop & Co., lost its substantial holdings in Bolivian mining when the Chileans occupied the Bolivian silver mines at Caracoles in 1879. In the 1880s a handful of American companies began to mine gold in Ecuador, but these were short-lived activities. Then in the next decade the South American Development Company of New York became an important factor in Ecuadorian gold mining. Unlike the other enterprises, it had a long life. A few Americans started to mine in Peru and, as we have seen, there were scattered U.S. stakes in mining in Colombia and Venezuela. In 1898 the Guggenheims initiated their smelter operations in Chile.[3]

Before 1900 there were also U.S. investments in South American agriculture. After the American Civil War, a colony of fleeing southerners settled in Campinas, in the state of São Paulo, Brazil, and began to farm. W. R. Grace invested in Peruvian sugar; Minor Keith planted bananas in Colombia. In all, however, the total stake was not large.[4]

As for utilities, an early American venture was the Central & South American Cable (later Telegraph) Company (see Chapter III). In the 1880s, an American, Theodore Vail, established telephone companies in Brazil, Argentina, and on the west coast of South America; his financing does not seem to have been American. In the 1890s, Vail, with British capital, invested in a power plant in Cordoba, Argentina, and in street cars in Buenos Aires; in 1907 he sold out to Belgian interests. The abortive activities of Tropical-American Company were noted in Chapter III. Americans are credited with having built street car lines in Rio de Janeiro in the 1860s, but here once more the financing of the operation was probably not American.* [5]

United States stakes in the South American oil industry before the turn of the century were mainly of two sorts: in distribution and in production. There were also a couple of refineries linked either with distribution or with production. While Standard Oil companies handled

* See Chapter VIII for small investments in Colombia and Venezuela.

most of the South American market, their business in the 1870s and 1880s was typically f.o.b. New York, Philadelphia, or Baltimore; by the 1890s, some shipments went directly to agents in key South American cities. With the exception of a short-lived oil refinery built by Standard Oil in Brazil in 1896 (and closed the next year when a tariff change made it no longer warranted), no U.S.-owned refineries processing imported crude oil existed in South America in the nineteenth century. Two Americans, Rollin Thorne and Henry Smith, had become associated with Peruvian oil developments in the 1860s and 1870s, but their interests were of short duration. In 1888 another American, Herbert W. C. Tweddle, purchased La Brea y Parinas property at Talara, in northwestern Peru, and erected a large petroleum refinery to process the *local* crude oil. Two years later Tweddle sold his Peruvian assets to an Englishman, William Keswick and then the London & Pacific Petroleum Company, a British firm controlled by Keswick, leased La Brea y Parinas enterprise. Later this business returned to American control.[6]

United States commercial and shipping interests in South America before 1900 included a wide variety of companies and individuals. Some of these, briefly noted in Chapter I, had a long history. In 1854 an enterprising young Irishman, 22-year-old William R. Grace, became a partner in Bryce & Company, an English firm engaged in shipbuilding and in the guano trade in Peru. Five years later, this Irishman married a daughter of an American ship captain—and so started his North American connections. Bryce, Grace, & Co. (as the firm soon came to be known) engaged in widespread trading activities; in the mid-1860s it opened an office on Wall Street in New York City, with W. R. Grace as manager. Grace established a line of sailing vessels from New York to Peru that eventually became Grace Lines.

In 1871 W. R. Grace left New York to return to Lima, Peru. He broke his ties with Bryce, and with Michael P. Grace organized Grace Brothers. After the war of the Pacific (1879–1883), Grace Brothers opened a branch in Valparaiso, Chile, which added to the other Grace branches in Peru (in Lima and Callao), in the United States (San Francisco and New York), and in England (London). The firm took on an American-Anglo-Peruvian character. Its founder, W. R. Grace, became an American citizen; his headquarters by the 1880s was definitely in

New York. (He was elected mayor of New York City in 1880 and 1884.) On the other hand, his brother Michael maintained connections with England; Michael Grace's daughter married Lord Donoughmore, one of the leading British investors in Peruvian railroads. In the mid-1880s, a company, formed by the heirs of the entrepreneur Henry Meiggs, transferred its debts and obligations to "Casa Grace" (as the firm was known in South America) and Michael Grace became an important factor in the financing of the Peruvian railroads and in handling Peru's foreign debt.

Through the liquidation of a private debt in 1884, Grace Brothers acquired the Cartavio hacienda—a sugar plantation in northern Peru. Five years later Casa Grace became involved in Bolivian affairs, aiding in a settlement between the Bolivian government and its foreign bondholders. With British associates, the Grace company formed a syndicate to operate nine Bolivian railroads and to build two more.

By the mid-1880s Casa Grace was a significant factor in business on the west coast of South America. In 1894 all the Grace enterprises were consolidated in an American corporation, W. R. Grace & Co. The Peruvian historian, Jorge Basadre, however, points out that in spite of the founder's American citizenship, the firm was as closely linked with British as with American interests. Not until the First World War, Basadre maintains, did W. R. Grace & Co. take on a character that was clearly North American. This may be true from the Peruvian viewpoint but by World War I, among Americans at home and abroad, W. R. Grace & Co. was considered "an old established American house." [7]

The records of Singer Manufacturing Company show the migration of American traders to Brazil in the 1850s. That company's first agent in Rio, Henry Milford, was an American. In the late 1850s William Van Vleck Lidgerwood, an American mechanical engineer, arrived in Campinas, in the state of São Paulo, and established an importing business. When American southerners came to Campinas in the 1860s, it is said they introduced new farm implements into Brazil; they offered a market for Lidgerwood, who soon sold not only American sewing machines but U.S.-made agricultural and industrial equipment as well. Lidgerwood was also for a time U.S. consul in Brazil.[8] Actually, many American consuls—not only in Brazil, but elsewhere as well—served both as businessmen and U.S. government representatives. It seems clear that by the last decade of the nineteenth century, in most ports and large cities in South America, U.S. merchants engaged in export-import trade. Rarely did these traders, or their firms, represent a single American company or handle a single commodity.

The amount of U.S. manufacturing in South America before 1900 was insignificant. The American engineer J. H. Johnston who had come to Peru in the 1870s to work on the Southern Railway, and Jacob Backus, a nephew of Henry Meiggs, started a prosperous beer-making enterprise in Lima. Other manufacturing activities by individuals could be cited, but none that was substantial. Diamond Match Company did some simple manufacturing in Peru and Brazil in the 1890s; it has been impossible to trace any other U.S. "international business" that had manufacturing plants in South America before the turn of the century; probably there were no others.

Briefly, then, during the late nineteenth century, although a number of American citizens visited South America, bringing with them engineering skills, entrepreneurial energy, and new products, they invested little capital. This was the case in railroads, mining, agriculture, utilities, oil, trade, and manufacturing. Cleona Lewis estimates that in 1897 U.S. direct investments in all South America totaled a bare $38 million—considerably less than the corresponding U.S. stake in the nearby Caribbean. Moreover, if we exempt some American trading firms, the cable company, and perhaps a handful of other businesses, American-financed enterprises in South America during the nineteenth century were not of long duration. So limited were the stakes that the British journalist W. T. Stead could write in 1902 that Americans have "done little or nothing to develop the South American continent." [9]

3

When the U.S. capital market became mature, by the early 1900s, U.S. funds in large amounts could, and did, venture into South America. The sizable investments were not in railroads, however. While U.S. money did go into financing the Madeira-Mamore Railroad (in the heart of the Amazon region), into the Guayaquil & Quito Railroad Company in Ecuador, and into railroads built in connection with mining projects, the main funds for South American railroads continued to be supplied by European investors.[10] It was mining and processing of various ores that attracted the most U.S. money to South America in the years before World War I.

4

"I came back to Chile [from Europe] at the beginning of this year and since then I have been busy looking for some important mining proposition to present to European capital," wrote Señor Marco Chiapponi, an Italian mining engineer, to the American engineer, William Braden. The letter was dated November 3, 1903. It continued:

> but your kind letter suggested to me that I could do a good deal better in addressing myself to you, as North American capital is perhaps more enterprizing and no one I know is in a better position than yourself to carry through successfully such a scheme . . .
>
> There are in Chile, Bolivia and Argentina hundreds of mining schemes, but the real fact is that if one looks for something really good, it is rather difficult to find one or two.
>
> I call really good a business which answers the following conditions:
>
> 1. Ore in sight enough to represent (on its profits) the capital necessary for buying the property and putting up plants.
>
> 2. Probable ore enough to represent at least the same amount.
>
> 3. Mining expectations such as to be an inducement.
>
> All calculations should be based on an interest on the capital of 20 per cent and a price of the metal 10 per cent less than the average of last 20 years.

Chiapponi then gave details on a copper deposit that met these specifications.

Early in 1904, following Chiapponi's suggestions, Braden raised $30,000 from E. W. Nash, president, and Barton Sewell, vice president, of American Smelting and Refining Company, Guy C. Barton, president of Omaha & Grant Smelting Co., and a few others. Then he left for Chile. Some 80 miles southeast of Santiago, at El Teniente in the Andes, he surveyed the deposit. Inaccessible and containing low-grade ore, it had not tempted European capital. Nonetheless, the size of the deposit made it promising. On the basis of his report, his sponsors recommended he purchase the property, which he did for $100,000 (U.S. dollars).

Then, on June 24, 1904 (less than eight months after the original proposition had come to Braden's attention), the Braden Copper Company was incorporated in Maine; its capital consisted of 625,000 each of preferred and common shares; Braden raised $625,000 on the preferred shares. This sum represented one of the first sizable entries of American capital into mining south of the equator.

During the nearly three hundred years the Spaniards ruled Chile—from 1541 to 1818—they had become aware of that country's vast copper resources. In Europe, however, copper was cheap, and importation from distant South America through the Straits of Magellan was not attempted. From 1830 to 1882, however, Chile became the world's largest copper producer; thousands of small miners eked out a living from the metal; some British capital was invested, and the American trader, Augustus Hemenway, had small mines at Carrizalillo. But in the 1880s the Chilean copper industry began to decline. Americans developed the rich copper deposits in western United States, where copper could be mined at a lower cost than in Chile. Accordingly, the United States came to replace Chile as the world's foremost supplier of copper. When Braden Copper Company was incorporated in 1904 the United States was still in first place. Chile by this time had fallen to sixth rank in copper output, after the United States, Mexico, Spain-Portugal, Japan, and Australia.

Why, with the United States in top position in copper production and nearby Mexico in second place, did any American even consider investing in the copper mines of distant Chile? The ability of certain men to risk and to adventure provides an explanation. The Americans who invested in Chile were interested in *any* good proposition, whether it lay in the arid lands bordering the Andes, in the Russian Caucasus, in Northern Mexico, or in the hills of Montana. Moreover, and of greater significance, from 1899 to 1903 technological innovations made possible for the first time the profitable mining of low-grade ore. The work of an American, D. C. Jackling, in copper metallurgy meant that ore once ignored could now be mined at a profit. The deposit Chiapponi and Braden had located in Chile had just such low-grade ore. The price of copper was high in 1904, and this stimulated interest in developing new enterprises.

Under a government decree of April 20, 1905, the Braden Copper Company was officially authorized to do business in Chile. With the first $625,000 Braden raised, he paid for the property, built a 35-mile road, established a community, constructed a concentrating plant, and a hydroelectric plant. The engineer got customs duties waived on construction equipment and machinery that he imported. The government aimed to restore Chile to first place in copper production, and perhaps the Americans would aid in achieving this goal.[11]

5

Prior to the formation of Braden Copper Company, Americans had sought and found foreign copper in Mexico and Canada; Amalgamated Copper Company officials had talked loudly of buying the Rothschild's Rio Tinto mine in Spain (an action that was never taken). There had been American capital involved in the Caucasus Copper Company, established in 1900 near Batum, and the Guggenheim Exploration Company had begun to seek foreign copper resources.[12] Braden Copper Company is especially important, however, because (1) it represents a sizable initial investment for that period; (2) it had a long history; and (3) it constituted the first major entry of Americans into the Chilean copper-mining industry—an industry in which Americans came to play the pre-eminent role. It is also important because it symbolized what was already typical of American investment abroad—the offering not only of capital, but of skills and technology to convert undeveloped resources into providers both of employment and profit.

Mining is costly, particularly in remote regions. Braden found he had to build a railroad since none existed. To pay for it, he sought added funds in the United States. The Guggenheims agreed to buy bonds, receiving common shares as a bonus and obtaining a first mortgage on the mine's output. They had already risked large sums in American and Mexican lead, silver, and copper mining; they had, as we have seen, started operating smelters in Mexico and at Antofagasta, in northern Chile. They put stiff conditions on the money they supplied, but not many men were ready to gamble on the low-grade ore at El Teniente. By June 1909 the Guggenheims had taken over the Braden enterprise, retaining the name Braden Copper Company. Through an issue of $4,000,000 of 6 per cent convertible bonds and after the retirement of the earlier bond issue and the preferred stock, the Guggenheims supplied $2,500,000 working capital in cash. They dispatched their own American engineers and staff to Chile and introduced new techniques. Braden was the first copper company in the world of any significance to utilize the flotation process in concentrating low grade ore. The Guggenheim engineers now sought more properties in Chile.[13]

Meanwhile, a lawyer and financier, A. C. Burrage (one of the founders of the Amalgamated Copper Company), visited London, where he learned that British interests controlled a huge ore deposit at Chuquicamata—in northern Chile (some 800 miles north of Santiago). The mines in the area had not been profitable because the usual methods of concentrating and smelting proved unsuitable. Earlier, Burrage had become interested in the Bradley process of ore treatment. (Anaconda tried the method, spent $750,000 on it, and declared it to be a failure.) Now Burrage planned to apply it in Chile. He envisaged mining all the ore in the deposit—and not just the high-grade streaks. As one writer put it, the British "failed to appreciate the possibilities of mass production" (so did many Americans). It was on the new technology that Burrage staked his success.

After a visit to Chuquicamata, Burrage obtained options on that mining area from the English companies there, from certain private Chilean investors, and also from the Chilean government. These options he offered to the Guggenheims, who in 1912 organized the Chile Exploration Company (Chilex) to take over the property. Daniel Guggenheim was president and Burrage was vice president of the new corporation. Whether the enterprise would succeed was a question; the risk was substantial. The ore was different from that at El Teniente, and different processes would have to be applied.

When the Guggenheims acquired this second Chilean copper-mining property, the Braden Copper Company was just starting production. The Guggenheims moved personnel from El Teniente to Chuquicamata. At Chuquicamata the Guggenheims' metallurgist, E. A. Cappelen-Smith, set out to perfect new methods of treating the low-grade oxide ore. The mine at Chuquicamata was an open pit mine; the copper ore was shoveled up; then the copper would be leached out of the ore in giant square vats filled with a dilute solution of sulphuric acid. The copper next went to a tankhouse for electrolytic precipitation; the resulting copper cathodes were then further refined and cast into shapes for shipment. At first there were metallurgical difficulties; considerable time would elapse before the enterprise would pay dividends. The Guggenheims' initial investment came to $12,000,000, and this was only a beginning; the mine required far more money to make it profitable.[14]

At Chuquicamata, as at El Teniente, a new community had to be created. Chuquicamata was in the nitrate-producing region of Chile. Americans built homes in the fashion of the nitrate camps; some were small two-family houses; many were barrack-type establishments. Everything was painted gray, accenting the bleakness of this desert region. No railroad had to be built since the line from La Paz, Bolivia, which passed through the nitrate fields and terminated at the port of Antofagasta, could be used. But the area was barren; drinking water had to be brought in by rail in tank cars and then carried on ox carts. Argentine cattle were driven on foot over the Andes range, a journey of fifteen days, most of it without food or water. At the oasis of San Pedro de Atacama, the cattle stopped for seven days for rest and food; then on arrival at Calama, some nine miles from Chuquicamata, the half-starved animals would again be fed and rested for twenty days before the slaughter. It was difficult to attract labor to Chuquicamata; few men wanted to go to this windswept, desolate spot, located at an altitude of slightly over 9,000 feet. "There is something wrong with this region; it affects your health," people would say superstitiously. The costs of developing the largest copper mines in United States were "inconsequential" compared with the costs here. "Everything that was required to sustain a population . . . had to be provided. A man couldn't exist there for 24 hours in its natural environment," Cornelius Kelley later explained to a congressional committee.[15]

At Chuquicamata, as at El Teniente, the Guggenheims found the Chilean government anxious to cooperate. The Chileans wanted a taxable industry. Company officials praised the government as "stable, progressive, and sympathetic." By 1914 development was well under way at both El Teniente and Chuquicamata—two of the three great Chilean copper properties. Chuquicamata was recognized as the largest known single copper deposit in the world. As yet, neither the Braden Company nor Chilex had paid dividends. By 1914, American investment in Chilean copper stood at $169 million (practically all of it in these two Guggenheim companies). American capital dominated the Chilean copper-mining industry; the money invested had all been exported from the United States.[16]

In spite of the developments in copper, nitrates in 1914 remained Chile's major industry, employing the most labor and producing the most revenue. Taxes on nitrate exports provided Chile's main source of income. In this industry, British, and to a lesser extent, German, money predominated. In 1909 the American consul in Santiago, Chile, reported that considerable American capital was being put into nitrates and "there seem to be good openings for further American investments." *
In 1912, du Pont, which had earlier (1907) opened an office in Chile to buy nitrates, purchased a nitrate *oficina* and completed a factory for the "elaboration of nitrate of soda." † It was not until the 1920s, however, that Americans assumed a significant role in the Chilean nitrate industry. An additional inroad into Chilean mining by American capital was Bethlehem Steel's leasing from a French company in 1913 the El Tofo iron ore mines.[17]

6

Mainly because of the huge stakes in copper, Chile obtained more American capital than any other South American country before World War I. American businesses were also interested in mining enterprises elsewhere. In the Peruvian Andes—at a height of over 14,000 feet—lay

* In 1909–1910 giant plans were made involving the consolidation of Chilean nitrate producers, in which several hundred million dollars were to be invested by J. P. Morgan, Kuhn, Loeb & Co., the First National Bank, and National City Bank. According to Charles R. Flint, the project was frustrated when U.S. Secretary of State Philander C. Knox insisted Chile pay for the damages to American properties in the war of the Pacific (1879–1883). Chile responded to Knox's ultimatum, expressing fear of having "her principal industry and source of income controlled by a corporation organized by the financial and industrial magnates of the United States." And that, as Flint relates, "was the end of the proposed consolidation" (*Memories of an Active Life*, pp. 68–72).
† Du Pont Nitrate Company, incorporated in Delaware, was formed to own and operate the property. Its capital was $1,600,000, of which $800,000 was in 7% cumulative non-voting shares and $800,000 was in common stock, all owned by E. I. du Pont de Nemours Powder Company.

the famous ore bodies of Cerro de Pasco, rich in copper, silver, lead, gold, and other minerals. In 1902, James B. Haggin, Henry C. Frick, Edward H. Clark (representing Mrs. Phoebe Hearst), J. P. Morgan, and others had formed the Cerro de Pasco Mining Company.* The new company had estimated that to develop the ore bodies would cost $5 million. The estimate was low. The company had to build 83 miles of railroad to connect with an existing line. It found coal, which warranted further investment. It had to bring Americans to do the simplest work, because skilled labor was absent. It had to train the Sierra Indian in minor mechanical tasks. The company's first smelter functioned improperly— at an altitude of 14,000 feet. There were also smelting difficulties because of the low-grade fuel. All this meant that by 1912 the investment had reached $25 million. None of this money had been generated in Peru; all came from the United States, and in its first decade the company paid no dividends. By this time the enterprise was Peru's largest copper producer.[18]

Meanwhile, another Peruvian venture took shape. Johnston and Backus—who had started the earlier mentioned beer-making company in Lima—now looked into mining. By 1912 their Sociedad Miñera Backus y Johnston del Peru, incorporated in that country, was building a silver-copper smelter at Casapalca, costing some $350,000. A year later the Company stood second only to Cerro de Pasco in Peruvian copper production (5,170 tons compared with 22,415 tons that year). How this property was financed is uncertain; I can find no evidence that the Americans sought funds from public sources in the United States.[19]

Also in the Cerro de Pasco region an American mining engineer, D. Foster Hewett, in 1905 discovered a vanadium mine, which Joseph M. Flannery of Pittsburgh purchased. Flannery single-handedly developed the property. His American Vanadium Company—formed in February 1906—introduced vanadium to the U.S. steel industry. By 1914 over 80 per cent of the world's supply of vanadium came from his mine, located in the Andes at roughly 16,000 feet. The ore was transported from the mine on the backs of llamas.[20]

In southeastern Peru, in the department of Puno, where 80 per cent

* Many of the group had been associated with Homestake Mining Company in the U.S.

of the gold of Peru was mined, the Inca Mining Company, a firm of American origin was in 1909 the largest enterprise. Two years later, its stock was sold to British investors.[21]

All these American investments resulted in a significant expansion in Peruvian mining. The activity was carried on under the Mining Law of November 8, 1890, which specified that for 25 years (or until 1915) there would be no new taxes or tax increases, a most favorable incentive.[22]

7

Bolivia's major export was tin. In 1914 American direct investment was not a significant factor in this industry. Mining engineer George Easley reported that the Pan-American Tin Company, controlled by Hoyt Metal Company, which in turn was a subsidiary of National Lead, was doing a small amount of tin-mining in Bolivia by 1909. This U.S.-controlled firm was an exception.[23]

Americans mined gold in Ecuador and Colombia. In 1913 a civil engineer, Francis G. Harvey, had brought to London samples of bauxite from British Guiana. He sought to attract British and German capital, but the Europeans showed no interest. Next he visited with a representative of Aluminum Corporation of America. Alcoa's management proved receptive. During 1914 and later Alcoa bought land in British Guiana, along the Demerara River, with an eye to mining bauxite, which was the basic raw material for aluminum production.[24]

8

While substantial U.S. capital flowed into South American mining, some new (and far less extensive) U.S. investments were made after 1900 in petroleum exploration, production, and refining. Herbert Hoover and his associates bought stock in the Lagunitos Oil Company, which operated in Peru under a sublease from a British company. Far more important was the entry of Standard Oil of New Jersey into Peruvian oil production. Standard Oil companies had since the 1870s been aware of the existence of commercial oil resources in Peru, but had not been interested in drilling for oil; they were more intent on marketing U.S.-

refined oil in Latin America. As Peruvian oil production mounted, Standard Oil subsidiaries purchased the output for resale in South America. As late as 1910, Standard Oil visitors to Peru reported, "It will be more profitable to buy production than to hunt for it, and to buy oil than to run the risks in this territory of producing it." As noted earlier, with the dissolution of Standard Oil in 1911, Jersey Standard, curtailed at home, contemplated more expansion abroad, including the purchase of foreign producing properties. The company's management now considered La Brea y Parinas property, at Talara in northern Peru at the very time when the Peruvian government threatened to reassess the tax basis and raise the taxes on the oil field.

Undeterred by the threat and acting through its Canadian affiliate—the Imperial Oil Company—Jersey Standard in 1913 acquired controlling interest in the London & Pacific Petroleum Company—the British firm which had leased La Brea y Parinas property. While the London & Pacific Company protested the proposed tax hike, claiming it "would amount to confiscation," Jersey Standard made a $1.5 million investment in geological work and improvements in producing, refining, storing, and transportation. The venture, when Jersey Standard invested, was a "going enterprise." Jersey Standard's affiliate, Imperial Oil Company, sent to Talara British and American engineers and skilled workers, as well as Canadian and American drillers. Soon Walter C. Teagle of Jersey Standard was purchasing added Peruvian facilities.* On September 10, 1914, Jersey Standard organized a Canadian affiliate, International Petroleum Company, Ltd., to acquire and operate all its Peruvian oil activities. I. P. C. became the leading oil producer and refiner in Peru. Its activities would subsequently involve the United States in considerable diplomatic controversy.[25]

Other U.S. investments were made in the nascent Colombian and Venezuelan oil industries.[26] In short, by 1914 Americans had just barely begun to invest in South American oil production; but the way was paved for massive participation in the decades to follow.

* Jersey Standard bought large blocks of stock in Hoover's Lagunitos Oil Company. Although it wanted more (it could not get it), Jersey Standard also purchased a minority interest in the British-owned Lobitos Oilfields Ltd., with an output equal to that of the London & Pacific Company.

9

The marketing plans of the U.S. mining and oil companies in South America are difficult to document. The Guggenheims apparently looked to worldwide copper markets—the United States and Europe primarily. Bethlehem, du Pont, and Alcoa were integrating their own operations and planned to return iron ore, nitrates, and bauxite to the United States. American Vanadium Company was shipping to the States, while Cerro de Pasco also seems to have had the American market in mind. On the other hand, Jersey Standard developed its Peruvian oil production with an eye to sales on the west coast of South America. One thing was clear. No American extractive enterprise in South America envisaged the host country as its primary market. No South American country had the population or the manufacturing facilities to absorb the projected output.[27]

The American companies in extractive-exporting enterprises in South America fit into the category of what are generally seen as "typical" investments by an industrial nation's corporations in less developed countries. Viewed in the context of all American business abroad, it is worth noting that massive investments by U.S. companies of this sort came relatively late in the history of U.S. direct foreign investment. It is only in the first decade of the twentieth century that we discover this so-called typical U.S. stake in South America.

10

Agricultural investment in South America by U.S. citizens and companies was small compared with the investment in extractive properties, especially that in mining. In 1914, $221 million had been invested in mining, $25 million in agriculture. Individual Americans bought farms, cattle ranches, and timberland in South America. In connection with their enterprises, mining companies often purchased land suitable for cultivation and cattle raising. At the time when Americans looked for rubber in Mexico, they likewise turned to South America. The Inca Mining Company's executives in 1901 discovered extensive rubber-growing properties in the Peruvian Andes, bordering on Bolivia, and formed the Inca Rubber Company, which acquired one million acres of land under a concession from the Peruvian government. In return for the grant, the company agreed to build a 150-kilometer road, to establish telegraph or telephone lines, to maintain the road, and "to permit free traffic over the road of missionaries, soldiers and officials traveling on business of the Government." The company could charge others a toll: "mules and horses . . . two cents each. Burros with freight or riders one cent each. . . . Llamas unloaded quarter cent each. Cattle one cent each. Sheep and hogs half cent each. Persons on foot, loaded or unloaded, half cent each." The fate of this enterprise is unrecorded.[28]

By 1903 Bolivia had granted the so-called "Acre concession" to a syndicate composed of British interests and U.S. Rubber Company representatives. The concession covered the Acre region of Bolivia that Brazil claimed. The Brazilian government accordingly sought to block the new enterprise: it failed to ratify a treaty with Bolivia providing for free navigation of certain confluents of the Amazon that extended into Bolivia, and it put prohibitive transit duties on goods imported into or exported from Bolivia via the Amazon River. Finally, after the Brazilian government paid a cash settlement to the syndicate for the disputed territory, the latter relinquished the concession. Brazil then paid Bolivia to acquire the disputed area. The U.S. Rubber Company "dropped" the project, directing its "energies . . . toward . . . other locations"—namely, Sumatra. Thus ended one potentially giant U.S. investment in South American agriculture.

The American entrepreneur Percival Farquhar made some investments in Brazilian rubber, as well as cattle ranches and timberland: none of these proved a pronounced success. In cattle ranching, the New York and Paraguay Company owned in 1914 some 780,000 acres in Paraguay plus some 17,000 head of cattle.* Substantial U.S. stakes in South Amer-

* Two Americans, William M. Baldwin and Joseph E. Stevens, who controlled the New York and Paraguay Company, pioneered in the manufacture of quebracho extract (used for tanning leathers) in the United States. From an initial importation of 50 tons of quebracho logs in 1897, they built up the business of the New York Tanning Extract Company and its subsidiary, the Argentine Quebracho Company, to a consumption of 100,000 tons of quebracho wood. They constructed a large extract plant in Brooklyn, N.Y., and another in Argentina. In 1914, they sold both factories to a British syndicate (Forestall Land Company), which obtained a practical monopoly of the manufacture of quebracho. Baldwin and Stevens renamed the New York Tanning Company the New York and Paraguay Company, and in 1914–1916 it was a going concern, selling quebracho logs and owning land and cattle. This company was the predecessor of International

ican agriculture included United Fruit Company's banana farms in Colombia and W. R. Grace's sugar plantation in Peru.[29]

11

American meatpackers did not integrate backward into cattle lands in the United States; nor did they do so in South America. Instead they integrated horizontally. With the exception of Cudahy Packing Company, all the large American packers made investments in meatpacking in South America: Armour, Swift, Sulzberger & Sons Company * and Morris. They did so in order to meet competition.

Before the days of refrigeration the United States had exported salted and pickled beef as well as live cattle. In the 1880s and 1890s, with refrigeration, American packers maintained and expanded foreign sales, exporting dressed beef, and until 1907 American beef predominated in world markets. During the first decade of the twentieth century, however, U.S. beef exports rapidly declined. The most significant reason was growing competition from Argentina.

Argentine beef had become competitive for two reasons. First, costs of U.S. production had risen, and second, Argentine output had increased, and its costs were lower than U.S. costs. In the United States in the 1890s more meat had been produced than consumed and prices of livestock had fallen. As a result of this and other factors, land previously devoted to stock raising had been put to alternative uses. More animals were raised on farms rather than on large ranches. As a consequence, in the early 1900s U.S. costs of production rose sharply. Meanwhile, the Argentine meatpacking industry developed. Financed by British and Argentine capital, the industry made huge profits during the Boer War (1899–1902). Added British capital and technology made the industry more efficient. Argentina raised its cattle on spacious pampas at a lower cost than proved possible in the United States. Soon Argentine beef captured European markets and even began to invade the American market.

Products Company. Charles Anderson Gauld refers to another American investment: the Paraguay Land & Cattle Company as a "50-50" deal between Percival Farquhar and Texas rancher Tex Rickard. There is no indication of the size of this enterprise.

* Name changed to Wilson & Co. in July 1916.

At this point the Chicago meatpackers—seeing their European markets being taken from them and their home markets threatened—responded by investing in the Argentine meat business. In self-defense Swift in 1907 bought an existing meatpacking plant in Buenos Aires; in 1909 National Packing Company * followed. By 1914 Sulzberger & Sons Company had a packing plant in the province of Buenos Aires. Swift also bought a meatpacking plant in Uruguay in 1912. These stakes by the Chicago businessmen have to be explained in entirely different terms from any of the other South American investments we have discussed (except, perhaps, Jersey Standard's investment in oil in Peru). The Chicagoans' primary motive appears to have been to maintain *foreign* markets—markets outside of the United States and outside the country where the investment was made. Their strategy proved effective. During the years 1910 to 1913 between 40 and 50 per cent of the total Argentine and Uruguayan beef exports were from plants owned by the American meatpackers.

The midwesterners next looked to Brazil. The Sulzbergers obtained a concession to construct a packing plant at Osasco, near São Paulo.† Work began on the plant in March 1914, but operations would not start until May 1915. The other American meatpackers would follow the Sulzbergers into Brazil.[30]

12

American investors in South America have been traditionally associated with "the development of mineral resources, export and allied activities, and public utility concessions," according to the Argentine-born Raul Prebisch. Yet, his statement notwithstanding, before World War I, U.S. investment in utilities in South America was minimal. (It has been estimated that only $3.7 million was the investment in 1914.) The mining companies, to be sure, made investments in power plants in connection with their operations. The cable company was still prominent.

---

* When in 1912 National Packing Company was dissolved, the ownership of this plant passed into the joint ownership of Morris and Armour.

† The concession went to a company called Continental Products, which was 23 per cent owned by the Sulzbergers and the rest by Farquhar's Brazil Land, Cattle & Packing Co. When in 1916 Sulzberger's U.S. company was renamed Wilson & Co., the Osasco plant came to be known as the Wilson plant.

But we noted earlier that the holdings of Vail in Argentina were sold to Belgian interests. In 1904 American entrepreneur Percival Farquhar organized the Rio de Janeiro Tramway, Light & Power Company. Most of its management was American, and it was often branded as an "octopus of Yankee imperialists." Yet the financing did not come from the United States; Farquhar found Canadian capitalists "were so much more willing than Wall Streeters to invest in Rio Light." * Farquhar also organized in 1905 the Bahia Tramway, Light & Power Company, which, again, was not U.S.-financed. In Chapter VIII we noted scattered investments in utilities by Americans in Venezuela and Colombia. But the total U.S. stake in South American public utilities was small. The era of massive U.S. participation in South American utilities was still ahead (the "tradition" was developed in the 1920s—not before).[31]

13

In 1902 a British journalist wrote of Argentina, Chile, and Peru as "commercial annexes of Great Britain." But, he added, "as Disraeli said, there is room in Asia for both Russia and England, so we may say that there is room in South America for both John Bull and Uncle Sam." [32]

As Americans invested in South America, trade increased. Whereas in 1900 U.S. imports from South America totaled $94 million, in 1913 they reached $218 million—that is, they more than doubled. U.S. investment in supply-oriented activities—such as the investments in mining—assisted this advance. Trading houses—many of them American—also participated in spurring the growth. Far more impressive was the rise in U.S. exports to South America. Whereas in 1900 these exports were a bare $38 million, in 1913 they equaled $146 million. Part of the reason was that American investors bought from familiar sources of supply. United States interests in Chilean mining, for example, stimulated U.S. exports of machinery. Many American exporters found that British and German companies in South America automatically purchased in their home country rather than in the United States. A manufacturer of power transmission appliances told the Federal Trade Commission in 1915

* This company became one of the largest light, power, and telephone companies in Brazil. In 1912 it became a subsidiary of Brazilian Traction, Light & Power Co., Ltd., of Toronto, Canada.

that "the investment of Chicago capital in packing houses in Buenos Aires insures the installation of American machinery in these plants, while houses controlled by British capital are equipped with English machinery." Other Americans learned more about South America and sought out the new markets.[33]

Although trade grew, up to World War I the majority of American-manufactured goods in Latin America—one 1911 estimate was 70 per cent—were marketed through commission houses. The great advantage of the commission house was that the U.S. seller had no merchandising expense other than a few catalogues and the commission (and sometimes the commission might be paid by the customer). The house handled the financing and the complexities of foreign trade (translation, customs duties, foreign exchange, taxes, documents, and so forth). A U.S. corporation exporting only on a casual basis found a commission house could sell its product far more economically than a salaried representative of the firm. Commission houses had representatives or correspondents in South America.[34]

Yet, when the volume of business grew, companies discovered—as they had earlier in the United States, and then in Europe, Canada, and Mexico—that if they were to sell effectively and to give proper service to their customers, they should have local representation.* As we saw in Chapter III, companies often appointed independent agents in foreign countries who agreed to sell and to service the enterprise's products. These agencies were bound by agreement and dealt *directly* with the home company. In South America such agencies were frequently run by

---

* Commission houses handled a variety of goods; they did not give consistently good service—sometimes because of lack of interest in and sometimes because of lack of knowledge of a particular product. It was a difficult business for a U.S. corporation to send its own man down to South America just to cope with a specific problem. The experiences of the Carbondale Refrigeration Company (of Carbondale, Pennsylvania) are informative. In 1901 this company installed a plant in Pernambuco, in northeast Brazil. Thirteen years later the Carbondale company sent a mechanic to service the plant. The man, unable to get direct connections to Pernambuco, had to go farther south to Bahia. From there he backtracked 200 miles on a coast steamer up to Pernambuco, where he did one hour's work, and then returned on the same steamer to Bahia. He waited five weeks for the arrival of the ship that would take him to New York. His journey totaled 10,000 miles; the mechanic did one hour's work, and with all the delays, the trip consumed nearly three months (Unsigned [1920] report of another traveler to Brazil, in "Brazil-Corporate Binder," International Division files, Otis Elevator Company, New York).

Americans. William T. Phelps, in Venezuela, was an agent for many American companies. In Brazil, Casa Pratt, owned by the American Charles Pratt, handled office machinery and similar products. The agency might also be a branch of a U.S. export-import house; W. R. Grace served as "agent" for many companies in Chile and Peru. Wessel, Duval & Co. in Chile sold such products as locomotives, Pullman cars, and air brakes. Sometimes, the agency might be owned and financed by local capital. The use of an on-the-spot agent involved no investment by the U.S. manufacturer, except possibly the credit line. It was the method adopted by many large U.S. companies in handling their South American business.[35]

The next step for many U.S. manufacturers in South America was to establish branch sales offices. In order to supply full service, to provide an adequate demonstration of the product, to offer satisfactory financing of sales, to keep the merchandising profit with the producer, to regulate inventories, and to control price, manufacturers required foreign branches.* This meant foreign investments by the United States companies. Whereas sales branches or subsidiaries had become the norm in European and Canadian trade by 1914, in South America U.S. companies were just beginning to make such investments. Table X.2 lists some of the U.S. firms which had established South American branches by 1914.[36]

In their extension of marketing arrangements to foreign lands, large American companies "mixed" their forms of doing business. In prosperous Argentina they might have a sales branch; in Chile, where the market was smaller, they might appoint an independent agent; in Ecuador, where they would sell infrequently, they might use a commission house.

In Europe and Canada, as we have seen, many companies established foreign plants in order to sell more effectively; this was far less evident in South America. Between 1900 and 1914 very few American companies undertook assembly, manufacturing, or refining for sale in a particular South American country. The market was still not large enough. Accord-

* Whereas in Europe, American industrials usually incorporated their sales subsidiaries in the host country (because of the tax situation, local legislation, and to avoid liability on the part of the parent), in Latin America sales extensions of American industrials were initially "branches" of a U.S.-incorporated company.

ing to Cleona Lewis, Singer Sewing Machine did assembly on its machine in three cities in South America.* As mentioned earlier, Diamond Match manufactured its simple product in Peru and Brazil. In 1904 W. R. Grace & Co. purchased a textile mill in Peru (known today as Inca Cotton Mill). Pullman Standard Car Export Corporation in 1912 started a shop in Rio for maintenance and assembly of passenger and freight cars; American Rolling Mill Company (ARMCO) that same year began to produce corrugated metal culverts for Brazilian drainage (a simple operation). Indeed, a handful of other American companies did a minimum of primitive assembly or manufacturing, all of which required only a negligible investment. A partial exception was Standard Oil of New Jersey, whose subsidiary, West India Oil Company, in 1911 acquired a minority interest in Compañía National de Aceites—an Austro-Hungarian company—which owned a refinery in Argentina. The refinery was used to process imported crude oil, and was required by Jersey Standard because of the tariffs on refined oil. Its output, however, was only 300 barrels a day in 1912 and 800 in 1914 (Jersey Standard's smallest refinery in the United States handled 2,500 barrels per day, and its largest at Bayonne 35,000 a day in 1912). In the main, American industrial concerns in South America—if not extracting or processing raw materials for export—served as sales and service enterprises.[37]

14

In 1914 U.S. trade and investment in South America seemed destined to grow. W. R. Grace was stimulating shipping on the west coast—and to some extent on the east coast. In 1913 Emmet J. McCormack and A. V. Moore formed the McCormack Company, Inc. and began the successful Moore-McCormack South American shipping line. The Panama Canal would open in August 1914, serving to tie the United States and South America closer together.[38]

In June 1914 the president of the National City Bank, Frank A. Vanderlip talked with a number of businessmen involved in foreign trade, including James A. Farrell, president of U.S. Steel. To his surprise, Vanderlip wrote in a personal letter, the people he interviewed told him that

---

* Singer officials in Latin America in the 1960s regard these early operations as simply sales branches (Interviews with Singer executives in South America, 1964).

what was demanded in the development of American foreign trade was a South American banking service. Since a very large expansion in U.S. trade with South America seemed in prospect, Vanderlip proposed that his bank undertake a modest trial in South American banking—requiring an expenditure of about $1,000,000. Farrell of U.S. Steel promised that his company (a large exporter to South America with investments in warehouses in key South American cities) would cooperate with National City Bank and that International Harvester, Armour, and Swift (all of which had investments in South America) would furnish a substantial amount of business. Farrell urged National City Bank to establish branches in Buenos Aires, Rio, and then elsewhere; he told Vanderlip that if the National City Bank did not take this step, some other bank would; Vanderlip concluded that his bank would thus be handicapped if it delayed entering the field. Accordingly, Vanderlip applied to the Federal Reserve Board to obtain permission for the National City Bank to open its first foreign branch in Buenos Aires; the application was approved, and in 1914 the new Argentine branch started to do business.[39]

In conclusion, between 1900 and 1914, U.S. corporations had begun to make large direct investments in South America. United States investors had been most attracted to South America by the minerals (mainly copper, but also other nonferrous metals, iron, and to some extent oil) and by meat (the large investments by the Chicago meatpackers in Argentina, Uruguay, and to a lesser extent Brazil were important). Likewise, they saw markets for the products of U.S. enterprise and made limited—but crucial—direct investments in sales outlets. Total U.S. direct investment in South America soared—if the figures are accurate—from $38 million in 1897 to $323 million in 1914. Nevertheless, in 1914 United States investment in South America still came nowhere near the British stake and, for that matter, remained less than U.S. interests in the Caribbean. Moreover, the direct investments of U.S. business were small compared with what would follow. Yet in practically every sector, probably excluding utilities, the foundations had been laid for the subsequent expansion of U.S. business in South America.[40]

Four

Summation

The Status of American International Enterprise—1914

The preceding chapters can leave no doubt that American businessmen were involved abroad in the years before 1914—sometimes through international * corporations and sometimes through companies that had stakes only in a single country. In fact, practically every prominent industrial tycoon in the late nineteenth and early twentieth centuries was in some manner interested in foreign business. Railroad leaders, such as Collis P. Huntington, E. H. Harriman, Cornelius Vanderbilt, and James J. Hill were likewise concerned. So too was J. P. Morgan, the era's key banker.†

Clearly, the alert American entrepreneurs sought opportunities beyond the national boundaries. Both the "push" of conditions at home (the growth of the firm and the economic environment in the United States) and the "pull" of prospects abroad (the possibilities of markets and sources of supplies) contributed to the rising direct foreign investment in the decades before 1914. United States government policies and actions had an impact, but only a small one, on the direct investment pattern; the influence was most pronounced in the Caribbean area.

The Americans who invested abroad before 1914 encountered some of the problems that their successors would meet. They recognized the need to develop strategies to cope with differences abroad: variations in host-country industry structure and host-country governmental attitudes and actions. In the process of expanding abroad, some U.S. companies adapted by joining cartels. Many American firms hired foreign nationals in each nation where they operated, used local directors, and admitted

---

* Here I am using the words "international" and "multinational" interchangeably.
† I do not refer to portfolio investments or underwriting, but to direct investment.

local capital.[1] Many had done so from the origin of their business abroad. The degree to which some companies had become international is evident in a 1907 letter from H. B. Thayer, Vice President of Western Electric, to an agent in Bangkok, Thailand:

> You speak of an anti-American attitude on the part of the [Government] Commission. We have offices and factories making our standard apparatus in Great Britain, Belgium, Germany, France, Russia, Austria, Italy, and Japan so that so far as this matter goes we are international rather than American. If there were time we could arrange to have the order go to any one of those countries that might be preferred.[2]

On the other hand, some U.S. companies—especially those that did business in nearby areas and in less developed countries—operated simply "extra-nationally," using methods and procedures adopted at home and merely extending the domestic enterprise.

In Mexico in 1914 American business met intense hostility. Once welcomed, U.S. enterprise now encountered pronounced difficulties. The ambivalence would be a harbinger for the future. In Canada, too, there had been hesitation on the part of the government and the public on how much U.S. capital was desirable, although no actions were taken to impede the flow of U.S. monies to the Dominion. American companies in the Caribbean faced innumerable obstacles in developing their operations. Americans were just beginning to make giant foreign investments in South America, and already they were clashing with some host governments (witness Jersey Standard's tax problems in Peru). In short, in the process of going abroad, American companies met unfamiliar conditions and shaped their strategies accordingly.

Yet how extensive actually was this pre-World War I foreign investment? The skeptic will counter that it is fine to say Americans were interested in foreign investments before the First World War, but that America was nevertheless a debtor in international accounts. Moreover, he argues, in 1914 U.S. foreign stakes were small compared with those of the major creditor nation, Great Britain, and also small in absolute terms. The skeptic will insist that U.S. business abroad was peripheral to most domestic enterprise, and that the companies that could be called "multinational" were few in number.

Table X.1. U. S. and European foreign investments in 1914
(book value in billions of dollars)

Country	Total
United States	$ 3.5[a]
Great Britain	18.3
France	8.7
Germany	5.6
Belgium, Netherlands, Switzerland	5.5

Source: W. S. Woytinsky and E. S. Woytinsky, *World Commerce and Governments,* New York: The Twentieth Century Fund, 1955, p. 191.

[a] Figures on direct and portfolio investments available only for the United States: $2.6 billion direct investment and $.9 billion portfolio investment.

It is true that in 1914 America was a debtor—a recipient of more foreign capital than the nation invested abroad. The skeptic is indeed correct that U.S. foreign investments were small compared with those of Britain, and, for that matter, France and Germany (see Table X.1). Regrettably, we do not have direct investment figures for the European nations and so have no basis for comparison on this score, but the totals support the skeptic. Mexico, Cuba, and Panama (and perhaps some other Central American countries) were probably the only nations in the world where U.S. foreign (direct or portfolio) investment in 1914 exceeded the British stake.[3]

The skeptic is also right in saying the size of U.S. direct investment in 1914 was small—the estimate is only $2.65 billion. This sum is less than the direct foreign investment *outflow* from the United States in certain individual years in the 1960s. Yet the skeptic is no historian. The historian wants to know how this figure fits into the then contemporary context. The Gross National Product of the United States in 1914 was only $36.4 billion. By simple arithmetic, *U.S. direct foreign investment in 1914 comprised a sum equal to 7 per cent of the U.S. GNP.* In the 1960s we talked about the huge direct investments abroad by U.S. business. In 1966, the GNP of the U.S. was $739.5 billion, while the book value of U.S. direct investments abroad totaled $54.6 billion—or *7 per cent* of our GNP.[4] Keeping this in mind, let us briefly summarize the U.S. direct investment in 1914 by area and by sector and then consider the last two objections of the skeptic: that foreign business was simply peripheral to domestic business and that the number of "multinational" concerns was negligible.

2

The evidence makes it clear that before 1914 American enterprise invested in developed, developing, and less developed countries around the world. The stakes differed according to the distance of the host country from the United States and according to the host country's state of economic development. This conclusion—derived from the data presented earlier—becomes explicit as we review in summary and schematically U.S. direct investment in 1914.[5]

The greatest U.S. direct investments in 1914 were in Canada ($618 million), which had just surpassed Mexico, the previous holder of first place. We have seen that U.S. companies investing in the Dominion sought both markets and sources of supply. Canada was nearby, and the per capita income was high enough to provide a market for U.S. goods. In the period before 1914 our evidence indicates that in order to sell in the Dominion, U.S. companies jumped over the tariff barrier and started the development of many Canadian secondary manufacturing industries. This was probably more important than the U.S. stakes "in the direction of perpetuating Canada's traditional status as a staple-producing economy." The Dominion was exceptional in the Western Hemisphere in attracting a large number of U.S. manufactories.[6]

Mexico ranked second only to Canada in having U.S. direct investment, estimated at $587 million in 1914. A major reason Mexico held this prominent position was its proximity to the United States. The U.S. investments there were dictated by the state of economic development. They predominated in mining and railroads. By 1914 stakes in oil production were rapidly mounting. The traditional pattern of a developed country investing in a less developed country prevailed.

As for the other nearby underdeveloped areas in the Western Hemisphere—the Caribbean islands and Central America (U.S. direct investment estimated at $371 million in 1914)—the main direct investments were in obtaining sources of supply. The stakes were in large part in agriculture. In South America ($323 million in U.S. direct investment in 1914), Americans sought raw materials and the giant investments were made in mining. Underdeveloped areas, with their low per capita income, did not warrant immense direct investments by U.S. companies in distribution and manufacturing to meet the demands in local markets; although the markets were tempting, only small investments were made in these sectors.

By contrast, the substantial U.S. direct investment in Europe ($573 million in 1914) was concentrated in selling, assembling, processing (including oil refining and blending plants), and manufacturing. U.S. manufacturing, petroleum, and insurance * companies made such entries. European markets were relatively familiar to Americans, who had emigrated from Europe or whose ancestors had crossed the Atlantic. Europe was "psychologically" nearby. Moreover, Europeans had a relatively high per capita income and could afford American products.

When we turn from the Western Hemisphere and Europe to consider U.S. stakes in more "distant" areas, we look toward regions that have not been treated in detail in this volume. The reason lies in the limited amount of U.S. direct investment. It is not that American businessmen were not concerned with investment in Asia, Oceania, and Africa; they were. The China trade, as we have seen, was very important to American development; investments in outposts in China were among the early U.S. stakes abroad. In political and business circles in the United States there was in the late nineteenth century enormous attention paid to Asian markets. As we have noted, the acquisition of the Philippines was viewed as a stepping stone to Eastern commerce. The actual investment did not reflect the rhetoric; [7] American direct investment in Asia in 1914 totaled only $120 million. The Orient was far away and relatively unknown to American businessmen; the risks and costs of investment rose with distance. The parts of Asia colonized by European powers were

* Selling only.

often inaccessible to U.S. enterprise. By 1914 U.S. direct investments in Asia—from the Ottoman Empire to China to the Philippines—were scattered and heterogeneous. By way of brief summary, they included:

(1) Outposts of trading and shipping firms (some with long histories). By 1914 roughly 80 American trading and shipping firms had such outlets in China alone.

(2) Independent American citizens with a wide range of small businesses (from retailing to manufacturing to sugar centrals). This was especially evident in the Philippines, where the American "colony" (not including the army of occupation) was estimated at from 10,000 to 20,-000 individuals in the early 1900s.

(3) Traders turned investors in projects (from railroads, to mines, to cotton mills). Before 1914 the American Trading Company had, for example, invested in other than trading enterprises in Korea, Japan, and in China; other American merchants had become investors in the Shanghai Rice Mill Company and the Shanghai Pulp and Paper Corporation.

(4) Financial syndicates holding concessions (for railroads, mining, or installing electrical and telephone facilities). Some of those started in China were by 1914 already out of business.*

(5) Fourteen Far Eastern branches of the International Banking Corporation.

(6) Sales outlets of the large U.S. insurance companies.

(7) Branches and subsidiaries of the giant U.S. manufacturing and petroleum enterprises (mainly for marketing, although a handful of companies were manufacturing in the Far East). Some large corporations were purchasing supplies and had direct outlets for this purpose (International Harvester in the Philippines and American Tobacco in Turkey

---

* For example, the American China Development Company, organized in 1895, obtained a concession to build the Hankow-Canton railway in April 1898. In July 1900 it made its first investments. The American shareholders then sold it to a Belgian syndicate—contrary to the provision in their contract, which prohibited the transfer of rights "to other nations." The Chinese demanded the agreement be voided. But in 1905, to restore the original state of affairs, the House of Morgan acquired control of the controversial company. The Chinese still wanted to void the contract and bought the properties for $6,750,000 (Remer, *Foreign Investments in China*, pp. 258–259). There were also the fruitless plans of E. H. Harriman to acquire the South Manchuria Railway and the Chinese Eastern Railway (Eckenrode and Edmunds, *E. H. Harriman*, pp. 98–99).

are examples). To my knowledge, only three international industrial corporations—Standard Oil of New Jersey and U.S. Rubber Company in the Dutch East Indies and Standard Oil of New York in China and Palestine—had investments or definite plans for investments * in raw materials. Stakes in Asia—as elsewhere—varied according to a country's state of development or underdevelopment. United States *manufacturing* companies had their key interests in Japan—a relatively developed nation—rather than in Turkey, India, or China. Although there was substantial U.S. direct investment in petroleum distribution in the Orient —"oil for the lamps of China"—the estimated total for *all* of Asia in 1914 was $40 million, which was less than one third of the U.S. direct investment in petroleum distribution in Europe. To repeat, Europe had the larger sum because it had the higher per capita income and thus offered the bigger market.[8]

As for Oceania ($17 million in U.S. direct investment in 1914), the explanation for the very low level of U.S. direct investment lies, I believe, primarily in the matter of distance plus unfamiliarity on the part of Americans. An added reason was that the low population of Australia meant a small sales potential. Yet because of the relatively high standard of living in Australia, as Table X.2 will show, aggressive U.S. manufacturing, oil, and insurance companies did make small investments, primarily in marketing.† About a handful went into manufacturing in Australia—for instance, American Tobacco (1894) and National Ammonia (1896). Swift, which opened a meatpacking plant in 1914 in Australia— for export—was an exception.[9]

Africa (a bare $13 million U.S. direct investment in 1914) was *terra incognita* for the American investor. Some trading firms, however, maintained outposts. The enterprising Guggenheims and other financial interests had invested in lucrative diamond mining and unprofitable rubber growing in the Belgian Congo. While no large U.S. corporate

---

* Standard Oil of New York made its Chinese contract in February 1914. It spent more than $2 million prospecting in 1914 (*China Year Book 1926*, p. 123).

† The figures in Table V.2 give the Oceania investment as $2 million in petroleum (which was all distribution), $5 million in sales organizations (again distribution) and $10 million in manufacturing. My own research indicates that the $2 million in petroleum distribution may be too low a figure, while the $10 million in manufacturing is probably too high. I would suggest that a number of investments that were in distribution were mistaken by Miss Lewis as being in manufacturing.

stakes appear to have existed in gold mining in South Africa, individual Americans in the Transvaal who managed the mines speculated in gold mining stock. As Table X.2 will indicate, certain U.S. manufacturing, oil, and insurance companies established direct distribution outlets in Africa, mainly in South Africa. There, a number of U.S. industrial companies opened sales branches to supply the needs of the gold miners. To this author's knowledge, no U.S. direct investments in manufacturing in Africa existed before World War I. The U.S. oil companies in Africa invested solely in marketing and not, up to 1914, in exploration, production, or refining. Indeed, on the whole, Africa was out of American businessmen's investment orbit. This could be attributed to several factors: to the European political dominance on that continent; to the distance from the United States; to the alternative opportunities for U.S. capital; and, chiefly, to the low per capita income of black Africa, which meant only small markets for American products.[10]

3

In 1914, mining held first rank in dollar totals among the sectors that attracted U.S. direct foreign investment (estimated $720 million—book value). This was because of the U.S. direct investments in South America and Mexico and the smaller stakes in Canada. Manufacturing was in second place (in 1914, $478 million), mainly because of U.S. direct investments in Canada and Europe. These figures, however, seem to be misleading. Mining required a substantial flow of U.S. capital. In terms used by economists, the mining enterprises involved "indivisibilities"—a large minimum investment was needed to get the project started. This was not true of most foreign manufacturing activities of this era. Generally, U.S. foreign investments in manufacturing grew gradually, in many cases using reinvested profits. The capital outflow in the years before 1914 for manufactories was usually small. It would appear that even though manufacturing ranked far below mining in terms of the book value of U.S. direct investment abroad in 1914, what is vastly more important is that *the foundations* for the subsequent expansion of U.S. manufacturing abroad had by this time already been laid. This root investment in manufacturing cannot be ignored.

Occupying third and fourth place in the sectors attracting U.S. foreign investments were agriculture ($356 million in 1914) and petroleum ($343 million in 1914). The figure for agriculture comprises mainly investments in the nearby areas: in the Caribbean (sugar and fruit) and Canada (timber). While the oil companies had begun to make some investments in oil production abroad, the petroleum stake was primarily in distribution (including some refining in consumer countries); it was worldwide, although more than one third of it was concentrated in Europe. It should be remembered that the United States was still a large oil exporter.[11]

4

The skeptic's claim that for major U.S. enterprises of the pre-World War I years foreign business was simply peripheral to domestic investment seems to be supported by the evidence. It does seem that with the exception of Standard Oil of New Jersey, Singer Sewing Machine, International Harvester, New York Life, and perhaps a handful of other large companies, foreign activities did not make a substantial contribution to the profits of U.S. enterprises. In 1914 the vast majority of American corporations were *not* multinational (this is true today as well). Many American corporations in 1914 had only obtained a foreign stake in a single country outside the United States—often a nearby country; many others had no interests abroad. Nonetheless, what is important is that foreign business was *not* peripheral in terms of the aspirations of the nation's key industrial leaders. Even though their domestic interests were generally larger and on the whole sources of greater profit, their vision of expanding abroad was very much in evidence. Not only did leaders in U.S. industry dream of American business not just in American terms, but in multinational terms—more important, by 1914 a number of major American enterprises actually had operations in many foreign nations.

In key markets abroad leading American companies had introduced small direct investments in sales outlets. This would be the first step for many companies in making direct investments abroad.* It is impossible

---

* Earlier we pointed out that too often people neglect the early sales branches and subsidiaries. Writers ask in their questionnaires: When did your firm first start to manufacture in a particular country? To understand the growth of international business the *questions* should be: When did your company first open any kind of operation in the particular country (sales, etc.)? And only then: When did your company first start to manufacture or refine in the particular country? (The dates—especially in the early years—will frequently be different.)

Table X.2. Some U. S. international companies—1914 Sales branches or subsidiaries in Asia, Africa, Oceania, and Latin America [a]

Company	Asia	Africa	Oceania	Latin America
Allis Chalmers				
Ault & Wilborg (later Interchemical)	Shanghai Manila	Johannesburg (1903)		Yes [b]
B. F. Avery				Buenos Aires (1910)
British-American Tobacco	Yes [c]		Yes [c]	Yes [c]
J. F. Case Threshing Machine				Yes
Chesebrough Mfg.				Yes
Columbia Phonograph	Hong Kong Shanghai		Sydney	
Colonial Oil				Yes
Dennison Mfg.				Mexico City (1912) Buenos Aires (1913)
Dorr		S. Africa (1912) Rhodesia (1912)	Melbourne (1911)	Mexico City (1908)
Eastman Kodak	Bombay	Capetown Cairo	Melbourne [c]	[d]
Equitable Life Assurance	Yes	Yes	Yes	Yes
Ford Motor				Buenos Aires (1913)
General Electric	Yes [c]	S. Africa (1898)	Australia (1898)	Yes
Goodyear				Mexico City (1911)
Ingersoll Rand		Johannesburg		
International Harvester	Yes		Australia (1912) New Zealand	Yes
International Steam Pump (later Worthington Pump & Machinery)	Calcutta		Sydney	Mexico City Buenos Aires

(continued)

Table X.2 (*continued*)

Company	Asia	Africa	Oceania	Latin America
National Cash Register			Australia (1893) N. Zealand (1907)	Yes
National Lead				Buenos Aires (1913)
National Paper & Type Co.				Buenos Aires (1913)
New York Life Insurance Co.	Yes	Yes	Yes	Yes
Parke, Davis	India China		Australia (1902)	
Remington Typewriter	India	S. Africa	Australia	Mexico City Buenos Aires (1911)
Sherwin-Williams	Yes	Durban Johannesburg	Yes	
Singer Sewing Machine	Yes	Yes	Yes	Yes [c]
Standard Oil of N.J. (& sub. West India Oil)				Yes [c]
Standard Oil of N.Y.	Yes [f]	Yes		
Texas Oil	Yes	Yes	Yes	Yes
United Shoe Machinery			Australia (1904) N. Zealand (1907)	Yes
U. S. Steel	Yes	Johannesburg	Sydney	Yes
Vacuum Oil	Bombay (1892) [e]	Yes	Australia New Zealand	

For sources and notes, see following page.

[209]

Sources: Corporate Annual Reports; company archives; Scudder Collection, Columbia University Library; company, industry, and diplomatic histories; Federal Trade Commission, Bureau of Corporations, and Department of Commerce reports. Charles W. Drees, ed. Americans in Argentina, Buenos Aires 1922 and William C. Downs, "The Commission House in Latin American Trade," Quarterly Journal of Economics, 26:118–139 (November 1911) were useful on Latin America. See note 36, Chapter IX, for more on Latin America and notes 6 and 7, Chapter X, for added references on Asia and Oceania.

a Date of establishment, when known, is in parentheses.
b "Yes" means more than one or two direct investments in sales branches or subsidiaries.
c Manufacturing or refining as well as sales.
d I have not verified such investments but circumstantial evidence indicates that they probably existed.
e May not have existed by 1914.
f Standard Oil of N.Y. had one of the largest investments in distribution:

ENTRIES ON ACCOUNTS OF STANDARD OIL OF NEW YORK, RE: ASIATIC BUSINESS

ASSETS	1903	1904	1905
Real Estate—Asiatic stations	$ 274,262.11	$ 439,632.23	$ 461,716.56
Construction—Asiatic stations	332,014.10	460,565.61	894,073.19
Office Furniture—Asiatic stations	17,088.18	23,727.90	34,277.00
Asiatic Floating Equipment	72,314.58	120,130.34	95,171.87
Accounts Receivable—Asiatic Books	407,989.49	611,867.48	2,431,563.88
Inventories—Asiatic Consignment	7,393,017.00	12,204,410.33	13,059,619.52
Cash—Asiatic stations	314,361.85	424,512.25	1,105,056.01
TOTAL ASSETS	8,810,992.31	14,284,846.14	18,081,478.03
Deduct Accounts payable	578,317.84	406,969.19	2,080,308.71
NET ASSETS	$8,232,674.47	$13,877,876.95	$16,001,169.26
Profits—Asiatic Consignment	2,228,141.74	1,669,819.64	1,875,432.32

The investment was large primarily owing to the need to carry heavy inventories, which were necessary because of the great quantities of oil in transit between United States and the distant Asiatic points. Source: Bureau of Corporations, Report on Petroleum Industry, pt. 3, pp. 589–590.

—in terms of space and evidence—to list every foreign sales branch and every foreign sales subsidiary of U.S. companies. In Canada and Europe they were clearly numerous. In 1907, for example, the British press reported there were 2,000 American firms in London and 10,000 American businessmen—doubtless an exaggeration, yet indicative of the expansion.[12] Table X.2 gives a rough indication of the extension of key U.S. manufacturing, oil, and insurance companies *outside of Canada and Europe* (the most popular places for expansion). The table is based on verified information that there was a *direct investment* in a sales outlet. Accordingly, entries for International Harvester do not reflect the 23 independent distributing agencies in South America, 15 in South Africa, 1 in Rhodesia, 8 in Australia, and 7 in Asia (1907). A business such as H. J. Heinz, with "agencies" in Latin America, Africa, and Australia, is omitted, because the agencies were apparently independent of the parent company. Similarly, Pabst Beer's foreign "agencies" are not included, since I cannot verify a direct investment. With the possible exception of B. F. Avery, and the definite exception of Colonial Oil and Standard Oil of New York, every company listed on Table X.2 had direct investments in sales and/or manufacturing or refining in Europe or Canada by 1914.* The table omits the numerous American trading houses with sales outlets around the world, as, for example, American Trading Company and Arkell & Douglas (together—16 branches on four continents), Carlowitz & Co. (7 branches in the Far East) or W. R. Grace & Co. (11 branches on the West Coast of South America).[13]

Today when we talk about multinational enterprise we do not refer to companies that simply have investments in sales outlets abroad. Writers always point to companies with direct investments in foreign manufacturing. At the reader has seen, Singer was the first American company to become multinational in these terms. By 1914, however, the number of U.S. manufacturing enterprises that had built or acquired foreign plants is larger than one might expect. Some of the companies that had more than two foreign factories are included on Table X.3.† The list excludes the many corporations with single manufactories in

* Note that two of the three exceptions were ex-Standard Oil companies, separated from Standard Oil in 1911 and thus still having special limited markets.
† Only verified operations are included.

Table X.3. The innovators: some manufacturing plants [a] built or purchased by American-owned companies between 1890 and 1914

Name	Britain	Germany	France	Austria	Italy	Russia	Canada	Elsewhere
Alcoa			×				×	
American Bicycle		×					×	
American Chicle	×						×	
American Cotton Oil							×	Holland
American Graphophone	×	×	×				×	
American Radiator	×	×	×	×	×		×	
American Tobacco [b]	×	×					×	Japan, Australia, Puerto Rico, Korea, China
Armour							×	Argentina
British-American Tobacco (see American Tobacco)								
Carborundum	×	×						
Chicago Pneumatic Tool	×	×					×	
Coca Cola							×	Cuba
Crown Cork & Seal							×	Mexico
Diamond Match	×	×					×	Brazil, Peru, Switzerland, South Africa
Eastman Kodak	×		×				×	Australia
Ford	× (mainly assembly)		× (only assembly)				×	
General Electric	×	d	d	d	d		e	Japan [d]
Gillette	×	×	×				×	
Heinz (H. J.)	×						×	Spain
International Harvester		×	×			×	×	Sweden
International Steam Pump	×	×	×	×			×	
Mergenthaler Linotype	×	×					×	
National Cash Register		×					×	
Norton		×					×	
Otis Elevator	×	×	×				×	
Parke, Davis	×					×	e	
Quaker Oats	e	×					×	
Sherwin-Williams	×						×	
Singer	e	×		e		×	e	
Stearns & Co. (Frederick) [f]							e	Australia
Swift							×	Argentina, Uruguay, Australia, Mexico

(continued)

Table X.3. (continued)

Name	Britain	Germany	France	Austria	Italy	Russia	Canada	Elsewhere
Torrington	×	×						
United Drug, Inc.	×						×	
United Shoe Machinery	×	×	×				×	
Western Electric	×	e	×	×	×	×	×	Belgium e, Japan
Westinghouse Air Brake	e	×	e			×	×	
Westinghouse Electric	×	×	×			×	×	

Sources: Corporate *Annual Reports;* company archives; Scudder Collection, Columbia University Library; *Moody's Manual;* company and industry histories; books on foreign investments; reports of the Mixed Claims Commission (United States and Germany); Marshall, Southard, Taylor, *Canadian-American Industry;* Federal Trade Commission, Bureau of Corporations, and Department of Commerce reports.

ª This list includes only American-financed concerns with manufacturing in more than one country. It includes direct investments with controlling interest—not just 100 per cent.

ᵇ Practically all these plants were transferred to Imperial Tobacco and British-American in 1902. The Korean factory was started after 1902 and closed by 1914; the Chinese factories were started after 1902.

ᶜ Plant built prior to 1890 by company or predecessor company.

ᵈ Agreements with manufacturing companies in which G.E. did not have controlling interest.

ᵉ Bulk packaging only.

ᶠ Acquired by Sterling Drugs in 1944.

foreign nations, for example, Burroughs Adding Machine Company, Electric Storage Battery Co., and Macguire Tramways in England; Julius Kayser & Co., Gramophone Company, and Steinway Pianos, in Germany; B. F. Goodrich in France; Pittsburgh Plate Glass and Federal Creosoting Company in Belgium; American Rolling Mill Company in Brazil. It also omits the numerous companies that established one or more plants in Canada.* [14]

* For instance, American Brake Shoe & Foundry (four plants by 1914), American Can (1912), American Cyanamid (1913), American Locomotive (1908), American Shipbuilding (1910–1911), Borden (1899), Computing-Tabulating-Recording (predecessor company, 1902), Deere (1911), Du Pont (1876 acquisition by American Powder Trust), Fairbanks,

Although the largest number of foreign stakes of U.S.-controlled international corporations was in the direction of sales and manufacturing,
U.S. companies had also made foreign investments in purchasing and
producing raw materials. The vast majority of such interests were by
companies that had interests only in a single country abroad. Some U.S.
businesses that had acquired raw material holdings in more than one
foreign country by 1914 are listed in Table X.4. The list is short. There
were far fewer companies with multinational extractive and agricultural
holdings than those with manufacturing stakes.

Interestingly, by 1914 certain American corporations were beginning
to make both market-oriented investments (sales outposts, manufacturing
plants, and oil refineries *) and supply-oriented investments (mines, oil
wells and refineries, farms, packing plants, plus purchasing outposts).
Table X.5 indicates some enterprises in these categories. Note that the
key "market-oriented" investments were in the developed countries in
the world and most supply-oriented stakes were in less developed areas
or in Canada.

In summary, it is significant that leading corporations in key industries in the United States were by 1914 involved in some kind of foreign
business. For the United States, which was still rich in raw materials, the
most remarkable phenomenon was not the search for supplies, but rather
the dispersal through investment of American technology abroad. Long
before 1914, while this country remained a debtor on international accounts, the U.S. companies with novel products and farsighted leadership came to make the most far-ranging entries into foreign lands. Not
only did these companies shape the development of industry in Canada,

---

Morse (1905), General Motors (predecessor companies), Goodyear (1910), International
Silver (1905), Ingersoll-Rand (by 1906), Link Belt (between 1905 and 1914), Neuralgyline
(by 1912; the company's name was changed to Sterling Products in 1917), Royal Baking
Powder (1906), Standard Sanitary (1910), Studebaker (predecessor company, 1909), U.S.
Rubber (1907), U.S. Steel (1913), Yates American Machine Tool (between 1905 and 1914).
The date in parenthesis—unless otherwise specified—indicates when the plant was built
or acquired. U.S. Dept. of Comm., Bureau of Foreign and Domestic Commerce, *American
Direct Investment in Foreign Countries*, p. 42, says American patent medicine and phar-
maceutical companies established at least fifteen manufactories in Canada between
1880 and 1913.

* In these years most but not all investments in oil refineries abroad were "market-
oriented" investments.

Table X.4. **Multinational extractive and/or agricultural holdings of U.S. companies acquired before 1914** [a]

Company	Country and/or region
Alcoa	France, British Guiana
Bethlehem Steel	Canada, Cuba, Mexico (?),[b] Chile [c]
General Asphalt	Venezuela, Trinidad
Guggenheim family [d]	Canada, Mexico, Chile, Belgian Congo
International Nickel	Canada, New Caledonia
International Salt	Spain, Italy [e]
Standard Oil of New Jersey	Canada, Rumania, Dutch East Indies, Peru, Mexico [f]
Standard Oil of New York	China, Palestine, Mexico [f]
United Fruit	Throughout the Caribbean
Virginia Carolina Chemical	Germany, Mexico

Sources: Same as for Table X.3, John Moody, *The Truth About Trusts,* and biographies of industrial leaders.

[a] The list excludes investments of men such as Bernard Baruch, Nelson W. Aldrich, Thomas Fortune Ryan, H. P. Whitney, J. P. Morgan, Minor C. Keith, and Herbert Hoover, who acquired personal holdings in mining and/or agricultural companies operating in two or more foreign countries. Baruch, Aldrich, Ryan, and Whitney had holdings in Mexico and the Congo; Morgan had holdings in Canada, Russia, and Peru; Keith had interests in the Caribbean and South America; Hoover had holdings in Peru and elsewhere. Some of these investments were direct investments, some were not.

[b] The San Toy Mining Co. in Mexico was said to be controlled by Schwab and other Pittsburgh capitalists (U.S. Senate, Subcommittee of the Committee on Foreign Relations, *Revolutions in Mexico, Hearings,* 41, 170, 692).

[c] The Chilean properties were leased.

[d] The Guggenheims were definitely direct investors; they operated through different companies in each country, but there was unquestionably Guggenheim influence on the management of these various enterprises.

[e] It is not clear that the company still owned these properties in 1914.

[f] The presidents of the companies, through Magnolia Petroleum Co. See Chapter VI.

but a large number invested in England—to exhibit the Republic's accomplishments in the former "workshop of the world." In 1901 a Britisher had concluded:

The most serious aspect of the American industrial invasion lies in the fact that these newcomers have acquired control of almost every

Table X.5. Some U. S.-owned companies with market- and supply-oriented direct foreign investments—1914

| Company | Market-oriented investments | | | Supply-oriented investments |
	Canada	Britain	Elsewhere	Country/countries
Alcoa	a	b	France, Europe b	f
Amalgamated Copper		b		Mexico
American Chicle	a	a		Mexico
American Tobacco			Cuba	Cuba, Turkey
Armour	a	b	Europe b	Argentina
British-American Tobacco	a		c d	England
Diamond Match		a	d	Canada
Du Pont	a			Chile
Guggenheim family		b	Europe b	f
International Harvester	a	a	c d	Philippines e Mexico (?)
International Nickel		b		f
Singer	a	a	c d	Russia (iron mines and timberlands to supply factory there)
Standard Oil of New Jersey	a		Europe b c	f
Standard Oil of New York			c	f
Swift & Co.	a	b	Europe b Mexico	Argentina, Uruguay, Australia
Texas Oil		b	c	Mexico
United Fruit		b	Europe b	f
U. S. Rubber	a	a		Sumatra
Virginia Carolina Chemical			Europe a	f

Sources: See note on sources in Tables X.2, X.3, and X.4.
[a] Existing operations more than just sales.
[b] Sales outlets only.
[c] See Table X.2.
[d] See Table X.3.
[e] Purchasing outlets only.
[f] See Table X.4.

new industry created during the past fifteen years . . . What are the chief new features in London life? They are, I take it, the telephone, the portable camera, the phonograph, the electric street car, the automobile, the typewriter, passenger lifts in houses, and the multiplication of machine tools. In everyone of these, save the petroleum automobile, the American maker is supreme; in several he is the monopolist.[15]

Had the same Britisher written in 1914, he would have to have added that with the Model T, the American maker was also supreme as far as the "petroleum automobile" was concerned.

I. Manuscript and Record Collections
Includes only collections either cited in the text or collections wherein the author obtained vital unpublished material.

Dearborn, Mich. Ford Motor Company Archives. Accession 76, Box 66. Foreign Dealer Contracts (1912–1913) and Accession 85. Ford Motor Company (1903–1919).

Madison, Wisc. State Historical Society of Wisconsin. McCormick Collection. Nettie Fowler McCormick Papers and Cyrus H. McCormick Papers.

———. ———. Singer Manufacturing Company Collection.

New York. American Radiator and Standard Sanitary Corporation. Records of American Radiator Company and Standard Sanitary Manufacturing Company

———. American Telephone and Telegraph Company. Records in Secretary's Office.

———. Columbia University Libraries. Department of Special Collections. Frank A. Vanderlip Papers and G. W. Perkins Papers.

———. ———. Graduate School of Business. Marvyn Scudder Financial Record Collection.

———. New York Life Insurance Company Archives. General Historical Records.

———. New York Public Library. Cruger Manuscripts, John Van Cortlandt Letter Book 1755–1760, and Philip Cuyler Letter Book, 1755–1760.

———. Otis Elevator Company, Records of International Division.

———. Western Electric Company Archives. General Historical Records.

Oakville, Ontario. Ford Motor Company of Canada, Ltd. Company Records.

Washington, D.C. National Archives. Record Group 59 (General Records of the Department of State). Record Group 76 (Records of International and Domestic Claims Commissions). Record Group 84 (Records of the Foreign Service Posts of the Department of State). Record Group 151 (Records of the Bureau of Foreign and Domestic Commerce, Department of Commerce).

West Orange, N.J. Edison National Historic Site, National Park Service, United States Department of the Interior. Papers of Thomas Alva Edison.

Windsor, Ontario. Ford Motor Company of Canada, Ltd. General Historical Records.

II. Companies Consulted

Many corporations provided valuable information, including interviews with prominent executives in the United States and abroad, company histories (some published and some in typescript), background papers (dealing with particular subsidiaries and their problems), along with published material (prospectuses, annual reports, company and industry journals, newspaper clippings, and specialized publications). It is unnecessary to document each piece of information from each corporation and to list each interview. Certain documents are cited in the notes. Executives of the following corporations (and subsidiaries or affiliates) in the United States and/or abroad made information available to the author.

Abbott Laboratories
Allis-Chalmers
Aluminium Ltd.
American and Foreign Power
American Cyanamid

American Metal Climax
American Radiator and Standard
  Sanitary
American Smelting and Refining
American Telephone and Telegraph
American Trading

Anaconda
Anderson, Clayton
Anglo-Lautero
Armour
Bethlehem Steel

Bristol-Myers
Burroughs
Cerro
Chesebrough-Pond's
Coca-Cola

Colgate-Palmolive
Corn Products
Deere
Du Pont (E. I.) de Nemours
Eastman Kodak

Firestone Tire and Rubber
Ford Motor
General Electric
General Motors

Goodyear Tire and Rubber
Grace (W. R.)
Gulf Oil
International Business Machines
International Harvester

International Packers
International Telephone and Telegraph
Johnson and Johnson
Kennecott Copper
Lilly (Eli)

Merck
Mobil Oil
National Cash Register
New York Life Insurance
Otis Elevator

Parke, Davis
Pfizer (Chas.)
Quaker Oats
Radio Corporation of America
Singer Sewing Machine

Smith Kline and French
Société Internationale Forestière
  et Minière du Congo
Sperry Rand
Standard Oil (N.J.)
Union Carbide

United Fruit
United Shoe Machinery
U.S. Rubber
Westinghouse Electric

III. **Government Documents (including the League of Nations and United Nations)**

A. Australia (all published in Melbourne).
Australia. Committee of Economic Enquiry. *Report.* 1965.
————. Department of Trade. *The Australian Pharmaceutical Products Industry.* 1960.
B. Canada (all published in Ottawa).
Canada. Department of Justice. Report of Commissioners, Combines Investigation Act. *Matches.* 1949.
————. Royal Commission on Canada's Economic Prospects. *Canada-United States Relations,* by Irving Brecher and S. S. Reisman. 1957.
————. ————. *The Canadian Automotive Industry,* by Sun Life Assurance Co. 1956.
————. ————. *Final Report.* 1957.
————. Task Force on the Structure of Canadian Industry. *Foreign Ownership and Structure of Canadian Industry.* 1968.
C. Costa Rica (published in San José).
Costa Rica. Laws, Statutes, etc. *Coleccion de las Leyes, Decretas y Ordenes.* 1886–
D. Great Britain (all published in London).
Great Britain. *Parliamentary Papers.* Vol. 7 (1841). First Report from Select Committee to Inquire into the Operation of the Existing Laws Affecting the Exportation of Machinery.
————. ————. Vol. 12 (1898). Report from Select Committee on Telephones.
————. ————. Vol. 96 (1899). Reports Respecting Telephone Service in Foreign Countries.
E. League of Nations
League of Nations. *Industrialization and Foreign Trade.* New York 1945.
————. *International Cartels,* by D. H. MacGregor. Geneva 1930.
————. *Review of the Economic Aspects of Several International Industry Agreements.* Geneva 1930.
E. United Nations (all published in New York)
U.N. Department of Economic Affairs, Fiscal Division. *International Tax Agreements.* Vol. 3. 1951.
————. Department of Economic and Social Affairs. *Foreign Capital in Latin America.* 1955.
————. Economic Commission for Latin America. *Towards a Dynamic Development Policy for Latin America,* by Raul Prebisch. 1963.
F. United States (all published in Washington, D.C.)
U.S. Bureau of Foreign and Domestic Commerce. *Special Consular Reports.* Nos. 1–86, 1890–1923.
————. *Monthly Summary of Commerce and Finance.* "Iron and Steel Trade" and "Lumber Trade." 1900.

U.S. Congress. House. *Report of Alien Property Custodian.* 65th Cong., 2nd sess. H. Doc. 840. 1918.

———. ———. Committee on Banking and Currency. *Money Trust Investigation. Hearings.* 62d Cong., 3d sess.

———. ———. Committee on Foreign Affairs. *Tin Investigation.* Report on H. Res. 404, 73d Cong., 2d sess. and H. Res. 71, 74th Cong., 1st sess.

———. ———. Committee on Merchant Marine and Fisheries. *Proceedings of the Committee on Merchant Marine and Fisheries in the Investigation of Shipping Combinations.* 62d Cong. 1913–1914.

———. ———. Committee on the Judiciary. *Trust Legislation. Hearings.* 63d Cong., 2d sess. Vol. 1. 1914.

———. ———. Committee on Ways and Means, *Private Foreign Investment.* Hearings before the Subcommittee on Foreign Trade Policy. 85th Cong., 2d sess. 1958.

———. Joint Economic Committee. *Foreign Government Restraints on United States Bank Operations Abroad.* 1967.

———. ———. Subcommittee on Inter-American Economic Relationships. *Private Investment in Latin America. Hearings.* 1964.

U.S. Congress. Senate. *American Branch Factories.* 71st Cong., 3d sess. Sen. Doc. 258. 1931.

———. ———. *American Branch Factories.* 73d Cong., 2d sess. Sen. Doc. 120. 1934.

———. ———. *Diplomatic History of the Panama Canal.* 63d Cong., 2d sess. Sen. Doc. 474. 1914.

———. ———. *Diplomatic Protection of American Petroleum Interests in Mesopotamia, Netherlands, East Indies and Mexico,* by Henry S. Fraser. 79th Cong., 1st sess. Sen. Doc. 43. 1945.

———. ———. Committee on Foreign Relations. *Investigation of Mexican Affairs.* Hearings and Report of Subcommittee on Foreign Relations. 66th Cong., 2d sess. Sen. Doc. 285. 2 vols. 1920 (Fall committee)

———. ———. Committee on Foreign Relations. *Revolutions in Mexico. Hearings.* 62d Cong., 2d sess. 1913 (Smith Committee).

———. ———. Committee on Foreign Relations. Subcommittee on American Republics Affairs. *United States-Latin American Relations.* 86th Cong., 2d sess. 1960.

———. ———. Committee on Interoceanic Canals. *Panama Canal.* Hearings. 62d Cong., 2d sess. 1912.

———. ———. Committee on Military Affairs. *Cartels and National Security.* Report of the Subcommittee on War Mobilization. 78th Cong., 2d sess. 1944.

———. ———. Committee on Military Affairs. *Economic and Political Aspects of International Cartels,* by Corwin Edwards. Subcommittee on War Mobilization, Monograph no. 1. 78th Cong., 2d sess. 1944.

U.S. Congress. Senate. Committee on Military Affairs. *Elimination of German Resources for War. Hearings.* 79th Cong., 1st sess. 1945–1946 (Kilgore Committee).

——. ——. Committee on Military Affairs. *Scientific and Technical Mobilization. Hearings.* 78th Cong., 1st sess. 1943 (Kilgore Committee).

——. ——. Committee on Patents. *Patents. Hearings.* 77th Cong., 2d sess. Parts 1–7. 1942 (Bone Committee).

——. ——. Committee on the Judiciary. *International Aspects of Antitrust.* Hearings before the Subcommittee on Antitrust and Monopoly. 89th Cong., 2d sess. 1967.

——. ——. Committee on the Judiciary. *Petroleum, The Antitrust Laws and Government Policies.* Report of Subcommittee on Antitrust and Monopoly. 85th Cong., 1st sess. 1957.

——. ——. Committee on the Judiciary. *A Study of the Anti-Trust Laws.* Hearings before Subcommittee on Antitrust and Monopoly. 84th Cong., 1st sess. Part 4. 1955.

——. ——. Special Committee Investigating Petroleum Resources. *American Petroleum Interests in Foreign Countries.* Hearings. 79th Cong., 1st sess. 1946 (O'Mahoney Committee).

——. ——. Special Committee Investigating the National Defense Program. *Investigation of the National Defense.* 77th Cong., 1st sess.–79th Cong., 1st sess. 1941–1945 (Truman Committee, 1941–June 1944).

U.S. Department of Commerce. Bureau of Foreign and Domestic Commerce. *American Direct Investments in Foreign Countries,* by Paul Dickens. Trade Information Bulletin, no. 731. 1930.

——. ——. *Daily Consular Trade Reports 1914.* 1914.

——. ——. *Foreign Capital Investments in Russian Industries and Commerce,* by Leonard J. Lewery. Miscellaneous Series, no. 124. 1923.

——. ——. Office of International Trade. *Factors Limiting U.S. Investment Abroad.* Parts 1 and 2, and Summary. 1953–1954.

——. ——. Office of International Trade. *Investment in Colombia.* 1953.

——. Bureau of Foreign Commerce. *Investment in Australia.* 1956.

——. ——. *Investment in Brazil.* 1961.

——. ——. *Investment in Chile.* 1960.

——. ——. *Investment in India.* 1961.

——. ——. *Investment in Indonesia.* 1956.

——. ——. *Investment in Japan.* 1956.

——. ——. *Investment in Mexico.* 1956.

——. ——. *Investment in the Philippines.* 1955.

——. ——. *Investment in the Union of South Africa.* 1954.

——. ——. *Investment in Turkey.* 1956.

——. Bureau of the Census. *Historical Statistics.* 1960.

U.S. Department of Commerce. Office of Business Economics. *Direct Private Foreign Investments of the United States.* 1953.

————. ————. *U.S. Business Investment in Foreign Countries.* 1960.

————. ————. *Survey of Current Business,* 1921+.

U.S. Department of Commerce and Labor. Bureau of Corporations. *Report of the Commissioner of Corporations on the Beef Industry.* 1905.

————. ————. *Report of the Commissioner of Corporations on International Harvester.* 1913.

————. ————. *Report of the Commissioner of Corporations on the Lumber Industry.* 1913–1914.

————. ————. *Report of the Commissioner of Corporations on the Petroleum Industry.* Part 3, "Foreign Trade." 1909.

————. ————. *Report of the Commissioner of Corporations on the Steel Industry.* 1911–1913.

————. ————. *Report of the Commissioner of Corporations on the Tobacco Industry.* 1909–1911.

————. Bureau of Manufactures. *Commercial Relations of United States with Foreign Countries, 1909.* 1911.

————. *Daily Consular and Trade Reports.* 1912.

————. ————. *Monthly Consular and Trade Reports 1905–1910.* 61 vols. 1905–1910.

————. Bureau of Statistics. *Consular Reports 1903–1905.* 12 vols. 1903–1905.

————. ————. *Foreign Commerce and Navigation 1867–1912.* 56 vols. 1867–1912.

U.S. Department of State. *Foreign Relations of the United States.* 1861+.

————. *List of Contracts of American Nationals with the Chinese Government.* 1925.

————. Bureau of Foreign Commerce. *Commercial Relations of the United States with Foreign Countries 1855/56–1902.* 54 vols. 1857–1903.

————. ————. *Consular Reports 1880–1903.* 72 vols. 1880–1903.

————. ————. *Special Consular Reports 1890–1903.* 26 vols. 1890–1903.

U.S. Federal Communications Commission. *Investigation of the Telephone Industry in the United States.* 1939.

U.S. Federal Trade Commission. *Electric Power Industry. Control of Power Companies.* 1927.

————. *Electric Power Industry. Supply of Electrical Equipment and Competitive Conditions.* 1928.

————. *Foreign Ownership in the Petroleum Industry.* 1923.

————. *Report on Cooperation in American Export Trade.* 1916.

————. *Report on International Electric Equipment Cartels.* 1948.

————. *Report on the Agricultural Implement and Machinery Industry.* 1938.

————. *Report on the Copper Industry.* 1947

U.S. Federal Trade Commission. *Report on the Copper Industry, Summary.* 1947.
———. *Report on the Meat-Packing Industry.* Summary and part 1. 1919.
———. Staff Report to Senate Select Committee on Small Business. *International Petroleum Cartel.* 1952.
U.S. Industrial Commission. *Reports of the Industrial Commission and Industrial Combinations.* 19 vols. 1900–1902.
U.S. Library of Congress. Legislative Reference Service. *Cartels and International Patent Agreements,* by Leisa G. Bronson, Public Affairs Bull. 32. 1944.
———. ———. *Expropriation of American Owned Property by Foreign Governments in the Twentieth Century.* 88th Cong., 1st sess. 1963.
U.S. Mixed Claims Commission, United States and Germany. *First Report of Marshall Morgan.* 1924.
———. *First Report of Robert W. Bonynge.* 1925.
———. *Report of Robert W. Bonynge.* 1934.
U.S. President. *A Compilation of the Messages and Papers of the Presidents 1789–1897.* Compiled by James D. Richardson. 10 vols. 1896–1899.
U.S. Special Mexican Claims Commission. *Report to the Secretary of State.* 1940.
U.S. Tariff Commission. *Mining and Manufacturing Industries in Colombia.* 1949.
U.S. Temporary National Economic Committee. *Investigation of Concentration of Economic Power. Hearings.* Parts 14–17, 20, 25. 1939–1940.
———. *Investigations of Concentration of Economic Power.* Monograph no. 6, "Export Prices and Export Cartels." 1940.
U.S. Treaties, etc. *Treaties and Other International Acts of the United States of America.* Edited by Hunter Miller. 8 vols. 1931–1948.
U.S. United States and Chilean Claims Commission. *The Alsop Claim.* The Case of the United States of America.
———. *Final Report of George H. Shields Before the United States and Chilean Claims Commission.* 1894.

IV. Court Cases
U.S. v. Aluminum Company of America, Eq. No. 85–73 (Southern District of New York 1940), *Brief of the Aluminum Company.*
U.S. v. American Sugar Refining Company. Testimony. Vol. 6. New York 1913.
U.S. v. American Tobacco Company, 164 Fed. 700 (Southern District New York 1908), revised and remanded 221 U.S. 106, 31 Sup. Ct. 632, 55 L. Ed. 663 (1911).
U.S. v. General Electric Co., 82 F. Supp. 753 (District New Jersey 1949).
U.S. v. General Electric Co., 115 F. Supp. 835 (District New Jersey 1953).
U.S. v. Imperial Chemical Industries, Ltd. 100 F. Supp. 504 (Southern District New York 1951).

U.S. v. Timken Roller Bearing Co., 83 F. Supp. 284 (Northern District Ohio 1849), modified and affirmed, 341 U.S. 593 (1951).

V. Foreign Investment and International Business
A. General

Adler, John H., ed. *Capital Movements and Economic Development. Proceedings of a Conference Held by the International Economic Association.* New York: St. Martin's Press, 1967.

Aharoni, Yair. *The Foreign Investment Process.* Boston: Division of Research, Graduate School of Business Administration, Harvard University, 1966.

Aitken, Thomas. *A Foreign Policy for American Business.* New York: Harper & Brothers, 1962.

Barlow, Edward R., and Wender, Ira T. *Foreign Investment and Taxation.* Englewood Cliffs, N.J.: Prentice-Hall, 1955.

————. *Management of Foreign Manufacturing Subsidiaries.* Boston: Division of Research, Graduate School of Business Administration, Harvard University, 1953.

Bauer, Raymond A., and Pool, Ithiel de Sola. *American Businessmen and International Trade.* Glencoe, Ill.: Free Press, 1960.

————, ————, and Dexter, Lewis Anthony. *American Businessmen and Public Policy.* New York: Atherton Press, 1963.

Behrman, Jack N. *Some Patterns in the Rise of the Multinational Enterprise.* Chapel Hill, N.C.: Graduate School of Business, University of North Carolina, 1969.

Benoit, Emile. "The Comparative Advantage of Producing Abroad." Typescript. 1961.

Blough, Roy. *International Business.* New York: McGraw-Hill, 1966.

Brewster, Kingman. *Antitrust and American Business Abroad.* New York: McGraw-Hill, 1958.

Cairncross, A. K. *Home and Foreign Investment 1870–1913.* Cambridge, England: Cambridge University Press, 1953.

Dunn, R. W. *American Foreign Investment.* New York: B. W. Huebsch and the Viking Press, 1926.

Ebb, Lawrence F. *Regulation and Protection of International Business.* St. Paul, Minn.: Western Publishing Co., 1964.

Fanning, Leonard M. *American Oil Operations Abroad.* New York and London: McGraw-Hill, 1947.

Fatouros, A. A. *Government Guarantees to Foreign Investors.* New York: Columbia University Press, 1962.

Fayerweather, John. *Management of International Operations.* New York: McGraw-Hill, 1960.

Feis, Herbert. *Europe, The World's Banker, 1870–1914*. New Haven: Yale University Press, 1930.

Fenn, Dan H., ed. *Management Guides to Overseas Operations*. New York: McGraw-Hill, 1957.

Friedmann, Wolfgang G., and Kalmanoff, George, eds. *Joint International Business Ventures*. New York: Columbia University Press, 1966.

———, and Pugh, Richard C. *Legal Aspects of Foreign Investment*. Boston: Little, Brown, 1958.

Fugate, Wilbur Lindsay. *Foreign Commerce and the Antitrust Laws*. Boston: Little, Brown, 1958.

Gaston, J. F. *Obstacles to Direct Foreign Investment*. New York: National Industrial Conference Board, 1951.

Goodrich, Carter. "Foreign Capital in the United States." Typescript. New York: Columbia University Library, n.d.

Hymer, Stephen. "The International Operations of National Firms." Ph.D. dissertation, Massachusetts Institute of Technology, 1960.

International Management Association. *Case Studies in Foreign Operations*. IMA Special Report No. 1. New York: International Management Association, 1957.

Jenks, Leland H. *The Migration of British Capital to 1875*. New York: Alfred A. Knopf, 1927.

Kindleberger, Charles P. *American Business Abroad*. New Haven: Yale University Press, 1969.

Lewis, Cleona. *America's Stake in International Investments*. Washington, D.C.: The Brookings Institution, 1938.

———. *The United States and Foreign Investment Problems*. Washington, D.C.: The Brookings Institution, 1948.

Meier, Gerald M. *Leading Issues in Development Economics*. Pp. 149–159. New York: Oxford University Press, 1964.

Mikesell, Raymond F., ed. *United States Private and Government Investment Abroad*. Eugene, Ore.: University of Oregon Press, 1962.

North, Douglass C. "The United States Balance of Payments 1790–1860" and Simon, Matthew. "The United States Balance of Payments, 1861–1900." In *Trends in the American Economy in the Nineteenth Century*. Studies in Income and Wealth, Vol. 24, pp. 573–715. Princeton: Princeton University Press, 1960.

Nurske, Ragnar. *Problems of Capital Formation in Underdeveloped Countries*. 1953 Reprint. New York: Oxford University Press, Galaxy Books, 1967.

———. "International Investment Today in the Light of Nineteenth Century Experience." *Economic Journal* 44 (December 1954):744–758.

Penrose, Edith. "Foreign Investment and the Growth of the Firm." *Economic Journal* 64 (June 1956):220–235.

Bibliography

Penrose, Edith. *The Large International Firm in Developing Countries: The International Petroleum Industry.* Cambridge, Mass.: M.I.T. Press, 1968.

Phelps, Clyde William. *Foreign Expansion of American Banks.* New York: Ronald Co., 1927.

Pierce, Harry H. "Foreign Investment in American Enterprise." In *Economic Change in the Civil War Era,* edited by David T. Gilchrist and W. David Lewis. Greenvale, Dela.: Eleutherian Mills-Hagley Foundation, 1964.

Polk, Judd, et al. *U.S. Production Abroad and the Balance of Payments.* New York: National Industrial Conference Board, 1966.

Robinson, Richard D. *International Business Policy.* New York: Holt, Rinehart and Winston, 1967.

Royal Institute of International Affairs. *The Problem of Foreign Investment.* London: Royal Institute of International Affairs, 1937.

Rubin, Seymour F. *Private Foreign Investment.* Baltimore: Johns Hopkins Press, 1956.

Singer, Hans. "Distribution of Gains Between Investing and Borrowing Countries" (1950). Reprinted in Hans Singer, *International Development,* pp. 161–172. New York: McGraw-Hill, 1964.

Southwestern Legal Foundation. *Proceedings of the 1959 Institute on Private Investment Abroad.* Albany, N.Y.: M. Bender, 1959.

Stahl, Everett. "Branch Factories in Foreign Countries." *Harvard Business Review* 8(1929):96–102.

Staley, Eugene W. *Raw Materials in Peace and War.* New York: Council on Foreign Relations, 1937.

Stead, W. T. *The Americanization of the World.* London: The "Review of Reviews" Office, 1902.

Vernon, Raymond. "Foreign-Owned Enterprise in the Developing Countries." *Public Policy* 15 (1966):361–380.

———. "International Investment and International Trade in the Product Cycle." *Quarterly Journal of Economics* 80 (1966):190–207.

———. "Long Run Trends in Concession Contracts." *Proceedings of American Society of International Law,* 61st Meeting. Pp. 81–89. Washington, D.C.: American Society of International Law, 1967.

———. *Manager in the International Economy.* Englewood Cliffs, N.J.: Prentice-Hall, 1968.

———. "Multinational Enterprise and National Sovereignty." *Harvard Business Review* 45 (March–April, 1967):156–172.

———. "Saints and Sinners in Foreign Investment." *Harvard Business Review* 41 (May–June, 1963):146–161.

Williamson, Jeffrey G. *American Growth and the Balance of Payments, 1820–1913.* Chapel Hill, N.C.: University of North Carolina Press, 1964.

Wilson, F. M. Huntington. "The Relation of the Government to Foreign Investment." *Annals of the American Academy of Political and Social Science* 48 (November 1916):298–311.

B. *Canada*

Aitken, Hugh G. J. *American Capital and Canadian Resources.* Cambridge, Mass.: Harvard University Press, 1961.

————. *The American Economic Impact on Canada.* Durham, N.C.: Duke University Press, 1959.

Canadian-American Committee. *Policies and Practices of United States Subsidiaries in Canada,* by John Lindeman and Donald Armstrong. Montreal (?): Canadian-American Committee, 1961.

Marshall, Herbert, Southard, Frank A., Jr., and Taylor, Kenneth W. *Canadian-American Industry.* New Haven: Yale University Press, 1936.

Moore, Elwood S. *American Influence in Canadian Mining.* Toronto: University of Toronto Press, 1941.

Safarian, A. E. *Foreign Ownership of Canadian Industry.* Toronto: McGraw-Hill Co. of Canada, 1966.

Southworth, Constant. "The American-Canadian Newsprint Industry and the Tariff." *Journal of Political Economy* 30 (1922): 681–697.

Viner, Jacob. *Canada's Balance of International Indebtedness 1900–1913.* Cambridge, Mass.: Harvard University Press, 1924.

Wilgus, W. J. *The Railway Interrelations of the United States and Canada.* New Haven: Yale University Press, 1937.

C. *Latin America*

Bernstein, Marvin, ed. *Foreign Investment in Latin America.* New York: Knopf, 1966.

Drees, Charles W., ed. *Americans in Argentina.* Buenos Aires, 1922.

Feuerlein, Willy, and Hannan, Elizabeth. *Dollars in Latin America.* New York: Council on Foreign Relations, 1941.

Gaither, Roscoe B. *Expropriation in Mexico.* New York: W. Morrow and Co., 1940.

Gordon, Wendell C. *The Expropriation of Foreign-Owned Property in Mexico.* New York: Graduate School of Arts and Science of New York University, 1941.

Historia Moderna de Mexico, El Porfiriata, La Vida Economica. Vol. 2. Mexico: Colegio de Mexico, 1965.

Kalmanoff, George. "Joint International Business Ventures in Mexico." Mimeographed. New York: Columbia University Library, 1959.

Meyer, Lorenzo. *Mexico y Estados Unidos en el Conflicto Petrolero (1917–1924).* Mexico: Colegio de Mexico, 1968

Mikesell, Raymond. *Foreign Investments in Latin America.* Washington, D.C.: Department of Economic and Social Affairs, Pan American Union, 1955.

Moore, J. R. "The Impact of Foreign Direct Investment on an Underdeveloped Economy: The Venezuelan Case." Ph.D. dissertation, Cornell University, 1956.

Osterheld, T. W. "History of the Nationalization of the Railroads in Mexico." *American Bankers Association Journal* 8 (1914):997–1003.

Pan American Petroleum & Transport Company. *Mexican Petroleum.* New York: Pan American Petroleum & Transport Co., 1922.

Phelps, Dudley Maynard. *Migration of Industry to South America.* New York and London: McGraw-Hill Book Co., 1936.

Pletcher, David. *Rails, Mines, and Progress: Seven American Promoters in Mexico, 1867–1911.* Ithaca: Cornell University Press, 1958.

Rippy, J. Fred. *British Investment in Latin America 1822–1949.* Minneapolis: University of Minnesota Press, 1959.

————. *The Capitalists and Colombia.* New York: The Vanguard Press, 1931.

————. "Investments of Citizens of the United States in Latin America." *The Journal of Business* 22 (1949):17–29.

Tischendorf, Alfred. *Great Britain and Mexico in the Era of Porfirio Díaz.* Durham, N.C.: Duke University Press, 1961.

Vernon, Raymond, ed. *How Latin America Views the U.S. Investor.* New York: Praeger, 1965.

————, ed. *Public Policy and Private Enterprise in Mexico.* Cambridge, Mass.: Harvard University Press, 1964.

Winkler, Max. *Investments of United States Capital in Latin America.* Boston: World Peace Foundation, 1928.

Wurfel, Seymour W. *Foreign Enterprise in Colombia.* Chapel Hill, N.C.: University of North Carolina Press, 1965.

Wythe, George. *Industry in Latin America.* New York: Columbia University Press, 1945.

D. Europe

Dunning, John H. *American Investment in British Manufacturing Industry.* London: Allen & Unwin, 1958.

Heindel, Richard Heathcote. *The American Impact on Great Britain 1898–1914.* Philadelphia: University of Pennsylvania Press, 1940.

Layton, Christopher. *Trans-Atlantic Investments.* Boulogne-sur-Seine, France: Atlantic Institute, 1966.

McCreary, Edward A. *The Americanization of Europe.* Garden City, N.Y.: Doubleday, 1964.

McKenzie, Fred A. *The American Invaders.* London: H. W. Bell, 1901.

Queen, George Sherman. "The United States and the Material Advance of Russia 1881–1906." Ph.D. dissertation, University of Illinois, 1941.

Servan-Schreiber, J. J. *The American Challenge.* Translated by Ronald Steel. New York: Atheneum, 1968.

Southard, Frank A. *American Industry in Europe.* Boston: Houghton-Mifflin, 1931.

Thwaite, B. H. *The American Invasion*. London: S. Sonnenschein & Co., 1902.

Williams, Francis. *The American Invasion*. New York: Crown Publishers, 1962.

E. *Asia*

Allen, George C., and Donnithorne, Audrey G. *Western Enterprise in Far Eastern Development*. New York: Macmillan, 1954.

————, ————. *Western Enterprise in Indonesia and Malaya*. London: G. Allen & Unwin, 1957.

Callis, H. G. *Foreign Capital in Southeast Asia*. New York: International Secretariat, Institute of Pacific Relations, 1942.

Hou, Chi-ming. *Foreign Investment and Economic Development in China 1840–1937*. Cambridge, Mass.: Harvard University Press, 1965.

Overlach, Theodore William. *Foreign Financial Control in China*. New York: The Macmillan Co., 1919.

Remer, C. F. *Foreign Investment in China*. New York: The Macmillan Co., 1933.

F. *Oceania*

Brash, Donald T. *American Investment in Australian Industry*. Cambridge, Mass.: Harvard University Press, 1966.

G. *Africa*

Frankel, S. Herbert. *Capital Investment in Africa*. London: Oxford University Press, 1938.

VI. **Company Histories and Business Biographies (including studies of particular companies in international business)**

Abbott, Lawrence F. *The Story of NYLIC*. New York: New York Life Insurance, 1930.

Ackerman, Carl. *George Eastman*. Boston and New York: Houghton Mifflin Co., 1930.

Adams, Frederick Upham. *Conquest of the Tropics*. Garden City, N.Y.: Doubleday, Page & Co., 1914 (United Fruit Co.).

Aitken, William B. *Distinguished Families in America, Descended from Wilhelmus Beekman*. New York: Knickerbocker Press, 1912.

Allen, Hugh. *The House of Goodyear*. Cleveland: Corday & Gross Co., 1943.

American and Foreign Power Company, Inc. *The Foreign Power System*. New York: American and Foreign Power Co., 1953 (booklet).

Armstrong, Theodore: *Our Company*. Dayton: National Cash Register Co., 1949.

Association of Edison Illuminating Companies. *Edison*. New York: Association of Edison Illuminating Companies, 1929.

Atkins, Edwin Farnsworth. *Sixty Years in Cuba, Reminiscences of Edwin F. Atkins*. Cambridge, Mass.: Riverside Press, 1926.

Babcock, Glenn D. *History of United States Rubber Company*. Bloomington, Ind.: Bureau of Business Research, Graduate School of Business, Indiana University, 1966.

Baldwin Locomotive Works. *History of the Baldwin Locomotive 1831–1923*. Philadelphia: privately printed, n.d.

Baruch, Bernard M. *Baruch: My Own Story*. New York: Holt, 1957.

Baxter, William T. *The House of Hancock*. Cambridge, Mass.: Harvard University Press, 1945.

Belden, Thomas Graham, and Belden, Marva Robins. *The Lengthening Shadow, The Life of Thomas J. Watson*. Boston: Little, Brown, 1962.

Bell, Alexander Graham. *Deposition of Alexander Graham Bell*. 1892.

Bernfeld, Seymour S. "A Short History of American Metal Climax, Inc." In *American Metal Climax, Inc. World Atlas*, pp. 1–16. New York: n.p., n.d. [1962].

Bezanson, Ann. "The Invention of the Safety Razor: Further Comments." *Explorations in Entrepreneurial History* 4 (1952):193–198.

Bridge, James Howard. *The Inside History of the Carnegie Steel Company*. New York: The Aldine Book Co., 1903.

Broderick, John F. *Forty Years with General Electric*. Albany: Fort Orange Press, 1929.

Buley, R. Carlyle. *The Equitable Assurance Society*. New York: Appleton-Century-Crofts, 1959.

———. *The Equitable Assurance Society of the United States 1859–1964*. 2 vols. New York: Appleton-Century-Crofts, 1967

Burgess, Eugene W., and Harbison, Frederick H. *Casa Grace in Peru*. Washington: National Planning Association, 1954.

Byars, William V., ed. *B. and M. Gratz, Merchants in Philadelphia 1754–1798*. Jefferson City Mo.: The Hugh Stephens Printing Co., 1916.

Candler, Charles Howard. *Asa Griggs Candler*. Atlanta, Ga.: Emory University Press, 1950.

Carr, Charles C. *Alcoa, an American Enterprise*. New York: Rinehart, 1952.

Carr, William H. A. *The Du Ponts of Delaware*. New York: Dodd, Mead, 1964.

Clark, Roscoe Collins. *Threescore Years and Ten, a Narrative of the First Seventy Years of Eli Lilly and Company 1876–1946*. Chicago: The Lakeside Press, R. R. Donnelly & Sons Co., 1946.

Cleland, Robert G. *A History of Phelps Dodge, 1834–1950*. New York: Alfred A. Knopf, 1952.

Clough, Shepard B. *A Century of American Life Insurance: A History of the Mutual Life Insurance Company of New York*. New York: Columbia University Press, 1946.

Cochran, Thomas C. *The Pabst Brewing Company*. New York: New York University Press, 1948.

———, and Reina, Reuben E. *Entrepreneurship in Argentine Culture*. Philadelphia: University of Pennsylvania Press, 1962.

Coon, Horace. *American Tel & Tel; the Story of a Great Monopoly*. New York: Longmans, Green and Co., 1939.

Corey, Lewis. *The House of Morgan.* New York: G. H. Watt, 1930.

Corti, Egon Caesar. *The Reign of the House of Rothschild.* Translated by Brian and Beatrix Lunn. New York: Cosmopolitan Book Corp., 1928.

Costa Rica Railway Co. *Concessions, Contracts and Decrees, 1879–1913.* Boston: privately printed, 1914.

Croly, Herbert. *Willard Straight.* New York: Macmillan Co., 1924.

Crowther, Samuel. *John H. Patterson.* Garden City, N.Y.: Doubleday, Page & Co., 1924.

———. *The Romance and Rise of the American Tropics.* Garden City, N.Y.: Doubleday, Doran & Co., 1929 (United Fruit).

Danielian, N. R. *A. T. & T., the Story of Industrial Conquest.* New York: Vanguard Press, 1939.

Davies, Robert Bruce. "The International Operations of the Singer Manufacturing Company 1854–1895." Ph.D. dissertation, University of Wisconsin, 1966.

———. "Peacefully Working to Conquer World Markets." *Business History Review* 43 (1969):299–325.

Diamond Match Company. *The Diamond Years.* n.p., 1956.

Donner, Frederick. *The Worldwide Industrial Enterprise.* New York: McGraw-Hill, 1967 (General Motors).

Dorian, Max. *The Du Ponts.* Translated by Edward B. Garside. Boston: Little, Brown, 1962.

Dutton, William S. *Du Pont.* New York: Charles Scribner's Sons, 1942.

Dyer, Frank Lewis, and Martin, Thomas Commerford. *Edison, His Life and Inventions.* 2 vols. New York and London: Harper & Brothers, 1929.

Eckenrode, H. J., and Edmunds, Pocahontas Wight. *E. H. Harriman, the Little Giant of Wall Street.* New York: Greenberg, 1933.

Emmet, Boris, and Jenck, John C. *Catalogues and Counters: A History of Sears, Roebuck.* Chicago: University of Chicago Press, 1950.

Engelbourg, Saul. "International Business Machines. A Business History." Ph.D. dissertation, Columbia University, 1954.

Everts, William W. *William Colgate, Christian Layman.* Philadelphia: American Baptist Publication Society, 1881.

Fetherstonhaugh, R. C. *Charles Fleetford Sise, 1834–1918.* Montreal: Gazette Printing Co. for the Bell Telephone Co. of Canada, 1944.

Flint, Charles R. *Memories of an Active Life.* New York and London: G. P. Putnam's Sons, 1923.

Forbes, Robert B. *Personal Reminiscences.* Boston: Little, Brown, 1882.

France, Boyd. *IBM in France.* Washington, D.C.: National Planning Association, 1961.

Garraty, John A. *Right-Hand Man: The Life of George W. Perkins.* New York: Harper, 1960.

Gauld, Charles Anderson. *The Last Titan: Percival Farquhar, American Entrepreneur in Latin America.* Stanford: University Press, 1964.

Geiger, Theodore. *The General Electric Company in Brazil.* Washington, D.C.: National Planning Association, 1961.

Gerretson, F. C. *History of Royal Dutch.* 4 vols. Leiden: E. J. Brill, 1953–1957.

Gibb, George Sweet, and Knowlton, Evelyn H. *The Resurgent Years 1911–1927.* New York: Harper, 1956.

Grace, J. Peter. *W. R. Grace and the Enterprises He Created.* New York: Newcomen Society in North America, 1953.

Gras, N. S. B., and Larson, Henrietta. *Casebook in American Business History.* New York: F. S. Crofts & Co., 1939.

Gray, James. *Business without Boundaries. The Story of General Mills.* Minneapolis: University of Minnesota Press, 1954.

Hammond, John Hays. *The Autobiography of John Hays Hammond.* 2 vols. New York: Farrar and Rinehart, 1935.

Hammond, John Winthrop. *Men and Volts. The Story of General Electric.* Philadelphia: J. B. Lippincott Co., 1941.

Hanke, Lewis. "A Note on the Life and Publications of Colonel George Earl Church." *Books at Brown* 20 (1965):131–163.

Hardin, Shields T. *The Colgate Story.* New York: Vantage Press, 1959.

Harrington, Fred. *God, Mammon, and the Japanese.* Madison: The University of Wisconsin Press, 1944.

Harvard University, Graduate School of Business Administration. "Moore-McCormack Lines, Inc." Case no. AM-P 181. Mimeographed. Boston: Graduate School of Business Administration, Harvard University, n.d.

———, ———. "United Fruit Company." Case no. ICH 150. Mimeographed. Boston: Graduate School of Business Administration, Harvard University, n.d.

Hatch, Alden. *American Express.* Garden City, N.Y.: Doubleday, 1950.

Haven, Charles T., and Belden, Frank A. *A History of the Colt Revolver.* New York: W. Morrow & Co., 1940.

Hidy, Ralph, and Hidy, Muriel. *Pioneering in Big Business.* New York: Harper, 1955.

Higgins, Benjamin, et al. *Stanvac in Indonesia.* Washington, D.C.: National Planning Association, 1957.

Hiriart, Luis. *Braden: Historia de Una Mina.* Santiago, Chile: Editorial Andes, 1964.

Hirschmeier, Johannes. *The Origins of Entrepreneurship in Meiji Japan.* Cambridge, Mass.: Harvard University Press, 1964.

Hoe, Robert. *A Short History of the Printing Press.* New York: R. Hoe, 1902.

Hoover, Herbert. *Memoirs.* Vol. 1. New York: Macmillan, 1952.

Huck, Virginia. *Brand of the Tartan: The 3M Story.* New York: Appleton-Century-Crofts, 1955.

Hudnut, James M. *Semi-Centennial History of New York Life Insurance Co.* New York: New York Life Insurance Co., 1895.

Hunt, Freeman, ed. *Lives of American Merchants.* 2 vols. New York: Derby & Jackson, 1858.

Hutchinson, William T. *Cyrus Hall McCormick.* 2 vols. New York: The Century Co., 1930, 1935.

International Harvester Co. *A Century of Progress 1831–1933,* n.p., n.d.

Jaffrey, Robert, ed. *1825–1925, A Centennial Review of the Business Founded by Augustus Hemenway of Boston in 1825 and Now Conducted by Wessel, Duval & Co.* New York: privately printed, 1925.

James, Marquis. *The Texaco Story: The First Fifty Years 1902–1952.* New York(?): Texas Co., 1953.

Josephson, Matthew. *Edison; a Biography.* New York: McGraw-Hill, 1959.

Kahn, E. J. *The Big Drink: The Story of Coca-Cola.* New York: Random House, 1960.

Kannappan, Subbiah, and Burgess, Eugene W. *Aluminium Limited in India.* Washington, D.C.: National Planning Association, 1961.

Kennan, George. *E. H. Harriman, a Biography.* 2 vols. Boston and New York: Houghton Mifflin Co., 1922.

Kepner, Charles David, Jr., and Soothill, Jay Henry. *The Banana Empire.* New York: Vanguard, 1935 (United Fruit).

———. *Social Aspects of the Banana Industry.* New York: Columbia University Press, 1936 (mainly United Fruit).

Kingsley, David P. *Militant Life Insurance and Other Addresses.* New York: New York Life Insurance Co., 1911.

Lane, Weaton J. *Commodore Vanderbilt.* New York: Alfred A. Knopf, 1942.

Larson, Henrietta. "A China Trader Turns Investor." *Harvard Business Review* 12 (1934):345–358.

Leech, Harper, and Carroll, John Charles. *Armour and His Times.* New York: D. Appleton-Century Co., 1938.

Lief, Alfred. *The Firestone Story.* New York: Whittlesay House, 1951.

———. *It Floats, the Story of Procter and Gamble.* New York: Rinehart, 1958.

Litchfield, P. W. *Industrial Voyage.* Garden City, N.Y.: Doubleday, 1954.

Lomask, Milton. *Seed Money: The Guggenheim Story.* New York: Farrar, Straus, 1964.

Longhurst, Henry. *Adventures in Oil: The Story of British Petroleum.* London: Sidgwick and Jackson, 1959.

Mackenzie, Catherine. *Alexander Graham Bell.* Boston and New York: Houghton Mifflin Co., 1928.

Manchester, Herbert. *Diamond Match Co.: A Century of Service and Progress 1835–1935.* New York: Diamond Match Co., 1935.

Marcossen, Isaac F. *Anaconda.* New York: Dodd, Mead, 1957.

———. *Metal Magic; the Story of American Smelting and Refining Company.* New York: Farrar, Straus, 1949.

Marcossen, Isaac F. *Wherever Men Trade: The Romance of the Cash Register.* New York: Dodd, Mead, 1945.

Marshall, James L. *Elbridge A. Stuart, Founder of Carnation Co.* Los Angeles: Carnation Co., 1949.

May, Stacy, and Plaza, Galo. *The United Fruit Company in Latin America.* Washington, D.C.: National Planning Association, 1958.

McCaffrey, E. D. *Henry J. Heinz.* New York: B. Orr Press, 1923.

McCormick, Cyrus. *The Century of the Reaper; an Account of Cyrus Hall McCormick.* Boston and New York: Houghton Mifflin Co., 1931.

McDonald, P. B. *A Saga of the Seas: The Story of Cyrus W. Field and the Laying of the First Atlantic Cable.* New York: Wilson-Erickson, 1937.

Moore, Austin Leigh. *John D. Archbold and the Early Development of Standard Oil.* New York: Macmillan, 1948.

Nevins, Allan, and Hill, Frank Ernest. *Ford.* 3 vols. New York: Scribner, 1954–1963.

———. *Study in Power, John D. Rockefeller.* 2 vols. New York: Scribner, 1953.

New York Stock Exchange Listing Statements. New York: F. E. Fitch, Inc., 1891–1914.

Northern Railway Company. *Costa Rica Railway Company, Ltd. and Northern Railway Company.* San José, Costa Rica: Northern Railway Company, 1953.

———, and United Fruit Company. *Concessions, Contracts, and Decrees 1892–1913.* Boston: United Fruit Co., 1914.

Oberholtzer, Ellis P. *Robert Morris, Patriot and Financier.* New York: The Macmillan Co., 1903.

O'Connor, Harvey. *The Guggenheims.* New York: Covici, Friede, 1937.

Otis, Fessenden N. *Isthmus of Panama: History of the Panama Railroad and of the Pacific Mail Steamship Company.* New York: Harper & Brothers, 1867.

Paine, Albert Bigelow. *In One Man's Life, Being Chapters from the Personal and Business Careers of Theodore N. Vail.* New York: Harper & Brothers, 1921.

Pinner, Felix. *Emil Rathenau und das elektrische zeitalter.* Leipzig: Akademische verlagsgesellschaft m.b.h., 1918.

Pollan, A. A. *The United Fruit Company and Middle America.* New York: n.p., 1944 (pamphlet).

"Pond's Chronology." Typescript, n.p., n.d. [1956 or later].

Poor, Laura Elizabeth, ed. *The First International Railway and the Colonization of New England; Life and Writings of John Alfred Poor.* New York: Putnam, The Knickerbocker Press, 1892.

Porter, Kenneth Wiggins. *The Jacksons and the Lees.* 2 vols. Cambridge, Mass.: Harvard University Press, 1937.

———. *John Jacob Astor.* 2 vols. Cambridge, Mass.: Harvard University Press, 1931.

Potter, Stephen. *The Magic Number.* London: Rinehart, 1959.

Pound, Arthur. *The Turning Wheel: The Story of General Motors Through Twenty-Five Years.* Garden City, N.Y.: Doubleday, Doran, 1934.

Price-Hughes, H. A., compiler. *B. T. H. Reminiscences Sixty-Years of Progress.* London: British Thomson-Houston Co., 1946.

Prout, Henry G. *A Life of George Westinghouse.* New York: Scribner, 1921.

Putnam, George H. *George Palmer Putnam: A Memoir.* New York and London: G. Putnam's Sons, 1912.

————. *Memories of a Publisher, 1865–1915.* New York and London: G. Putnam's Sons, 1915.

Pyle, Joseph Gilpin. *The Life of James J. Hill.* 2 vols. Garden City, N.Y.: Doubleday, Page & Co., 1917.

Richter, Ernest. "The Amalgamated Copper Company." *Quarterly Journal of Economics.* 30 (1916):406.

Roe, Richard. "The United Shoe Manufacturing Company." *The Journal of Political Economy* 22 (1914):43–63.

Sanford, Peleg. *The Letter Book of Peleg Sanford, Newport Merchant, 1666–1668.* Providence: Rhode Island Historical Society, 1928.

Simonds, William Adams. *Edison: His Life, His Work, His Genius.* Indianapolis: The Bobbs-Merrill Co., 1934.

Sims, William Lee, II. *"150 Years"* . . . *The Future! Colgate-Palmolive.* New York: Newcomen Society in North America, 1956.

Spender, J. A. *Weetman Pearson.* London: Cassell and Co., 1930.

Stalson, J. Owen. *Marketing Life Insurance.* Cambridge, Mass.: Harvard University Press, 1942.

Stehman, J. Warren. *The Financial History of the American Telephone and Telegraph Company.* Boston and New York: Houghton Mifflin Co., 1925.

Stewart, Watt. *Henry Meiggs, Yankee Pizarro.* Durham, N.C.: Duke University Press, 1946.

————. *Keith and Costa Rica: A Biographical Study of Minor Cooper Keith.* Albuquerque: University of New Mexico Press, 1963.

Swanberg, W. A. *Citizen Hearst.* New York: Scribner, 1961.

Swift & Co. *Yearbooks.* Chicago: Swift & Co., 1912, 1913, 1914.

Terrell, John Upton. *Furs by Astor.* New York: Morrow, 1963.

Thompson, Craig. *Since Spindletop; a Human Story of Gulf's First Half Century.* Pittsburgh: Gulf Oil, 1951.

Thompson, John F., and Beasley, Norman. *For the Years to Come, a Story of International Nickel.* New York: Putnam, 1960.

Thornton, Harrison John. *The History of the Quaker Oats Company.* Chicago: University of Chicago Press 1933.

Toshiba. *History.* Tokyo 1964 (in Japanese).

Vernon, Raymond, et al., compilers. Research Reports on Business Abroad. Prepared for Multinational Business Project. Dittoed. Boston: Harvard Graduate School of Business Administration, 1965+.

Watson, Thos. J. *Men—Minutes—Money*. New York: International Business Machines Corporation, 1934.

Western Electric Co. *The Western Electric Company and Its Place in the Bell System*. New York: Western Electric Co., 1938.

Whyte, Adam Gowans. *Forty Years of Electrical Progress; the Story of G.E.C.* London: E. Benn, 1930.

Wiegman, Carl. *Trees to News. A Chronicle of the Ontario Paper Company's Origin and Development*. Toronto: McClelland & Stewart, 1953.

Wilkins, Mira, and Hill, Frank Ernest. *American Business Abroad: Ford on Six Continents*. Detroit: Wayne State University Press, 1964.

———. "An American Enterprise Abroad: American Radiator Company in Europe 1895–1914." *Business History Review* 43 (1969):326–346.

Williams, Gattenby [pseud. for William Guggenheim]. *William Guggenheim*. New York: The Lone Voice Publishing Co., 1934.

Wilson, Charles. *The History of the Unilever*. 3 vols. New York: Frederick A. Praeger, 1968.

Wilson, Charles Morrow. *Empire in Green and Gold*. New York: Henry Holt & Co., 1947.

Winkler, John K. *Five and Ten, The Fabulous Life of F. K. Woolworth*. New York: R. M. McBride & Co., 1940.

———. *Morgan, the Magnificent*. New York: Vanguard Press, 1930.

———. *Tobacco Tycoon, The Story of James Buchanan Duke*. New York: Random House, 1942.

Young, Desmond. *Member for Mexico. A Biography of Weetman Pearson, First Viscount Cowdray*. London: Cassell, 1966.

Young, Sidney. "Cananea Consolidated History." Cananea, Sonora, Mexico, 1920. Typescript. New York: Anaconda Co.

VII. Commerce and Industry

Abrams, M. A. "The French Copper Syndicate 1887–1889." *Journal of Economic and Business History* 4 (1932):409–428.

Adams, Walter, ed. *The Structure of American Industry*. New York: Macmillan, 1950.

Aitken, Hugh F. J. "Government and Business in Canada: An Interpretation." *Business History Review* 38 (1964): 4–21.

Andrews, E. B. "The Late Copper Syndicate." *Quarterly Journal of Economics* 3 (1889):508–516.

Bailyn, Bernard. "Communications and Trade: The Atlantic in the Seventeenth Century." *Journal of Economic History* 13 (1953):378–388.

Bailyn, Bernard. *The New England Merchants in the Seventeenth Century.* Cambridge, Mass.: Harvard University Press, 1955.

Bain, Harry Foster, and Read, Thomas Thornton. *Ores and Industry in South America.* New York: Harper & Brothers, 1934.

————. *Ores and Industry in the Far East.* Rev. and enl. ed. New York: Council on Foreign Relations, 1933.

Bauer, P. T. *West African Trade.* Cambridge, England: Cambridge University Press, 1954.

Beard, Miriam. *A History of Business.* 2 vols. Ann Arbor: University of Michigan Press, Ann Arbor Paperbacks, 1963.

Bennett, Norman R., and Brooks, George E., Jr., eds. *New England Merchants in Africa, A History Through Documents 1802 to 1865.* Brookline, Mass.: Boston University Press, 1965.

Berenson, Conrad, ed. *The Chemical Industry.* New York: Interscience Publishers, 1963.

Berge, Wendell. *Cartels; Challenge to a Free World.* Washington, D.C.: Public Affairs Press, 1944.

Bernstein, Marvin D. *The Mexican Mining Industry, 1890–1950.* Albany: State University of New York, 1965.

Berthold, Victor H. *History of the Telephone and Telegraph in Brazil 1851–1921.* New York: no publisher listed, 1922.

Bishop, John Leander. *A History of American Manufactures from 1608 to 1860.* 2 vols. Philadelphia: E. Young & Co., 1864.

Briggs, Charles F., and Maverick, August. *The Story of the Telegraph and the History of the Great Atlantic Cable.* New York: Rudd & Carleton, 1863.

Bright, Arthur A. *The Electric Lamp Industry.* New York: Macmillan Co., 1949.

British Electrical and Allied Manufacturers' Association. *Combines and Trusts in the Electrical Industry.* London: British Electrical and Allied Manufacturers' Association, 1927.

Bruchey, Stuart, ed. *Cotton and the Growth of the American Economy.* New York: Harcourt, Brace & World, 1967.

————. *The Roots of American Economic Growth.* New York: Harper & Row, 1964.

Bruck, W. F. *Social and Economic History of Germany 1888–1939.* New York: Russell & Russell, 1962.

Buck, Norman S. *The Development of the Organization of Anglo-American Trade 1800–1850.* New Haven: Yale University Press, 1925.

Casson, Herbert. *The History of the Telephone.* Chicago: A. C. McClurg & Co., 1910.

Caves, Richard E. and Holton, Richard H. *The Canadian Economy.* Cambridge, Mass.: Harvard University Press, 1959.

Centennial Seminar on the History of the Petroleum Industry. *Oil's First Century.* Boston: Harvard Graduate School of Business Administration, 1960.

Chandler, Alfred D., Jr. *Strategy and Structure.* Cambridge, Mass.: M.I.T. Press, 1962.

―――. "The Beginnings of 'Big Business' in American Industry." *Business History Review* 33 (1959):1–31.

Clark, Victor S. *History of Manufacturers in the United States.* 2 vols. Washington, D.C.: Carnegie Institution of Washington, 1916, 1928.

Cochran, Thomas C. *The American Business System, A Historical Perspective 1900–1955.* Cambridge, Mass.: Harvard University Press, 1957.

―――, and Miller, William C. *The Age of Enterprise.* Rev. ed. New York: Harper & Row, Harper Torchbooks, 1961.

Cole, Arthur H. and Williamson, Harold. *The American Carpet Manufacturers.* Cambridge, Mass.: Harvard University Press, 1941.

Collie, Muriel F. *The Saga of the Abrasives Industry.* Greendale, Mass.: The Grinding Wheel Institute, 1951.

Cox, Reavis. *Competition of the American Tobacco Industry, 1911–1932.* New York: Columbia University Press, 1933.

Day, Clive. *A History of Commerce.* Rev. and enl. ed. New York: Longmans, Green and Co., 1922.

Depew, Chauncey, ed. *1795–1895 One Hundred Years of American Commerce.* New York: D. O. Haynes & Co., 1895.

Donnan, Elizabeth, ed. *Documents Illustrative of the History of the Slave Trade to America.* 4 vols. Washington, D.C.: Carnegie Institution of Washington, 1930–1935.

Downs, William C. "The Commission House in Latin American Trade." *Quarterly Journal of Economics* 26 (1911):118–139.

Dumbell, Stanley. "Cotton Market in 1799." *Economic Journal, Supplement,* January 1926, pp. 141–148.

Easterbrook, W. T. and Aitken, Hugh G. J. *Canadian Economic History.* Toronto: Macmillan Co. of Canada, 1956.

Edminster, Lynn Ramsay. *The Cattle Industry and the Tariff.* New York: The Macmillan Co., 1926.

Edwards, Junius David, Frary, Francis C., and Jeffries, Zay. *The Aluminum Industry.* New York: McGraw-Hill Book Co., 1930.

Elliott, William Yandel, et al. *International Control of Non-Ferrous Metals.* New York: The Macmillan Co., 1937.

Fayle, C. Ernest. *A Short History of World Shipping.* New York: L. MacVeagh, The Dial Press, 1933.

Firestone, O. J. *Canada's Economic Development, 1867–1953.* London: Bowes & Bowes, 1958.

Gates, William B. *Michigan Copper and Boston Dollars*. Cambridge, Mass.: Harvard University Press, 1951.

Gray, Lewis Cecil. *History of Agriculture in Southern United States to 1860*. 2 vols. Washington, D.C.: The Carnegie Institution of Washington, 1933.

Guerra y Sanchez, Ramiro. *Sugar and Society in the Caribbean; an Economic History of Cuban Agriculture*. Translated by Marjory M. Urquidi. New Haven: Yale University Press, 1964.

Guthrie, John A. *The Economics of Pulp and Paper*. Pullman, Wash.: State College of Washington Press, 1950.

————. *The Newsprint Paper Industry*. Cambridge, Mass.: Harvard University Press, 1941.

Habakkuk, H. J. *American and British Technology in the Nineteenth Century*. Cambridge, England: Cambridge University Press, 1962.

————, and Postan, M., eds. *The Cambridge Economic History of Europe*. Vol. 6. Cambridge, England: Cambridge University Press, 1965.

Hacker, Louis M. *The World of Andrew Carnegie, 1865–1900*. Philadelphia and New York: J. B. Lippincott Co., 1968.

Hall, Courtney Robert. *History of American Industrial Science*. New York: Library Publishers, 1954.

Hall, Douglas. *Ideas and Illustrations in Economic History*. New York: Holt, Rinehart and Winston, 1964.

Halsey, Frederic M. *Railway Expansion in Latin America*. New York: The Moody Magazine and Book Co., 1916.

————. *The Railways of South and Central America*. New York: Francis Emory Fitch, 1914.

Hammond, M. B. *The Cotton Industry*. New York: Macmillan Co., 1897.

Hanson, S. G. *Argentine Meat and the British Market*. London: Oxford University Press, 1937.

————. *Economic Development in Latin America*. Washington, D.C.: Inter-American Affairs Press, 1951.

Harrington, Virginia. *The New York Merchant on the Eve of the Revolution*. New York: Columbia University Press, 1935.

Hartendorp, A. V. H. *History of Industry and Trade of the Philippines*. Manila: American Chamber of Commerce of the Philippines, 1958.

Haynes, Williams. *The American Chemical Industry*. 6 vols. New York: D. Van Nostrand Co., 1945–1954.

————. *The Stone That Burns; the Story of the American Sulphur Industry*. New York: D. Van Nostrand Co., 1942.

Henderson, W. O. "The American Chamber of Commerce for the Port of Liverpool." In *Transactions of the Historical Society of Lancashire and Cheshire for the Year 1935*. Liverpool, England, 1935.

Hexner, Ervin. *International Cartels.* Chapel Hill, N.C.: Duke University Press, 1945.

———. *International Steel Cartel.* Chapel Hill, N.C.: Duke University Press, 1943.

Hill, James J. *Highways of Progress.* New York: Doubleday, Page & Co., 1910.

Holcombe, A. N. *Public Ownership of Telephones on the Continent of Europe.* Boston and New York: Houghton, Mifflin Co., 1911.

———. "The Telephone in Great Britain." *Quarterly Journal of Economics* 21 (1906):96–135.

Howard-White, F. B. *Nickel, an Historical Review.* London: Methuen, 1963.

Hughlett, Lloyd J., ed. *Industrialization of Latin America.* New York: McGraw-Hill Book Co., 1946.

Hunter, Alex, ed. *The Economics of Australian Industry.* Melbourne: Melbourne University Press, 1963.

Innis, Harold Adams, and Lower, A. R. M., eds. *Select Documents in Canadian Economic History, 1783–1885.* Toronto: University of Toronto Press, 1933.

Jack, Andrew B. "The Channels of Distribution for an Innovation: the Sewing Machine Industry in America 1860–1865." *Explorations in Entrepreneurial History* 8 (1957):113–141.

Johnson, Emory R., et al. *History of Domestic and Foreign Commerce of the United States.* 2 vols. Washington, D.C.: Carnegie Institution of Washington, 1915.

Joralemon, Ira. *Romantic Copper.* New York: D. Appleton-Century Co., 1935.

Keller, Morton. *The Life Insurance Enterprise 1885–1910.* Cambridge, Mass.: Harvard University Press, 1963.

Kingsbury, J. E. *The Telephone and Telephone Exchanges.* London: Longmans, Green and Co., 1915.

Knowles, L. C. A., and Knowles, C. M. *The Economic Development of the British Overseas Empire.* 2 vols. London: G. Routledge & Sons, 1924, 1930.

Knox, F. A., Baxter, C. L., and Slater, D. W. *The Canadian Electrical Manufacturing Industry.* Toronto, 1955.

Lebkicher, Roy, et al. *ARAMCO Handbook.* Haarlem, The Netherlands: J. Enschede, 1960.

Lenczowski, George. *Oil and State in the Middle East.* Ithaca: Cornell University Press, 1960.

Levy, Hermann. *Monopolies, Cartels, and Trusts in British Industry.* London: Macmillan & Co., 1927.

Lewis, Howard T. *The Motion Picture Industry.* New York: D. Van Nostrand, 1933.

Liefmann, Robert. *Cartels, Concerns and Trusts.* London: Methuen & Co., 1932.

Lieuwen, Edwin. *Petroleum in Venezuela.* Berkeley: University of California Press, 1954.

Liu, Kwang-Ching. *Anglo-American Steamship Rivalry in China 1862–1874*. Cambridge, Mass.: Harvard University Press, 1962.

Longrigg, Stephen Hemsley. *Oil in the Middle East, Its Discovery and Development*. London: Oxford University Press, 1954.

Mahoney, Tom. *The Great Merchants*. New York: Harper, 1955.

————. *The Merchants of Life; An Account of the American Pharmaceutical Industry*. New York: Harper, 1959.

Main, O. W. *The Canadian Nickel Industry*. Toronto: University of Toronto Press, 1955.

Mason, Edward S. *Controlling World Trade; Cartels and Commodity Agreements*. New York and London: McGraw-Hill Book Co., 1946.

McDiarmid, O. J. *Commercial Policy in the Canadian Economy*. Cambridge, Mass.: Harvard University Press, 1946.

McLean, John F., and Haigh, Robert W. *The Growth of Integrated Oil Companies*. Boston: Division of Research, Graduate School of Business Administration, Harvard University, 1954.

Mitsubishi Economic Research Institute. *Mitsui-Mitsubishi-Sumitomo*. Tokyo: Mitsubishi Economic Research Institute, 1955.

Mitsubishi Economic Research Bureau. *Japanese Trade and Industry*. London: Macmillan and Co., 1936.

Moody, John. *The Truth About Trusts*. New York: Moody Publishing Company, 1904.

Morison, Samuel Eliot. *The Maritime History of Massachusetts 1783–1860*. Boston: Houghton Mifflin Co., 1941.

Nelson, Ralph L. *Merger Movements in American Industry 1895–1956*. Princeton: Princeton University Press, 1959.

Nevins, Allan. *Sail on, The Story of the American Merchant Marine*. New York: U.S. Lines, 1946.

Nicholls, William H. *Price Policies in the Cigarette Industry*. Nashville, Tenn.: Vanderbilt University Press, 1951.

North, Douglas C. *The Economic Growth of the United States 1790–1860*. Englewood Cliffs, N.J.: Prentice-Hall, 1961.

————. *Growth and Welfare in the American Past*. Englewood Cliffs, N.J.: Prentice-Hall, 1966.

Odell, Peter R. *An Economic Geography of Oil*. London: Bell, 1963.

Pan, Shu-Lun. *Trade of the United States with China*. New York: China Trade Bureau, 1924.

Parsons, A. B. *The Porphyry Coppers*. New York: American Institute of Mining and Metallurgical Engineers, 1933.

————, ed. *Seventy-Five Years of Progress in the Mineral Industry 1871–1946*. New York: American Institute of Mining and Metallurgical Engineers, 1947.

Penrose, Edith. *The Economics of the International Patent System.* Baltimore: Johns Hopkins Press, 1951.

————. *The Theory of the Growth of the Firm.* New York: Wiley, 1959.

Plummer, Alfred. *International Combines in Modern Industry.* 3rd ed. London: Pitman, 1951.

Porritt, Edward. *Sixty Years of Protection in Canada 1846–1907.* London: Macmillan and Co., 1908.

Porter, Robert P. *Industrial Cuba; Being a Study of Present Commercial and Industrial Conditions, with Suggestions as to the Opportunities Presented in the Island for American Capital, Enterprise and Labor.* New York and London: G. P. Putnam's Sons, 1899.

Powell, Fred Wilbur. *The Railroads of Mexico.* Boston: The Stratford Co., 1921.

Reavis, L. U. *An International Railway to the City of Mexico.* St. Louis, Mo.: Woodward, Tiernan & Hale, 1879.

Read, Oliver, and Welch, Walter. *Tin Foil to Stereo.* Indianapolis: Howard W. Sams and Bobbs-Merrill, 1959.

Reid, C. Lestock. *Commerce and Conquest.* London: C. & J. Temple, 1947.

Reid, James D. *The Telegraph in America.* New York: Derby Brothers, 1879.

Richards, G. Tilghman. *Typewriters.* London: Science Museum, 1938.

Ripley, William Z. *Trusts, Pools and Corporations.* Rev. ed. Boston: Ginn and Co., 1916.

Schlesinger, Arthur M. *The Colonial Merchants and the Revolution, 1763–1776.* New York: F. Ungar Pub. Co., 1957.

Shwadran, Benjamin. *Middle East, Oil, and the Great Powers.* New York: Praeger, 1955.

Simon, Matthew, and Novack, David E. "Some Dimensions of the American Commercial Invasion of Europe 1871–1914." *Journal of Economic History* 24 (1964):591–605.

Southworth, J.R. and Homs, Percy C. *El Directorio Oficial Minero de Mexico.* Vol. 9. Pub. bajo la authorizacion del gobierno. Mexico, 1908.

————. *Las Minas de Mexico.* Vol. 9. Pub. bajo la authorizacion del gobierno. Mexico, 1905.

Spurr, Josiah Edward. *Marketing of Metals and Minerals.* New York: McGraw-Hill, 1925.

Steigerwalt, A. K. *The National Association of Manufacturers, 1895–1914.* Ann Arbor: Bureau of Business Research, Graduate School of Business Administration, University of Michigan, 1964.

Stevens, William S., ed. *Industrial Combinations and Trusts.* New York: Macmillan Co., 1913.

————. *The Powder Trust, 1872–1912.* Philadelphia: University of Pennsylvania, 1912.

Stocking, George Ward, and Watkins, Myron W. *Cartels in Action*. New York: The Twentieth Century Fund, 1946.

————. *The Potash Industry*. New York: R. R. Smith, 1931.

Strassmann, W. Paul. *Risk and Technological Innovation, American Manufacturing Methods during the Nineteenth Century*. Ithaca: Cornell University Press, 1959.

Thompson, Robert Luther. *Wiring a Continent, The History of the Telegraph Industry in the United States, 1832–1866*. Princeton: Princeton University Press, 1947.

Van der Haas, H. *The Enterprise in Transition. An Analysis of European and American Practice*. London: Tavistock Publications, 1967.

Vanderlip, F. A. *The American "Commercial Invasion" of Europe*. New York: Republished from Scribner's Magazine, 1902.

Vernon, Raymond. *The Dilemma of Mexico's Development*. Cambridge, Mass.: Harvard University Press, 1963.

Wallace, D. H. *Market Control in the Aluminum Industry*. Cambridge, Mass.: Harvard University Press, 1937.

Webb, Herbert Laws. *The Development of the Telephone in Europe*. London: Electrical Press, 1910.

Weller, Charles Edward. *The Early History of the Typewriter*. La Porte, Ind.: Chase & Shepard, 1921.

Whittlesey, Charles R. *National Interest and International Cartels*. New York: The Macmillan Co., 1946.

Wiebe, Robert H. *Businessmen and Reform*. Cambridge, Mass.: Harvard University Press, 1962.

Williamson, Harold F., and Daum, Arnold R. *The American Petroleum Industry 1859–1899*. Evanston, Ill.: Northwestern University Press, 1959.

————, et al. *The American Petroleum Industry 1899–1959*. Evanston, Ill.: Northwestern University Press, 1963.

Woodruff, William. *Impact of Western Man*. New York: St. Martin's Press, 1967.

Woytinsky, W. S., and Woytinsky, E. S. *World Commerce and Governments*. New York: Twentieth Century Fund, 1955.

Young, John Parke. *The International Economy*. 4th ed. New York: Ronald Press, 1963.

VIII. United States Diplomatic Histories

Bailey, Thomas A. *A Diplomatic History of the United States*. 6th ed. New York: Appleton-Century-Crofts, 1958.

Beale, Howard K. *Theodore Roosevelt and the Rise of America to World Power*. New York: Crowell-Collier Publishing Co., Collier Books, 1962.

Bemis, Samuel Flagg, ed. *The American Secretaries of State and Their Diplomacy*. 10 vols. New York: Alfred A. Knopf, 1927–1929.

Bemis, Samuel Flagg, ed. *A Diplomatic History of the United States.* 3d ed. New York: Henry Holt and Co., 1950.

———. *The Latin American Policy of the United States.* New York: Harcourt, Brace and Co., 1943.

Bisson, T. A. *America's Far Eastern Policy.* New York: International Secretariat, Institute of Pacific Relations, 1945.

Blount, James H. *The American Occupation of the Philippines 1898–1912.* New York and London: G. P. Putnam's Sons, 1913.

Bradley, Harold Whitman. *The American Frontier in Hawaii; The Pioneers 1789–1843.* Stanford University Press, 1942.

Campbell, Charles S. *Special Business Interests and the Open Door Policy.* New Haven: Yale University Press, 1951.

Cline, Howard F. *The United States and Mexico.* Cambridge, Mass.: Harvard University Press, 1953.

Crichfield, George W. *American Supremacy; The Rise and Progress of the Latin American Nations and Their Relations to the United States under the Monroe Doctrine.* 2 vols. New York: Brentano's, 1908.

Cronon, E. David, ed. *The Cabinet Diaries of Josephus Daniels, 1913–1921.* Lincoln, Neb.: University of Nebraska Press, 1936.

Dennett, Tyler. *Americans in Eastern Asia.* New York: The Macmillan Co., 1922.

DeNovo, John A. *American Interests and Policies in the Middle East.* Minneapolis: University of Minnesota Press, 1963.

Dulles, Foster Rhea. *America in the Pacific; a Century of Expansion.* Boston and New York: Houghton Mifflin Company, 1932.

Ellis, Lewis Ethan. *Reciprocity, 1911; A Study in Canadian-American Relations.* New Haven: Yale University Press, 1939.

Feis, Herbert. *Petroleum and American Foreign Policy.* Stanford: Food Research Institute, Stanford University, 1944.

Finnie, David H. *Pioneers East: The Early American Experience in the Middle East.* Harvard Middle Eastern Studies, vol. 13. Cambridge, Mass.: Harvard University Press, 1967.

Griswold, A. Whitney. *The Far Eastern Policy of the United States.* New York: Harcourt, Brace and Co., 1938.

Healy, David F. *The United States in Cuba 1898–1902.* Madison: The University of Wisconsin Press, 1963.

Hill, Lawrence F. *Diplomatic Relations Between the United States and Brazil.* Durham, N.C.: Duke University Press, 1932.

Ise, John. *The United States Oil Policy.* New Haven: Yale University Press, 1924.

Jenks, Leland. *Our Cuban Colony.* New York: Vanguard Press, 1928.

Jessup, P. C. *Elihu Root.* New York: Dodd, Mead & Co., 1938.

LaFeber, Walter. *The New Empire.* Ithaca: Cornell University Press, 1963.

Leopold, Richard W. "The Emergence of the America as a World Power: Some

Second Thoughts." In *Change and Continuity in Twentieth Century America,* edited by John Braeman, et al. New York: Harper & Row, 1964.

May, Ernest R. *Imperial Democracy: The Emergence of America as a Great Power.* New York: Harcourt, Brace & World, 1961.

McCormick, Thomas J. *China Market.* Chicago: Quadrangle, 1967.

Merk, Frederick. *Manifest Destiny and Mission in American History.* New York: Alfred A. Knopf, 1963.

Moore, John Bassett. *History and Digest of the International Arbitrations to Which the United States Has Been a Party.* 6 vols. Washington, D.C.: Government Printing Office, 1898.

Munro, Dana G. *Intervention and Dollar Diplomacy in the Caribbean 1900–1921.* Princeton: Princeton University Press, 1964.

———. *United States and the Caribbean Area.* Boston: World Peace Foundation, 1934.

Offutt, Milton. *Protection of Citizens Abroad by the Armed Forces of the United States.* Baltimore: The Johns Hopkins Press, 1928.

Parks, E. Taylor. *Colombia and the United States.* Durham, N.C.: University of North Carolina Press, 1935.

Pratt, Julius W. *Expansionists of 1898.* Baltimore: The Johns Hopkins Press, 1936.

Rauch, Basil. *American Interest in Cuba: 1848–1855.* New York: Columbia University Press, 1948.

Rippy, J. Fred. *Rivalry of the United States and Great Britain Over Latin America 1808–1830.* Baltimore: The Johns Hopkins Press, 1929.

———. *The United States and Mexico.* Rev. ed. New York: F. S. Crofts & Co., 1931.

Varg, Paul A. *Making of a Myth, The United States and China 1897–1912.* East Lansing: Michigan State University Press, 1968.

———. "The Myth of the China Market, 1890–1914." *The American Historical Review* 73 (1968):742–758.

Vevier, Charles. *The United States and China 1906–1913.* New Brunswick: Rutgers University Press, 1955.

Williams, Benjamin H. *Economic Foreign Policy of the United States.* New York: McGraw-Hill, 1929.

Williams, William Appleton. *The Tragedy of American Diplomacy.* Rev. ed. New York: Dell Publishing Co., 1962.

Wilson, Henry Lane. *Diplomatic Episodes in Mexico, Belgium, and Chile.* Garden City, N.Y.: Doubleday, 1927.

IX. General Works (for background)

Ackerman, Carl. *Mexico's Dilemma.* New York: George H. Doran Co., 1918.

Basadre, Jorge. *Historia de la Republica del Peru.* Vols. 3, 4, 6. 5th ed. Lima: Ediciones "Historia," 1961–1962.

Bell, Edward I. *The Political Shame of Mexico.* New York: McBride, Nast & Co,. 1914.

Bulnes, Francisco. *The Whole Truth About Mexico.* New York: M. Bulnes Book Co., 1916.

Calvert, Peter. *The Mexican Revolution 1910–1914.* Cambridge, England: Cambridge University Press, 1968.

Cooper, Clayton Sedgwick. *The Brazilians and Their Country.* New York: Frederick A. Stokes Co., 1917.

————. *Understanding South America.* New York: George H. Doran Co., 1918.

"Canadian National Problems," *The Annals of the American Academy of Political and Social Science* 45 (1913).

Childe, Gordon. *What Happened in History.* New York: Penguin Books, 1946.

Forbes, W. Cameron. *The Philippine Islands.* 2 vols. Boston and New York: Houghton Mifflin Co., 1928.

Friedman, Milton, and Schwartz, Anna Jacobson. *A Monetary History of the United States.* Princeton: Princeton University Press, 1963.

Hayes, Carlton J. H. *A Generation of Materialism 1871–1900.* New York: Harper, 1941.

Herring, Hubert. *A History of Latin America.* 2d ed. New York: Alfred A. Knopf, 1964.

Johnson, Harry G. *Economic Nationalism in Old and New States.* Chicago: University of Chicago Press, 1967.

Link, Arthur S. *Wilson: The New Freedom.* Princeton: Princeton University Press, 1956.

————. *Wilson: The Struggle for Neutrality.* Princeton: Princeton University Press, 1960.

Manchester, Alan K. *British Preeminence in Brazil, Its Rise and Decline.* New York: Octagon Books, 1964.

May, Stacy. *Costa Rica.* New York: Twentieth Century Fund. 1952.

Nehemkis, Peter. *Latin America.* New York: Alfred A. Knopf, 1964.

Noyes, Alexander Dana. *Forty Years of American Finance.* New York: G. P. Putnam's Sons, 1909.

Pinson, Koppel S. *Modern Germany.* 2d ed. New York: Macmillan, 1966.

Ravignani, Emilio, ed. *Asambleas Constituyentes Argentinas 1813–1833.* Vol. 1. Buenos Aires: Jacob Peuser, 1937.

Rippy, J. Fred. *Latin America and the Industrial Age.* 2d ed. New York: G. P. Putnam's Sons, 1947.

Rostovtzeff, Mikhail I. *Rome.* Translated by J. D. Duff. New York: Oxford University Press, Galaxy Book, 1960.

————. *The Social and Economic History of the Roman Empire.* 2d ed. 2 vols. Oxford: Clarendon Press, 1957.

Royal Institute of International Affairs. *The Middle East.* 2d ed. London: Royal Institute of International Affairs, 1954.

Tannenbaum, Frank. *The Mexican Agrarian Revolution.* Washington, D.C.: The Brookings Institution, 1930.

Wilson, Charles Morrow. *Challenge and Opportunity; Central America.* New York: H. Holt and Co., 1941.

X. Directories, Handbooks, and Conference Proceedings

American Exporter. *Export Trade Directory.* 1912, 1919–1920.

American Institute of Mining Engineers. *Transactions of the American Institute of Mining Engineers.* 32 (1902).

Angel, J. L. *Directory of American Firms Operating in Foreign Countries.* 6th ed. New York: World Trade Academy Press, 1966.

The Copper Handbook. Houghton, Mich. 1901.

Dictionary of American Biography.

Filsinger, Ernest. *Exporting to Latin America; a Handbook for Merchants, Manufacturers and Exporters.* New York: D. Appleton and Co., 1919.

Figueroa, Pedro Pablo. *Diccionario Biografico de Estranjeros en Chile.* Santiago, Chile: Imprenta Moderna, 1900.

The Mineral Industry. 1893–1915. New York: Engineering and Journal, 1893–1915.

Moody's Industrial Manual: American and Foreign. 1909 to date. Title varies. New York: Analyses Publishing Co., 1909–1914, Moody's Investors Service, 1914–date.

Moody's Manual of Railroad and Corporation Securities. 1900–1924. Title varies. New York: Moody Manual Co., 1900–1918, Poor's Publishing Co., 1919–1924.

National Foreign Trade Convention. *Official Report of the National Foreign Trade Convention,* 1914–date. New York: National Foreign Trade Convention Headquarters, 1914–date.

Stewart, Charles F., and Simmons, George B. *A Bibliography of International Business.* New York: Columbia University Press, 1964.

Vernon, Raymond. "The Multinational Corporation: A Bibliography." Mimeographed. Boston: Harvard Graduate School of Business Administration, 1966.

XII. Periodicals (includes only those used in connection with this study)

American Economic Review

Annals of the American Academy of Political and Social Science

Business History Review

Business International

Business Topics

Business Week

Bibliography

Canadian Motor
Columbia Journal of World Business
Commercial and Financial Chronicle
Comments on the Argentine Trade
Economic Journal
Explorations in Entrepreneurial History
Explorations in Entrepreneurial History, series 2
Fortune
Harvard Business Review
Inter-American Economics Affairs
Journal of Business
Journal of Commerce
Journal of Economic History
Merchant's Magazine
National City Bank Monthly Letter
New England Historical Society Register
New York Times
Political Science Quarterly
Quarterly Journal of Economics
Wall Street Journal
Western Electric News
World Business (Chase Manhattan Bank)

Notes

Chapter I: The Trader Becomes an Investor

1. Gordon Childe, *What Happened in History*, Pelican ed., New York 1946, 89–90; M. Rostovtzeff, *Rome*, Galaxy Books, New York 1960, 263; C. Lestock Reid, *Commerce and Conquest*, London 1947; Bernard Bailyn, "Communications and Trade: The Atlantic in the Seventeenth Century," *Journal of Economic History*, 13:378–388 (Fall 1953).

2. I have found especially useful on colonial mercantile activities, manuscript data on various merchants in New York Public Library (see bibliography); Charles M. Andrews, *The Colonial Period of American History*, 4 vols., New Haven 1938; Carl Bridenbaugh, *Cities in the Wilderness, Urban Life in America, 1625–1742*, Capricorn ed., New York 1964, 29–41, 175–188; *The Letter Book of Peleg Sanford, Newport Merchant, 1666–1668*, Providence 1928, p. iv; Emory R. Johnson et al., *History of Domestic and Foreign Commerce of the United States*, Washington, D.C., 1915, vol. I; William T. Baxter, *House of Hancock*, Cambridge, Mass. 1945; Virginia Harrington, *The New York Merchant on the Eve of the Revolution*, New York 1935; Arthur Schlesinger, *The Colonial Merchants and the Revolution*, New York 1957.

3. Baxter, 95; *New England Historical Genealogical Society Register*, 26:43 (1872); Harrington, *The New York Merchant*, 178 (Kilby).

4. W. B. Aitken, *Distinguished Families in America Descended from Wilhelmus Beekman*, New York 1912, 56, 134; Harrington, 186–187; Cruger Manuscripts, NYPL.

5. Harrington, 194–197, and Aitken, 134.

6. John Van Cortlandt to Abraham Maw in Virginia, Feb. 16, 1764, and to Newton and Gordon in Madeira, Apr. 3, 1764, John Van Cortlandt Ltr. Bk., NYPL.

7. Marcus Lee Hansen, *The Atlantic Migration 1607–1860*, New York 1961, 47–48; Elizabeth Donnan, ed., *Documents Illustrative of the History of the Slave Trade to America*, Washington, D.C. 1932, 1935, vol. III, and IV, 235.

8. Andrews, vol. IV, chap. 10 (excellent on mercantilism; the quotation is from p. 335); Douglass C. North, *The Economic Growth of the United States, 1790–1860*, Englewood Cliffs, N.J. 1961, 19, expounds the thesis that British policy possibly aided American merchants. This was, of course, the position taken by George Louis Beer, *The Old Colonial System*, 2 vols., New York 1912.

9. Gordon C. Bjork, "The Weaning of the American Economy: Independence, Market Changes, and Economic Development," *Journal of Economic History*, 24:541–560 (December 1964); Alexander Hamilton, "Report on Manufactures," Dec. 5, 1791, in Alexander Hamilton, *Works*, ed. Henry Cabot Lodge, New York 1904, III, 294; U.S. Dept. of Comm., Bureau of Census, *Historical Statistics*, Washington, D.C. 1960, 547 (cotton exports). The cotton gin, invented in 1793, was responsible for the United States' becoming a major cotton exporter.

10. Tyler Dennett, *Americans in Eastern Asia*, New York 1941, 42 (South and North Pacific); Samuel Eliot Morison, *Maritime History of Massachusetts*, Boston

1941, 66 (Shaw & Randall); N. S. B. Gras and Henrietta Larson, *Casebook in American Business History,* New York 1939, 119 (Perkins).

11. Kenneth Wiggins Porter, *John Jacob Astor,* 2 vols., Cambridge, Mass. 1931, I, 165, 167, 169, chaps. 7 and 8; II, 607–612.

12. M. B. Hammond, *The Cotton Industry,* New York 1897, 278–291, Stanley Dumbell, "Cotton Market in 1799," *Economic Journal, Supplement,* January 1926, 141–148, Lewis Cecil Gray, *History of Agriculture in Southern United States to 1860,* Washington, D.C. 1933, II, 718, and Norman Sydney Buck, *The Development of the Organisation of Anglo-American Trade 1800–1850,* New Haven 1925, 4ff (cotton market but little on U.S. business in Liverpool). W. O. Henderson, "The American Chamber of Commerce in the Port of Liverpool, 1801–1908," in *Transactions of the Historical Society of Lancashire and Cheshire,* 85:2 (1933); participants were mainly Liverpool merchants interested in the cotton trade; Buck, 107–108 (American merchants in England, dealing in British manufactured goods, 1808ff); Stuart Bruchey, ed., *Cotton and the Growth of the American Economy,* New York 1967, 229 (refers to American cotton merchant's branch house in Liverpool in 1810).

13. C. F. Remer, *Foreign Investments in China,* New York 1933, 242. Russell & Co. was formed by two Americans, Philip Ammidon and Samuel Russell. It started doing business in Canton on Jan. 1, 1824—"for transaction of commission business, [to] offer the public our services for that line" (Robert Forbes, *Personal Reminiscences,* Boston 1882, 339). The predecessor of Russell & Co. was Samuel Russell & Co., formed some six years earlier (*ibid.,* 336–337). J. P. Sturgis and Co. was the Canton agent of Bryant and Sturgis in Boston (Porter, II, 619). Olyphant & Co. was a branch house of a New York concern (*ibid.,* 637–638).

14. Harold Whitman Bradley, *The American Frontier in Hawaii, The Pioneers, 1789–1843,* Stanford, Calif. 1942, 82 (Honolulu); Forbes, 355 (Manila), R. Jaffray, *1825–1925 Centennial Review,* New York 1925, 19 (Alsop), 7 (Hemenway); Charles R. Flint, *Memories of an Active Life,* New York 1923, 73 (Hale); Morison, 218, and John Winkler, *Morgan,* New York 1930, 44 (Peabody); Buck, 73, 94–96 (Humphreys & Biddle), 107, 153–155 (other Americans in England); Norman R. Bennett and George E. Brooks, Jr., *New England Merchants in Africa, A History through Documents 1802–1865,* Boston 1965, xxvi, 189, 226–227 (an American resident in Majunga, Madagascar, 1830s and 1840s), xxvii, 216ff (an American resident in Zanzibar), 210, 223, 344 (other Americans resident in Bombay and Zanzibar, acting for American traders). David H. Finnie, *Pioneers East: The Early American Experience in the Middle East,* Cambridge Mass. 1967, 30, 26 (four U.S. merchant "houses" in Smyrna in 1827, the first established in 1811).

15. Douglass C. North, "The United States Balance of Payments 1790–1860," *Studies in Income and Wealth,* Princeton 1960, vol. XXIV; Harrington, 126–

163; Cleona Lewis, *America's Stake in International Investment,* Washington, D.C. 1938, 174.

16. Gras and Larson, 92–98, 119–113 (investments of U.S. traders). Astor had a permanent representative in China from 1817 to 1823, until the man died (Porter, II, 614). Perkins & Co. was in China from 1803 to 1829, until Cushing returned home and Forbes died (Forbes, 340–341); James P. Sturgis & Co., Russell, Sturgis & Co., and Russell & Sturgis of Manila were all merged into Russell & Co. (Morison, 273). Examples of short-lived companies abound. American Exporter, *Export Trade Directory 1912* (Harvey & Outerbridge, Bowring & Company; Arkell & Douglas); Jaffray, 7–13 (Hemenway). Arkell & Douglas no longer exists in the 1960s.

17. Flint, 8–9 (Americanization of W. R. Grace); telephone conversation with executive Melchior, Armstrong & Dessau, 1961, and American Exporter, *Export Trade Directory 1919–1920* (Americanization).

18. Aitken, 56, 134.

19. Bradley, 237, 244–245 (Honolulu); Basil Rauch, *American Interest in Cuba, 1848–1855,* New York 1948, 191 (Drake Brothers and Company); Jaffray, 48 (Hemenway); U.S. & Chilean Claims Commission, *The Final Report of George H. Shields,* Washington, D.C. 1894, 35–36, and U.S. & Chilean Claims Commission, *The Alsop Claim,* Washington, D.C. 1910, passim. On Feb. 16, 1879, Chilean forces occupied the Bolivian silver mines at Caracoles, and by the end of March the entire Bolivian littoral was under Chilean control. The U.S. Government represented the surviving partners (and their heirs) of Alsop & Company in their claims against the Chilean government for the sum lost in the war. Charles Morrow Wilson, *Empire in Green and Gold,* New York 1947, chap. 4, esp. 77 (United Fruit's predecessor); Eugene W. Burgess and Frederick Harbison, *Casa Grace in Peru,* Washington, D.C. 1954, 22, 26. Another example of this pattern in a different part of the world was in Formosa where two traders built a port. See F. R. Dulles, *Americans in the Pacific,* Boston 1932, 76.

20. Lewis, 192–193; Clyde William Phelps, *The Foreign Expansion of American Banks,* New York 1927, 8–9; Lewis Corey, *The House of Morgan,* New York 1930, 43; Gras and Larson, 550; Charles W. Drees, *Americans in Argentina,* Buenos Aires 1922, 151. Boston-born Samuel B. Hale also invested in Argentine railways (the Western Railway) and in 1842 he started cattle ranching with 25,000 acres.

Chapter II: New Stakes Abroad

1. The 1830s and 1850s were the key decades of foreign capital inflow; in the 1840s there was a return or repudiation of borrowed funds (Douglass North, "U.S. Balance of Payments 1800–1860," *Studies in Income and Wealth,* Princeton 1960, XXIV, 584). North does not deal with outflow for U.S. direct invest-

ments abroad. There is no book on the role of foreign capital in American economic development. For a start, see Cleona Lewis, *America's Stake in International Investment*, Washington, D.C. 1938, 7–30, 52, 68–70, 78–80, 88, 100, 110; Carter Goodrich, "Foreign Capital in the United States," unpubl. typescript, and Harry H. Pierce, "Foreign Investment in American Enterprise," in David I. Gilchrist and W. David Lewis, *Economic Change in the Civil War Era*, Greenvale, Del. 1965, 41–53 (on portfolio investments).

2. The relationship between American business abroad and the U.S. government is in itself deserving of a book. In this volume it will be touched on only briefly. Useful are: Record Group 59, National Archives (State Department records); Post Records, NA; published reports of consular representatives have appeared at various intervals. The best source on treaties is Hunter Miller, ed., *Treaties and Other International Acts of the United States Government*, 8 vols., Washington, D.C. 1931–1948. On claims see RG 76, NA, and John Bassett Moore, *History of International Arbitrations*, 6 vols., Washington, D.C. 1898, esp. vol. II.

3. Herbert Marshall, Frank A. Southard, Jr., and Kenneth W. Taylor, *Canadian-American Industry, a Study in International Investment*, New Haven 1936, 11, 4, 3, 8–9 (Canadian investments); Testimony of Matthew Curtis to Select Committee of British Parliament, "First Report from Select Committee Appointed to Inquire into the Operation of the Existing Laws Affecting the Exportation of Machinery," *Parliamentary Papers*, 1841, VII, 112 (Dyer). U.S. Dept. of Comm., Bureau of Foreign and Domestic Commerce, *American Direct Investments in Foreign Countries* (by Paul Dickens), Washington, D.C. 1930, 34 (1829 Mexican mining venture); Fred Wilbur Powell, *The Railroads of Mexico*, Boston 1921, 96 (stage coach route); Claims against Mexico under the Convention of 1839, RG 76, NA (other investments); see also Moore, II, 1276ff (Mexico); Basil Rauch, *American Interest in Cuba*, New York 1948, 31; J. Fred Rippy, "Investments of Citizens of the United States in Latin America," *Journal of Business*, 22:18, January 1949 (Cuban sugar investment, 1828); E. F. Atkins, *60 Years in Cuba, Reminiscences of Edwin F. Atkins*, Cambridge, Mass. 1926, 123–124 (early U.S. investments in Cuban sugar); Ravignani, Emilio, ed., *Asambleas Constituyentes Argentinas 1813–1833*, Buenos Aires 1937, vol. I, entries for July 19, 1813, and Aug. 2, 1813, 56, 60 (brickmaking and boat service). I am indebted to Mr. Pedro Vulovic for pointing out this reference to me. Edmond John Haslop, "Americans in Argentina," *Comments on Argentine Trade*, 16:14, April 1937 (Stephen Hallett); Moore, II, 1485–1487, 1497–1543 (splendid on Hopkins in Paraguay); see also Misc. Claims #21, RG 76, NA; F. R. Dulles, *Americans in the Pacific*, Boston 1932, 155–566 (Hawaii); Lewis, 293 (Russia).

4. Leland Jenks, *Our Cuban Colony*, New York 1928, 19 (Cuban railroad); *Dictionary of American Biography*, XX, 63, and Frederick M. Halsey, *Railway Expansion in Latin America*, New York 1916, 11, 34–35 (Wheelwright).

5. Watt Stewart, *Henry Meiggs, Yankee Pizarro*, Durham, N.C. 1946, 18, 23.

Colonel George Earl Church, another U.S. entrepreneur in Latin America, undertook work as an engineer in 1860 on the Great Northern Railway between Buenos Aires and San Fernando. See Lewis Hanke, "A Note on the Life and Publications of Colonel George Earl Church," *Books at Brown,* 20:132 (1965).

6. Based on data in works cited in nn. 3–5 above, plus various claims commission reports. Reports of Chilean Claims Commission of 1892 indicate that the U.S. government considered money earned abroad and invested abroad by Americans as an "American direct investment abroad." Meiggs was an outstanding example of a fugitive from American justice.

7. See RG 76, NA, and Moore, *International Arbitrations,* esp. vol. II.

8. Lewis, 12.

9. Miriam Beard, *A History of Business,* Ann Arbor, Mich. 1963, II, 161; Emory R. Johnson et al., *History of Domestic and Foreign Commerce of the United States,* Washington, D.C. 1915, II, 124–25; W. T. Easterbrook and Hugh G. J. Aitken, *Canadian Economic History,* Toronto 1956, 298–299, 313 (Great Western); Robert Luther Thompson, *Wiring a Continent,* Princeton 1947, 299–300, 306, 433–434, and *Dictionary of American Biography,* VI, 358 (Atlantic cable). George Haven Putnam, *George Palmer Putnam, A Memoir,* New York 1912, 33–34, 49, 99–100 (the branch of Wiley and Putnam shut down in 1847).

10. Letter printed in Putnam, 74–78 (addressed to New York *Commercial Advertiser,* April 1844).

11. Adelaide Hasse, *Index to U.S. Documents Relating to Foreign Affairs,* Washington, D.C. 1914, 232–234, gives voluminous citations on isthmian transit projects from 1824 to 1839. Hunter Miller, *Treaties,* Washington, D.C. 1937, V, 154 ("golden moment"), 115–143 (treaty on Isthmus transit rights); Polk's message to Senate, Feb. 10, 1847, *ibid.,* 156 (railroad or canal); Fessenden N. Otis, *Isthmus of Panama: History of the Panama Railroad and of the Pacific Mail Steamship Company,* New York 1867, 16–17 (Congress and mail contracts; Aspinwall's plans); *Dictionary of American Biography,* I, 396 (Aspinwall).

12. Otis, 16–22; Halsey, 4, 106–111.

13. Frederick Merk, *Manifest Destiny and Mission in American History,* New York 1963, 128, 134–135, 139, 142. Merk writes that the Tehuantepec route was most favored by President Polk and his cabinet during the Mexican War. This interpretation hardly meshes with the President's own message to the Senate, Feb. 10, 1847, in which he referred to the Isthmus of Panama as "the most practicable for a railroad or canal"—Powell, 149–152, Merk, 208, and Misc. Claims #174, RG 76, NA (Tehuantepec Railroad Company).

14. Halsey, 134–135.

15. Included here are only four examples, but see J. Fred Rippy, *Capitalists and Colombia,* New York 1931, 45–50, for more interoceanic plans; see also Hasse, 252–261.

16. 31st Cong., 1st sess., H. Ex. Doc. 75, 173–180 (copy August 1849 contract);

34th Cong., 1st sess., S. Ex. Doc. 68, 100–102 (charter of Accessory Transit Co., Aug. 14, 1851); enclosures with letter of David Ogden to W. H. Seward, May 3, 1864, Misc. Ltrs., RG 59, NA (splendid on Accessory Transit Co. and size of investment; includes a letter from Vanderbilt, March 26, 1856); Thomas A. Bailey, *A Diplomatic History of the American People,* 6th ed., New York 1958, 275, 488 (Clayton-Bulwer Treaty); 33rd Cong., 1st sess., S. Ex. Doc. 8 (1852-1853 problems in Nicaragua), esp. 14 ("crave protection"), 16 ("depredations on the property"); Milton Offutt, *The Protection of Citizens Abroad by the Armed Forces of the United States,* Baltimore 1928, 32–35; 33rd Cong., 1st sess., S. Ex. Doc. 85 and 33rd Cong., 1st sess., H. Ex Doc. 126 (events of May, June, July 1854); Pierce message to Congress, Dec. 4, 1854, printed in James Richardson, *Messages of the President,* Washington, D.C. 1897, V, 280–284 (for recital of events and justification of Hollins); Claims of Citizens of the United States against Nicaragua, 1879, in Misc. Claims #235, RG 76, NA (property losses of Accessory Transit Company and losses of Central American Transit Company, incorporated New Jersey March 28, 1862); throughout Weaton J. Lane, *Commodore Vanderbilt,* New York 1942, 87–138, has been helpful; Moore, II, 1560–1565 (Costa Rica claims of Vanderbilt); data from Lane indicate Vanderbilt profited.

17. Otis, 59–69 (Panama railroad); Pierce's message to Congress, Aug. 21, 1856, and Buchanan's 1st Annual Message, Dec. 8, 1857, in Richardson, V, 416, 447 (safe passage); Offutt, passim, notes two such interventions before 1861 and a large number thereafter. Otis, 46 (passengers); Halsey, 112–118 (Panama railroad history); U.S. Senate Hearings before the Committee on Interoceanic Canals, *Panama Canal,* 62nd Cong., 2nd sess., Washington, D.C. 1912, 243–245.

18. While much of Panama's "American" character came after the Canal was built, even before its construction there was already a large American community in Panama. See Rippy, 50–52; F. U. Adams, *Conquest of the Tropics,* New York 1914, 35 (banana planting along Panama Railroad).

19. U.S. Dept. of Comm., Bureau of Census, *Historical Statistics,* Washington, D.C. 1960, 545, 547 (exports); W. Paul Strassmann, *Risk and Technological Innovation, American Manufacturing Methods during the Nineteenth Century,* Ithaca 1959, 117 (America's world position); H. J. Habakkuk, *American and British Technology in the Nineteenth Century,* Cambridge, Eng. 1962, 4–5 (U.S. products and mechanization); J. Leander Bishop, *A History of American Manufactures from 1608 to 1860,* Philadelphia 1864, II, 524–527 (lists exhibitors at the Crystal Palace).

20. "Agreement signed by Burgess & Key," London, Aug. 3, 1851; Burgess & Key, "Memorandum for Dr. Black, *London Illustrated News,*" Aug. 23, 1851; and Burgess & Key to C. H. McCormick, June 8, 1871, all in Nettie Fowler McCormick Manuscripts, McCormick Collection, State Historical Society of Wisconsin. See also William T. Hutchinson, *Cyrus H. McCormick,* New York 1935, II, 406.

21. Charles T. Haven and Frank A. Belden, *A History of the Colt Revolver,* New York 1940, is the basic source on Colt. It gives a picture of the factory at Pimlico near Vauxhall Bridge, 1853–1857, p. 347, and a contemporary description, 345–349. It reprints a report of the Committee on Patents, December 1853, in which Colt's reasons for the London factory are given, 337. See *ibid.,* 336–339, 86 (machinery quotation), 89 (end London manufactory), 124 (licenses).

22. John Dunning, in *American Investment in British Manufacturing Industry* (London 1958, 17), calls this the first American participation in British manufacturing industry; it is not the first, since the Colt enterprise preceded it.

23. U.S. Dept. of Comm., Bureau of Census, *Historical Statistics,* Washington, D.C. 1960, 565.

Chapter III: The Appearance of Modern International Business

1. William Woodruff, *Impact of Western Man,* New York 1967, 237 (conquest of distance).

2. Alfred D. Chandler, Jr., in "The Beginnings of 'Big Business' in American Industry," *Business History Review,* 33:1–31 (Spring 1959), argues that big business developed in the United States in the 1880's and 1890's based on the extension of railroads and the growth of urban centers. He demonstrates for U.S. business a pattern in establishing a domestic sales network. We will show a similar pattern in establishing a foreign network.

3. *Historical Statistics of the United States,* Washington, D.C. 1960, 564–565 (balance-of-payments figures). The earliest general estimates of the book value of U.S. direct investments abroad are in Cleona Lewis, *America's Stake in International Investment,* Washington, D.C., 1938, 578ff. These estimates are reproduced in Table V.2.

4. The information on Singer comes in large part from the Singer Manufacturing Company Manuscripts, State Historical Society of Wisconsin, Madison, Wisconsin. Other data come from the Scudder Collection, Graduate School of Business Library, Columbia University. Citations for material from the Singer Manuscripts at Wisconsin will include Acquisition number, box, volume, or carton number, letter book number (if appropriate), plus the designation S. Mss. This chapter was completed before my attention was drawn to Robert Bruce Davies'. "The International Operations of the Singer Manufacturing Company, 1854–1895," unpubl. Ph.D. diss. University of Wisconsin 1966, and Robert B. Davies, "Peacefully Working to Conquer World Markets," *Business History Review,* 43:299–325 (Autumn 1969). Mr. Davies deals with some of the same material as I am covering.

5. Statement by I. M. Singer, in "Applicant's Petition, Statement, Account, and Testimony, in the Matter of the Application of Isaac M. Singer for the Extension of Letter Patent . . . granted to him Nov. 4, 1856," New York 1870, 6–7, copy in Acq. 2, Carton 3, S. Mss.

6. Singer's first French patents were Aug. 12, 1851, and Apr. 13, 1852; see data in Acq. 2, Carton 1, S. Mss. and statement by I. M. Singer, n. 5 above.

7. Chas. L. Fleishman (a company lawyer) and W. F. Proctor (later to become a vice president of Singer Manufacturing Company), Paris, to I. M. Singer & Co., Apr. 5, 1855, Acq. 2, Box 35, S. Mss. (terms of the sale, which took place Mar. 23, 1855).

8. I. M. Singer & Co. to Callebaut, Paris, Apr. 24, 1855, and to W. F. Proctor, Paris, July 16, 1855, both in Acq. 2, Carton 1, S. Mss.

9. I. M. S. & Co. to Chas. L. Fleishman, Paris, Dec. 14, 1855 (manufactory understood to be completed), Aug. 29, 1856, and May 29, 1858 (problems); Charles Callebaut v. Isaac M. Singer & Edward Clark, May 10, 1858 (litigation), all in Acq. 2, Carton 1, S. Mss. See also John Munroe & Co., Paris, to I. M. S. & Co., July 28, 1862, Acq. 1, Box 2, Ltr. Bk. 5, Broderick to I. M. S. & Co., Mar. 14, 1863, Acq. 1, Box 7, Ltr. Bk. 15, Fleishman to I. M. S. & Co., Apr. 2, 1862, Acq. 1, Box 7, Ltr. Bk. 16, Fleishman to President of Singer Manufacturing Company, Feb. 12, 1864, Acq. 1, Box 8, Ltr. Bk. 26; and Fleishman to I. Hopper, President of Singer Mfg. Co., Oct. 19, 1866, Acq. 1, Box 28, Ltr. Bk. 63, all in S. Mss.

10. Andrew B. Jack, "The Channels of Distribution for an Innovation: The Sewing Machine Industry in America, 1860–1865," *Explorations in Entrepreneurial History*, 9:120, 121, 124, 125–132, 134 (February 1957).

11. *Jornal do Comercio*, Nov. 11, 1858, and Dec. 2, 1858 (Brazilian ads); "Statement of Machines Sold in Foreign Countries," Acq. 2, Carton 1, Alexander Anderson to F. G. Bourne, Mar. 10, 1896, Acq. 2, Box 29 (Kimball in Glasgow 1860), W. E. Broderick, London, to I. M. S. & Co., Jan. 22, 1862, Acq. 2, Carton 1, S. Mss. ("pioneers"); Broderick to I. M. S. & Co. Jan. 4, 1862, Acq. 1, Box 1, Ltr. Bk. 2, S. Mss.

12. F. G. Bourne, "American Sewing Machines," in Chauncey Depew, ed. *1795–1895 One Hundred Years of American Commerce*, New York 1895, II, 535 and 525 (Civil War; Howe); "Applicant's Petition," n. 5 above, 186–183 (premiums on foreign exchange); Broderick to I. M. S. & Co., Feb. 25, 1862, Acq. 1, Box 1, Ltr. Bk. 4, S. Mss. (competition); Acq. 1, Boxes 8 and 16, S. Mss. (frequent reference in letters to Wheeler & Wilson's role).

13. Broderick to I. M. S. & Co., Feb. 15, 1862, Acq. 1, Box 1, Ltr. Bk. 4, S. Mss. (Broderick's remittances and branch offices); F. Neidlinger, Hamburg, to I. M. S. & Co., Apr. 8, 1863, Acq. 1, Box 7, Ltr. Bk. 16, S. Mss.

14. See December 1864 letters of Woodruff to Singer Mfg. Co., Acq. 1, Box 16, Ltr. Bk. 38, S. Mss. esp. letter of Dec. 16, 1864.

15. Acq. 1, Boxes 8, 10–21, S. Mss. (business in 1864–1865).

16. See Woodruff letters, Acq. 1, Box 24, Ltr. Bks. 54–55; Woodruff to Singer Mfg. Co., Sept. 1 and 8, 1866, Acq. 1, Box 26, Ltr. Bk. 59 (. . . *my delicate little body*"); Sept. 22, 1866, Acq. 1, Box 27, Ltr. Bk. 60 ("to the dogs"); Nov. 21, 1866, Acq. 1, Box 28, Ltr. Bk. 63, S. Mss.

17. Woodruff to Singer Mfg. Co., Jan. 18, 1867, Acq. 1, Box 30, Ltr. Bk. 66; Mar. 16, 1867, Acq. 1, Box 31, Ltr. Bk. 68 (Woodruff's visit to States); June 19, 1867, Acq. 1, Box 33, Ltr. Bk. 72 (McKenzie investigating), S. Mss.

18. Bourne, 535. The record of premiums on foreign remittances does show a sharp drop in 1867; see "Applicant's Petition," n. 5 above, 186–193.

19. Woodruff to Singer Mfg. Co., Dec. 7, and Nov. 27, 1867, Acq. 1, Box 36, Ltr. Bk. 79; Acq. 1, vol. 116 (London accounts, 1867), S. Mss.

20. "Report of the Proceedings on the Occasion of Breaking the Ground for Singer Manufacturing Company's New Factory, May 18, 1882," 21, 32, Acq. 1, Carton 4; Acq. 2, Carton 1 (balance sheet); J. K. Macdonald to Singer Mfg. Co., Sept. 14, 1867, Acq. 1, Box 35, Ltr. Bk. 76 (100 units); Anderson to Bourne, n. 11 above (200 units and background on the history of Singer plants in Glasgow), all in S. Mss.

21. Acq. 1, Boxes 37–53; Acq. 1, vol. 117; Acq. 2, Boxes 1–6, S. Mss.

22. Acq. 2, Box 1 (sewing machines sold); Woodruff to Edward Clark (President), May 19, 1877, Acq. 2, Box 2, S. Mss.

23. Woodruff to Clark, Mar. 24, 1878, Acq. 2, Box 2, S. Mss.

24. Bourne, 535 (competitive sales); "Principal Offices and Branches," Acq. 1, vol. 117, S. Mss.

25. Geo. McKenzie, London, to Woodruff, Apr. 17, 1879, Acq. 2, Box 2, S. Mss.

26. London Committee Minutes, Acq. 2, Box 41 (London Office activity); Acq. 2, Boxes 6–8 (Neidlinger correspondence); New York office activity is inferred by process of elimination and reading between the lines.

27. "Report of Proceedings . . . New Factory"; Barr & Knox to Singer Mfg. Co., Feb. 26, 1883, Acq. 2, Box 7 (probable cost of Kilbowie factory, exclusive of land, law expenses, surveying, architects and measures, fees and the cost of all fixed plant and machinery—boilers, engines, and so on—was estimated at £178,805, or $868,264). Full cost figures are not available.

28. London Committee Minutes, Acq. 2, Box 41, S. Mss. (market allocations).

29. Tom Mahoney, *The Great Merchants*, New York 1955, 67 (1873 Montreal assembly plant); William Close, Montreal to Geo. McKenzie, Sept. 22, 1881, Acq. 2, Box 5; Close to Singer Mfg. Co., May 23, 1882, Acq. 2, Box 6; Close to McKenzie, Mar. 22, 1883, Acq. 2, Box 8 (all on reasons for factory); Close to all Canadian branches, Nov. 5, 1883, Acq. 2, Box 7 ("We have been shipping you for some time past, machines manufactured in Montreal."). Geo. Neidlinger, Hamburg, to Geo. McKenzie: Mar. 4, 1882, Acq. 2, Box 7 ("enormous duty"); Aug. 1, 1882, Acq. 2, Box 6 (plans for factory); Dec. 22, 1883, Acq. 2, Box 8 (progress), and Robert Gillespie, Floridsdorf, Austria, to McKenzie, Dec. 20, 1883, Acq. 2, Box 8 ("We [in Austria] have now cast five times and I must say that we are getting on pretty fair. . .").

30. Depew, 345 (locomotive exports); *History of the Baldwin Locomotive Works*, n.p. [1923], passim.; Isaac F. Marcosson, *Wherever Men Trade: The*

Romance of the Cash Register, New York 1945, 192 (by the mid-1880s John H. Patterson of National Cash Register was selling cash registers abroad); see also Theodore Armstrong, *Our Company,* Dayton 1949, 79, and Samuel Crowther, *John H. Patterson,* Garden City, New York 1924, 268; William T. Hutchinson, *Cyrus Hall McCormick,* New York 1935, II, chaps. 11 and 15, and esp. p. 285; also Cyrus H. McCormick, Jr., London, to Cyrus H. McCormick, July 8, 1878, Cyrus McCormick Mss., State Historical Society of Wisconsin (reaper sales abroad). In 1881 the Remington Company wrote to the Singer representative in Germany, "We have a very handsome business in Great Britain and quite a trade in France and have received many orders and many applications for the agency from Germany." The company wanted to know if the Singer representative would undertake to sell the typewriters (see E. Remington & Sons, New York, to George Neidlinger, Aug. 16, 1881, Acq. 2, Box 5, S. Mss.). The Singer representative did not undertake the task, and in 1883 Remington arranged for direct representation in Germany, then in France in 1884, in Russia in 1885, in England 1886, and so on throughout Europe. See Tilghman Richards, *Typewriters,* London 1938, 7 (Remington's direct representation); Otis data from files of Otis Elevator Company, New York.

31. John Dunning, *American Investment in British Manufacturing Industry,* London 1958, 18, 32; Herbert Marshall, Frank A. Southard, and Kenneth W. Taylor, *Canadian-American Industry,* New Haven 1936, 11, 13, 14.

32. R. L. Thompson, *Wiring a Continent,* Princeton 1947, 10, 14, 15 (Morse was interested in foreign patents), 69 (Canadian situation), 289 (formation of Western Union), 371 (cable to Russia), 306, 321, 434 (transatlantic cable); Marshall et al., 125 (Montreal Telegraph); Lloyd P. Hughlett, ed., *Industrialization of Latin America,* New York 1946, 109, and *DAB,* XVI, 521 (Scrymser).

33. Marshall et al., 125–126 (Dominion Telegraph & Great Northwestern); Hughlett, 109 (International Ocean Telegraph); *Moody's Public Utilities 1928* (Commercial Cable Co.); *DAB,* XII, 76 (Mackay); *Foreign Relations of the U.S.,* passim.

34. J. E. Kingsbury, *The Telephone and Telephone Exchanges,* London 1915, 191–206 (the telephone in Europe and abroad); Catherine MacKenzie, *Alexander Graham Bell,* Boston 1928, 183ff (Bell in England); *Deposition of Alexander Graham Bell* (1892) in suit brought by the United States to annul the Bell patents, 80–82, 89, 363 (background information); "Edison Telephone Company" files, in Edison National Historic Site Archives, West Orange, N.J. (hereafter cited as EA); Matthew Josephson, *Edison,* New York 1959, 149–155; A. N. Holcombe, "The Telephone in Great Britain," *Quarterly Journal of Economics,* 21:96–135, November 1906 (an excellent article); British Parliamentary Papers, Select Committee Report, *Telephones,* London 1898, vol. XII, passim.

35. Kingsbury, 191–206; files, Secretary's Office, American Telephone and Telegraph Company (International Bell Telephone Company, Continental Telephone Company, Tropical Telephone Company); Victor M. Berthold, *History*

of the Telephone and Telegraph in Brazil, New York 1922, 52ff; F. R. Welles, "The Early Days of the Company Abroad," *Western Electric News,* 1:1–3, July 1912 (excellent article by founder of Western Electric's activity in Belgium; also has data on International Bell Telephone Company); Julien Brault, *Le Téléphone en 1888—histoire de la téléphonie,* Paris 1888, 243 (Oriental Telephone Company); H. B. Thayer to Leggett, May 25, 1905, Western Electric Archives, Western Electric Company, New York (Hong Kong and Oriental Telephone Company); British Parliamentary Papers. *Reports Respecting Telephone Service in Foreign Countries,* London 1899, vol. XCVI, passim, A. N. Holcombe, *Public Ownership of Telephones on the Continent of Europe,* Boston 1911, passim, esp. 25, 27, 31, 269–272, 358, 359, 374, 383; *Electrical World,* July 3, 1897 (I.B.T.C.); Dept. of State of New York to author, Nov. 15, 1963 (dissolution documents).

36. American Bell Telephone Company, *Annual Reports,* 1880, 1881, 1882, 1883, 1885 (Canadian holdings); R. C. Fetherstonhaugh, *Charles Fleetwood Sise,* Montreal 1944, 112–131 (excellent on Canadian telephone situation).

37. F. R. Welles, "The Early Days of the Company Abroad," *Western Electric News* 1:2 (July 1912); Welles files, Western Electric Archives, esp. Welles to Barton, Jan. 1, 1890 (Western Electric abroad); W. E. Leigh, "Some Features of Our Foreign Business," *Western Electric News,* 2:1–3 (October 1913); *Electrician,* 4:77, 78, 81, February 1885 (Montreal factory—1882; patent situation).

38. Gourard to G. P. Lowrey, Jan. 31, 1879, EA; Josephson, 188ff (Morgan link); see EA, passim., on Morgan's interest in Edison's foreign business; Edison to Drexel, Morgan & Co., Oct. 18, 1881; Theodore Waterhouse to Egisto P. Fabbri, Dec. 16, 1881 (new company); memo in Edison's hand on course to be followed by London company, [1882]; Arnold White, Secretary of Edison Electric Light Company Ltd. to Edison, Sept. 28, 1882 (problems); Charles Batchelor to Edison, Oct. 3, 1882 (Edison's opposition to British lamp manufacture); Lowrey, Paris, to Edison, Oct. 23, 1881; E. H. Johnson to Edison, Nov. 2, 1881 (Swan); data on The Edison and Swan United Electric Company, Ltd.—all in EA.

39. See 1880–1881 files on Edison Electric Light by foreign country; Articles of Association, February 1882 for all three French companies, and list of subscribers, EA.

40. Koppel S. Pinson, *Modern Germany,* 2nd ed., New York 1966, 227, and Felix Pinner, *Emil Rathenau und das elektrische zeitalter,* Leipzig 1918, 90ff (Rathenau's role). Batchelor to Edison, Oct. 9, 1882, and J. F. Bailey to Edison, Dec. 13, 1882 (relations with Siemens); 1883 agreements with Siemens & Halske, wherein the latter agrees not to attack or oppose Edison's incandescent electric light patents in exchange for other benefits; 1882–1883 files on Edison Electric Light in foreign countries, esp. Batchelor to Insull, Apr. 25, 1882, and J. F. Bailey to Edison, Oct. 21, 1883; Hammer to Edison, July 16, 1883 ("to deal directly with you"), Batchelor to Edison, Dec. 9, 1883 (foreign bankers' villainy)—all in EA.

41. Batchelor to Edison, Feb. 8, 1884 (the deception); file on Edison Electric

Light Company of Europe, Ltd., 1884 (minutes of shareholder and board of directors meetings, reports to the directors by the officers, bondholders, and other interested parties); Minutes of the Board of Directors, Edison Electric Light Company of Europe, Ltd., Jan. 21, 1885 (approval of arrangements)—all in EA.

42. Data in 1880–1881 files on Edison Electric Light by foreign country; Frazar and Co., Yokohama, to Edison, Aug. 5, 1885, and to F. R. Upton, Apr. 29, 1886, EA (Japan); American Trading Co. to Edison, Oct. 24, 1885, EA and Fred Harrington, *God, Mammon and the Japanese,* New York 1944, 128 (Korea); Marshall et al., 15 (Canadian Co.); Theodore Geiger, *The General Electric Company in Brazil,* Washington, D.C. 1961 (Edison in Brazil); Frank Lewis Dyer and Thomas Commerford Martin, *Edison, His Life and Inventions,* New York 1929, I, 376 (Chile); U.S. Dept. of State, Bureau of Foreign Commerce, *Commercial Relations of the U.S. with Foreign Countries, 1900,* I, Washington, D.C. 1901, 688 (Argentina); R. G. B. Davis to Edison, Sept. 18, 1884, EA (notation by Edison); Stewart to Edison, Jan. 10, 1885 (failure of Kendall & Co.), and Edison comment on Stewart's Nov. 18, 1885, letter, EA.

43. S. B. Eaton to Edison Electric Co. of Europe, Sept. 9, 1891, EA (December 1886 fusion); Deutsche Edison Gesellschaft to Edison Electric Light Co. of Europe, Aug. 1, 1885, EA (asking for ratification German-French contracts); A. E. G. to National City Bank, Jan. 23, 1925, in Prospectus, Scudder Collection, Columbia University (name change 1887); "Plan for Edison General Electric Co.," n.d. [1888?], EA (A. E. G.'s participation in formation Edison General Electric).

44. John Winthrop Hammond, *Men and Volts, The Story of General Electric,* Philadelphia 1941, 57, 69–70 (Brush), 91 (Thomson-Houston); Dunning, 23 (Brush-licensing); Gourard to Insull, Dec. 31, 1881, EA (Brush); Geiger, 37 (Brush and Thomson-Houston); General Electric, *Annual Report,* Jan. 31, 1893; Prospectus of the Canadian General Electric Co., Ltd., Apr. 1, 1922, indicates that the Canadian company acquired at formation the "exclusive right in perpetuity to manufacture and sell in Canada the products developed by General Electric Co." Canadian General Electric Co., *Annual Report 1905,* Scudder Collection (G.E. majority ownership at origin).

45. Henry G. Prout, *A Life of George Westinghouse,* New York 1921, 62 (brakes exported), 269 (manufactory in France); U.S. Dept. of State, Bureau of Foreign Commerce, *Commercial Relations of the U.S. with Foreign Countries, 1899,* II, Washington, D.C. 1900, 183 (stipulation in French contracts); Prout, 62 (manufacture in England), 262 (Germany and Russia), 113 (Westinghouse Electric Co. in U.S.), 263 (Westinghouse in London); Scudder Collection (date of formation Westinghouse Electric Co.).

46. "Pond's Chronology," typescript, n.d. [1956 or later?] sent to the author by Chesebrough-Pond's, Inc. William Haynes, *American Chemical Industry,* New York 1949, VI, 60–61. Burroughs died, and in 1910 Wellcome became a British

subject; thus the company became a British-controlled firm. Marshall et al., 14 (cites *Monetary Times* on Wyeth); Frederick Stearns & Co., Prospectus, January 1917, Scudder Collection; Tom Mahoney, *The Merchants of Life*, New York 1959, 79 (Parke Davis).

47. Carl W. Ackerman, *George Eastman*, Boston 1930, 4, 28, 42, 52–53, 58, 92–93, 94, 137. Marshall et al., 13 (American powder trust in Canada); William S. Dutton, *Du Pont*, New York, 1942, 180 (the Gunpowder Trade Association).

48. H. F. Williamson and Arnold R. Daum, *American Petroleum Industry*, Evanston 1959, 322, 338 (percentage oil exports); Austin Leigh Moore, *John D. Archbold and the Early Development of Standard Oil*, New York 1948, 64, and Allan Nevins, *Study in Power, John D. Rockefeller*, New York 1953, I, 40, 42 (Rockefeller & Co.); Ralph W. Hidy and Muriel E. Hidy, *Pioneering in Big Business*, New York 1955, 42–43 (foreign investments of Ohio-Standard), 143 (end of Standard's first foreign refinery); see Nevins, II, 117 (problems of Galician refinery; Nevins appears to be mistaken in his comment that it survived the "foolish enmity.").

49. Hidy and Hidy, 46 (formation of Standard Oil Trust), 126 (Thompson & Bedford, Chesebrough, Vacuum Oil), 127 (New York Standard), 128 (Waters-Pierce and Archbold and Conill; Canadian sales); Williamson and Daum, 516–519 (Baku-Tiflis line), 632, 636 (Russian competition); Nevins, II, 119–122 (oil war); Hidy and Hidy, 132ff (Russian competition), 144 (Tweddle); Bureau of Corporations, *Report of the Commissioner of Corporations on the Petroleum Industry*, pt. III, "Foreign Trade," Washington, D.C. 1909, 442ff (England), 331ff (Germany); Hidy and Hidy, 152 (East of Suez trade).

50. "Tabulation showing the year in which the New York Life began to do business in foreign countries," prepared for the author by Rose Hoey, New York Life Insurance Co., Feb. 14, 1963; J. Owen Stalson, *Marketing Life Insurance*, Cambridge, Mass. 1942, 827 (per cent of foreign business); NYLIC, Board of Trustees, Minutes, December 1882, NYLIC Archives (reasons for purchase Paris building); James M. Hudnut, *Semi-Centennial History of the New York Life Insurance Company, 1845–1895*, New York 1895 (Berlin and Vienna buildings and receipts from foreign business); Lawrence P. Abbott, *The Story of NYLIC*, New York 1930, 127–128 (foreign government requirements); Shepard Clough, *A Century of American Life Insurance, A History of the Mutual Life Insurance Company of New York*, New York 1946, 162; Morton Keller, *The Life Insurance Enterprise, 1885–1910*, Cambridge, Mass. 1963, 89, 90, 105 (Mexico).

Chapter IV: Factors Influencing the Growth of Business Abroad

1. *Commercial & Financial Chronicle*, December 1897, 1147 (the Austrian minister); Fred A. McKenzie, *The American Invaders*, New York 1901, 12 (the

Englishman's comments). McKenzie's book was published in England before it was published in New York; Alexander Dana Noyes, *Forty Years of American Finance*, New York 1909, 302–303 (details of Morgan's offer); B. H. Thwaite, *The American Invasion*, London 1902; and W. T. Stead, *The Americanization of the World*, London 1902.

2. John W. Gates, Chairman of American Steel and Wire, before the U.S. Industrial Commission, *Preliminary Report on Trusts and Industrial Combinations*, Washington, D.C. 1900, I, 9; G.E. *Annual Report* (Jan. 31, 1898); *Fortune*, August 1935, 75 (Sherwin-Williams slogan was adopted in 1895); Howard K. Beale, *Theodore Roosevelt and the Rise of America to World Power*, New York 1962, 80 (quotation from Depew).

3. Letterheads, New York Life Insurance Company Archives, New York; Morton Keller, *The Life Insurance Enterprise 1885–1910*, Cambridge, Mass. 1963, 94. Herbert Hoover, *Memoirs*, New York 1957, I, 29ff, 76–77; Isaac Marcosson, *Metal Magic*, New York 1949, 63 (Guggenheims). American interest in foreign trade at this time is brought out in A. K. Steigerwalt, *The National Association of Manufacturers 1895–1914*, Ann Arbor, Mich. 1964; and Ernest R. May, *Imperial Democracy: The Emergence of America as a Great Power*, New York 1961.

4. Alfred D. Chandler, "The Beginnings of 'Big Business' in American Industry," *Business History Review*, 33:1–31 (Spring 1959); *U.S. Industrial Commission Report*, Washington, D.C. 1900–1902, vols. I–XIX. Mira Wilkins, "An American Enterprise Abroad: American Radiator Company in Europe 1895–1914," *Business History Review*, 43:327, Autumn 1969 (example of response to U.S. depression); U.S. Dept. of Comm., Bureau of Census, *Historical Statistics of the United States*, Washington, D.C. 1960, 544 (exports of manufactured goods); Ralph L. Nelson, *Merger Movements in American Industry 1895–1956*, Princeton 1959; John Moody, *The Truth About Trusts*, New York 1904.

5. *Historical Statistics*, 564 (net exporter of capital); Nelson, 6 (large-scale capital market and mergers).

6. *Foreign Relations of the U.S.*; RG 59, NA; Walter LeFeber, *The New Empire*, Ithaca 1963; Ernest May, *Imperial Democracy: The Emergence of America as a Great Power;* Charles S. Campbell, *Special Business Interests and the Open Door Policy*, New Haven 1951, 12; *Foreign Relations of the U.S. 1909*, xv, xx (Taft comments); Herbert Croly, *Willard Straight*, New York 1924, 295 (other Taft statements); F. M. Huntington Wilson, "The Relation of Government to Foreign Investment," *Annals of the American Academy of Political and Social Science*, 68:298–311, November 1916 (F. M. Huntington Wilson was assistant secretary of state in the Taft administration). Richard W. Leopold, "The Emergence of America as a World Power: Some Second Thoughts," in John Braeman et al., eds., *Change and Continuity in Twentieth Century America*, New York 1964, 4 (United States as a world power). It is not claimed here that

the only reason for U.S. government action was to aid U.S. business. The author believes strongly that political considerations always took priority over economic considerations in Washington. Nonetheless, government spokesmen did emphasize their belief in giving aid to U.S. business abroad.

7. Company records and RG 59, NA; see also U.S. Dept. of State, *Foreign Relations of the United States;* George Sweet Gibb and Evelyn H. Knowlton, *The Resurgent Years 1911–1927,* New York 1956, 107 (oil and the State Department); Perkins to McCall, Aug. 31, 1899, Box 8, Perkins Papers, Special Collections, Columbia University (insurance firm and the State Department).

8. Sections 1, 2, and 3 of the Sherman Act include the phrase "restraint of trade . . . with foreign nations." R. Liefmann, *Cartels, Concerns and Trusts,* New York 1933; Alfred Plummer, *International Combines in Modern Industry,* 3rd ed., London 1951 (1st ed., 1934); Ervin Hexner, *International Cartels,* Chapel Hill 1945; George Stocking and Myron W. Watkins, *Cartels in Action,* New York 1946; and William S. Stevens, ed., *Industrial Combinations and Trusts,* New York 1913, 160–184 (copies of international agreements involving American companies). See also court cases against leading companies; Bureau of Corporations, Federal Trade Commission, Temporary National Economic Committee, and U.S. Tariff Commission reports. The hearings of the Kilgore, Truman, and Bone committees during World War II have pertinent data on these early relationships. Likewise, company records have been used. While the conclusions are her own, the author owes a great debt to the conceptualizations of Alfred Plummer. In the text she has tended to avoid where possible the use of the word "cartel," because of the negative connotation it has come to evoke. When it is used, its meaning is limited to formal restrictive agreements between or among otherwise *independent* concerns, designed to control prices, amounts produced, and/or major methods of marketing. Richard D. Robinson found in a survey of 172 American companies that "not infrequently . . . the initial ownership share held by an American firm in a foreign enterprise had been received in payment for intangible assets." He does not note that the existence of these intangible assets provided the *magnet* to attract local foreign capital. See his *International Business Policy,* New York 1964, 170.

9. The literature on the rise of nationalism in Canada and Europe is prolix. Any standard Canadian history tells the story; on European nationalism, see Carlton J. H. Hayes, *A Generation of Materialism 1871–1900,* New York 1941, chap. VI.

10. On Latin America see chapters VI, VIII, and IX below.

11. The distinction between "extra-national" and the "genuine" multinational corporation is from "Report of the Task Force on the Structure of Canadian Industry," *Foreign Ownership and Structure of Canadian Industry,* Ottawa 1968, 33.

Chapter V: Expanding Abroad

1. William B. Gates, *Michigan Copper and Boston Dollars,* Cambridge, Mass. 1951, 64; M. A. Abrams, "The French Copper Syndicate, 1887–1889," *Journal of Economic and Business History,* 4:409–428 (May 1932); Gates, 82–83 (Calumet & Hecla; 1892 agreement and its fate); *Engineering and Mining Journal,* Sept. 28, 1895, 294, Oct. 26, 1895, 389, and June 13, 1896, 561 (Rothschilds and Anaconda).

2. Scudder Collection, Columbia University, and Amalgamated Copper Company, Application for Listing on New York Stock Exchange, Feb. 14, 1910 (Amalgamated's aim). See Chapter VI on Amalgamated in Mexico. *Mineral Industry 1892,* 3 (Lewisohn Bros.); *Copper Manual 1899,* II, 380 (Lewisohn Bros.' London house); Secretary of State, New Jersey (date of formation United Metals); Harvey O'Connor, *The Guggenheims,* New York 1937, 111–112 (United Metals Selling Company was initially owned by the Lewisohn brothers, H. H. Rogers, William Rockefeller and other individuals); *Copper Manual 1904,* III, 167 (activity UMSC). UMSC handled copper for companies outside Amalgamated; in 1901 it made a ten-year contract with the American Smelting and Refining Company to sell that company's copper output at a commission of one per cent. See also *Moody's 1914,* 612 (Amalgamated's acquisition of UMSC); O'Connor, *The Guggenheims,* 111–112, 118, 123, 281, and *Commercial and Financial Chronicle,* March 19, 1910, 788 (ASARCO); F. Ernest Richter, "The Amalgamated Copper Company," *Quarterly Journal of Economics,* 30:406 February 1916 (Guggenheims' largest dealers).

3. Testimony of John D. Ryan, U.S. House, Judiciary Committee, *Hearings on the Clayton Act,* 63rd Cong., 2nd sess. (1914), I, ser. 7, pt. 11, 435.

4. Allan Nevins, *Rockefeller,* New York 1953, II, 123 (quote), 124 (no general agreement); Ralph W. Hidy and Muriel E. Hidy, *Pioneering in Big Business,* New York 1955, 237; H. F. Williamson and Arnold R. Daum, *American Petroleum Industry,* Evanston, Ill. 1959, 650, and Dept. of Commerce and Labor, Bureau of Corporations), *Report of Commissioner of Corporations on the Petroleum Industry,* Washington, D.C. 1909, pt. III, pp. 88–89 (henceforth cited as *Bur. of Corps. Rep. on Petroleum Industry*).

5. *Bur. of Corps. Rep. on Petroleum Industry,* pt. III, 89, 92 (Europe), 287–291ʳ (Far East); Hidy and Hidy, 520, 563–564 (Europe), 549, 553 (Far East).

6. *Bur. of Corps. Rep. on Petroleum Industry,* 51–52 (Standard Oil holdings 1907). Hidy and Hidy indicate that in 1897 Standard Oil officials first went to Rumania in search of concessions; in 1904 they first acquired leases to oil lands there (p. 516); see Chapter VI of this volume for the acquisition by Waters-Pierce (a Standard Oil affiliate) of oil lands in Mexico in 1902. See also F. C. Gerretson, *History of Royal Dutch,* Lieden 1953, II, 46; Hidy and Hidy, 502, 780 (Dutch East Indies), 499–501 (Burma); *Foreign Relations of the U.S. 1922,* II,

352–354 (1902 Burmese situation); Hidy and Hidy, 498 (Japan). The Jersey Standard subsidiary, International Oil Company, Ltd., built a modern refinery in Japan which was sold to Nippon Petroleum Company along with the subsidiary's small production activity. International Oil Company, Ltd.'s activities in Japan were from 1900 through 1906.

7. Hidy and Hidy, 522.

8. George Sweet Gibb and Evelyn H. Knowlton, *The Resurgent Years,* New York 1956, 8 (effects of dissolution); Hidy and Hidy, 712–713 (Jersey Standard's share); "Chesebrough Manufacturing Company," typescript, Nov. 17, 1911, Scudder Collection, Columbia University Library; Chesebrough-Pond's Inc., "The Story of Chesebrough-Pond's Inc.," n.d. [1964?], 4–5; Hidy and Hidy, 126 (Chesebrough's Latin American outlets); "Company History [Chesebrough-Pond's]," typescript, 1960, communication to author by company. "History of the Company [Socony-Mobil]," typescript, n.d. [ca. 1955] in files of Mobil Oil Southern Africa (Pty.), Ltd.; Hidy and Hidy, 525, 488–489, 778 (Vacuum Oil: blending plants in Germany, Hungary, Austria, England, and Russia); Edward Prizer, President of Vacuum Oil Co., to Secretary of State, Oct. 27, 1918, RG 59, 763.72113A/510, National Archives (Vacuum Oil's European operations); Hidy and Hidy, 126 (Vacuum Oil—1892 office in Bombay) and 528 (exports of Vacuum Oil to Australia, New Zealand, Egypt, Portugal, and South Africa 1910). Interviews with Mobil Oil officials, summer 1965, in Egypt, West Africa, and South Africa, indicate that in these places, as well as in Australia in the early years of the century, Vacuum Oil sold more than lubricating oil. Lisbon, Portugal, was the point from which the Vacuum Oil trade on the west coast of Africa was supervised and supplied: interviews with Mobil Oil officials in Accra, Lagos, and Monrovia, summer 1965. The South African business of Vacuum Oil started with exports as early as 1882. In 1897 Vacuum Oil, London, sent two representatives to canvass the South African market. A branch of the London Vacuum Oil Company, which was wholly owned by Vacuum Oil in New York, was opened in Johannesburg in 1902 and then in other South African cities. In that same year Colonial Oil Company started marketing refined oil products in South Africa—mainly illuminating parafin. Colonial Oil Company and Vacuum Oil Company in 1908 amalgamated to form Vacuum Oil Company of South Africa, Ltd., which handled the whole range of petroleum products. Vacuum Oil Company was the first oil company in South Africa ("History of the Company," cited above, and Eric Rosenthal, *Mobil in South Africa,* Capetown 1962). Vacuum Oil also merged with Colonial Oil in Australia. See *Moody's 1914* (Vacuum Oil's use of Mobiloil name; also on Colonial Oil). Hidy and Hidy, 483 (Borne, Scrymser; Galena Signal Oil Co.); Chapter VI below (Waters-Pierce).

9. Gibb and Knowlton, 681 (foreign deliveries), 76 (small oil production), 91 (Dutch East Indies). Pp. 185–186 above (Peruvian oil). J. A. Spender, *Weetman Pearson,* London 1930, 202 (Mexico).

10. John A. De Novo, *American Interests and Policies in the Middle East 1900–1939,* Minneapolis 1963, 169 and RG 59, 867.6363/1, 4, NA (New York Standard in Near East); Paul Reinsch, American Minister to Peking to Secretary of State, Feb. 12 and 16, 1914, RG 59, 893.6363 (N.Y. Standard in China; 893.6363/1 includes contract).

11. *Bur. of Corps. Rep. on Petroleum Industry,* 54, 64, and Williamson and Daum, 660 (Pure Oil); Hidy and Hidy, 571 (Jersey Standard's purchase); Marquis James, *The Texaco Story,* [N.Y.?] 1953, 31; see Chapter VI for more on the Mexican oil investments.

12. *U.S. v. Aluminum Company of America,* Eq. No. 85–73, Southern District of New York 1940, Brief of the Aluminum Company, 103, 580–590, 599.

13. William S. Dutton, *Du Pont,* New York 1942, 120 (Gunpowder Association; no date is given on this agreement); Max Dorian, *The Du Ponts,* Boston 1962, 140 (South Africa); William S. Stevens, ed., *Industrial Combinations and Trusts,* New York 1913, 176–183 (copy of 1897 agreement); see Chapter IX below for du Pont's Chilean investment.

14. Dept. of Commerce and Labor, Bureau of Corporations, *Report of Commissioner of Corporations on the Tobacco Industry,* Washington, D.C. 1909, pt. I, 69–70, 82–84, 88, 165, 169ff (activities of American Tobacco in foreign business); U.S. Industrial Commission, *Report on Trusts and Industrial Combinations,* Washington, D.C. 1901, XIII, 322, 327 (testimony of Duke); *U.S. v. American Tobacco Co.,* 221 U.S. 106; Stevens, 416–424 (texts of decrees in *U.S. v. American Tobacco*); Reavis Cox, *Competition in the American Tobacco Industry,* New York 1933, 73, 71 (Duke and British-American).

15. E. Rathenau to Thomas Edison, Feb. 19, 1889, Edison National Historic Site Archives, West Orange, N.J.; G.E., *Annual Reports 1893–1900;* Canadian General Electric Co., Ltd., *Annual Report 1905;* Canadian General Electric Co., Prospectus, Toronto, July 2, 1907, Scudder Collection; Federal Trade Commission, *Electric-Power Industry, Supply of Electrical Equipment and Competitive Conditions,* 70th Cong., 1st sess., Sen. Doc. No. 46, Washington, D.C. 1928, 144, 142; *B. T. H. Reminiscences Sixty Years of Progress,* compiled by H. A. Price-Hughes, London 1946, 9; Frank A. Southard, *American Industry in Europe,* Boston 1931, 19; Federal Trade Commission, *Report on Cooperation in American Export Trade,* Washington, D.C. 1916, pt. I, 278; Toshiba, *History,* Tokyo 1964. (I am indebted to General Electric officials in Japan for translations of the relevant sections of this Japanese language history of Toshiba—the company that came into existence as a result of the later merger of Tokyo Electric and Shibaura Engineering.) See also George Stocking and Myron W. Watkins, *Cartels in Action,* New York 1946, 322 (A. E. G.) and 321 (Japanese Company); F.T.C., *Electric-Power Industry,* 145.

16. Interview with William Rogers Herod, New York March 11, 1964; G.E., *Annual Reports.* G.E.'s strategy was not always effective. In China, a U.S. government representative learned from an American General Electric salesman that

he "had considerable difficulty in competing with Japanese agents of the General Electric Company, *who are supposed to confine themselves to Japan* [my italics] . . . The Japanese company in question in competing in China with General Electric Company advertises itself . . . as a branch of General Electric Company and purports to put in General Electric Company machinery, whereas it puts in an inferior manufactured Japanese product, thereby injuring the good name of General Electric Company" (see Julean Arnold, Chefoo, China, to Secretary of State, June 28, 1913, RG 59, 893.6463/3, NA).

17. Henry G. Prout, *A Life of George Westinghouse,* New York 1921, 263–264, 271–272; *Commercial and Financial Chronicle,* July 29, 1899, 232.

18. Thomas J. Watson, *Men—Minutes—Money,* New York 1934, 257, 358 (International Time Recording Co. business); Saul Engelbourg, "International Business Machines, A Business History," unpubl. diss. Columbia University 1954, 281, 284–285; Robert Sheehan, "What Grows Faster than IBM? IBM Abroad," *Fortune,* November, 1960; Boyd France, *IBM in France,* Washington, D.C. 1961, 3–14.

19. Mira Wilkins and Frank Ernest Hill, *American Business Abroad: Ford on Six Continents,* Detroit 1964, 14–19; *Canadian Motor,* Toronto, 1906, inside leaf (Olds); Sun Life Assurance Co. of Canada, *The Canadian Automotive Industry,* Ottawa, 1956, 3 (McLaughlin and Studebaker); Arthur Pound, *The Turning Wheel,* Garden City, N.Y. 1934, 63; General Motors, *Annual Report 1911;* Wilkins and Hill, 22–25, 37–39, 434–435, and passim.

20. The best sources on the German potash industry are H. R. Tosdale, "The German Potash Syndicate," in W. Z. Ripley, *Trusts, Pools and Corporations,* rev. ed., Boston 1916, 795–832, and George Ward Stocking, *The Potash Industry,* New York 1931, although practically all the books cited in Chapter IV, n. 8, deal with this situation. John Moody, *The Truth about Trusts,* New York 1904, 324 (Virginia-Carolina purchase). Investor's Agency, "International Agricultural Corporation," Feb. 18, 1913, Scudder Collection; Stocking, 117–123, esp. 121 (contracts); *Moody's 1911,* 3067 (investment).

21. Stocking, 123 (law enacted May 25, 1910); International Agricultural Corporation, *Annual Report for Year Ended June 30, 1913,* and Investor's Agency Report (response of I.A.C.); I.A.C., *Annual Reports* (option not taken up).

22. S. T. Morgan, President, Virginia Carolina Chemical Company, to Stockholders, July 19, 1911, with *Annual Reports* (first quote). Investor's Agency, "Virginia Carolina Chemical Co." Sept. 10, 1912, and May 13, 1913; and S. T. Morgan to Blair & Co., June 18, 1914 (second quote) all in Scudder Collection; Stocking, 132 (in 1911 all independent mines not yet in the Syndicate were to reenter); I.A.C. *Annual Report 1913* (Syndicate "controls the world's supply of potash.")

23. S. T. Morgan to stockholders, Sept. 2, 1913, with *Annual Reports,* Scudder Collection; *Moody's 1914,* 322 (sulphur mines in Mexico).

24. Diamond Match, *1897 Annual Report.* The British subsidiary of Ameri-

can Radiator was called National Radiator Company, Ltd. (data from files of American Radiator and Standard Sanitary Corporation). There are many examples of disguised American origins.

25. Ann Bezanson in "The Invention of the Safety Razor: Further Comments," *Exploration in Entrepreneurial History,* 4:197, May 15, 1952, for example, gives patent law as reason for Gillette's 1907–1908 German factory.

26. Mira Wilkins, "An American Enterprise Abroad: American Radiator Company in Europe 1895–1914," *Business History Review,* 43:326–346 (Autumn 1969) provides an example of such a pattern.

27. F. A. Vanderlip, "Report on Trip to St. Petersburg," Apr. 15, 1901, Vanderlip Papers, Special Collections, Columbia University.

28. Cyrus H. McCormick, Jr., "Private and Confidential Interviews Regarding Russian Factory—St. Petersburg Interviews," July 1909, Nettie Fowler McCormick Papers, Wisconsin State Historical Society, Madison. (The spelling of the Russian names is McCormick's.) International Harvester, *Annual Report 1911.* For a description of other American investments in Russia, see George Sherman Queen, "The United States and the Material Advance in Russia, 1881–1906," unpubl, diss. University of Illinois 1941, 164–221.

29. Wilkins, "An American Enterprise Abroad" (n. 26 above).

30. G. C. Allen and Audrey G. Donnithorne, *Western Enterprise in Far Eastern Economic Development,* New York 1954, 231, 233. Data from Ministry of International Trade and Industry, Tokyo, indicate increase in number of U.S. businesses.

31. Lawrence P. Abbott, *The Story of NYLIC,* New York 1930, 127–128 (reserves); Morton Keller, *The Life Insurance Enterprise 1885–1910,* Cambridge, Mass. 1963, 108 (Equitable in Switzerland); McCall to Perkins, Oct. 7, 1892, Box 5, Perkins Papers, Special Collections, Columbia University; see also correspondence in Box 8 (Swiss situation).

32. Kingsley to Perkins, July 31, 1896, Box 6, Perkins Papers.

33. Keller, 107–108 (Austria), 108–109 (Germany); von Nimptsch to Perkins, Sept. 26, 1899 (von Nimptsch's friends) and Perkins to McCall, Aug. 31, 1899 (Austria and Switzerland) in Box 8, Perkins Papers; James M. Hudnut, *History of New York Life Insurance Company, 1895–1905,* New York 1906, 41–42, and John Garraty, *Right Hand Man,* New York 1960, 61–62, 69–70 (German situation); NYLIC, "By-Laws of the NYLIC, 1899," as amended, in Archives, NYLIC.

34. Translation of letter from Witte to New York Life Insurance Company, Oct. 7, 1899, Box 7, Perkins Papers; Perkins to McCall, Oct. 22, 1899, Box 8, Perkins Papers; R. Carlyle Buley, *The Equitable Life Assurance Society,* New York 1959, 71–81 (Equitable's foreign business and the problems).

35. Keller, 276–277; NYLIC, Final Report of the Special Committee of the Board of Trustees, June 27, 1907, Scudder Collection (quote).

36. "Remarks on Existing Laws and European Business," June 17, 1908, pub-

lished in Darwin P. Kingsley, *Militant Life Insurance and Other Addresses,* New York 1911, 223–224; Walter Buckner, "Memorandum to the Board of Directors," Oct. 13, 1938, NYLIC Archives (Italian situation); Keller, 277 (Italy).

37. J. Owen Stalson, *Marketing Life Insurance,* Cambridge, Mass. 1942, 825–826 (insurance in force); Archives, NYLIC (NYLIC insurance in force).

38. Clyde William Phelps, *Foreign Expansion of American Banks,* New York 1927, 160, 85–86, 147 (general); American Exporter, *Export Trade Directory,* New York 1912, 176 (New York banks with foreign branches are listed); Alden Hatch, *American Express,* Garden City, N.Y. 1950, 93, 100. "International Banking Corporation," Vanderlip Papers, Special Collections, Columbia University Library; Joint Economic Committee, *Foreign Government Restraints on United States Bank Operations Abroad,* Washington, D.C. 1967, 15–16 (26 foreign branches); National City Bank of New York, *Monthly Letter,* Jan. 14, 1914, and Chapter IX herein (National City Bank). Among the U.S.-incorporated banks establishing branches abroad before World War I were Farmers' Loan and Trust Co. (Paris and London 1906), Trust Company of America (London 1887—established by a predecessor bank), and the Mutual Insurance Company-dominated Guaranty Trust Co. (London 1897). Some American banks went into business in Mexico and the Caribbean (see Chapters VI and VIII).

39. Fred A. McKenzie, *The American Invaders,* New York 1901, 59, points out that many of the chief U.S. firms had set up factories in England; "American drugs manufactured in this country [England] probably very largely exceed the import trade." The drug companies also started to manufacture in Canada. See Chapter III above. McKenzie, 64–65 (Heinz and Horton).

Chapter VI: The "Spillover" to Mexico

1. Cleona Lewis, *America's Stake in International Investment,* Washington, D.C. 1938, 578ff (size of investments); reproduced in Table V.2 herein.

2. Hubert Herring, *A History of Latin America,* 2nd ed. rev., New York 1961, 339.

3. Victor Braschi, "Mexican Railroad System," *Transactions of American Institute of Mining Engineers* (New York), 32:262 (1902), henceforth cited as *Transactions.*

4. Fred Wilbur Powell, *The Railroads of Mexico,* Boston 1921, 123; *Commercial and Financial Chronicle,* 31:240, Sept. 4, 1880 (Mexican and U.S. railroad competition) and 31:109–110, July 31, 1880.

5. Herring, 340; David M. Pletcher, *Rails, Mines, and Progress,* Ithaca 1958, 24–25 (Díaz's concession policy and that of his successor Manuel Gonzalez).

6. Powell, passim.

7. *Ibid.,* 137.

8. J. Fred Rippy, *The United States and Mexico,* rev. ed., New York 1931,

312. *Historia Moderna de Mexico, El Porfiriato, La Vida Económica,* Mexico 1965, II, 1077–1086 (henceforth cited as *Historia de Mexico*).

9. Braschi, *Transactions,* 262. In giving federal assistance to railways, Díaz was in keeping with other nineteenth-century governments, in Europe, the United States, Canada, and Latin America. See Carter Goodrich, *Government Promotion of American Canals and Railroads, 1800–1890,* New York 1960, 6–7.

10. Luis Salazar, "Mexican Railroads and the Mining Industry," *Transactions,* 303.

11. *Ibid.,* 332.

12. Richard E. Chism, "A Synopsis of the Mining Laws of Mexico," *Transactions,* 5; see also, *Cananea Herald,* Apr. 4, 1903, for similar expression of opinion.

13. Isaac Marcosson, *Metal Magic. The Story of American Smelting and Refining Company,* New York 1949, 45; see also Gatenby Williams [pseud. for William Guggenheim], *William Guggenheim,* New York 1934, 74ff.

14. The number of U.S. mining companies entering Mexico between 1890 and 1910 runs into many hundreds. A 1902 report indicated 294 Mexican mining ventures belonging to American companies and individuals (Lewis, 203). This number increased. If anyone wished to list such companies, he would find their names in *Mineral Industry* and *Engineering and Mining Journal* of these years. See also Marvin D. Bernstein, *The Mexican Mining Industry, 1890–1950,* Albany, N.Y. 1964, chaps. 3–5; J. R. Southworth, *Las Minas de Mexico,* Mexico 1905, vol. IX, and J. R. Southworth and Percy C. Homs, *El Directorio Oficial Minero de Mexico,* Mexico 1908, vol. IX (lists mining companies by districts); *Historia de Mexico,* 997–998; U.S. Senate, Subcommittee of the Committee on Foreign Relations, *Revolutions in Mexico, Hearings,* 62nd Cong., 2nd sess., Washington, D.C. 1913 (henceforth cited as *Revolutions in Mexico*); U.S. Senate, Subcommittee of the Committee on Foreign Relations, *Investigations of Mexican Affairs, Hearings,* 66th Cong., 2nd sess., Washington, D.C. 1920, pt. 9, 1428 and 1463 (financing); henceforth cited as *Fall Committee Hearings.*

15. Marcosson, 50–53.

16. *Mineral Industry 1905,* 139.

17. Ira B. Joralemon, *Romantic Copper, Its Lure and Lore,* New York 1934, 136ff, and Pletcher, 219–259 (William C. Greene); Sidney Young, "Cananea Consolidated History," Cananea, Sonora, Mexico 1920—unpublished typescript by the Secretary of that company in Secretary's Office, Anaconda Company, New York (for financial and corporate history of the Cananea companies). The Greene-Cananea enterprise was by the end of 1906 linked to the Amalgamated group by common management and direction and by some of the same large stockholders. In 1910—the first time Amalgamated publicized its investment in the Mexican mining operation—its holding was only 4 per cent. See Amalgamated Copper Company, Application for Listing on the New York Stock Exchange, Feb. 14, 1910.

18. R. G. Cleland, *A History of Phelps Dodge,* New York 1952, 131; Joralemon, 216–217.

19. *Mineral Industry 1905,* 144, and William Yandell Elliott et al., *International Control of Non-Ferrous Metals,* New York 1937, 405.

20. Young, "Cananea Consolidated History."

21. *Mineral Industry 1902,* 254 (Mexico's rank), and previous and subsequent volumes for comparative purposes; *Moody's 1910* (Consolidated Batopilas Silver Mining Co.).

22. Marcosson, 46, 64–69, 210–212 (Towne, ASARCO); John Moody, *The Truth About Trusts,* New York 1904, 45–46 (Data, not wholly accurate, on ASARCO). *Mineral Industry 1903,* 473–476; Harvey O'Connor, *The Guggenheims,* New York 1937, has a large amount on the Guggenheims in Mexico. (The family is reported to have objected to this book.)

23. In the bound volume of Annual Reports of ASARCO, in the Scudder Collection, Columbia University, the map is included between the April 1904 and April 1905 reports.

24. Edwin Ludlow, "The Coal Fields of las Esperanzas, Coahuila, Mexico," *Transactions,* 140, 144, 146.

25. William White, "The Steel-Plant at Monterrey," *Transactions,* 344.

26. *Transactions,* passim.

27. *Cananea Herald,* April 4, 1903; *Mineral Industry 1902,* 270, and *1903,* 473.

28. *Cananea Herald,* Apr. 4, 1903 (taxes).

29. Joralemon, 161–162, and Pletcher, 236–252; Southworth and Homs, 9.

30. Powell, 175–177 (reasons for acquisition of railroad based on Díaz Dufoo's 1910 biography of Limantour); T. W. Osterheld, "History of the Nationalization of the Railroads of Mexico," *American Bankers Association Journal,* 8:997–1003 (May 1916); Southworth and Homs, 9 (quote from government publication).

31. Southworth and Homs, 9 (quote), 17 (840 U.S. companies); Bernstein, chap. VI (other reservations about U.S. investment).

32. W. A. Swanberg, *Citizen Hearst,* New York 1961, 29; Investor's Agency, "Report on American Chicle Company," Nov. 10, 1911, Scudder Collection, Columbia University; Rippy, *The United States and Mexico,* 313–315; *Special Mexican Claims Commission Report,* Washington, D.C. 1940, 303, 142–143, 560; *Fall Committee Hearings,* pt. 9, 1375–1378; *Revolutions in Mexico,* passim, and *Historia de Mexico,* 1106–1115 (other land holdings).

33. Dept. of Commerce and Labor, Bureau of Manufactures *Commercial Relations of the U.S. with Foreign Countries 1909,* Washington, D.C. 1911, 509–518 (plantations in Mexico); Lewis, 283–284 (rubber); Bernard Baruch, *My Own Story,* New York 1957, 213–214. Baruch's details do not exactly coincide with the far more complicated presentation in *Moody's 1909* and *Moody's 1911.* Our summary extracts data common to the three sources. Intercontinental had an investment in Mexico in 1911 said to equal $1,250,000 (*Moody's 1911*); *Special*

Mexican Claims Commission, 287 (Mexican Crude Rubber Co.) and 118–119, 241, 522 (other rubber ventures).

34. *Moody's 1914* (Mexican Telegraph Co. and Mexican Telephone and Telegraph); Charles Anderson Gauld, *The Last Titan: Percival Farquhar, American Entrepreneur in Latin America,* Stanford, Calif. 1964, 55 and 61 (Pearson); Bernstein, 42–43, and *Historia de Mexico,* 1086–1089 (other U.S. utilities); *Revolutions in Mexico,* 87 (Cananea); Miguel S. Wionczek, "Electric Power," in Raymond Vernon, ed., *Public Policy and Private Enterprise in Mexico,* Cambridge, Mass. 1964, 21–33.

35. U.S. Senate Special Committee Investigating Petroleum Resources, *American Petroleum Interests in Foreign Countries, Hearings,* 79th Cong., 1st sess., Washington, D.C. 1946, 333–334; Address by Edward L. Doheny, Dec. 6, 1921, published in Pan American Petroleum & Transport Company, *Mexican Petroleum,* New York 1922, 25.

36. Ralph W. Hidy and Muriel E. Hidy, *Pioneering in Big Business,* New York 1955, 128; *Revolutions in Mexico,* 464, 777, 779 (Pierce and Mexican Central Railway).

37. Doheny address (n. 35 above), 17; *American Petroleum Interests in Foreign Countries,* 334–335; *Historia de Mexico,* 1128 (Waters-Pierce); Alfred Tischendorf, *Great Britain and Mexico in the Era of Porfirio Díaz,* Durham, N.C. 1961, 125 (Pearson); *Mineral Industry 1915,* 540–541 (historical tables).

38. When United Shoe Machinery Company set up "a company well capitalized . . . to manufacture machine made shoes in San Luis Potosi," the Singer office in Mexico advised Singer Manufacturing Company in New York that machines could be sold to United Shoe. Mexican Office, Singer Co. to New York office, Jan. 3, 1903, Acq. 1, vol. 6, Singer Mss., Wisconsin State Historical Society.

39. *Cananea Herald,* Apr. 4, 1903; Joralemon, 163.

40. Rippy, 316.

41. *Statistical Abstract 1906,* 206, and *1910,* 346 (trade figures); William C. Downs, "The Commission House in Latin American Trade," *Quarterly Journal of Economics,* 26:121 (November 1911).

42. *Historia de Mexico,* 1154 (British and U.S. investment compared). I have found no evidence to substantiate the assertion of Edward I. Bell in *The Shame of Mexico* (New York 1914, 35) that American mining and rubber interests in northern Mexico desired U.S. government intervention there in the Díaz era.

43. Rippy, 320–331, *Revolutions in Mexico,* 5, Francisco Bulnes, *The Whole Truth About Mexico,* New York 1916, 121–127, and Carl W. Ackerman, *Mexico's Dilemma,* New York 1918, 55 (anti-American sentiment); *Daily Consular and Trade Reports,* July 18, 1912, 316 (more U.S. than Mexican capital in Mexico—1911); Bulnes, 145 (Mexican War heritage), 198–199 (contributions of American capital).

44. *Fall Committee Hearings,* 2639 (oilmen's disenchantment); Tischendorf,

124, 146, Peter Calvert, *The Mexican Revolution 1910–1914,* Cambridge, England 1968, 24, 27, and J. A. Spender, *Weetman Pearson: First Viscount Cowdray,* London 1930, 188–189 (Díaz and the British); Bulnes, 201 (description of Limantour); Hawley Copeland to President Woodrow Wilson, Feb. 24, 1913, RG 59, 812.00/6684, National Archives. Copeland equates Standard Oil and Waters-Pierce interests. For the view that Standard Oil did not control Waters-Pierce, see Hidy and Hidy, 448–451, George Sweet Gibb and Evelyn H. Knowlton, *The Resurgent Years,* New York 1956, 19–20, and Shelburne Hopkins' testimony, *Revolutions in Mexico,* 792; *ibid.* 777–785 (more on Pierce and the railroads).

45. Regrettably, neither volume on the history of Standard Oil of N.J.—Hidy and Hidy nor Gibb and Knowlton—clarifies the role of Waters-Pierce and Standard Oil in the 1911 revolution. Cleona Lewis, 222, citing works by Arthur Pound and Samuel Taylor Moore, Ludwell Denny, and Pierre L'Espagnol de Tramerye, states "Pierce . . . gave financial assistance to the forces opposing Díaz." Copeland, in the letter cited in n. 44 above, writes that a retired manager of Waters-Pierce in Mexico (Cullinan by name), who it "was generally understood . . . was kept on the payroll" of Waters-Pierce and whose wife was on "very friendly terms with the Madero family," it could be "assumed" assisted in "arranging funds for the Madero revolution" or acted "as go-between, between Madero and Standard Oil, when he organized his revolution." Such evidence is only circumstantial. Díaz's son, after the fall of the dictator, attributed his father's demise to Pierce (Lorenzo Meyer, *Mexico y Estados Unidos en El Conflicto Petrolero [1917–1942],* Mexico 1968, 43). Lawrence Converse, a 22-year old American officer in Madero's army, stated to a U.S. Senate Committee that Madero told him "Standard Oil interests were backing them [Madero's forces] in their revolution." Standard Oil, Converse said, would get an oil concession as a reward (*Revolutions in Mexico,* 104–105, 108; see also 319, 460–468, 507). The El Paso agent's *informant* referred to in the footnote, p. 129, reported Troxel carried a letter from John D. Archbold, "authorizing him to make contracts." The agent did not see the letter, and Standard Oil denied its existence. The denial by Standard Oil may have been honest, but an element of doubt remains. Gibb and Knowlton, sympathetic historians of Standard Oil of New Jersey, indicate that the company did on occasion send independent agents to act for it and that at times it made public statements that were not entirely genuine (Gibb and Knowlton, 86–87, 354).

Standard Oil had been considering oil concessions in Mexico (Hidy and Hidy, 775, n. 29). After the Díaz ouster, it again looked closely at the prospects. Gibb and Knowlton suggest this "may have been" because "of the temporary reversal of fortunes of the English [Lord Cowdray]" in the Madero revolution (p. 84). Calvert has excellent data on Waters-Pierce, Standard Oil, and the Mexican Revolution; he concludes that neither Waters-Pierce nor Standard Oil ever made a substantial loan to the Madero forces (pp. 76–84). To summarize, many people at the time and subsequently believed that either through Waters-Pierce or directly (and the two were generally undifferentiated), Standard Oil was involved in the revolution. There is evidence that both Waters-Pierce and Standard Oil itself would gain from the overthrow of Díaz, but while there is considerable unsubstantiated *circumstantial* evidence that Waters-Pierce and Standard Oil aided the revolution, I have seen no satisfactory proof of participation or non-participation. I have not seen the records of either Waters-Pierce Company or Standard Oil of New Jersey. Calvert's accounting of the sources of Madero funds (pp. 82–83) is convincing, but still does not answer the question of whether Standard Oil and/or Waters-Pierce in any way participated in the revolution.

46. Bell, 35 and chaps. IV and V; Meyer, 41 (Guggenheim's discontent with Limantour). Testimony of James W. Malcolmson in *Revolutions in Mexico,* 139–140, claims Americans with the mining companies were "neutral."

47. Doheny to Taft, May 5, 1911, RG 59, 812.00/1666, NA. John R. Phillips, whose company had agricultural holdings in Mexico, told a Senate Committee that he had learned the Taft administration planned to intervene in Mexico, that "The American Smelting & Refining Co. practically closed down all its smelters for a short time [in the spring of 1911], and the managers were asked to come to New York." Soon after their arrival in New York he continued, "the word went out that there was to be no intervention." Phillips implied a connection. See Phillips testimony in *Revolutions in Mexico,* 321.

48. Calvert, 99–100 (Madero's views toward foreign investments); *Revolutions in Mexico,* 88 (Cananea Co.); Harvey O'Connor, *The Guggenheims,* New York 1937, 333–334 and ASARCO, *Annual Report 1912* (ASARCO); *Revolutions in Mexico,* 136 (other mining companies); *Fall Committee Hearings,* 2639–2640 (favors to Madero; Fall has been called a "spokesman for Doheny oil interests," so this is not evidence from a hostile witness); Hopkins testimony in *Revolutions in Mexico,* 754, and *Fall Committee Hearings,* 2524–2525.

49. *Engineering and Mining Journal,* 93:389, Feb. 24, 1912 (quote); *Revolutions in Mexico,* 6, 12, 28, 46, 80, 88, 158–159, 371–372, 544–548, 598–599, 601–602, 692, 697–723, 798–803, 817 (damage to U.S. property); Vernon, 35 (Mexican Light & Power); R. Carlyle Buley, *The Equitable Assurance Society of the United States,* New York 1959, 80; *Foreign Relations of the United States 1912,* 731–805 (general conditions) and 783, 786, 789, 790, 835, 838, 840 (arms); *Revolutions in Mexico,* 136–137 (El Tigre) and 92 (Cananea Co. representative); Bell, 123–124, argues that the rubber interests of Rockefeller and Aldrich opposed Madero, because they would "be coerced to buy at an excessive price . . . properties of the Maderos"; Bell, 160–161 (Guggenheims' views); I have seen no other data to substantiate Bell's argument that the Guggenheims made their opposition to Madero well known in Washington and at the American Embassy in Mexico.

50. *Foreign Relations of the United States 1912,* 827 (new taxes); see also Meyer (48–49), who points out that the oil companies balked at other Madero

actions besides the new taxes in mid-1912; *Fall Committee Hearings,* 529 (Texas Company), and Craig Thompson, *Since Spindletop,* n.p. 1951, 96 (Gulf); Hopkins testimony in *Revolutions in Mexico,* 793, and Gibb and Knowlton, 20 (Magnolia); Hopkins testimony in *Revolutions in Mexico,* 791, 793 and Gibb and Knowlton, 85 (Doheny); Spender, 171, 184–185, 169, 202, and Gibb and Knowlton, 85 (Lord Cowdray).

51. Herring, 355–356 (chronology); Copeland to Woodrow Wilson, Feb. 24, 1913, RG 59, 812.00/6684, and Lind to Bryan, Oct. 8, 1913, RG 59, 812.00/9127, NA (English oil money); Calvert (196ff) argues there was no truth to the involvement of English oil money. Henry Lane Wilson, *Diplomatic Episodes in Mexico, Belgium and Chile,* New York 1927, 286–287; Arthur Link, *Wilson,* Princeton 1956, II, 348–349 (views of Ambassador and American colony), 349–350 (Woodrow Wilson's feelings); E. David Cronon, ed., *The Cabinet Diaries of Josephus Daniels,* Lincoln, Neb. 1963, 43 (quote). Compare this with the Copeland letter cited above; clearly Wilson was influenced by Copeland's communication.

52. Lind to Bryan, Oct. 8, 1913, RG 59, 812.00/9127, NA (quote); Link, II, 351 (copper companies and Doheny); Spender, 170 (Cowdray and Pierce); *Special Mexican Claims Commission,* Washington, D.C. 1940, passim.; *Fall Committee Hearings,* passim., and *Mineral Industry 1913,* 317 and 319ff. (damages and problems); ASARCO, *Annual Report 1913,* and for more details, *Special Mexican Claims Commission,* Decision No. 15, 59–88; Isaac F. Marcosson, *Magic Metal—The Story of American Smelting and Refining Company,* New York 1949, 231; *Foreign Relations of the United States 1914,* 758–761 (forced loans to rebels 1913) and 762 (government threats); *EMJ,* 97:137, Jan. 10, 1914; Bell, 352–353 (general conditions).

53. *Fall Committee Hearings,* 1372–1379 (plantations); Vernon, 35 (utilities); Meyer, 58 (appeal to Wilson); *Foreign Relations of the United States 1914,* 762 (expropriation threat); Tampico to Washington, D.C. Nov. 19, 1913, RG 59, 812.6363/16, NA; U.S. Dept. of Comm., Bureau of Foreign and Domestic Commerce, *American Direct Investments in Foreign Countries,* Washington, D.C. 1930, 19 ("most prolific"); *Mineral Industry 1913,* 318 (production figures); Bell, 347–348 (activity of oil companies).

54. Link, II, 392–401 (details of the intervention); Meyer, 58–61 (takes a different view of the intervention, which I am not convinced is valid); Herring, 357–358; *Fall Committee Hearings,* 1380; O'Connor, *The Guggenheims,* 334.

Chapter VII: The "Spillover" to Canada

1. Irving Brecher and S. S. Reisman, *Canada-U.S. Economic Relations,* Royal Commission on Canada's Economic Prospects, Ottawa 1957, 114, and Hugh G. J. Aitken, John J. Deutsch, W. A. Mackintosh, Clarence L. Barber et al., *The American Economic Impact on Canada,* Durham, N.C. 1959, vii (emphasizes the

stable and orderly government in Canada and the friendly relations that served to encourage U.S. investment).

2. Hugh G. J. Aitken, "Government and Business in Canada: An Interpretation," *Business History Review*, 38:14 (Spring 1964), and W. T. Easterbrook and Hugh G. J. Aitken, *Canadian Economic History*, Toronto 1956, 416 (Cooke's activity); Herbert Marshall, Frank A. Southard, and Kenneth W. Taylor, *Canadian-American Industry*, New Haven 1936, 113–123 (other railroad investments); William J. Wilgus, *The Railway Interrelations of the United States and Canada*, New Haven 1937, is poor on this subject.

3. E. S. Moore, *American Influence on Canadian Mining*, Toronto 1941, 9ff (the best source); Marshall et al., 6–10, 87–102, 109–112; *Mineral Industry, Monetary Times* and *Commercial and Financial Chronicle*, passim; John F. Thompson and Norman Beasley, *For the Years to Come, A Story of International Nickel of Canada*, New York 1960, 21, 24, 25–40, 114, 142–143; *Mineral Industry, 1892*, 346; *ibid. 1903*, 492; O. W. Main, *The Canadian Nickel Industry*, Toronto 1955, 16 (Canadian Copper-Orford contract), 27 (second arrangement); *Copper Handbook 1901*, 88 (Canadian Copper output).

4. Moore, 25 (Bethlehem); Moore, 19–22, and Marshall et al., 109–112 (asbestos); Milton Lomask, *Seed Money: The Guggenheim Story*, New York 1964, 23, and Cleona Lewis, *America's Stake in International Investment*, Washington, D.C. 1938, 212 (Nipissing silver), 209–210 (Yukon gold), 583–584 (statistics on mining investment).

5. *Commercial and Financial Chronicle*, Aug. 5, 1899, 281 (International Paper); Marshall et al., 6 (Ontario); U.S. Dept. of Comm., Bureau of Foreign and Domestic Commerce, *Daily Consular and Trade Reports*, Feb. 11, 1914, 554 (Prairie Provinces and British Columbia); *Commercial Relations of U.S. with Foreign Countries 1909*, 424 (90 per cent figure); Lewis, 591 ($101 million; the figure includes speculative and other land holdings); *Daily Consular and Trade Reports*, Feb. 11, 1914, 554 (estimated $100 million U.S. investment in 1913 in land in British Columbia and the Prairie provinces, a figure which excludes investment in timber rights and investment in land and timber rights in Quebec and Ontario).

6. Moore, 17, 26, 28, 30 (smelting); L. C. A. Knowles and C. M. Knowles, *The Economic Development of the British Overseas Empire*, London 1930, II, 554–555 (mineral processing); Moore, 10–11 (Whitney); Marshall et al., 31 (flour milling) and 6 (export duties on timber); Edward Porritt, *Sixty Years of Protection in Canada*, London 1908, 366 (Ontario government ruling re timber); Marshall et al., 36–37 (pulpwood legislation); Constant Southworth, "The American-Canadian Newsprint Paper Industry and the Tariff," *Journal of Political Economy*, 30:683 (October 1922).

7. L. Ethan Ellis, *Reciprocity 1911*, New Haven 1939, 136 (role U.S. newspapers); Marshall et al., 45 (Ontario Paper Co.); Lewis, 595 (figures).

8. *U.S. v. Aluminum Co. of America,* Eq. #85–73, Brief of Alcoa, Southern District of New York, 1940, 103; Muriel F. Collie, *The Abrasives Industry,* Greendale, Mass. 1951, 62 and passim.; American Cyanamid, *Annual Report 1913;* Interview with Bruce Crawford, Johannesburg, So. Africa, July 29, 1965.

9. Chapter III (Western Union); F. C. Fetherstonhaugh, *Charles Fleetford Sise, 1834–1918,* Montreal 1944, 208, 180 (U.S. interests in Canadian Bell; see Chapter III for background); Marshall et al., 139–140 (other U.S. interests); Lewis, 603 (estimate of U.S. investment).

10. Hidy and Hidy, 151, 256–257; U.S. Dept. of Comm. and Labor, Bureau of Corporations, *Report of Commissioner of Corporations on the Petroleum Industry,* Washington, D.C. 1909, pt. III, "Foreign Trade," 52 (Imperial fully integrated).

11. Raymond A. Bauer, Ithiel de Sola Pool, and Lewis Anthony Dexter, *American Business and Public Policy,* New York 1963, 135, and E. R. Barlow and Ira T. Wender, *Foreign Investment and Taxation,* Englewood Cliffs, N.J. 1955, 20, 39, as well as Marshall et al., 231, have noted that Canadian operations are frequently excluded when American businessmen discuss their "foreign" business. The Department of Commerce found in tabulating materials on foreign business that it had to specify Canadian as "foreign" or it would be excluded. Brecher & Reisman note "Many American companies have come to regard their Canadian operations as simply an extension of their domestic market" (115). Such conditions were true from the genesis of U.S. business in Canada.

12. Marshall et al., 73 (first "branch" plant in 1870); U.S. Dept. of Comm., Bureau of Foreign and Domestic Commerce, *American Direct Investments in Foreign Countries,* by Paul Dickens, Trade Information Bull. #731, Washington, D.C. 1930, 42 gives a pharmaceutical branch plant in 1860; this may be an error.

13. *Commercial Relations of U.S. with Foreign Countries 1909,* 437 (New Brunswick), 480–481 (Toronto), 483 (Windsor).

14. Theodore H. Boggs, Address, National Foreign Trade Convention, *Official Report 1925,* 373 (200 plants 1912). See Chapter X herein for more on Canadian plants.

15. L. W. Serrell (patent lawyer) to Edison, June 4, 1881, Edison Archives, W. Orange, N.J., wrote "I have received word from my correspondent in Canada that your lamps were duly received and advertised in the 'Free Press' and that the Commissioner of Patents informed that it would be sufficient to save the patent." Two years later the Edison Electric Light Company was established in Canada and manufacture began. Marshall et al., 15. Compare this with the experience of Bell; see *The Electrician,* 4:78, 82 (February 1885). Bell lost his patent for noncompliance with the "working clause." Porritt, 410 (quote).

16. William Close, Montreal, to Geo. R. McKenzie, Mar. 22, 1883, Acq. 2,

Box 8, Singer Mss., State Historical Society of Wisconsin (Singer factory in Montreal); Unsigned Statement [by Gordon McGregor], n.d. [June 1904?], Secretary's office, Ford Motor Company of Canada, Oakville, Ontario (Ford); Hugh Allen, *The House of Goodyear,* Cleveland 1943, 218 (Goodyear); Cyrus McCormick, *The Century of the Reaper,* Boston 1931, 132–133 (International Harvester); Report of Theo. Ahrens, President of Standard Sanitary Manufacturing Company to its Board of Directors, in Minutes, Board of Directors, Jan. 24, 1907, and Report of Ahrens to Board, Jan. 25, 1912, Secretary's office, American Radiator and Standard Sanitary Corporation. Marshall et al., 202 (tariff motivation).

17. *American Branch Factories Abroad,* Sen. Doc. 258, 71st Cong., 3rd sess., 34; O. J. McDiarmid, *Commercial Policy in the Canadian Economy,* Cambridge, Mass. 1946, 209 (Canadian policy). The direct connection is obscure; possibly, the presence of competition from lower priced British goods may have spurred investment. We know of the indirect connection—that is, the feeling that England would reciprocate and American firms ought to be in a position to take advantage of the reciprocity. There are many other reasons for the expansion abroad accelerating after 1897. Because this was true worldwide and not only into Canada, I tend not to place much weight on this legislation as a primary cause of the growth. Mira Wilkins and Frank Ernest Hill, *American Business Abroad, Ford on Six Continents,* Detroit 1964, 18–19 (Ford).

18. Porritt, 410–411 (industry incentives), 411–412 (quotes from the Toronto *Globe*), 27, 366, 399–400 (steel rails).

19. Lewis, 595 (figures).

20. Clifton Sifton, "Reciprocity," in the issue on "Canadian National Problems," *The Annals,* 14:20–28, January 1913 (splendid article); James J. Hill, *Highways of Progress,* New York 1910, 85–101; Robert H. Wiebe, *Businessmen and Reform,* Cambridge, Mass. 1962, 95–96; Ellis, passim.

21. Sifton, 27.

22. Brecher & Riesman, 115; data from archives, New York Life Insurance Company; *Daily Consular and Trade Reports,* Feb. 11, 1914, 554 (estimate of investment size from *Monetary Times*); Marshall et al., 215 (general services).

23. Marshall et al., 215, 266 (explains the absence of U.S. interest in terms of the basic differences in the banking systems of the two countries and "the statutory requirement that a majority of the directors of every [Canadian] bank must be British subjects domiciled in Canada").

24. Wilkins & Hill, 18–19 (Ford); Sherwin-Williams Co. of Canada, Ltd., *Annual Report 1913* and Sherwin-Williams Co. (U.S.), Prospectus 1920, both in Scudder Collection, Columbia University; International Harvester, *Annual Report 1907; U.S. v. Aluminum Co. of America,* Eq. No. 85–73, Brief of Alcoa, Southern District of New York, 1940, 582–583, 587–598 (Alcoa); George Sweet Gibb and Evelyn H. Knowlton, *The Resurgent Years 1911–1927,* New York 1956, 95–97 (Jersey Standard); data on specific diplomatic discussions obtained directly

from Jersey Standard; financial records of Western Electric Archives, New York, indicate that "pursuant to an agreement dated Dec. 31, 1913, Western Electric Company (Illinois) transferred all its common stock investments in foreign allied and subsidiary companies to Electrical Properties, Limited (Canada) whose name was changed as of October 31, 1914 to Western Electric Company, Limited (Canada) but retained its investments in notes and accounts of and advances to those companies. In exchange for the stock investments Western Electric received capital stock and bills payable from Electric Properties." The United States had a corporate income tax in 1909; it was deemed constitutional in 1913 and reimposed that year. Canada did not have corporate income taxes until 1917; Easterbrook and Aitken, 504 (Canadian taxes); under such circumstances, it would be clearly desirable for a Canadian corporation to be recipient of foreign profits and to make expenditures abroad out of its surpluses.

25. Based on company histories. See also insights in Canadian-American Committee, "Policies and Practices of United States Subsidiaries in Canada," n.p. 1961, 26.

26. S. Morley Wicketts, "Canada and the Preference," in *Annals*, 40–41.

27. A. E. Safarian, *Foreign Ownership of Canadian Industry*, Toronto 1966, 10 (by 1913 U.S. investment represented 22 per cent of the long-term foreign capital invested in Canada).

Chapter VIII: The "Spillover" to the Caribbean

1. Robert P. Porter, *Industrial Cuba*, New York 1899, 356, 354 (railroads in Cuba); Dana G. Munro, *Intervention and Dollar Diplomacy in the Caribbean 1900–1921*, Princeton 1964, 17 (San Domingo Improvement Company).

2. Watt Stewart, *Henry Meiggs, Yankee Pizarro*, Durham, N.C. 1946 (Meiggs); for Meiggs' railroad concession see Decree XXIV, July 20, 1871, *Coleccion de las Leyes, Decretos y Ordenes*, San José, Costa Rica, 127; Northern Railway Company, *Costa Rica Railway Company, Ltd. and Northern Railway Company*, San José, Costa Rica 1953, 6. The biography of Minor C. Keith, Watt Stewart, *Keith and Costa Rica*, Albuquerque 1964, does not do justice to this fascinating figure. Costa Rica Railway Company, *Concessions, Contracts, and Decrees, 1879–1913*, Boston 1914 (contains originals and translations); Northern Railway Company and United Fruit Company, *Concessions, Contracts, and Decrees, 1892–1913*, Boston 1914. We were guided through these by Don Porfirio Gongora, who was for many years Minor Keith's lawyer.

3. Cleona Lewis, *America's Stake in International Investment*, Washington, D.C. 1938, 602 (Guatemala railroad); Walter LaFeber, *The New Empire, 1860–1898*, Ithaca, New York 1963, 219ff (Nicaraguan canal); J. Fred Rippy, *Capitalists and Colombia*, New York 1931, 54–57, and Frederic M. Halsey, *Railway Expansion in Latin America*, New York 1916, 68–71 (Colombian railroads; British-

German financing); George W. Crichfield, *American Supremacy*, New York 1908, II, 250 (Venezuelan railroad).

4. Leland H. Jenks, *Our Cuban Colony*, New York 1928, 36 and *Mineral Industry 1897*, 944 (mining in Cuba); Lewis, 584 (estimated mining investment in Cuba and West Indies at only $3 million in 1897); Julius W. Pratt, *Expansionists of 1898*, Baltimore 1936, 250–251 ($6 million 1897 estimate for mining investment in Cuba); Porter, 321 ($8 million estimate for U.S. stake in Cuban mining in 1898), 319–320 (names of iron companies); John Moody, *The Truth about Trusts*, New York 1904, 295ff (asphalt companies); Crichfield, 250 (Venezuela); J. Fred Rippy, "Investments of Citizens of the United States in Latin America," *Journal of Business*, 22:19 (January 1949); Bureau of the American Republics, *Honduras*, Washington, D.C. 1892, 50–52 (lists mining companies in Honduras).

5. Frederick Upton Adams, *Conquest of the Tropics*, Garden City, N.Y. 1914, 38–48; Stacy May and Galo Plaza, *The United Fruit Company in Latin America*, Washington, D.C. 1958, 4–5; Samuel Crowther, *Romance and the Rise of the American Tropics*, Garden City, N.Y. 1929, 171–172; C. M. Wilson, *Empire in Green and Gold*, New York 1947, 28, 77, 88, 82; Douglas Hall, *Ideas and Illustrations in Economic History*, New York 1964, Chap. 4 (early banana trade from Jamaica).

6. Porter, 284; Jenks, 33–35; Edwin Farnsworth Atkins, *Sixty Years in Cuba, Reminiscences of Edwin F. Atkins*, Cambridge, Mass. 1926, 1, 37, 67.

7. Adams, 54–68, Crowther, 143–161, Wilson, 36–68, May and Plaza, 5–6 (Keith). On Keith's other interests, interviews with Don Porfirio Gongora and Don Fernando Castro, San José, Costa Rica, July 23, 1964.

8. Atkins, 108, 121, 139 (U.S. tariff policies), 208ff (problems in Cuba 1895–97); Lewis, 590–591 (investments in agriculture).

9. Charles Anderson Gauld, *The Last Titan: Percival Farquhar*, Stanford, Calif. 1964, 13, 23; Porter, 361 (telegraph); Crichfield, II, 250 (Venezuela).

10. See Chapters III and V above.

11. Lewis, 606 (figures; the investment in northern Venezuela and Colombia surely did not exceed $3 to $5 million).

12. LaFeber, 218ff (Nicaragua); Milton Offutt, *Protection of Citizens Abroad by the Armed Forces of the United States*, Baltimore 1928, 79 (Panama); Atkins, 160, 174 (calls for aid); *Foreign Relations of the United States 1895*, 1216–1220, and *ibid., 1896*, 674ff. (Cuba).

13. Pratt, 231–278 (American business attitude toward the Spanish-American war); Acq. 2, Box 30, Singer Mss., State Historical Society of Wisconsin, contains a collection of Spanish newspaper attacks on Singer, Equitable Insurance Company, and New York Life Insurance Company. See, for example, *El Pueblo*, May 16, 23, June 4, 5, 6, 7, 8, 9, 10, 11, 12, 14, 15, 16, 17, 18, 20, 1898 and *El Pais*, May 11, 15, 23, 30, June 6, 10, 13, 1898. The reaction of Singer to these attacks is interesting; its British manager in Madrid instructed company representatives

to "display the Spanish flag and put some posters in a conspicuous position, stating that we are not Americans but that the business belongs to an Englishman established in Spain for the last 30 years." The company opened a subscription among employees to raise funds for the Spanish fleet! See letters of the manager Edmund Adcock, Apr. 25 and 28, 1898, to company managers in Spain in the same Acquisition box.

14. Testimony in *U.S. v. American Sugar Refining Company, et al.*, New York 1913, VI, 3024, 3026 (B. H. Howell investment); *Journal of Commerce*, Aug. 22, 1900, and Jan. 20, 1902 (United Fruit); *Commercial Relations of the U.S. 1909*, 598 (40 per cent figure); *U.S. v. American Sugar Refining Company*, VI, 3008, 3035, 3018 (Cuban-Sugar), 3357 (Havemeyer's interests). Other important sugar companies in Cuba included Trinidad Sugar Manufacturing Company, Cape Cruz Company, Guantanamo Sugar Company, Francisco Sugar Company, Washington Sugar Company. See data in Scudder Collection, Columbia University Library. Minor C. Keith was involved in Cuban sugar independently of United Fruit: Stewart, *Minor C. Keith*, 178.

15. Porter, 306 and 306n; U.S. Bur. of Corps., *Report on Tobacco Industry*, Washington, D.C. 1909, pt. 1, 150, 182 (Puerto Rican cigarettes and cigars), 11, 159ff, 193 (Havana Tobacco), 156, 193 (growing tobacco).

16. Gauld, 13–14 (American Indies Company); Lewis, 325 (Havana Electric Railway).

17. Thomas Cochran, *The Pabst Brewing Company*, New York 1948, 246; Charles Howard Candler, *Asa Griggs Candler*, Atlanta 1950, 141 (Coca Cola); Lewis, 606 (growth figures).

18. *Moody's 1907*, 2265; see Report of Nicaraguan Mixed Claims Commission of 1910, presented Jan. 20, 1915, in RG 76, National Archives, for other Nicaraguan concessions.

19. See n. 5 above for books on United Fruit Co. as well as Charles David Kepner, Jr. and Jay Henry Soothill, *The Banana Empire*, New York 1935. There is a need for an excellent history of the company based on company records; *Journal of Commerce*, Nov. 6, 1899 (acreage); Adams, 76 (reasons for diversification); Munro, 18–19 (United Fruit in the early 1900s had 50 per cent interest in Vaccaro Bros. and 60 per cent interest in Hubbard-Zemurray Company in Honduras); Edgerly & Crocker, "Special Letter—United Fruit Company," Jan. 2, 1915, Scudder Collection (directors' decision); Preston to Committee on Merchant Marine and Fisheries in House of Representatives, Jan. 27, 1913, copy of testimony in Scudder Collection (acreage in 1913).

20. Contract Costa Rican Government and Tropical Trading and Transport Co. (a subsidiary of United Fruit Company), Oct. 22, 1900, in Northern Railway Company and United Fruit Company, *Concessions, Contracts and Decrees*, 26; Decree of July 7, 1909, in *ibid.*, 83; Harvard Business School Case, ICR #150, "United Fruit Company" (other contracts).

21. Hall, 77 (share of banana imports); *Journal of Commerce,* July 3, 23, 1902, and *New York Times,* Aug. 23, 1902 (Preston's 1902 arrangements); *Journal of Commerce,* Nov. 20, 1903, July 5, and Aug. 4, 1904 (purchase in 1903 of ½ interest); Adams, 118 (100 per cent control); United Fruit Company, *Prospectus,* June 1, 1907, Scudder Collection. Later, as American big business began to worry about antitrust action (1911–1914), United Fruit spoke about the competition it met and denied monopoly.

22. Northern Railway and United Fruit Company, *Concessions, Contracts,* 50, 57 (Costa Rica); Gauld, 53ff; Halsey, 142ff; data from office United Fruit Company, Guatemala City, Guatemala. Adams, 326, and Munro, 17 (Keith's ambition); Stewart, 142–143 (diversity of Keith's interests); *Journal of Commerce,* Nov. 6, 1899 (railroads at origin); Investor's Agency, Appraisal of United Fruit, Nov. 17, 1914, Scudder Collection (railroads, 1914); May and Plaza, 18 (Tropical Radio).

23. Preston to Committee on Merchant Marine and Fisheries (contribution of United Fruit). The company also helped establish and subsidized a department for the study of tropical diseases at Tulane University—the first of its kind in the United States.

24. *Foreign Relations of the United States* series covering 1900–1914. The best book on dollar diplomacy is Dana G. Munro, *Intervention and Dollar Diplomacy in the Caribbean 1900–1921,* Princeton 1964; see also F. M. Huntington Wilson, "The Relation of the Government to Foreign Investment," *Annals of the American Academy of Political and Social Science,* 68:304, November 1916 (quote); Wilson was assistant secretary of state in the Taft administration. *Congressional Record,* 58th Cong., 3rd sess., 1904, 19 (Roosevelt Corollary); Offutt, 96–160, and Munro, passim. (interventions). In Nicaragua in 1910 the largest American businesses were the United States and Nicaragua Company, the Central American Commercial Company (with a concession to manufacture ice), and the Bluefields Steamship Company, Ltd., later the Bluefield Fruit and Steamship Company (with exclusive rights to traffic on the Escondido River). According to Munro (18, 172–173), United Fruit owned a substantial portion of this company. Revulsion against the Bluefield company's "monopolistic" concession was considered "one of the causes" of the revolution of 1909 in which Zelaya was overthrown. Certain U.S. business interests appear to have participated in the overthrow of Zelaya (for details see Munro, 117ff). In the ensuing upheaval there was damage to the properties of the following large American companies in Nicaragua: Mining Exploration Company (with properties in eastern Nicaragua), the Anderson Pine Timber Concession (exclusive rights to cut pine timber on government land in the northeastern part of the republic), and Atlantic Fruit Company. See Report of Nicaraguan Mixed Claim Commission of 1910, presented Jan. 20, 1915, in RG 76, National Archives.

25. Offutt, 112ff; Samuel Flagg Bemis, *The Latin American Policy of the United States,* New York 1943, 163–164, 166.

26. Rippy, *Capitalists and Colombia,* 57–62 (investments in Colombia); J. A. Spender, *Weetman Pearson,* London 1930, 210 (General Asphalt); RG 59, 821.6363/34, NA (State Department, on Standard Oil of New York in Colombia; these records only report and do not indicate any affirmative diplomatic action on the part of the department). Rippy, 131, and E. Taylor Parks, *Colombia and the United States,* Durham, N.C. 1935, 467 (say "Standard Oil"); Lewis, 225 (says "Standard Oil of N.J.," but gives no source).

27. *Foreign Relations of the U.S.,* 1904–1914, especially *1913,* 308 (Knox quote); Spender, 210 (Lord Cowdray; contract withdrawn Nov. 24, 1913); see also Peter A. R. Calvert, *The Mexican Revolution 1910–1914,* Cambridge, England 1968, 174ff; RG 59, 821.6363/9, NA (Bryan quote—letter is dated Nov. 18, 1913).

28. Crichfield, II, 128–141; *Foreign Relations of U.S. 1901,* 541–543 (warship); RG 84, NA has extensive records on the New York & Bermudez Company; *Foreign Relations of the U.S. 1908,* 786–793 (summation of the case); Crichfield, II, 251 (Orinoco company).

29. Crichfield, II, 251–253 (U.S. and Venezuela Company), 259 (quote); *Foreign Relations of the U.S. 1908,* 793–796, 804–805, 820 (breaking relations) and *Foreign Relations of the U.S. 1909,* 609ff., 613 (quote from Bacon), 624–627 (settlements). The details of relations involving direct investments are invariably omitted from the standard treatment, but always included are the relations with Venezuela and her foreign bondholders. These had broader implications, for a German stake in the Caribbean seemed threatening. In 1902 Venezuela defaulted on her foreign loans and was pressed by European powers for settlements; Germany, Great Britain, and Italy sent warships. German ships bombarded Puerto Cabello, and Theodore Roosevelt protested. Samuel Flagg Bemis, *A Diplomatic History of the United States,* 3rd ed., New York 1950, 522–525; John Parke Young, *The International Economy,* 4th ed., New York 1963, 568–569.

30. Edwin Lieuwen, *Petroleum in Venezuela,* Berkeley 1954, 7, 11–14 (General Asphalt); Foster Bain and Thomas Thornton Read, *Ores and Industry in South America,* New York 1934, 331 (Shell purchased controlling interest in January 1913).

31. Bemis, *Latin American Policy,* 163–164, 166.

32. Every standard diplomatic history and most economic histories of the United States have a section on these events. Such international lawyers as John Bassett Moore have commented at length. Bemis and Munro in the books cited above are excellent. Herbert Feis, Jacob Viner, and many others have participated in discussions about the policies—mainly in relation to loans— with which we have not been concerned here. See interesting round-table dis-

cussion on Foreign Investment at the University of Chicago, June 18 to June 30, 1928 (mimeographed copy in Columbia University Library), esp. pp. 178ff. See also B. H. Williams, *Economic Foreign Policy of the United States,* New York 1929. The Smedley Butler quotation is in this instance from Max Gordon's letter to *Columbia University Forum,* 6:48 (Winter 1963). It is often cited. On the opposite side, Young, 568, 616–618, argues that the entire U.S. policy in the Caribbean was "to forestall European intervention . . . The protection of property was incidental." Wilson's article, cited in n. 24 above is very valuable on the rationale for government intervention.

33. This point has been made by Munro, 531, and Bemis, *Latin American Policy,* 166.

34. U.S. Senate Subcommittee of the Committee on Foreign Relations, *Investigation of Mexican Affairs, Hearings,* 66th Cong., 2nd sess., Washington, D.C. 1920, pt. 9, 1389, 1465–1466; pt. 13, 1912 and passim (Mexican government spurs to investment); L. C. A. Knowles and C. M. Knowles, *The Economic Development of the British Overseas Empire,* London 1930, II, 553 (quote on Canadian gains). See also text above.

Chapter IX: The South American Experience

1. Wessel, Duval & Co., *A Centennial Review,* New York 1925, 25; Isaac Marcosson, *Metal Magic, The Story of American Smelting and Refining Company,* New York 1949, 69; *Engineering & Mining Journal,* 74:13 (July 5, 1902).

2. *Dictionary of American Biography* (Meiggs and Wheelwright); Watt Stewart, *Henry Meiggs, Yankee Pizarro,* Durham, N.C. 1946; Lewis Hanke, "A Note on the Life and Publications of Colonel George Earl Church," *Books at Brown,* 20:131–163, 1965; Frederic Halsey, *Railway Expansion in Latin America,* New York 1916, 5, 12, 36; Jorge Basadre, *Historia de la Republica del Peru,* Lima, 5th ed., 1962, VI, 2907–2908; U.S. Claims Commission, *The Alsop. Claim,* Washington, D.C. 1910 (involves members Wheelwright family).

3. U.S. and Chilean Claims Commission, *The Final Report of George H. Shields,* Washington, D.C. 1894, 35–37 and U.S. and Chilean Claims Commission, *The Alsop Claim,* passim; *Mineral Industry 1892,* 558; U.S. Dept of State, Bureau of Foreign Commerce, *Commercial Relations of the U.S. with Foreign Countries 1900,* I, Washington, D.C. 1901, 170–171 (Ecuador); n. 1 above (Guggenheims).

4. C. H. Soper, São Paulo, to Singer Sewing Machine Co., Feb. 11, 1944, in Singer Sewing Machine Company files, São Paulo (outlines a vast amount of research into Singer history in Brazil; it deals with U.S. southerners in Brazil). See p. 176 herein on Grace and Chapter VIII on Keith's investments. Charles W. Drees, ed., *Americans in Argentina,* Buenos Aires 1922, 166 (other U.S. investments).

5. *Report of George H. Shields,* 11–12; *DAB,* XVI, 521 (Central & South American Cable Company, organized in 1879, began operations in 1882); Albert Bigelow Paine, *In One Man's Life,* New York 1921, 205–212, 221; Charles Anderson Gauld, *The Last Titan: Percival Farquhar, American Entrepreneur in Latin America,* Stanford, Calif. 1964, 65–66 (Rio Streetcar).

6. Ralph W. Hidy and Muriel E. Hidy, *Pioneering in Big Business 1882–1911,* New York 1955, 258, 527–529; Bur. of Corps., *Report of Commissioner of Corporations on the Petroleum Industry,* Washington, D.C. 1909, pt. III, "Foreign Trade," 86, 310, 631; Basadre, VI, 2814 (Thorne and Smith); *Mineral Industry 1892,* 564, and Basadre, 2816 (Tweddle's activity: transfer of the property to Tweddle occurred Feb. 3, 1888; Tweddle's sale to Keswick).

7. J. Peter Grace, *W. R. Grace (1832–1904) and the Enterprises He Created,* New York 1953, 11–15; Charles R. Flint, *Memories of an Active Life,* New York 1923, 8 (Grace New York office—1865); Basadre, III, 1297 (New York office—1862); Clayton Sedgwick Cooper, *Understanding South America,* New York 1918, 215 (says New York branch established 1868), 218 (W. R. Grace & Co. incorporated); Wessel, Duval & Co., *A Centennial Review,* 22; Basadre, VI, 2752–2758, 2771–2772 (Michael Grace); Eugene W. Burgess & Frederick H. Harbison, *Casa Grace in Peru,* Washington, D.C. 1954, 92 (Peruvian interests), 26 (sugar); Cleona Lewis, *America's Stake in International Investments,* Washington, D.C. 1938, 319–320 (Bolivia); RG 59, 832.635/16, National Archives (State Department records describe Grace as "an old-established American house").

8. Soper letter cited in n. 4 above; Robert Bruce Davies, "The International Operations of Singer Manufacturing Co.," unpubl. diss., University of Wisconsin, 1966, 77 (identifies Milford as a former bookkeeper for Singer in New York).

9. *Mining & Metallurgy,* 26:509, November 1945, and Stewart, 258 (Backus & Johnston); Diamond Match, *Annual Reports 1897, 1898, 1899;* Lewis, 606 (investment estimate). J. F. Rippy, "Investments of Citizens of the United States in Latin America," *Journal of Business,* 22:17–21, January 1949, puts considerable emphasis on 19th-century investments, but he too accepts that most were ephemeral. W. T. Stead, *The Americanization of the World,* London 1902, 87 (quote).

10. Halsey, passim; Gauld, 128 (Madeira-Mamore); U.S. Dept. of State, *Foreign Relations of the United States 1915,* I, 343 (Guayaquil & Quito Ry).

11. A. B. Parsons, *Porphyry Coppers,* New York 1933, 134–142 (excellent on Braden); Luis Hiriart, *Braden: Historia de una Mina,* Santiago 1964, 7–65 (tells same story; there is some discrepancy in dates in the two books); Foster Bain and Thomas Thornton Read, *Ores and Industry in South America,* New York 1934, 219, 210, 213ff; *Mineral Industry 1904,* 122 (national rankings in copper industry); Bain and Read, 219 (Jackling); Parsons, 143–156; Pope Yeatman, "Report on Braden Copper Company," Sept. 1, 1911, Scudder Collection, Columbia University (general activity); *Mineral Industry 1906,* 226 (high price and its stimulus to development).

12. John Moody, *Truth About Trusts,* New York 1904, 5 (Rio Tinto); George Sherman Queen, "The United States and the Material Advance of Russia, 1881–1906," unpubl. diss., University of Illinois, 1941, 204, and W. Y. Elliott et al., *International Control of Non-Ferrous Metals,* New York 1937, 410 (Caucasus Copper and J. P. Morgan involvement); Marcosson, 63 (Guggenheims).

13. Parsons, 143, 145, 148.

14. Bain and Read, 221; Marcosson, 197; Parsons, 261; Harvey O'Connor, *The Guggenheims,* New York 1937, 348; visit to the property, summer 1964. In 1913 Chile Copper Company, a holding company, was formed. It took over the stock of the Chilex Company; it was controlled by the Guggenheims.

15. Visit to Chuquicamata, summer 1964, and interviews there; interview with Charles Brinckerhoff, New York 1963; Marcosson, 198, and Parsons, 262 (general conditions), 558 (meat); Temporary National Economic Committee, *Hearings,* Washington, D.C. 1940, pt. 25, 13102 (Kelley's comment).

16. O'Connor, 349 (praise of Chilean government); Lewis, 584 (size of investment).

17. George Wythe, *Industry in Latin America,* New York 1945, 197–198, Williams Haynes, *American Chemical Industry,* New York 1945, II, 58–59; Dept. of Comm. & Labor, Bureau of Manufactures, *Commercial Relations of U.S. 1909,* Washington, D.C. 1911, 668 (nitrates); du Pont, *Annual Report 1907* and *Annual Report 1912;* Bain and Read, 249 (Bethlehem). Of all the steel companies, Bethlehem had the greatest and earliest interest in foreign iron ore properties. Bethlehem went to mine ore in Chile, not because of scarcity of ore in the U.S., but on account of the comparative cheapness of water freights as against rail costs. *Engineering & Mining Journal (EMJ),* 97:80 (Jan. 10,1914); data on French company from Bethlehem Iron Ore Company, La Serena, Chile.

18. Lewis, 237; Bain and Read, 283, 296; Hughes and Dier, "Report on Cerro de Pasco Copper Company," Nov. 21, 1919. Scudder Collection, Columbia University; *Mining and Metallurgy,* 26:509 (November 1945); *Mineral Industry 1906,* 235, 236.

19. *Mineral Industry 1912,* 222, and *1913,* 178; *Mining and Metallurgy,* 26:509 (1945); American financial manuals throw no light on the financing of this company.

20. "American Vanadium Company," folder in Scudder Collection, Columbia University; Haynes, II, 228, *EMJ,* 93:83 (Jan. 6, 1912).

21. The Inca Mining Company was profitable: started in 1895, by 1904 it had earned over $2,500,000. With the cost of the property, roads, telephone line and equipment deducted from this sum, its few shareholders were pleased to net $600,000. "History of the Inca Mining Co." [1904?], Scudder Collection, Columbia University; *Mineral Industry 1911,* 314 (sale to British).

22. Basadre, VI, 2879.

23. Testimony of George A. Easley, Report of Subcommittee of House Committee on Foreign Affairs, *Tin Investigation,* Washington, D.C. 1935, 754.

24. *EMJ*, 111:363, Feb. 19, 1921.
25. George Sweet Gibb and Evelyn H. Knowlton, *The Resurgent Years, 1911–1927*, New York 1956, 96 (Lagunitos Oil Co.); Hidy and Hidy, 529 (quote); Basadre, VI, 2815–2816 (The Peruvian government in March 1911 demanded remeasurement of La Brea y Parinas oil fields, which would result in higher taxes. The initial measurement had been made in January 1888.); Gibb and Knowlton, 95–97 (acquisition by Imperial Oil and so on). See p. 175 above for history of La Brea y Parinas property. The International Petroleum Company took outright ownership of the properties purchased; it subleased La Brea y Parinas property, which was, as mentioned, leased by the London & Pacific Company. My forthcoming book on the Emergence of Multinational Enterprise: American Business Abroad, 1914 to the Present will deal with this controversy.
26. See Chapter VIII.
27. Du Pont, *Annual Report 1912;* Testimony of A. V. Davis, *U.S. v. Aluminum Co. of America,* Eq. No. 85–73, Southern District of New York 1940, Brief of the Aluminum Company, 46–48 (Alcoa); *EMJ*, 97:80, Jan. 10, 1914 (Bethlehem); *ibid.*, 93:83, Jan. 6, 1912 (American Vanadium); *Mineral Industry 1913*, 178 (Cerro); Hidy and Hidy, 529, and Gibb and Knowlton, 198 (Jersey Standard).
28. Lewis, 583–584, 590–591 (investment estimates); J. Fred Rippy, *Capitalists and Colombia,* New York 1931, 58–59 (agriculture—Colombia); Pamphlet, "History of the Inca Mining Company and the Inca Rubber Company of Peru," Home Office, Bradford, Pa., n.d. [1904?], Scudder Collection, Columbia University Library (text of the May 16, 1902 concession).
29. U.S. Rubber, *Annual Report 1903;* Reprint of Press Release, Jan. 25, 1926, in U.S. Rubber, *Annual Report 1925;* Lawrence F. Hill, *Diplomatic Relations Between the U.S. and Brazil,* Durham, N.C. 1932, 285–290 (Acre concession); Gauld, 142, 201, 213, 216, 71, 221. (Farquhar's investments); "Confidential Draft on Paraguay Project" [1916], folder "A.I.C.," Vanderlip Papers, Special Collections, Columbia University; Lewis, 591, is mistaken when she notes the investment of International Products Company in 1914; the company did not exist then. Samuel Crowther, *Romance and Rise of the American Tropics,* Garden City, N.Y. 1929, 183 (United Fruit in Colombia); P. 176 above (Grace sugar plantation).
30. Swift & Co., *Year Book 1927*, 38; *ibid. 1918,* 19; Federal Trade Commission, *Report on the Meat Packing Industry,* Washington, D.C. 1919, pt. I, 88 (Sulzberger-Wilson), 164–165, 167 (per cent of business), 181–182 (Brazilian enterprise). The F.T.C. report described the Brazil Land, Cattle & Packing Co. as a subsidiary of Brazilian Railways. Gauld, 161, 164 (Brazil Land, Cattle & Packing Co. & Brazil Railways).
31. Raul Prebisch, *Toward a Dynamic Development Policy for Latin America,* New York 1963, 53 (quote); Lewis, 603 (statistics); Gauld, 66, 69, 75, 82, and Clayton Sedgwick Cooper, *The Brazilians and Their Country,* New York 1917, 141 (Rio Co.); Gauld, 83–86 (Bahia Co.).

32. Stead, 85, 87.

33. *Statistical Abstract 1912,* 410, and *Statistical Abstract 1913,* 350 (trade statistics); Federal Trade Commission, *Report on Cooperation in American Export Trade,* Washington, D.C. 1916, I, 75 (American machinery quote), 66–75 (investment and increase in exports). The F.T.C. explicitly disassociated itself from any advocacy of capital investment in other countries by American manufacturers or the U.S. government *as a means* of increasing trade with such nations (*ibid.,* 66).

34. William C. Downs, "The Commission House in Latin American Trade," *Quarterly Journal of Economics,* 26:119, November 1911; Ernest B. Filsinger, *Exporting to Latin America,* New York 1920, chap. 5.

35. Downs, 129, 130, 132; Filsinger, 54; Company annual reports; data on William T. Phelps and Charles Pratt obtained in Caracas and Rio; Acc. 76, Box 66, Ford Archives, Dearborn, Mich. (contracts with foreign agencies); Wessel, Duval & Co., *A Centennial Review.*

36. For sources on some Argentine branches, see Charles Drees, ed., *Americans in Argentina,* Buenos Aires 1922, 119 (G.E.); *Comments on Argentine Trade,* 4:46, April 1925 (J. F. Case). United Shoe Machinery Co. records in Buenos Aires indicate office opened in 1903; *Notarial Deed,* Oct. 4, 1904, United Shoe Machinery Co. files, Buenos Aires, (presidential decree, giving branch official recognition, was Aug. 12, 1904) Drees, 112 (Ault & Wilborg). Information from Ministry of Economy, Buenos Aires, Argentina, *New York Times,* Jan. 17, 1964 (Singer); D. M. Phelps, *Migration of Industry to South America,* New York 1936, 11, says Singer opened branch in Buenos Aires in 1906. Actually, Singer *Manufacturing* Co. had operated in Latin America for years, but in 1904 this company established a new U.S. subsidiary called Singer Sewing Machine Co., which in 1904–1906 introduced its branches in Latin America. *Comments on Argentine Trade,* 4:6, March 1925 (Avery & Sons); booklet published by International Steam Pump Co. [n.d. 1911?] bound with I.S.P.C.'s *Annual Reports,* Scudder Collection; letter of J. W. Earle (president of Union Typewriter) to A. Barton Hepburn, Apr. 23, 1912, Scudder Collection; Drees, 106 (National Paper); N. S. B. Gras and Henrietta Larson, *Casebook in Business History,* New York 1939, 445 (Dennison); information from office of National Cash Register Company, Buenos Aires, Argentina (NCR); Drees, 128 (National Lead); Mira Wilkins and Frank Ernest Hill, *American Business Abroad: Ford on Six Continents,* Detroit 1964, 434 (Ford: 1913 is the date the Board gave authority for branch in Argentina; 1914, the date property was first rented). National City Bank of New York, Monthly Letter, July 1915, 8–9, and Federal Trade Commission, *Report on Cooperation in American Export Trade,* Washington, D.C. 1916, I, 236 (U.S. Steel, warehouses in S. America); Bureau of Corporations, *Report of Commissioner of Corporations on the Petroleum Industry,* pt. III, "Foreign Trade," Washington, D.C. 1909, 86, 310, 631; Hidy and Hidy, 527 (doing busi-

ness in South America), 529 (Standard Oil—Brazil); Gibb and Knowlton, 197, 639 (Standard Oil—Brazil); Hidy and Hidy and Gibb and Knowlton disagree on the date of organization of Standard Oil—Brazil; 1911 is the date given by the Dept. of State, West Virginia, where the company was incorporated (the predecessor company Empreza Industrial de Petroleo was formed in 1896).

37. Lewis, 600 (Singer); Diamond Match, *Annual Reports, 1897, 1898, 1899;* Burgess and Harbison, 22 (1904 date of Grace entry into textiles); Wythe, 151 and Phelps, 12 (Pullman Standard); *New York Times,* Nov. 11, 1962 (ARMCO). Secretary's office, Esso-Argentina (West India Oil acquired a 20 per cent interest in Compañía National de Aceites in 1911; in 1921 it completed the acquisition of all of the stock); Gibb and Knowlton, 198 (reason for acquisition), 678 (comparative statistics).

38. Cooper, *South America,* 209 (Grace); Harvard Business School Case, #AM-P 181, "Moore-McCormack Lines, Inc."

39. Frank A. Vanderlip to James Stillman (Chairman of the Board, National City Bank), June 5, 1914, Vanderlip Papers, Special Collections, Columbia University. At the first meeting of the National Foreign Trade Convention in May 1914, one matter of concern was the need for more American banking facilities in South America; see *Official Report of the National Foreign Trade Convention,* passim. See also Dept. of Comm., *Commercial Relations of U.S. 1909,* 642 (lack of U.S. banking facilities in Argentina). Joint Economic Committee, *Foreign Government Restraints on United States Bank Operations Abroad,* Washington, D.C. 1967, 16 (National City Bank's first overseas branch—1914).

40. Lewis, 606 (figures); U.S. Senate, Committee on Foreign Relations, Subcommittee on American Republics Affairs, *United States-Latin American Relations,* 86th Cong., 2nd sess., Washington, D.C. 1960, 283, 295–296 (U.S. v. British investment).

Chapter X: The Status of American International Enterprise

1. Charles P. Kindleberger, *American Business Abroad,* New Haven 1969, 180, gives these three items as criteria for multinational corporations.

2. Thayer to C. G. Edward, Edward & Co., Bangkok, Siam, Oct. 9, 1907, Western Electric Archives, New York.

3. U.S. Dept. of Comm., Bureau of the Census, *Historical Statistics of the United States,* Washington, D.C. 1960, 565 (international investment position); Herbert Feis, *Europe, the World's Banker 1870–1914,* New Haven 1930, passim (European investment); W. S. Woytinsky and E. S. Woytinsky, *World Commerce and Government,* New York 1955, 195 (distribution of British investment).

4. See Table V.2 (1914 figure on U.S. direct investment); *Survey of Current Business* (balance-of-payments data); U.S. Dept. of Comm., *Long Term Economic Growth, 1860–1965,* Washington, D.C. 1966, 167 (Kendrick's National Bureau

of Economic Research estimate of GNP—1914); *Survey of Current Business,* September 1967, 40 (1966 direct investment figures); *Economic Report of the President,* Washington, D.C. 1967, 213 (1966 GNP).

5. All investment figures are from Table V.2 above.

6. Hugh G. J. Aitken, "The Changing Structure of the Canadian Economy," in Aitken et al., eds., *The American Economic Impact on Canada,* Durham, N.C. 1959, 9. Aitken writes, "At the risk of oversimplification it can be said that the influence of the United States upon the character of Canadian development is in the direction of perpetuating Canada's traditional status as a staple-producing economy." The evidence I have presented earlier would indicate that this was not true in the years before 1914. See also L. C. A. Knowles and C. M. Knowles, *The Economic Development of the British Overseas Empire,* London 1930, II, 553, for an argument along the same lines as mine. A. E. Safarian, in *Foreign Ownership of Canadian Industry,* Toronto 1966, and Herbert Marshall, Frank A. Southard, Jr., and Kenneth W. Taylor, in *Canadian-American Industry,* New Haven 1936, put emphasis throughout on investments in secondary manufacturing.

7. Paul A. Varg, "The Myth of the China Market, 1890–1914," *The American Historical Review,* 73:742–758 (February 1968), has pointed to "the gap between the rhetoric and actualities" of the China trade, 1890–1914. This was true of investment as well as trade.

8. General data on investment in Asia come from company records, interviews in Asia and the United States, as well as American Exporter, *Export Trade Directories;* James H. Blount, *The American Occupation of the Philippines,* New York 1912; W. Cameron Forbes, *The Philippine Islands,* 2 vols., Boston 1928; A. V. H. Hartendorf, *History of Industry and Trade of the Philippines,* Manila 1958, 58–59; C. F. Remer, *Foreign Investments in China,* New York 1933; Chi-ming Hou, *Foreign Investment and Economic Development in China 1840–1937,* Cambridge, Mass. 1965; F. R. Dulles, *Americans in the Pacific,* Boston 1932; Charles Vevier, *United States and China,* New Brunswick 1955; A. W. Griswold, *Far Eastern Policy of the United States,* New York 1938; Charles S. Campbell, *Special Business Interests and the Open Door Policy,* New Haven 1951; Fred Harrington, *God, Mammon and the Japanese,* New York 1944; Tyler Dennett, *Americans in Eastern Asia,* New York 1941; G. C. Allen and Audrey G. Donnithorne, *Western Enterprise in Far Eastern Economic Development, China and Japan,* New York 1954; G. C. Allen and Audrey G. Donnithorne, *Western Enterprise in Indonesia and Malaya,* London 1957; John A. DeNovo, *American Interests and Policies in the Middle East 1900–1939,* Minneapolis 1963, 38–42, 169, and Chapter III; *Foreign Relations of the United States;* U.S. Dept. of State, Bureau of Foreign Commerce, *Commercial Relations of the U.S.* Specific data: Remer, 262 (130 firms; his figure includes not only export-import concerns but all companies; I have reduced the figure to 80); Blount, 440 (size of the

American colony in the Philippines); Harrington, 156ff (Korean developments); American Trading Company Records, New York; Remer, 252 (Shanghai companies); "International Banking Corporation," Vanderlip Papers, Special Collections Columbia University; Clyde William Phelps, *Foreign Expansion of American Banks,* New York 1927, 147; Morton Keller, *The Life Insurance Enterprise 1885–1910,* Cambridge, Mass. 1963, 276; U.S. Dept. of Commerce and Labor, *Report on Petroleum Industry,* Washington, D.C. 1909, pt. 3, 589–590; D. M. Fisk, "A Brief History of the First Sixty Years of Texaco," unpubl. paper 1964; U.S. Dept. of Comm. and Labor, Bureau of Corporations, *Report on the Tobacco Industry,* Washington, D.C. 1909; F.T.C., *Report on Cooperation in American Export Trade,* Washington, D.C. 1916, pt. 2, 202, 216–217, 221–222, 236, 242; Toshiba, *History,* Tokyo 1964 (I am indebted to G.E.-Japan's officials for translations of the Japanese text); International Harvester, *Horizons, Foreign Centennial Issue,* n.p. 1951, 29–30; Chapter V above (oil companies); U.S. Rubber, *Annual Report 1910;* Lewis, 588. Figures for Asian and European petroleum distribution are those given on our Table V.2. All of the $40 million was in distribution in the east; Miss Lewis was unaware of Standard Oil of New Jersey's investment in the Dutch East Indies. Her European figure ($138 million) includes refineries (for distribution) and also some oil production in Rumania.

9. The best book on U.S. direct investment in Australia is Donald T. Brash, *American Investment in Australian Industry,* Cambridge, Mass. 1966; on U.S. sales and manufacturing investments before World War I, see Brash, 21, 312 (National Ammonia Co.), 292 (International Harvester), 298 (G.E.), 304 (Henry Disston & Sons), 310 (Swift), 316 (Parke, Davis), 317 (Frederick Stearns & Co), 320 (Helena Rubinstein), 325–326 (Kodak). Brash, however, neglects to note that the first U.S. company to manufacture in Australia was American Tobacco. See Bureau of Corporations, *Report on the Tobacco Industry,* pt. I, 69–70, 165. See also on early U.S. stakes in Australia and New Zealand, F.T.C., *Report on Export Trade,* pt. 2, 202, 216–217, 221–222, 236, 242; Commonwealth of Australia, Dept. of Trade, *The Australian Pharmaceutical Products Industry,* Melbourne 1960, 77; Theodore Armstrong, *Our Company,* Dayton, Ohio 1949, 90; Carl Ackerman, *George Eastman,* Boston 1930, 179; International Steam Pump Co., *Annual Report 1911;* International Harvester, *Horizons, Foreign Trade Centennial Issue,* n.p. 1951, 29–30; Bureau of Corporations, *Reports on Petroleum Industry,* pt. 3, 589–590; R. Carlyle Buley, *The Equitable Life Assurance Society of the United States 1859–1964,* New York 1967, I, 471–478; F.T.C., *Report on the Meatpacking Industry,* Washington, D.C. 1919, pt. 1, 87 (Swift).

10. Bernard M. Baruch, *My Own Story,* New York 1957, 209–211 and Société Internationale Forestière et Minière du Congo, *Status,* Bruxelles 1950 (details on the concessions in the Congo); interview with Albert van de Maele (a director of *Forminière*), New York, Apr. 19, 1965 (Guggenheims in the Congo); interviews, Johannesburg, 1965; company histories, annual reports, *Mineral Industry*

1905, and S. Herbert Frankel, *Capital Investment in Africa,* London 1938, and interviews throughout the African continent, 1965.

11. Based on figures in Table V.2.

12. In June 1914, 50 per cent of National Cash Register Co.'s sales were foreign. F. B. Patterson to F. S. Moseley & Co. and Union Trust Co., Sept. 25, 1924, Scudder Collection, Columbia University. Richard Heathcote Heindel, *The American Impact on Great Britain 1898–1914,* Philadelphia 1940, 206 (American firms in London).

13. International Harvester, *Annual Report 1907;* Stephen Potter, *The Magic Number,* London 1959, 98 (Heinz); Thomas Cochran, *The Pabst Brewing Company,* New York 1948, 246–247; American Exporter, *Export Trade Directory,* New York 1912.

14. Data from company *Annual Reports, F.T.C. Reports, Moody's,* files from the Secretary's office, International Division, or archives of particular companies; Scudder Collection, Columbia University Library; company and industry histories; reports from Mixed Claims Commission (U.S. and Germany); Marshall et al. is invaluable.

15. Fred A. McKenzie, *The American Invaders,* New York 1901, 31.

Two

International Business